University of Toronto Italian Studies

The Science of Buffoonery:
Theory and History
of the Commedia dell'Arte

The Science of Buffoonery:
Theory and History of the Commedia dell'Arte

edited by

Domenico Pietropaolo

University of Toronto Italian Studies   3

Dovehouse Editions Inc.
1989

Canadian Cataloguing in Publication Data

Main entry under title:

  The Science of buffoonery: theory and history of the commedia dell'arte

(University of Toronto Italian studies; 3)
Based on presentations at an international symposium held
  November 22–24, 1985, at the University of Toronto.

Bibliography: p.

ISBN 0–919473–67–9

  1. Commedia dell'arte. I. Pietropaolo, Domenico, 1949– . II. Series.

PQ4155.S34 1988   809'.917   C88–090231–0

Copyright ©1989, Dovehouse Editions Inc.

For orders write to:

  Dovehouse Editions Inc.
  32 Glen Ave.
  Ottawa, Canada
  K1S 2Z7

For information on the series write to:

  University of Toronto Italian Studies
  c/o The Department of Italian
  University of Toronto
  21 Sussex Ave.
  Toronto, Canada, M5S 1A1

Typeset by the HUMANITIES PUBLICATION CENTRE, University of Toronto

Manufactured in Canada   Printed by Imprimerie Gagné Ltée

CONTENTS

Acknowledgements

Several people have contributed to the preparation of this volume. I am especially grateful to Laurie Detenbeck, Massimo Ciavolella, Don Beecher, and Michael Dunleavy. In organizing the conference (University of Toronto, November 22–24, 1985), I received valuable assistance from Amilcare Iannucci, Michael Sidnell, Kathy Pearl, Carla Quattrociocchi, Tina Cosentini, Maria Bonfa, Ralph Blasting, and Laurie Detenbeck. To all of them I am very grateful.

Gabriele Erasmi

The *commedia dell'arte* and the Greek Comic Tradition

The year 1429 must be reckoned among the important dates in the history of comedy. It was the time when Italian humanists became aware of Nicholas of Cusa's momentous discovery of Codex Ursinus Vaticanus 3870 (D) which contained, in addition to four of the eight already known Plautine comedies, twelve more, hitherto unknown.[1] The availability, at this point, of a corpus of 26 Roman comedies (six by Terence and twenty by Plautus) provided the humanists not only with a better understanding of ancient comedy, but also with a range of plots and characters sufficiently vast to allow for the possibility of generating, within that range and on the basis of those forms, a new modern comic theatre. If this process began as translation of Plautus and Terence, it soon moved to imitation and adaptation, and to the search for a language that would vividly recreate the language of the ancients. As that language could not fail to express contemporary attitudes, so too the characters and locations moved to the modern world, some of those characters undergoing changes, others being added from the theatrical plots of *novelle* in Boccaccio and others. If certain aspects of character and plot remained constant, this was only partially due to the Humanists' fastidious respect for the rules they came to codify for ancient comedy;[2] much of it was the consequence of the cleverness of the ancient plots and their similarity to plots and characters in Boccaccio's *Decameron*.[3] Moreover, as characterization was limited to the private sphere of human life, the ancient characters could be deemed universal and such that only marginal changes would be necessary to make them live again on the stage of the modern world. We might say that, precisely because the Roman playwrights had successfully adapted Greek New Comedy to the Roman world, its further adaptation to the modern world that was transpiring in the Renaissance was bound to be similarly successful.

The publication of the *editio princeps* of Plautus in 1472,[4] followed in the next year by the Aldine edition of Terence[5] (the *edition princeps* had been published three years earlier in Strasbourg),[6] led in the following years to a number of performances, in the original and in translation, of the plays of Plautus and Terence. Soon these were mixed with new plays from what came to be called the *commedia erudita*.[7]

In this context, it is particularly distressing that Vespasiano da Bisticci, who died in the years when all this experimentation was being carried out with such great enthusiasm, could toss so nonchalantly the notion that the library of Federigo da Montefeltro at Urbino boasted, among its 93 Greek manuscripts,[8] the complete works of Menander, and this without arousing an interest similar to the one caused by the finding of the twelve comedies of Plautus.[9]

Menander was, after all, the source of a good number of the plays of Plautus and Terence,[10] and we would naturally assume that the Humanists would pursue that lead, even if no such book was ever available.[11] Only the *Fragments* of Menander were eventually edited in Paris, in 1553, by Guillame Morel.[12] The fact is that the Humanistic interest in Greek authors was limited to Plato and Aristotle, and Latin translations were often preferred to Greek originals. According to Remigio Sabbadini,

la rassegna delle biblioteche ci dimostra che come il Rinascimento fu originariamente latino, così si conservò sostanzialmente latino anche quando vi penetrò l'elemento greco . . .Unica città in cui la grecità paresse mettere salde radici, possiamo dire essere stata Firenze. A S. Marco di Venezia i codici greci entrarono per donazione di un greco, Bessarione. A Urbino un principe munifico, Federigo introdusse con gli autori latini anche i greci; e se qualcuna di Padova, come S. Giustina, aumentò il suo patrimonio con libri greci, lo dovette alla larghezza di un fiorentino, Palla Strozzi. In Pesaro gli autori greci vennero accolti sì, ma nella veste latina. E a Roma Niccolo V, che diede la prima forte spinta alla ricerca degli scrittori greci, non è quello stesso che li voleva tutti tradotti in latino e che nelle traduzioni si fece quanto zelante promotore altrettanto liberale rimuneratore? Del resto il suo canone bibliografico e, al pari del suo, i canoni di Ugolino Pisani e di Pier Candido Decembrio non ammettevano autori greci se non nella versione latina.[13]

It is therefore quite possible that, if indeed a Menander was available at Urbino, interest in his works might have been delayed by the fact that the recovery of Plautus was only then providing its fruits with the early stagings and translations of his plays. Thus, it was only through Roman adaptations of Greek New Comedy that modern theatre emerged in Italy.

Old comedy, however, had been available for some time. Manuscripts of Aristophanes had been in the possession of Guarino, Aurispa, Gaspare de Verona, Lianoro de' Lianori, Francesco Barbaro, Lorenzo Valla, Bessarione, and Poliziano.[14] Yet the *editio princeps*, with only nine plays, appeared only on the 15 July, 1498. In a long preface, Musurus addressed the "Philhellenes" commending the nobles of Venice for their growing interest in Greek learning.[15] In Florence, Arsenios Apostolis, who had been put in charge of a school of Greek instituted by Pope Leo, collaborated with Franchini on another edition of Aristophanes published by the Giunta (they were the archrivals of the Aldine Press), which appeared in February of 1525.[16] In 1516, the same Giunta had published in Florence the *Thesmophoriazousae* and the *Lysistrata*.[17] A full edition of the eleven plays appeared finally in Basel in 1532.[18] Arsenios Apostolis was very fond of Aristophanes[19] and it was perhaps at his instigation that the *Plutus* was performed in the original in Florence.[20] While since 1476 the works of Plautus and Terence were being performed all over Italy,[21] it would seem that this may very well have been the only revival of Aristophanes at the time.

The *Plutus* was easily the best known of the comedies of Aristophanes: it was the most widely read in the Byzantine period[22] and, through the influence of the Greek immigrants, it became the favourite one among the Humanists.[23] Leonardo Bruni even attempted to translate it in Latin and succeeded in completing the translation of the first act.[24] The relative popularity of the *Plutus* might have stemmed from the fact that it was one of the most self-contained of the plays of Aristophanes: it did not contain barbs directed at contemporaries, there were only a few references to Athenian customs, and no learned references. It was simple and edifying. Unlike many of his other plays, this one did not cause the reader, as Plutarch had earlier complained, to need the assistance of "a grammarian to explain the personal allusions."[25] Moreover, the *Plutus* was a play in which anonymous individuals and their common concerns dominated the stage; even the God that bestows riches is a poor blind man who tries to avoid making too many interested friends. The presence, finally, of an amusing servant, Cario, helps the comedy resemble, a bit more, the patterns of New Comedy, as they were evident in Plautus and Terence.

The *Plutus* was imitated by Agostino Ricchi in *I tre tiranni*, written in 1530, a play in which three characters, old Girifalco, young Filocrate, and noble Chrisaulo become, because of their actions and circumstances, symbols respectively of Love, Fortune and Greed.[26]

Earlier, toward the end of 1512 or at the beginning of 1513, in the wake of the return of the Medici to Florence, Eufrosino Bonini, who taught Greek in Florence, had composed a *Commedia di Giustizia*, which was too a re-make of the *Plutus*.[27] Instead of blind Wealth he introduced blind Fortune, who reacquires her sight thanks to the cures administered by physicians, rather than through the intervention of Asclepios. By playing on the Italian word for physicians, *medici*, Bonini was able to allude to the Medici family, in whose palace the play was performed. The comedy thus became a very thinly veiled allegory that praised the restoration of the Medici as the cause of the renewed political fortunes of the city. Whatever its merits, the comedy is of some interest for its employing the device of using fictional characters to allude to or represent real characters in political life. It matters little that Bonini used this device to flatter, rather than attack the then powerful Medici. What is important is the fact that the author was evidently aware that Aristophanes had employed a similar device in the *Knights*, the play that attacks Cleon, who, after his victory at Sfacteria, had become the dominant political figure in Athens. Apparently fearful of retaliation—beatings are mentioned in the first lines of the play[28] —the costume makers had refused to make a comic mask of Cleon. It is said that Aristophanes played the role himself without a mask "smearing his face with red dye."[29] He changed the name of Cleon into Paphlagon and had one of the characters say (lines 227–233):

These clever people in the audience and I, and God, can all be counted on. Don't be afraid. His likeness isn't good; Our mask designers were so scared of him they would not reproduce the fellow's face. But he'll be known. The audience is smart.

The point is that, while on other occasions Aristophanes attacked individuals directly by putting them on the stage with a mask that imitated their features (it is said, for instance, that at the performance of *The Clouds* Socrates was in the audience and at one point stood up to let the people compare his mask on the stage with his own face),[30] he could make his attack perhaps even more pointed by staging actions and featuring individuals that, through a transparent allegory, would mirror real situations and characters. While Bonini looked at the *Plutus*, he evidently contaminated something from *Knights*. There *Demos* is rejuvenated and invigorated so that he can do away with the innovations of Paphlagon-Cleon.

Bonini's message is that the confusion of republican Florence can be done away with the reinvigorating return of the Medici.[31] His effort may very well have inspired Machiavelli to write, in *La Mandragola*, another and more aristophanesque allegory on the return of the Medici. If Parronchi's interpretation is correct, Callimaco is none other than Lorenzo de' Medici; Nicia, who bears the name of the Greek leader of the Peloponnesian war and is, as well, a character in the *Knights*, represents Pier Soderini, while Lucrezia, the virtuous wife corrupted by Callimaco, is then Florence.[32] *La Mandragola* is the reverse of the *Commedia di Giustizia* and, while employing the forms of New Comedy, it must be deemed, in the final analysis, inspired by Aristophanes. Indeed, even its most novel character, Fra Timoteo, can be seen as an adaptation of the character of Socrates in *The Clouds*. Socrates corrupts society through the use of sophistry. Fra Timoteo, Lucrezia's spiritual guide, corrupts her with the same means and proves that what is evil is acutally good.[33]

Machiavelli wrote another comedy, unfortunately lost, *Le maschere*, where, as an adaptation of *The Clouds* and other comedies by Aristophanes, he attacked many of his contemporaries in Florence.[34] Given Machiavelli's political passions and comic talent, it is not surprising that Aristophanes would influence him to write in the same spirit. It is also not surprising that neither Machiavelli nor his nephew had the courage to divulge *Le maschere*, for the imitation of Aristophanes could be perpetrated successfully only in a free society.[35]

All his comedies were in the final analysis political, referred specifically to contemporary events, and satirized individuals prominent in Athens. From another point of view, his comedies did not have well crafted plots: the latter were merely the explication of paradoxical ideas aroused by the frustrations caused by political events and a war that was slowly destroying Athens: what if we could rejuvenate the people from a senility that makes them the victims of the likes of Cleon (*Knights*)? What if women were to go on a sex strike? Men would forget war and think only of making love (*Lysistrata*). What if an individual, weary of the war, were to make a private peace with the enemy? Others might do the same (*Acharnians*). What if we could bring back from Hades the likes of Aeschylus and the spirit of Marathon and Salamis (*Frogs*)? Is there a way to kidnap that elusive woman that is Peace and make her our consort (*Peace*)? Why is wealth so unfairly distributed? The God must be blind. What if we could cure him (*Plutus*)? And then, what if economic equality could be enacted (*Ecclesiazousae*)? Can we come to terms with the Gods (*Birds*)? What are the advantages and consequences of listening to the Sophists (*Clouds*)? Does democracy need all this gigantic apparatus of public servants (*Wasps*)? Aristophanes' plots would become fantastic scenarios pursuing the implications of these questions, and, as the questions arose in the context of contemporary events in Athens, the characters would be either taken directly from life or they might become thinly disguised under a different mask. That Aristophanes' comedies could be actually staged was the result of the amazing tolerance of Athenian political institutions.

Aside from the fact that, already around 1525, Greek studies were declining in Italy,[36] it is clear that Aristophanes' kind of theatre could not appeal to the Humanists. Its concerns were not easily applicable to the Italy of Great Lords where intellectuals profited from their protection. Its plots, moreover, could not constitute a repertoire from which it would be possible to generate other plots. At best, only some structural devices could be employed. In remaking Plautus' *Menechmi* into *I simillimi*, Giovan Giorgio Trissino attempted to restore the function the chorus had in Aristophanes, the one of linking the different parts of the comedy without breaking it into acts. It was apparently an isolated attempt and it remains a historical curiosity.[37]

One of the lessons that could be drawn from Aristophanes was that, whenever the action on the stage can encompass the emotions of the audience and refer to the real world outside of the theatre, it succeeds in making the imitation of life unfolding on the stage much more like life itself. Thus, almost from the beginning *commedia erudita* moved the action from ancient Greece to the cities of Italy and the present time, provided its characters with a contemporary quality of language and manners and, on occasion, though timidly, referred to contemporary problems. The sorry state of the Church could be reflected in the figure of Fra Timoteo, the corruption of the Roman court and the hypocrisy of courts in general could be referred to in Ariosto's *Cassaria* as well as the rapacity of the Spaniards.[38]

On occasion also, comedy could regain its aristophanesque quality and satirize individuals and groups well known to the audience. Thus in 1662, when *commedia erudita* had long been superseded by the practices of *commedia dell'arte*, Giovanni Alfonso Borelli, in a letter to Marcello Malpighi, referred to a play by Pietro Castelli, professor of medicine at Messina, where the latter attacked the protagonists in a contemporary medical controversy:

. . .si agitò tutta questa disputa dai soliti personagi delle commedie Pantaloni, Zanni, Medici, Speziali, Armeni ed altri simili, e so che la detta commedia ridusse in disperazione la parte contraria tanto, che arrivarono ad archibusate ed altre dimostrazioni.[39]

These and perhaps other instances would be exceptions. The political climate would permit only limited freedom of speech and none at all in political matters. Political satire and protest could only be expressed anonymously and Pasquino would be its only form.

More recently, Kenneth McLeish has stressed the fact that Aristophanes' theatre implies a great deal of physical acting to complement verbal acting and that Aristophanes made use, repeatedly, of routines similar to the *lazzi* of *commedia dell'arte*; these would be possible thanks to the existence of groups of skilled professional performers.[40] This is not new; what is new and useful is that McLeish approaches the physical aspects of performance of Old Comedy with the vocabulary and attitudes derived from vaudeville and *commedia dell'arte*. This helps us in our understanding of Aristophanes, particularly since performances of Aristophanes' comedies are still rare, and no tradition has yet been established for satisfactory performances. But is there a historical connection between Aristophanes and *commedia dell'arte*? I doubt that more than analogy can be established. When the comic actor emerges, he is always an individual who colors the parts that he is allowed to choose for himself with his physical characteristics. Once on the stage, the character lives only through the actor.[41] Aristophanes, however, shows that early drama was far more explicit in suggesting specific physical actions through stage directions than was later drama and these were important ingredients in performance.[42]

An element of comic improvisation, similar to the *lazzi* of *commedia dell'arte*, was certainly part of the performances of New Comedy,[43] and, in the plays of Menander, there are also clear implications that, in the choral interludes, actions and text were left to the resources of the performers. In the *diskolos* (lines 230–232), the nature of the choral interlude and its possible physical routines are announced as follows:

There are people coming
with offerings for Pan. They've had a drop to drink;
this is not time to get involved with them . . .

We can easily imagine the chorus staggering on stage, performing pratfalls and other routines and singing bawdy songs. The other interludes are announced by the simple word *Xorou* inserted where they should occur. The same device, with slight variations, characterizes the *Epitrepontes* and the *Perikeiromene*.[44] At the end of the first scene, a chorus of drunkards is usually announced and we are left with the implication that it will keep reappearing during the remaining choral interludes. That device was maintained by Plautus in one instance of the *Bacchides*,[45] while elsewhere flute playing provides an interlude.[46]

Having accepted a division in 5 acts,[47] *commedia erudita* provided musical interludes which may have led later to the introduction of comic interludes. In any case, early performances must have shown the necessity of relying more and more on the skill of the actor. Some of the

performances of Plautus and Terence were deemed boring, partially because of the language.[48] But even as the language became more natural
and spontaneous—we may remember here Ruzzante's insistence on the
natural—success depended more and more on comic characterization. As
the plots of *commedia erudita* were based on an endless declension and
conjugation of the original plots of Plautus and Terence, increased by a
few more from Boccaccio, they became predictable. Only the actor, recognizable for a specific comic type he created, could maintain the interest,
and the comic aspect of comedy resided mainly in the figure of the servant.

In the prologue to the *Amphitruo* (lines 60–63), Plautus had already
recognised this fact:

nam me perpetuo facere ut sit comoedia
reges quo veniant et di, non par arbitror.
quid igitur? *quoniam hic servos quoque partis habet*
faciam sit, proinde ut dixi, tragicomoedia.

(it does not seem to me appropriate that it be
completely a comedy since there are Gods and Kings.
What then? *Since there is also the role of the servant*
I'll make it, as I just said, a tragicomedy.)

In his first play, Ariosto seems to have adhered to Plautus' prescription.
He reproduced the tricksters of Plautus and maintained the connection
with Roman comedy by having them, like Chrysalus in *Bacchides* (lines
925ff.), compare their deeds to those of a victorious general. He did also
something else: he did not give them Greek names but Italian nicknames
suggesting a type. Volpino is he who plans the tricks, Fulcia he who
sustains the action when Volpino comes into problems. In his second
comedy, *I suppositi*, Ariosto retained the type of the dull faithful servant
who gets easily confused, giving him the same name it had in *Cassaria*,
Nebbia, 'Foggy.'

The identification of the actor with a specific type, although his role
may vary, was one of Ruzzante's contributions to the evolution of the
genre. When and where the role of the servant was taken over by the
zanni is not too clear; nor is it clear how and when they originated.[49]
There is little doubt, however, that they lent their mask, their physical,
verbal idiosyncracies and regional accent to the servants of Plautus, and
supplied anew the buffoonery and slapstick implied in the original Plautine creations. The type of the *miles gloriosus*, which from Menander
had made his way into the comedies of Livius Andronicus, Terence and
Plautus acquired almost immediately Spanish characteristics.[50] The colorless *sbirro spagnolo* of Ariosto's *Lena*, revamped as the captain in many

other plays will exist, with many different names, well into the eighteenth century, making his appearance even in *opera buffa*.[51] As the trickery of servants is always at the expense of a number of old men, the *senes* of Roman comedy, these will be cristallised in Pantaloon and the Doctor,[52] the latter a new type, already adumbrated in the Machiavellian Nicia and Ariosto's Cleandro, which satirizes the stupidity underlying the pretence of learning.[53] These basic types exist, however, as the deceivers and the deceived in plots revolving around young lovers. In Plautus and Terence, the females are often colorless presences, while the males are funny only as caricatures of helpless despair.[54] The tradition of courtly love and Petrarchan manners gave the lovers emerging in *commedia dell'arte* a very prominent role, which could then be parodized in the loves of servants. The role of the female servant was also present in Roman comedy, both as a trickster and as a staid maid, and these were maintained in the countless variations presented in *commedia dell'arte*. Of the odious figure of the *parasitus*,[55] still present in *commedia erudita*, only his appetite for food and drink is retained and blended into the characterization of the *zanni*. The *meretrix* and the *laena*, prominent figures in *commedia erudita*, were probably the victims of censorship in the post Tridentine atmosphere of the Counter-Reformation and eventually disappeared; some of their characteristics, however, survived in less offensive types.[56]

Commedia dell'arte, as Ireneo Sanesi showed long ago, is merely the outcome of the evolution of *commedia erudita*.[57] Bound to the type of plots described in Plautus and Terence, compelled to seek an endless number of variations and additional complications to make them interesting, it found it necessary to work these out in *scenari*. As these plots revolved around a limited number of basic characters, the emergence of the professional actor, specialized in one of these roles, freed him from the limitation of a prepared text, and gave him freedom to exercise his creativity to the point that the actor literally disappeared behind the mask he impersonated. If the specific "masks" originated outside the framework of *commedia dell'arte*, as the famous passage from the dialogue by Massimo Troiano dating from 1568 and describing a performance of improvised comedy seems to imply,[58] soon they were to take this or that role within the still classical framework of the comic scenario, accepting its function but modifying its persona.

With the decadence of the actor, and the inevitable rigidity and repetition of his role, the author became preeminent again as the creator of character and situation,[59] but the original debt that *commedia erudita* contracted with Plautus and Terence, and through them with Menander and

Greek New Comedy, was maintained and extended. Only the political demise of the type of world that had seen the birth of *commedia erudita* first, and its evolution as *commedia dell' arte* later, would put eventually an end to the almost exclusive hold that Menander and his Roman epigones had on comedy.

McMaster University

NOTES

1 The discovery had been made in 1425, but news of it reached Poggio Bracciolini in 1429; the latter "urged Cardinal Orsini to lose no time in securing the Plautus, and, by the end of the year, Nicolaus had arrived in Rome bringing with him the MS of four of the eight known plays and of twelve that were new, which is still one of the treasures of the Vatican Library. In the recension of Plautus which gradually became current in Italy, Poggio was aided by Gregorio Corero of Venice." See John Edwin Sandys, *A History of Classical Scholarship*, vol. 2 (Cambridge University Press, 1908), p. 34. See also, by the same author, the *Harvard Lectures on the Revival of Learning* (Cambridge University Press, 1905), p. 39. See also Remigio Sabbadini, *Le scoperte dei codici latini e greci ne' secoli XIV e XV* (Firenze: Sansoni, 1905 [1967]), pp. 111–112, and *Le scoperte dei codici latini e greci ne' secoli XIV e XV: Nuove ricerche* (Firenze: Sansoni, 1914 [1967]), pp. 16–17, 240–41. The comedies of Plautus which were already known in the Middle Ages were *Amphitruo, Asinaria, Aulularia, Captivi, Curculio, Casina, Cistellaria* and *Epidicus*. For the *Codices* of Plautus, see W. M. Lindsay's edition of Plautus (Oxford: Clarendon Press, 1904 [1965]), pp. iv and xx.

2 These were the units of time, place and action; the division into five acts; the necessity of a prologue; a stock of set characters; and such Aristotelian notions as *peripeteia* and *anagnorisis* (*agnizione* for Giraldi). Originally also, comedies were to be written in verse; musical interludes were adopted from the practice of Plautus, and there was at least one attempt to revive the chorus. For these and other relevant notions see Ireneo Sanesi, *La commedia* in *Storia dei generi letterari italiani* (Milano: Vallardi, 1911), p. 223ff. and the Introduction to Douglas Radcliff-Umstead, *The Birth of Modern Comedy in Renaissance Italy* (Chicago and London: University of Chicago Press, 1969), pp. 2–10. A useful synthesis is provided by Nino Borsellino's Introduction to *Commedie del Cinquecento* (Milano: Feltrinelli, 1962), pp. xviii–xxi.

3 For the debts of *commedia erudita* to Boccaccio see the many references in the aforementioned works by Radcliff-Umstead and Sanesi. See also Borsellino, pp. xv–xviii.

4 Sandys, *A History of Classical Scholarship*, vol. 2, p. 103.

5 This is the first Italian edition of Terence, which Sanesi, p. 135, erroneously considered to be the *princeps*.

6 Sandys, vol. 2, p. 103. See also George E. Duckworth, *The Nature of Roman Comedy* (Princeton: University Press, 1971), p. 439. For the manuscript tradition and the merits of these early Renaissance editions of Plautus and Terence, see pp. 437–441.

7 For the early performances of Plautus and Terence, see Vito Pandolfi, *Il teatro del Rinascimento e la Commedia dell'Arte* (Roma: Lerici, 1969). Each of the chapters of the first part provides a fairly exhaustive account of performances both of Latin and Italian comedies in each of the major Italian centres of the Renaissance. See also Sanesi, ch. 3.

8 For the library at Urbino and its Greek holdings, see Sabbadini, 1905, p. 200, Note 78.

9 Vespasiano's reference to the Menander is in *Vite* I, 327; it is referred to by Jacob Burckhardt, *The Civilization of the Renaissance in Italy* (New York: Mentor, 1961), pp. 157–58. See also Harry Thurston Peck, *A History of Classical Philology* (New York: MacMillan, 1911), p. 273f. Both Thurston Peck and Burckhardt believed in the existence of such a volume on the basis of Vespasiano's phrase "tutte le opere" and felt that the book may have disappeared during the sack of Urbino by the troops of Cesare Borgia in 1501. It is strange, however, that Vespasiano is the only one to refer to such a book; considering, moreover, that he was one of the most important copyists and booksellers of the time, and acted as an agent for Cosimo and Nicholas V, besides Federigo da Montefeltro, it seems unlikely that only one copy was produced and that it escaped the notice of the printing presses, which produced in 1498, the year of Vespasiano's death, an edition of Aristophanes, an author of less potential interest to the Humanists.

10 Plautus' *Aulularia, Bacchides, Cistellaria, Poenulus* and *Stichus* were derived from Menander, but there may have been others. Terence's *Andria, Heauton Timorumenos, Eunuchus,* and *Adelphoe* were adapted from Menander. In addition Terence contaminated in these other plays of Menander. See Duckworth, pp. 52–54 and 59–60. In the case of Terence, such was his dependance on Menander that he was called *dimidiatus Menander* (Suetonius, *Vita Terenti*, V).

11 While it cannot be excluded, of course, that Vespasiano had indeed seen a whole Menander, it would appear that, in the West, the last author who had read Menander was Sidonius Appolinaris who, in the fifth century, had drawn a comparison between Terence's *Hecyra* and Menander's *Epitrepontes*. In the East, where Greek studies continued to flourish, there are only a few references to Menander, while there are many to the work of Aristophanes. Psellus (1018–1078), who "describes himself lecturing on Homer, Menander and Archilochus" only makes reference to *Menandreia* (see Sandys, vol. 1, pp. 411–412), presumably gnomic excerpts, while he deals extensively with Aristophanes. The very learned Tzetzes (1110–1180) does not mention Menander among the more than 400 authors that he read. Anna Comnena, one of his patrons, is acquainted with Aristophanes, but not with Menander. Finally, Thomas Magister (1282–

1328) writes commentaries on the plays of Aristophanes, but not on Menander (see Sandys, vol. 1, pp. 418ff, and 430). One is, therefore, a bit sceptical about the existence of manuscripts of Menander beyond the fifth or sixth century A.D. In spite of his reputation that had earlier caused him to be ranked among the very best in Greek literature, his works, with the only exception of Egypt which has yielded many extensive fragments in this last century, must have been dispersed and lost sometime between the fifth and the tenth century.

12 Sandys, vol. 2, p. 105.
13 Sabbadini, 1905, p. 204.
14 Sanesi, p. 139.
15 See Deno John Geanakoplos, *Greek Scholars in Venice* (Cambridge, Mass: Harvard University Press, 1962), p. 122.
16 Geanakoplos, p. 186f.
17 Sandys, vol. 2, p. 104.
18 Sandys, vol. 2, p. 105.
19 Geanakoplos, p. 181.
20 Sanesi, p. 141. He does not mention, however, Arsenios.
21 See Pandolfi, passim; Sanesi, pp. 140–144.
22 See the introduction to the *Plutus* by Moses Hadas in *The Complete Plays of Aristophanes* (New York: Bantam, 1962), p. 463.
23 Sanesi, p. 199.
24 Sanesi, p. 139.
25 Quoted by Sandys, vol. 1, p. 305f.
26 See Sanesi, pp. 268–272; Radcliff-Umstead, pp. 189–195.
27 See Sanesi, p. 199f.
28 *Knights*, 4–5.
29 Mary R. Lefkowitz, *The Lives of the Greek Poets*, (Baltimore: The Johns Hopkins University Press, 1981), p. 108.
30 See Hadas, p. 101.
31 One of the historical circumstances of Aristophanes' *Plutus* is that, in 388 B.C., Athens was experiencing an economic recovery. Conon had brought to Athens Persian gold. Thus, as Benjamin Bickley Rogers wrote, "very welcome to the whole audience must have been the restoration of Wealth, at the close of the comedy, to his long-deserted home in the Athenian Treasury." See the Introduction to the *Plutus*, p. 361, in the Loeb Classical Library Edition of Aristophanes (Cambridge, Mass: Harvard University Press, 1924 [1979]). Thus, in Bonini's play, Fortune would be similarly restored to Florence.
32 See Francesco Gaeta's *Nota introduttiva* to Niccolò Machiavelli, *Il teatro e tutti gli scritti letterari* (Milano: Feltrinelli, 1965), p. xiv.
33 It is probably excessive to see in Lucrezia's willingness to believe Fra Timoteo, Florence faithfulness to Savonarola. Timoteo is not exactly an "unarmed prophet." His role is far closer, as a fraudulent advisor, to the one of Socrates in *The Clouds*.

34 Sanesi, pp. 202–203; Radcliff-Umstead, p. 117.

35 Many a critic has expressed admiration for the implied tolerance of Athenian institutions and leaders with respect to the attacks brought forth by the writers of Old Comedy.

36 See Sandys, vol. 2, p. 100.

37 Sanesi, p. 255.

38 *Cassaria*, Act 3, scene 3; Act I, scene 5. Radcliff-Umstead, p. 85, points out that Leo X, initially enthusiastic about Ariosto's comic talent, chose not to have *Il Negromante* performed in Rome since he was displeased with references to "ecclesiastical abuses" and "Leo X's wholesale business in indulgences at high prices."

39 *The Correspondence of Marcello Malpighi*, vol. 1, ed. Howard B. Adelmann (Ithaca and London: Cornell University Press, 1975), p. 115 in a letter from Pisa dated January 19, 1662.

40 Kenneth McLeish, *The Theatre of Aristophanes* (New York: Taplinger, 1980). See, in particular, pp. 18–21, 26–28, 94–100 and passim.

41 Similar notions are expressed by Pandolfi, p. 148.

42 As McLeish aptly shows, the Aristophanesque texts are full of indications for the performance of comical physical actions and vocal effects which are an integral part of the play. On occasion also, the entrance on stage of a drunken character, for instance, may indicate that his actions were left to the comic skill of the performer.

43 See the Introduction to *The Diskolos of Menander*, ed. E. W. Handley (Cambridge, Mass: Harvard University Press, 1965), p. 6f., where Handley implies that the dramatist's reliance on popular stock characters meant that these would be recognizable to the audience through their acting devices. He also refers to allusions to scenes from tragedy, which again would derive their effect from both verbal and physical acting.

44 See *Epitrepontes*, lines 33–35:
    Let's go since a bunch
    of drunken youths is approaching
    and I don't think it's time to get involved with them
and *Perideiromene*, lines 71–76:
    Slaves! a bunch of drunken youths
    is approaching. I congratulate the mistress
    on her bringing the girl inside—that's
    being a mother. And now I must find my master. . . .

45 *Bacchides*, 106: simul huic nescioquoi, turbare qui huc it, decedamus <hinc>.

46 *Pseudolus*, 573–573a:
    exibo, non ero vobis morae;
    tibicen vos interibi hic delectaverit.
On this matter of choral interludes and act division, see Handley's commentary, pp. 171–174 and Duckworth, pp. 98–101.

47 Sanesi, pp. 223–230.

48 See, for instance, Isabella d'Este's letter of February 3, 1502, where she complains about a performance of *Bacchibes* as "tanto longa e fastidiosa." Quoted by Sanesi, p. 145. For examples of early translations, see Sanesi, pp. 146–150.

49 See Pandolfi, p. 148ff. It would seem, however, that, between 1510 and 1520, these characters were already common. See Pandolfi, p. 169.

50 See Pandolfi, pp. 178–182.

51 See, for instance, Pergolesi's *La serva padrona* and Valentino Fioravanti's *Le cantatrici villane*. Probably the last representation and caricature of the braggart soldier is Belcore in Donizetti's *L'elisir d'amore* where, however, he has lost his Spanish accent, and his rank has been reduced to that of a sergeant.

52 See Pandolfi, pp. 174–182.

53 See Pandolfi, pp. 174–182; for the *senes* in Roman Comedy, see Duckworth, pp. 242–249. For the transformation, in *comedia erudita* and *commedia dell'arte*, of one of the *senes* into the Doctor, see again Duckworth, on "professional types," pp. 261–262. The Doctor, "an amusingly pompous practitioner," appears in *Menechmi*, 889ff; there are also lawyers in *Peonulus*, 515ff. and *Phormio*, 458ff. Elaine Fantham reminded us that the type of Doctor may have been ultimately derived from the philosopher such as we find in Aristophanes' *The Clouds*.

54 For the women in Plautus, and Terence, see Duckworth, pp. 253–261; for the *adulescentes*, see pp. 237–242. For the later *Innamorati*, see Pandolfi, pp. 182–83.

55 For the ancient *parasitus*, see Duckworth, p. 265ff.

56 The *meretrix* in ancient comedy is of two types: one, the lover, blends with the *virgo* and thus continues to exist as the female lover; the other, clever and mercenary, will find its way into some of the characteristics of female servants of the *commedia dell'arte*.

57 See Sanesi's conclusions, pp. 434–445.

58 See Pandolfi, p. 148.

59 It is in this context that Goldoni's theatrical reforms acquire their meaning and their importance.

Elaine Fantham

The Earliest Comic Theatre at Rome: Atellan Farce, Comedy and Mime as Antecedents of the *commedia dell'arte*

It would be foolish to deny the indirect influence of Roman literary comedy—the adaptation of Greek New Comedy which my colleague, Gabriele Erasmi, has traced—upon the *commedia erudita*, and through these Italian literary comedies on the *commedia dell'arte*. Yet inevitably students of drama hanker for a more direct or significant continuity from the Roman comic theatre, and inevitably must be disappointed from the very nature of the evidence. Popular comedy persists as an underground tradition, with elements of stage business and mimicry that can only be observed and copied, not described: echoes of children's games, street humour, caricatures of accent and gesture from notorious contemporaries like Charlie Chaplin or Richard Nixon, while the aspects of literary comedy preserved on the page are perhaps the least significant characteristics of the subgenre.

Roman comic theatre can be classified into four types of entertainment, whose chronological relationship is not a straightforward sequence.[1] First come the Atellan farces, brought to Rome from Oscan Atella in Campania, traditionally unscripted and based on improvisation; these were beloved by the Italians before and after the flowering of Greek-style comedy, from the fourth century before Christ to the first century of our era and beyond. Chronologically second—at Rome itself—is the adaptation of Greek urban comedy, itself a post-classical form at Athens, as the so-called *Palliata*, a genre identified at Rome by its foreign costume, the *Pallium* worn by Greek citizens. Part of the appeal of the genre was the licence of depicting another society in which—as in English versions of French farce—anything goes. The *Palliata* flowered, refined itself and withered within the hundred years from 240 to 140 B.C., fathering some relatively successful by-products; these were variations in a local Italian setting called *Togatae*, comedy in Roman dress, or *Tabernariae*, Market comedies. Little is known of these, but their most successful exponent, the dramatist Afranius, freely declared that he had made over plots from Greek comedy. Since this sub-genre fell between two stools, lacking either the uninhibited earthiness of Atellan farce or the authentic sophistication of Greek comedy, it faded fast and can be safely dismissed. More difficult to assess is the long-lasting and versatile entertainment called Mime, emerging from Greek Alexandria to become the Roman favourite after the decline of the formal *Palliata*, to dominate the stages of the Empire and enrage the Christian Fathers by its open eroticism. Three of these genres are relevant to the *commedia dell'arte*, but they are not all equally knowable, and I shall devote most of my discussion *not* to the form closest to the *commedia*, but to the Greek-style comedy about which we, and the authors of the *commedia* also, had most information.

Affinities between the Atellan farces and the *commedia* are most likely coincidence rather than actual inheritance, and must be handled with an additional *Caveat*: theatre histories have repeatedly used the known *commedia* itself to explain the less known Atellane. Roman scholars like Varro or the later commentators on Juvenal who provide most of our fragmentary evidence about the form and content of Atellane and even about Mime may never have watched a performance. Indeed one of our main sources, Isidore the seventh century A.D. bishop of Seville, drew his picture of the Atellane from the learned etymologising Varro and the lexicon of Verrius Flaccus. Already in 1589 as Norbert Jouard has pointed out in his *La commedia dell'arte et la comédie latine* (Paris: Edition Hermès, 1982, p. 20) Niccolo Rossi was assimilating the new *commedia* and its leading roles of Francatrippa, Brighella and Pantalone to the mimes and Atellanes of Ancient Rome for which his only evidence was those learned dictionaries and his extrapolation from the *commedia* itself; he had no access, and nor do we, to the details of ancient performance. It would be fair to argue that he imagined the ancient forms on the basis of the modern. The scanty evidence has not significantly increased in the last century and you can read in the modern reprint of De Amicis' study *La commedia popolare latina e la commedia dell'arte* (Naples, 1882) almost all that we have to build on.

The Atellanes works with four rustic types differentiated by their vices: perhaps the favourite was the greedy, lustful, credulous Maccus, a natural dupe whom Italian art-historians have recognised in the hook-nosed, sharp-chinned hunchback depicted in ancient Campanian pots and statuettes;[2] de Amicis sees them as ancestors of Pulcinella or Arlecchino. Many of the titles from the literary Atellanes of the last century before Christ star Maccus in unusual situations and impostures such as *Maccus the Virgin, Maccus the Innkeeper, Maccus in Exile, Maccus Enlisted, Maccus Demobilised, Maccus the Election Agent* and *The Twin Maccuses.* Another leading role is Bucco, named from the Latin word for mouth or jaw, who seems to have been a mighty talker and eater; Jouard associates him with Brighella. Contrasted with these is Pappus the old dotard, a clear forerunner of Pantalone: he too gives the name to comedies such as *Pappus in Second Place*, seemingly an election comedy, and *The Second Auctioneer.* Surviving lines of this text show the old man in love. He has gone to Venus' temple to supplicate for success. Shortly after his son and a friend discuss the situation: "Do you want to make your stepmother desert the silly old fool?" "Father, I brought you out here on purpose to scold you for your folly"[3] (Pomponius 131, 142–44). Most likely we have here the standard adultery plot of later mimes or Catullus' Poem XXVII, in which the old and impotent marry a flighty young girl and suffer for it. The last type of the Atellane, Dossennus, is the most awkward to reconcile with the *commedia*; de Amicis[4] compares him with the *dottore*, but the ancient sources do not specify any characteristics of Dossennus except greed; there is no firm proof that he was pedantic or long-winded, or associated with a particular profession. The plots hinged on the mutual deceptions of this quartet, and titles indicate that plays usually started from an impersonation or change of trade and worked through the humour of trickery and exposure. Gesture was important—Tertullian protests at the performer's vulgar gestures and mimicry is suggested by, for example, these lines from Pomponius' *The Miller*: "He can be instantly glad or gloomy, leaping for joy or wincing in grief" (Pomponius fr. 124f). In Atellane, unlike the mime, the players were masked, and an amateur could take part without the social disqualifications visited on regular mime and comic actors.[5]

Our evidence from the first century of the empire showed that Atellanes combined the old stock roles with current parody of emperors and their favourites, alluding to recent scandals of Nero or Domitian. With such a fixed cast the plays must have depended, like the *commedia*, on the creative powers of the troupe leader devising a new situation and sequence of scenes around which the performers would ad-lib. One or two elements of the *commedia* seem to have been missing; the young lovers are not implied by any ancient testimonia, though scenes of groping and fondling are described. Nor is there any hint of the braggart soldier, Matamoros. The predominantly small-town context offers scenes from court and local politics, from trades like fulling and milling, and from domestic situations like the man who marries money (two plays called *The Dowered Wife*) or local events like vintages and auctions, but have no occasion to bring in the stateless mercenary captains. Similarly there is little to suggest an equivalent for the *dottore*; this is a world of knockabout and buffoonery and basic humour of greed, lust and the lavatory.

Mime—not of course a silent genre in antiquity—contributed the erotic component in ancient popular theatre; in its most common form the triangle of stupid cuckold, scheming young bride and eager adulterer.[6] Its leading players became famous in the sophisticated city and its recurring themes were of the lover hidden hastily in the chest—like Sir John Falstaff—at the husband's unexpected return. Such age old rituals depend on the agility and mimicry of the performers. There were other mimes— of mythological travesty, of intrigue and poisoning and sham deaths—but the seduction motif is easily the most frequent. Some of the apparent affinities with the *commedia* seem to me problematic: for example the costume. The *centunculus* or multi-coloured patchwork tunic of the male mime and the *ricinium* of the female are not attested in the same sources that report the types of plot closest to *commedia*. The costume sounds like that of Harlequin, but it also suggests that of the court jester or clown. Again, none of our sources offers any account of typical gesture or stage business. This is not to deny the relevance of mime or its stepchild Pantomime, essentially a form of dance entertainment, to the prehistory of the *commedia*; simply to acknowledge that we cannot make useful inferences.

We fall back, then, on the scripted comedy adapted from the formal five-act Greek play, typically a domestic intrigue centred on the young lover and his apparently unsuitable beloved and his frustrations at the hands of a skinflint father, a cruel slaveowner or an arrogant soldier rival; intrigues in which the real hero is not the ineffectual bourgeois youth but his flamboyant servant, an exhibitionist, disrespectful, unscrupulous and bibulous slave of dubious age and origin. Two recent books have suggested a new approach to Roman comedy of special interest to students of the *commedia*: Gianna Petrone's *Teatro antico e inganno* (Palermo, 1985) and Niall Slater's *Plautus and the Theatre of the Mind* (Princeton, 1985).[7] Slater argues that Plautus, whose stage name, Maccus, suggests that he had learned his skills as performer in the Atellane, adapted the formal Greek scripts so as to stress the element of improvisation by writing into the dialogue of his leading slaves sequences in which they are forced to respond to crisis and share with the audience their indecision and constant risk of breakdown and discovery. In this way Plautus gave to Greek comedy the appeal of the Atellane and made his Greek slaves into recognisably Italian intriguers and *improvvisatori*. It has long been recognised that Plautus altered the balance of the sentimental Menandrian comedies, shrinking the more genteel roles and building up the accent on lowlife by multiplying or expanding the servant roles and stressing the greedy parasites: *quantus sit Dossennus edacibus in parasitis*, as Horace put it (*Epistles* 2.1.173)[8] To this we might add Plautus' transformation of the countrymen, usually treated with some respect by Menander, into bumpkins to be mocked and beaten, and his grotesque exaggeration of the exotic mercenary soldiers, already foreigners in the Greek city states, and inflated in absurdity in the Roman adaptations. Only one type from the *commedia* is lacking—the *dottore*. Hellenistic Greece and Rome do not have professional lawyers to intervene in family entanglements with their jargon and details of wills, contracts and lawsuits; the role of professional intruder in the household has to be taken on by the chef, essential to many of the comic plots, or far more rarely, the physician.[9]

I would like to illustrate the features common to Plautus comedy and the *commedia* from two plays, both of which have developed these elements beyond their prominence in the original Greek models, no doubt because they were already popular components in Atellan farce. The first play is *Pseudolus* ("Le Menteur") in many ways Plautus' masterpiece, because of his loving exaltation of the slave protagonist. The plot is triggered by the need of young Calidorus to pay for the purchase of his slave girlfriend before she can be spirited off to the Near East by the rival, the foreign captain, Polymachaeroplagides; but the young man appears only in Acts 1 and 3. He is naïive, polite and without interest; his girl, like many girls in comedy, has no speaking role, and leaves the stage forever halfway through Act 3. It is typical of Roman comedy, as it seems to be of the *commedia*, that lovers' endearments are offset by the more cynical comments of the eavesdropping servant who mediates between the audience and the sweet young things. Pseudolus is an improvisor eager to exercise his skill at the expense of the father or the slaveowner and his chief characteristic is a splendid relish for self-dramatisation. He is either up-front presenting his view of the action to the audience (he even compares himself to the playwright as creator of the action)[10] or downstage putting on an act and assuming striking poses for his old master and the kindly neighbour; the element of display is overt. We might consider his entry in Act 3 to give his master some fairly insubstantial good news.

PS.:   I'll give my man a grandiose greeting.
CAL.: Whose is that resounding Hail?
PS.:   Ho there, hey there, ho there master, lord and master, you I say,

> Pseudolus' own chief commander, see, I bring you three times three,
> a triple trinity of blessings, joy, rejoicing jointly shared,
> all this won by my devices, cunning, trickery and fraud.
> CAL.: How the rascal camps it up!
> PS.: Stand forth and greet me, boldly stride
> and offer me your outstretched hand in hopeful salutation.
>
> (*Pseudolus* 702–05)

The verbal pirouettes demand matching stage movements—and yet we have no clue in the text to their nature. Pseudolus and others who have so many traits of the *zanni* are sometimes described in terms of their gestures, but there is no hint of dance-steps or somersaults such as abound in the *commedia*.[11] On the contrary, when Pseudolus dances, as he does in the finale, he is supposed to be stepping out: he is recalling how he celebrated his young master's success with exotic Ionian dancing and song until the repeated toasts of wine got the better of his feet and threw him. As he reports the occasion he reenacts it, but this is set apart as a dance, and the corollary is that the normal movements of these comics lacked the real elasticity of a Truffaldino. Besides the leading slave, the play also features a professional impostor, Simia, who outplays Pseudolus at his own games, and two old dupes—the master, who is allowed to keep his dignity until the very last scene where he must dance as a forfeit to recover the money he lost in the wager, and the slave dealer who forfeits both his cash and his dignity, for in Plautus money rather than sex lubricates the action. One more detail. When I first read about the *commedia* I was struck by the exploitation of dialect; not just the differentiation of peasant and city dweller, but for example, Beolco's Paduan peasant, Florentine noble, Venetian *dottore* and Bergamasque soldier, or Goldoni's Doctor from Bologna and Bergamasque servants. I asked myself whether we could detect any such dialect variation in Roman comedy; here it seemed Roman comedy differed from both the *commedia* and its Greek models. Since about 1960 we have in Menander's comedy *The Shield* a scene of imposture in which the young gentleman impersonates a physician by putting on the Doric vowels of Cos, the home of Hippocrates' School of Medicine, and gives his nonsensical diagnosis in a regional accent.[12] What is there in our Latin texts to compare? The Romans noticed the speech of men from other Italian communities,[13] and even in a Greek setting may stop to mimic their phrases. But the playwright can hardly provide an equivalent in Latin for regional variation between the different types of Greek in his model.

Greek phrases in Roman comedy are usually smart-set vocabulary like gastronomic French, or slave-argot, not a demarcator for the foreigner, since all the stage roles are supposedly Greek. The only language variation in the whole corpus of Roman comedy is the Punic, partly genuine, partly nonsensical, spoken by the Carthaginian uncle of Plautus' *Poenulus*. To return then to *Pseudolus*, how does Plautus handle the nearest thing to a foreigner, the Macedonian captain's batman? His speech has been infected with the bombast of his military master, and he is mercilessly mocked by the old men who are convinced he is the hired impostor sent by Pseudolus. It is, it seems to me, inevitable that this foreign servant, mocked for his funny clothing and accused of being his master's fancy boy, was also equipped with a comic accent to increase his absurdity. Latin never adopted the convention used by Greek of indicating dialect and accent variation in writing; it is for us to imagine the humour of accent wherever it is made possible by the script. *Pseudolus* could be played as *commedia dell'arte*, with its old men, its dominant gesticulating trickster, and its sequence of confrontations and imposture and confidential self-commendations to the audience.

I have chosen the *Casina*[14] as my second exhibit: it was the model for Machiavelli's *Clizia* and has often been compared with the Atellan farce, largely because of its Pantalone-type protagonist. For the old lecher Lysidamas of *Casina* has fallen in love, and on his first entry rhapsodises about his new enjoyment of life like Pappus in the Atellan *Pappus in second place*; he preens and boasts of his perfume and offers every opportunity for mimicry, and this Pantalone, not any intriguing slave, is the leading figure, destined for mockery and physical abuse. Scholars have even related the name of the play to the old Oscan word *casnar* or *casinar*, which Varro tells us meant "old fellow,"[15] and was the equivalent of Pappus the dotard. A second point of affinity is the recurring contrast of town and country servant, which opens the play, between the sophisticated young squire (or groom), Chalinus, and the earthy bailiff, Olympio. These two are being pushed by the opposing intrigues of husband and wife as rival claimants for the hand in marriage of the sweet young maiden, Casina. The contrast of their manners must have been reinforced by a distinction of accent and clothing; at the same time the opening scene offers vivid scope for mimicry as the countryman threatens his urban rival with hard labour fetching water on the farm, and describes with vivid quotation the luscious endearments that his future bride will offer him. Later scenes display the intrigue of his old master to enjoy a stolen night with the young bride of his rival.

Similar contrast of town and country is prominent in the opening servant dialogue of *Mostellaria* or the differentiated rivals for the favours of Phronesium in *Truculentus* "The Boor"; there the young townsman must compete with a country boor and his servant, and a braggart soldier whose pretensions are quickly faced down by the greedy courtesan. *Casina* has two set-piece scenes, (and here I do not know whether I am describing something characteristic of the *commedia*): in the first the old master and his wife draw lots, each ostensibly on behalf of the servant he is sponsoring as husband for the bride. The alarums and confusion of the lot-drawing scene depend heavily on stage business like peering and prodding and gestures of elation or despair. In the second episode the women of the intrigue disguise the now defeated bailiff as the future bride and solemnly escort "her" over the threshold into the house. The whole sequence is cast as song, not spoken dialogue, and there follows a series of melodramatic vignettes as first the maidservant in the plot rushes out pretending that the bride has gone mad and is armed with a sword, then the groom enters his nuptial chamber to emerge shellshocked from the encounter with his overmuscular bride. Each of these scenes calls for vigorous mimicry and a variety of leaps and bounds that will fill an otherwise unoccupied stage—but there is no word in the text. The Roman theatre offers no description of *lazzi*, not even any allusions to cartwheels and cabrioles, but the scenes must depend for their appeal on the antics of the performer. In keeping, the play will end with the abject old lecher beaten and cudgelled in full flight from his hoped for consummation, surrounded, mocked and forgiven by the women as the "bride" still in wedding finery strides in demanding his conjugal rights.

I have said little about one of the controlling aspects of the *commedia* about which much is known, and one that was important in ancient comedy also: this is the mask. We are told by Greek sources that the mask determined the dramatic personality (the original meaning of *persona* is "mask") and that the comic playwright about to compose the script for a scene would take and hold in front of him the masks of his leading roles to gain insight into their behaviour. Marble reliefs and painted frescoes alike show masks as symbols of the play, by themselves or set out before the dramatist in his study.[16] Wearing one of the masks of an old man or young woman (for in Greek comedy lovers too wore masks) the actor let it define his role as if he became a Brighella, Pantalone or Matamoro. How was it in Roman comedy? Cicero tells us that the *sanniones* who have sometimes been seen as forerunners of the *zanni* make their effect with their eyes, their expressions and their whole bodies,[17] but these are clowns or mime-artists, not performers in comedy or Atellan farce. The ancient commentators on Terence believed that his actors originally performed in comedy without masks, and many textbooks on Roman drama assume this as beyond dispute: we can point to another Ciceronian text that seems to say that masks were only adopted within Cicero's own youth, because a star performer wished to hide his squint.[18] Yet Plautine characters refer to masks and describe each other in terms that presume a set mask for each role. Here for instance is Pseudolus as described by the man he has duped when he is asked for an identification:

> A redhaired fellow with big round belly, thick in
> the calf and swarthy skinned
> his head was huge, his eyes were piercing, ruddy
> cheeks, and then his feet!
> They were enormous. . . . (*Pseudolus* 1218–20)

The Romans had seen Greek comedy masked in Southern Italy. It is hard to believe they took over the Greek costumes which gave their name to the plays and not the vivid character masks we see used as decorative motifs all over Roman domestic architecture. They loved the humour of human appetites, of rustic horseplay, of repartee and artful abuse. They found slaves more interesting than lovers and money marginally more absorbing than sex: in all these respects we may point to affinities with the *commedia* rather than argue for direct influence, but these very affinities explain why it was so easy for the improvisors of *commedia dell' arte* to compose their scenarios as permutations and combinations of the erudite Renaissance offspring of Plautine comedy.

University of Toronto

NOTES

1 The classic survey of evidence for the Roman comic theatre is till *The Roman Stage*, 3rd ed. (London, 1964) by William Beare. Other studies of Roman Comedy such as *The Nature of Roman Comedy*, 2nd ed. (Princeton, 1967) by George Duckworth limit themselves to adaptations of Greek comedy, and to the text rather than to matters of production and staging.

2 For illustrations see *The History of the Greek and Roman Theatre* (Princeton, 1961) by Margete Bieber, figures 538–39 and 817–24.

3 The titles and excerpts are my own translation from *Scaenicae Romanorum Poesis fragmenta* Vol. 2 (3rd ed.) edited by Otto Ribbeck.

4 De Amicis pp.28–29.

5 The chief testimony is Livy 7.2.12 based on Varro's works of theatre history now lost.

6 On this type see "The Adultery Mime" by R. W. Reynolds, *Classical Quarterly*, 40, 1946, pp. 77–84.

7 For a comparative review of both books see Erich Segal in *TLS*, July 12, 1985.

8 "How he plays the Atellan grotesque in his greedy parasites." The implication is that Plautus stressed this aspect of his parasite roles to assimilate them to Dossennus in the beloved Atellane. On these modifications see *Elementi plautini in Plauto* by Eduard Fraenkel (Rome, 1960), the updated translation from his original German *Plautinisches im Plautus* of 1922.

9 For intrusive caterers in Plautus see the *Aulularia* and *Mercator*; for a physician see *Menaechmi* 889–956. Both types occur in Menander. See below, note 12.

10 On Pseudolus' role see "The transformations of Pseudolus" by John Wright, in *Transactions of the American Philological Association*, Vol. 105, 1974, pp. 403–16.

11 On Roman acting techniques see Bieber (note 2) c.15 with illustrations. Although commentators on Terence's comedies distinguish between *Motoriae*, plays of lively action, and *Statariae*, plays of static dialogue, the evidence of illustrations in the Terentian manuscripts suggest a largely static presentation with movement confined to hands and arms. This is also suggested by Quintilian's comments on the similarity between the gesture of the lawcourt and the comic stage in *Institutio Oratoria* 11.3. (On which see Fantham, *Phoenix* 36, 1982, pp. 243–263.) The only account of stage gesture in Plautus' scripts is the commentary on the improvising slave's mime at *Miles Gloriosus* 210–25; this too speaks only of the upper body. It is most likely that, except in scenes of action and dramatic upset, stage behaviour was naturalistic without stylization. In contrast as I have suggested, scenes of drunken celebration or panic called for full scale character dancing or even acrobatics.

12 See now the translation of W. G. Arnott in *Menander* Vol. 1 (Loeb Classical Library, Cambridge, Mass., 1979) pp. 74–81.

13 Compare Plautus *Trinummus* 609 "Just nicely so, as the Praenestine puts it" mocking the idiom of nearby Palestrina.

14 For a recent translation of *Casina* see *Plautus: The Darker Comedies*, tr. James Tatum (Baltimore, 1983). There is a good philological commentary on the play by W. T. MacCary and M. M. Willcock (Cambridge, 1976). Professor Willcock is currently preparing a commentary on *Pseudolus*, of which the last edition with English commentary is that of E. H. Sturtevant (New Haven, 1932).

15 Varro *de Lingua Latina* 7.29 and 96. See also 7.95 on Dossennus/Manducus and 6.68 on Bucco.

16 See "The Poet and the Mask" by T. B. L. Webster in *Classical Drama and its Influence: Essays presented to H. D. F. Kitto* (London, 1965) pp. 5–15.

17 Cicero, *de Oratore* 2.251.

18 Cicero, *de Oratore* 3.221. On the evidence for masks in productions of comedy at Rome see Beare (note 1) Appendix I, pp. 303–09.

Douglas Radcliff-Umstead

The Erudite Comic Tradition of the *commedia dell'arte*

Although one might argue for an antithesis between the amateur, fully written erudite comedies of strict classical style produced in Italy throughout the sixteenth century and the improvised plays performed by the professional actors of the *commedia dell'arte* beginning by the fourth decade of that same century, careful examination will reveal a rapport of mutual inspiration and reinforcement. The designation of "erudite," "learned," or "regular" to the comic theatre of late Renaissance Italy refers to plays structured in five acts according to classical unities of time and space (but not necessarily that of action) on the model of the ancient Latin plays of Plautus and Terence. In an attempt to trace the origins of the *commedia dell'arte* some historians have succumbed to the temptation to assert a direct line of continuity from the ancient mimed Atellan farces with their grotesquely masked characters like Maccus and Buccus through the performances during medieval times of buffoons, jesters, acrobats, and mountebanks in public squares or at the banquets of nobles and well-to-do merchants. The laughable antics of devils in the sacred plays of the Middle Ages would appear to anticipate the nimble tricks of Harlequin, Pulcinella, and the Zanni in the *commedia dell'arte*. Unfortunately documentation does not exist to support the theory of an unbroken tradition of popular buffoonery. To appreciate the theatrical style, the subject matter, the stage practice, and a great deal of the character types of the *commedia dell'arte*, we must look to the inspiring example of erudite comedies.[1]

Performances of comedies played a major role in the public life of "elite" society in sixteenth-century Italy. The production of comic drama occupied the attention of courtiers, bureaucrats, and leading artists. In festively decorated palace courtyards or in the great halls of the government centres of republican communes, artists like Raphael, Giulio Romano, Bronzino, and Vasari created elaborate stage sets with scenery designed according to the rules of vanishing-point perspective. Every year the pre-Lenten celebration of carnival provided the perennial occasion for performing comedies. The public wearing of masks, parades of colourful floats, jousts, tournaments, and privately sponsored banquets and balls all highlighted the carnival-time festivities which also featured the production of comic plays. Special state occasions like weddings between lordly families, visitations by foreign dignitaries, and the birth of an heir to the throne would call for splendid celebrations that usually included the performance of comedies. The comic art, which forever celebrates the joyous rebirth of life and society, entered fully into the political symbolism of the late Renaissance Italian city states.[2]

Indeed the very number of comedies written and actually staged during the sixteenth century in Italy is astounding, attesting to the enthusiasm and dedication of the individuals responsible for the productions. This modern comic theatre with its aspiration to classical perfection arose as the culminating moment of a century and a half of striving by humanistic scholars to achieve the formal order and balance of ancient Roman comedy. The discovery in 1428 by Nicholas Cusanus of twelve previously unknown Plautine comedies started a period of intense study on the drama of antiquity. By the second half of the fifteenth century humanists abandoned writing Latin comedies on the pattern of vernacular sacred plays and adopted the form of Plautus and Terence. With the introduction of printing, scholarly editions of the comedies by the two ancient Roman playwrights became available as modes for emulation and for translation in modern languages. Venice became the most active urban centre for the staging of humanistic comedies like those of Tito Livio dei Frulovisi (d. ca. 1456) and Giovanni Armonio Marso (working around 1502) with performances by students or monks. Vernacular translations of the works of Plautus and Terence led by the last quarter of the fifteenth century to productions in Rome, Florence and Ferrara. All the humanistic research, the writing of new Latin plays on the ancient model, and stagings by municipal and courtly authorities finally by the onset of the sixteenth century encouraged Italian writers to compose original plays in their own living language. Bold pioneers at the start, like Ludovico Ariosto at the Este court in Ferrara writing five comedies and Niccolò Machiavelli in political exile in the Tuscan countryside composing his plays *La Mandragola* (1518) and *La Clizia* (1524), reflected the influence of humanism by carefully following classical structure in their drama. Other comic playwrights of the first wave in the sixteenth century include Cardinal Bernardo Dovizi da Bibbiena with *La Calandria* for production during the carnival of 1513 in the duchy of Urbino and that scourge of princes Pietro Aretino with five comedies that carried the convention of classical drama nearly to the breaking point. Public service almost seemed to require composition of a comedy, as with the Florentine statesman Donato Giannotti writing *Il Vecchio amoroso* around 1533 and the future political assassin Lorenzino de' Medici presenting his *Aridosia* in 1536 for staging in the Tuscan capital. Even in the first generation of comic playwrights there emerged a figure who combined the roles of actor and author: Angelo Beolco (ca. 1496–1542), the Paduan writer generally called Ruzante after the peasant character who reappears throughout several of his stage works. Romantic criticism in the second half of the nineteenth century regarded Beolco as an outcast who established the *commedia dell'arte* by forming his own dramatic troupe and improvising plays that he later wrote down in completed form. The fact that certain characters like Ruzante, Menato, and Gnua return in various plays suggests the creation of fixed masked types anticipating those of the *commedia dell'arte*. But Beolco's recurring characters display markedly different traits in individual plays according to dramatic circumstances. Also Beolco's acting troupe was made of gifted amateurs rather than professional performers. The Paduan playwright most closely approximated the later style of the *commedia dell'arte* by permitting his actors a wide scope for improvisation of comic tricks and by creating verbally teasing situations where his playful character Ruzante frustrates an anxious listener by delaying a crucial message with a meandering tale. For Angelo Beolco belongs to the first generation of Renaissance playwrights in his devotion to the cultural traditions of humanism that brought about the revival of classical-style comedy.[3]

Toward the middle of the sixteenth century a second wave of comic dramatists appeared on the scene just as literary critics were formulating an elaborate theory on the nature of comedy following the publication, the translation from Greek to Latin and the explication of Aristotle's *Poetics* in the 1530's and 1540's. Critics like the Ferrarese rhetorician Giambattista Giraldi Cintio with his *Discorso intorno al comporre delle commedie e delle tragedie* of 1545 joined Aristotle's observations on comic struture to Horace's recommendations in the *Ars Poetica* to develop a new canon of dramatic practice. Two of the comic playwrights working during that era of critical restriction were the Florentines Anton Francesco Grazzini (called "Il Lasca") and Giovan Maria Cecchi, who continued the momentum established by Machavelli. While retaining the form, many of the character-types, and comic devices of Plautus and Terence, Lasca would declare in the prologue of his play *La Strega* that a modern dramatist must

represent contemporary customs since people lived in a manner far different from that of ancient Athens or Rome.[4] An erotic frenzy pervades many
of Cecchi's comedies as that playwright clearly acknowledged, as in his
drama *Le Maschere*, the carnival function of comedy to be the remedy and
antidote to purge minds of inhibiting thoughts. Both Lasca and Cecchi
participated in the civic and intellectual life of the Tuscan capital where
comedy performed by amateurs served as an ornament of the restoration
of the Medicean family under Duke Cosimo I.

Among the playwrights of the second generation Andrea Calmo (b. 1509
or 1510) recalls Beolco in being both an actor and dramatist. This Venetian deliberately adapted the earlier stage works of Beolco, Ariosto, and
Machiavelli to create plays of a review or vaudeville nature uniting parody
or caricature in a joyous kaleidoscopic picture of the cosmopolitan city
on the lagoon. Calmo's plays anticipate the scenarios of the *commedia
dell'arte* in that each one is an overwhelming compendium of the major character-types and humorous devices of Renaissance comedy. The
servant figures and other characters from the working classes in Venice especially parallel the madcap clowns like Harlequin and Zanni. Just as the
masked actors in the *commedia dell'arte* would represent characters from
various regions of Italy with their comically incomprehensible dialects, so
too in Calmo's plays like *La Spagnolas* there prevails a linguistic chaos
with Venetian-speaking merchants, a Bergamask porter, a German charcoal burner, a pedantic tutor orating in Ragusan, a Dalmatian mercenary
soldier amidst echoes of Spanish and modern Greek. Pursuing his acting
career during the 1540s and 1550s, Calmo was attempting in his plays to
use his stage experience to develop a theatre of wide public appeal just as
the troupes of the *commedia dell'arte* succeeded in achieving.[5]

By the close of the sixteenth century there arose the last generation of
comic dramatists at Naples with Giordano Bruno and Giambattista Della
Porta. In his play *Il Candelaio* (1582) the rebellious philosopher Bruno
was endeavouring to deconstruct the conventions of Renaissance classical theatre. Composed in seventy-five scenes over five acts, *Il Candelaio*
works through a superabundance of structural and stereotypical elements
like a formal argument, an antiprologue, and a proprologue along with
nineteen characters to crowd the stage with its nocturnal representation
of the Neapolitan underworld. The scientist and magical researcher Della
Porta deftly combined Plautine intrigue with Terentian sentiment to produce a large number of comedies like *La Fantesca* and *Gli Duoi Fratelli
Rivali*. Della Porta's plays achieved such European-wide popularity that
their plots came to serve as scenarios for productions by companies of

the *commedia dell'arte*.[6] All the various Italian cities where the erudite comedy flourished were to contribute motives, character-types, and plot situations for the emerging professional acting troupes.

Performance of comedies entered into the spectacles of civic life in late Renaissance Italy, not only during carnival season but also on the festive days of local patron saints and on the anniversary of major historical events. Along with comedies, the other important literary genre of carnival celebration in Tuscany was that of songs (*canti carnascialesch*) that accompanied and illustrated the themes of pageant floats. Frequently the same persons who wrote the carnival songs and prepared the decorations of the pageant parades were the ones responsible for staging comedies: the *brigate* (informal associations of friends). These were all amateur groups who enjoyed designing and constructing sets, working on costumes, and acting in the plays provided in the case of Florence by writers like Lasca and Cecchi. In addition to the loosely constituted *brigate* there were also the formally chartered learned societies or academies that staged dramas. Academies such as the "Umidi" ("The Damp Ones") in Florence, the "Intronati" ("The Thunder-Struck") in Siena, and the "Infiammati" ("The Enflamed Ones") in Padua encouraged their members to submit plays for production before select guests. In Florence during each week of the pre-Lenten season one of the responsibilities of the "king" elected by the "Umidi" for a seven-day term would be to arrange a banquet with an appropriate celebration such as a verse competition or performance of a comedy by members of the academy. Academic honours and titles eventually came to exercise a powerful appeal on the professional actors of the *commedia dell'arte*, who named their companies the "Gelosi" ("The Zealous Ones"), the "Confidenti," the "Uniti," the "Accesi" ("The Ardent Ones"), and the "Fedeli" ("The Faithful Ones") in the style of the academies. Isabella Andreini, the leading actress of the Gelosi company, prided herself on being a member of the "Accademia degli Intenti" in Pavia.[7] Along with the theatrical activities of the *brigate* and academy in Florence, the religious mutual aid societies known as lay confraternities occasionally mounted productions of profane comedies in addition to their usual sacred dramas until late in the sixteenth century when Archbishop Alessandro de' Medici forbade them to stage plays of a secular nature. One can readily see how widespread the production of comedies had become in Italian municipalities, with the result that the *commedia dell'arte* through its deliberate intention to attract the masses arrived at a popular audience never reached before by the *brigate*, the academies, or the confraternities.

Venetian society of the patrician class delighted in banquets highlighted
by performance of individual buffoons or by small troupes of amateurs
putting on humorous skits called "comedie". Young members of the
aristocracy formed entertainment companies called the "Compagnie della
Calza" from their colorful stockings and took names like the "Immortali",
the "Eterni" or the rustic "Zardinieri" and "Ortolani" ("Gardeners"). Angelo Beolco's company, often consisting of five men and two women,
used to take part in the festivities with the young nobles at the palaces of
the most prominent patrician families. At those occasions the amateur actors had the opportunity to perform on the same program with some of the
most skilled comic artists of the day, like the great clown Zuan Polo and
his son Cimador. Throughout the sixteenth century there were numerous
encounters between the amateurs with their literary culture and the professional performers with their practical experience which would lead to the
high degree of refinement in the style of the *commedia dell'arte* companies like the Gelosi under the direction of the actor-impresario Francesco
Andreini. It had been one of those early professional comedians, the Luc-
chese performer Francesco Nobili who was called Cherea after a Terentian
character, that had introduced the Venetians to vernacular productions of
Plautine comedies in the first decade of the sixteenth century. The impressive skill of actors like Cherea, Zuan Polo, and Cimador lay in their ability
to improvise a wide range of roles for the enjoyment of their audiences:
the parts of necromancer, peasant, cowardly warrior, learned professor.
Singing, acrobatic suppleness, and mime all enhanced the tour-de-force
performances of the great actors. The gala atmosphere of private patrician
entertainment in Venice brought together the comic talents of local nobles,
amateurs from the *terra firma* regions of the Venetian realm like Padua,
and the most accomplished actors of Italy.[8]

Courtly productions possessed a noted advantage over those of private
groups or religious associations: the full financial support of a reigning
dynasty like the Estense in Ferrara and the Gonzaga in Mantua who sought
through spectacles to affirm their splendour and authority. By sponsoring
performances of ancient Roman comedies or of modern plays on the classical pattern the noble lords demonstrated their dedication to humanistic
culture. In organizing the staging of his comedies Ludovico Ariosto had
all the resources of the Ferrarese court at his command. Productions could
take place for a sizable audience in the courtyard of the ducal palace of
the Este if weather permitted or else in a grand hall. By 1530 the Estense
palace even had its own theatre, but a fire destroyed it a year later. For
those ducal performances an author-organizer like Ariosto could call on

the services of local artisans for the staging and enlist as actors enthusiastic courtiers, functionaries, pages, students and even immediate members of the duke's family. It had long been the practice of the ruling families to hire the professional buffoons to participate in the triumphal processions and court pageants. Toward the end of the fifteenth century, as Mantua entered a period of staged magnificence with Isabella D'Este as the wife of Marquis Francesco Gonzaga from 1490 to 1539, courtly entertainments attracted some of the leading comic spirits of the day such as the original Fritellino and the versatile Zafarano (Ercole Albergati), whose roles could range to a tragic Orpheus in Poliziano's play. Especially for the lavish intermezzi with elaborate ballets and allegorical and mythological tableaux that occurred between the acts of erudite comedies there was a pressing need for the services of professional actors, dancers and singers. Therefore one can see how from the initial period that Italian courts undertook to promote the staging of comedies as a regular feature of state spectacles, paid actors and entertainers contributed their skills to creating visual, musical and choreographic display for the occasion. Because actors moved from court to court seeking employment in pageants, plays, and banquets, they had the opportunity for a broad exposure to humanistic culture in general and classical comedy in particular. The courtly receptiveness to career actors and performers would continue into the second half of the sixteenth century when the Estense and the Gonzaga rulers patronized the early companies of the *commedia dell'arte* such as the Gelosi. Staging of comedies by amateurs and later by professional actors advanced the political symbolism of the dynastic houses that wished to express their magnificence to the state's dutifully impressed subjects.[9]

Depending upon its urban location for performance, erudite comedy would attract aristocratic audiences, members of the upper middle class in a city like Florence where in good weather friends gathered in the gardens of the hosts sponsoring productions, and the circles of scholars and literati in academies. Among the entertainments offered by some bordelloes the acting of a licentious comedy might alternate with the reading of a lascivious tale from the *Decameron*. Nuns in convents also put on comedies, some of which were probably three-act farces of a rather edifying nature; townswomen and their female servants attended those performances while husbands and men-servants had to wait outside the all-female enclaves. Plays composed for production by children in schools would definitely be of a didactic character. Some of the academicians, like the Intronati of Siena, directed their plays to the "most worthy ladies" whose affections they hoped to sway with their romantic dramas. But even a playwright like Angelo Beolco whose stage works portrayed the struggles of starving peasants did not intend his dramas for a broad public crossing all classes but for patricians and academicians. It would fall to the troupes of the *commedia dell'arte* to take the subject matter of the erudite comedy to a popular audience.

Although Italy did not have a permanent theatre building until Palladio's Teatro Olimpico at Vicenza in 1580, the improvised performing spaces in palaces and municipal buildings could take advantage of the best developed stagecraft in Europe. The importance of spectacle in public affairs had encouraged artists to design elaborate stage machinery for brilliant visual effects. As would occur with the sets for plays of the *commedia dell'arte*, the *mise-en-scène* for erudite comedies would be a street with private residences and public buildings, especially a church. Prologues to comedies situate the dramas in specific cities and sometimes on precise streets as when Machiavelli indicates the "Via dello Amore" in Florence as the scene for *La Mandragola*. Ariosto chose his home city Ferrara as the setting for his second comedy *I Suppositi* and his fourth *La Lena*: mentioning the arrogance and greed of petty officials, having characters carry out their daily tasks as they refer to monasteries and gardens in the city even to naming the very street where the dramatist lived. Donato Giannotti humorously informs his audience in the prologue to *Il Vecchio amoroso* that they are sitting in the Arno River watching the events of a drama taking place in the university town of Pisa. The court environment of Mantua under the Gonzaga dukes closes around the title character of Aretino's comedy *Il Marescalco* in a stage scene between the palace and the stables where the farrier is in the ruler's employ: although the duke never shows himself, his presence dominates the theatrical space. Annibal Caro intended his comedy *Gli straccioni* of 1543 to be a political commentary on the decadence of Rome's aristocracy and the reformistic program of the Farnese pontiff Paul III to re-establish order in the holy city while restoring its physical grandeur and splendor. The buildings of the street scenes in erudite comedies have functioning doors, windows and balconies as would often be the case for productions of the *commedia dell'arte*. In a carnival sequence in Act IV, sc. 4 of *Il Vecchio amoroso* young men on the street throw oranges up to flirtatious girls standing on balconies as was the custom in Pisa during pre-Lenten celebrations. Along with the unity of place which the *commedia dell'arte* observed in the traditions of erudite comedy, the unity of time restricted action to less than twenty-four hours, which would be represented by the onset of dusk, terrifying nocturnal scenes for misadventures, and the brilliant arrival of dawn. The lavishness of the tableaux in the intermezzi would counter-balance the unique setting of the comedy in production. Within the simplicity of *mise-en-scène* and the limit of time there frequently were extremely complicated plots and sub-plots as the major characters and their servants conspired to achieve amorous and commerical victories. Except that the erudite plays required the classical five acts rather than the three which came to characterize the *commedia dell'arte*, a remarkable similarity of dramatic style would continue from the learned to the popular theatres.[10]

In determining the appropriate language for erudite comedies Italian dramatists participated in the *questione della lingua* that had preoccupied authors since the time of Dante. While Machiavelli advocated the use of contemporary Tuscan, the diplomat Baldesar Castiglione recommended a composite literary language from various Italian dialects along with foreign words. The poet Pietro Bembo suggested a return to the golden age of the Trecento with the Tuscan of Petrarch's verse and Boccaccio's prose in the *Decameron* as the proper models for Italian writers. Although Ariosto was an Emilian, he followed the counsel of the Venetian Bembo to write in the tradition of Petrarch and Boccaccio. While generally Bembo's proposal prevailed, writers of comedies resorted to other Italian dialects for a variety of reasons—usually for humorous effect as would occur in the regional type characters of the *commedia dell'arte*. Calmo's plays represent the greatest possible linguistic diversity. In the prologues to several of his plays Beolco defended the Paduan dialect as the most natural choice for the language of his characters, but in his classical-style comedy *L'Anconitana* there are two prologues, one in Tuscan and the other in Paduan, while within the play the servants of peasant origin speak Paduan, the adventurous lovers use Tuscan, and a rich merchant expresses himself in Venetian. Throughout Italian Renaissance comedy porters speak Neapolitan or Bergamask to arouse the audience's laughter. Pedants, lawyers, and physicians flaunt their learning with lengthy phrases in Latin. The Sienese comedy *Amor Costante* (1536) by the Intronato academician Alessandro Piccolomini features entire scenes in Spanish, a poetaster resorting to a ridiculously Italianized Neapolitan, and a German student from the University of Pisa (the play's setting) speaking a barbaric Italian with a few words of his native language. The *commedia dell'arte* in Italy would continue the comic contrasting of languages with the Venetian Pantalone, the Bolognese Dottor Gratiano, and the Neapolitan Pulcinella.

In addition to the debate over the suitable language for comedies, playwrights and theorists argued over the use of prose or verse. The example of Plautus and Terence influenced the choice of verse, but many dramatists felt that since comedy (unlike tragedy) should be a mirror of every-day life with most characters drawn from the middle and lower classes, prose would be the most natural means to represent daily existence. Even among the writers who preferred verse most sought a meter like the blank verse of hendecasyllable lines that achieved versimilitude by best resembling the prose of everyday speech. Both Ariosto and Cecchi reflect the confusing arguments by first composing some of their comedies in prose and then later recasting them into verse, usually with a loss of colloquial liveliness. Whether opting for prose or verse dramatists aimed at recapturing the nuances of different classes and social groups. Cecchi used his expert knowledge of farming and peasant life to have his rural characters refer to the exact names for crops and other foodstuffs. Merchants speak about marriage in similes drawn from the world of trade and high finance while priests offer advice in unctuous tones of sentences high-lighted by biblical illustrations. Machiavelli and Cecchi excel in revealing the stupidity of certain characters (especially older husbands about to be made cuckolds) who attempt to display their wisdom by constantly quoting proverbs. Young lovers usually express their ardent desire in mellifluous Petrarchistic phrases, a trait that will carry over into the *commedia dell'arte*. Beolco especially anticipates the verbal comic tricks of future Harlequins in Ruzante's tantalizingly repetitious stories that intentionally hold up in delivering the desired communication. Monologues abound in these comedies to demonstrate the inventiveness of astute servants and the hyperbolic eloquence of inflamed lovers. Erudite comedy created for the professional actors of the *commedia dell'arte* a rich linguistic tradition to be used in the improvised speeches of their scenarios.

It is in the wide range of character-types that regular classical comedy particularly influenced the popular theatre. Playwrights had before them the comic types of Plautus and Terence, figures from the sacred drama (*sacra rappresentazione*) of the fifteenth century, and the amusing examples of the life around them. Ancient comedy provided models for the parasite and the braggart warrior. Whereas in the world of Hellenistic Greece and republican Rome, parasites formed a class that attached themselves to wealthy patrons by performing useful errands and relieving the boredom of banquets, in Italian Renaissance comedies the parasites frequently appear as brokers, enjoying a social status far inferior to that of servants as they lend themselves to advancing the intrigues of individuals who offer them fine repasts. For although a dramatist like Machiavelli could portray the parasite Ligurio as a creature of superior intelligence and loyalty, parasites in erudite comedies distinguish themselves generally only by their gluttony to anticipate the insatiable hunger of the Zanni in the later *commedia dell' arte*.[11] In their portrayal of the braggart warrior Plautus and Terence had turned to the representation of mercenary captains in the New Attic Comedy, emphasizing the opulence and the cowardice of the military figures with their booty won in Eastern wars. Renaissance Italy possessed two equivalents of the *miles gloriosus*: the mercenary soldiers selling their dubious services to the contending communes and the *bravo* (thug) who might be a street criminal or the "strong-arm man" of a lordly family. In erudite comedies the braggart soldier is often impoverished despite claims to have snatched wealth from the ruins of demolished cities. Another original feature of the cowardly warrior in Italian plays appears in his literary affectations, speaking in an ultra-refined Petrarchistic language to show himself the *capitano innamorato* or else displaying his expertise in military tactics and dueling ceremonies. But when the danger of a challenge to arms menaces these boastful soliders, they take to flight as their better part of valor. Since Spanish occupation weighed heavily on Italians during the sixteenth century, the braggart warrior in comedies is often a Spaniard like Captain Marrada in *Amor Costante* reduced to a lowly police role in Pisa and usually frustrated in his amorous quests. Beolco succeeded in creating the most original and touchingly pathetic braggart in his *Parlamento de Ruzante* about the starving peasant Ruzante going to fight in the war of the League of Cognac only to come home more impoverished than ever and to face a thrashing from a *bravo* to whom he has lost his wife. All those comic warriors share their flair for *braggadocio* as they swagger about boasting of their conquests over thousands of opponents. This figure of the braggart captain would participate in numerous dramas of the *commedia dell' arte*, yet with an ambivalence not generally present in erudite comedies where the solider is almost always an object of ridicule. Francesco Andreini recounted his role in the books of *Le Bravure del Capitano Spavento* (published in 1607 and 1618) as the archetype of the strutting paragon of bravado. But in some of the *commedia dell' arte* scenarios the warrior moves away from the rodomontades of a Captain Matamoros to emerge as a dignified hero who deserves and wins the love of a fair maiden.[12] While the parasite remained a character-type too closely identified with Antiquity to become part of the popular theatre realized by the *commedia dell' arte*, the braggart warrior in the variations achieved by the playwrights of the erudite comedy could move into the gallery of parts as the Neapolitan or Spanish captain of the professionally acted dramas.

Comedy across the ages had delighted in presenting the pretentions of the *senex* or *vecchio*: the older man who acts as a blocking figure or *alazon* because he allows a senescent erotic passion to dominate him or yields to a miser's lover of gold.[13] Nicomaco in Machiavelli's *Clizia* (inspired by Plautus' *Casina*) as well as Teodoro Catellini in Giannotti's *Il Vecchio amoroso* and Filippo in Cecchi's *La Stiava* (both modeled on Plautus' *Mercator*) all illustrate elderly merchants so inflamed with sensual desire for a young woman that they oppose themselves against wives and sons in a battle of authority. Although these tyrannical father-figures hold many traits of rage, insistence on control, and temporary erotic obsession in common with the later Pantalones of the *commedia dell' arte*, the characters in the erudite comedies tend to be of a far more advanced age than the robust Venetian merchant in the improvised plays: generally around seventy although they refer to erroneous family record books to claim they are in their fifties. All-consuming greed that blinds a father to his daughter's pregnant condition and the danger to their family's honour rules the miser Ghirigoro de' Macci in Giovan Battista Gelli's comedy *La Sporta*, which the playwright based on Plautus' *Aulularia*. But regular Italian comedies do depict fathers who are consistently dignified even when they find themselves in bewildering circumstances like the Sicilian Filogono in Ariosto's *I Suppositi* who arrives in Ferrara and discovers an impostor in his son's place. Also most of the fathers who briefly succumb to a late sexual frenzy do recover their dignity and give way realistically to permit their sons to wed the young women of proved good family background. Like Pantalone, the older men in erudite comedies hold positions of respect in bourgeois society that they must regain from any fleeting passion.[14]

There is hardly a single classical-style comedy whose cast does not have a host of servants. Usually the hero turns to a wily man-servant to devise tricks (*beffe*) to outwit the miserly father or the possessive mother to obtain the funds for the youth to free a beloved girl from a cruel procurer. Although Italian Renaissance society did practice a limited form of slavery,[15] most of the servants are free men who like the attendant Corbolo in Ariosto's *La Lena* pit themselves explicitly against the slaves in the plays of Plautus and Terence to surpass the ancient models in cunning. Sometimes the number of servants in an individual drama is so large that a choral quality emerges from the dynamism of their action to promote the central plot as in Ariosto's first comedy *La Cassaria*. The servants in Aretino's comedies *Lo Ipocrito* and the *Talanta* differ remarkably from the slaves of ancient Roman comedy. In *Lo Ipocrito* the servants are background figures who comment on the events happening around them while in the *Talanta* the attendants Costa and Fora represent the force of pure animal appetite in the war between hunger and poverty that they intend to win by robbing a delicatessen owner of his precious goods.[16] Like the Zanni, Pedrolinos and Harlequins of the *commedia dell' arte*, the servants in erudite comedies alternate between feats of utter gluttony and the devising of masterful strategems in a battle of skill and desire.

Peasant characters possess many of the same traits as town servants, and in some of the dramas by Beolco the circumstances of warfare and famine compel peasants to take posts as servants in cities. Cecchi also pictures in his play *Il Figliuol Prodigo* the wonderment of peasants visiting Florence on a trip to purchase clothes for a family wedding: on beholding some masks in a shop window a peasant boy thinks they are flayed faces. Throughout many of the comedies the age-old resentment between city and countryside predominates as peasants attempt to cheat absentee urban landlords and their stewards of an excessive share of already meager crops. Occasionally a peasant manages, as in Cecchi's farce *La Serpe Ovvero La Mala Nuora*, to outsmart two venal physicians by playing a country bumpkin to elicit a medical opinion and proposed treatment while merely paying with a vague promise of future delivery of foodstuffs. As the recurring figure in many of Beolco's works the shrewd rustic Ruzante displays those nearly diabolical characteristics of appetite and erotic longing that will distinguish Harlequin as the master rascal of the *commedia dell' arte*. Resourcefulness for basic physical survival impels the rural figures of regular Italian comedies just as the clowns of the masked theatre will play the scoundrel to overcome the threat of poverty and hunger.[17]

Three related character-types of the erudite comedy were to crystalize in the Dr. Gratiano of the professional dramas: the pedant, the lawyer, and the physician. As mentioned earlier, that vain trio resorted to Maccheronic Latin to impress listeners with their superior education and spurious wisdom. Although Plautus' *Bacchides* provides the example of the tutor Lydus and that same author's *Menaechmi* features an overbearing physician, Italian Renaissance life and literature from the novella through Latin humanistic comedy offer countless instances of this modern character-type. The pedant from the early *Calandria* through the late *Candelaio* is usually a private tutor of decidedly pederastic tendencies that deny him participation in the triumph of romantic love which closes innumerable dramas. The blocking figure of the pedant with his distortion of culture and abuse of authority must suffer, as does Bruno's Manfurio in *Il Candelaio* with extreme physical pain and financial loss, the mocking *beffa* that exposes his façade of academic superiority. Among the scenarios in the collection by the troupe director Flaminio Scala, the *Teatro delle favole rappresentative* of 1611, is one entitled *Il Pedante* in the continuing tradition of ridiculing the Latin-spouting scholar who forever fails to communicate worthwhile lessons.[18]

Lawyers and physicians were figures of popular satire in the sacred dramas of the Renaissance because of their mercenary demands of high fees from the clients and patients whom they regarded with contempt as they cloaked their incompetence with incomprehensible Latin. Since Italian society was particularly litigious, authors of comedies frequently represented attorneys as grasping professional types intent on achieving financial profit from the troubles of their fellow citizens. Dr. Cleandro in Ariosto's *I Suppositi* appears as a creature swelling with ostentatious egotism as he boasts of accumulating a fortune of 15,000 ducats from his legal practice. Messer Nicia Calfucci in Machiavelli's *Mandragola* and Messer Ambrogio in Cecchi's *L'Assiuolo* along with countless other attorneys all throughout erudite comedies, the *commedia dell'arte* and comic opera possess a vainglory which causes them to believe themselves invincible in their careers or virilely attractive men of the world. Physicians in Cecchi's plays are called wallet emptiers who place monetary profit over patients' welfare. While clients languish in agony, the medical practitioners of Cecchi's farces fawn over each other with exaggerated ceremoniousness. Generally in Renaissance comedy the physician ranks along with snake charmers and other charlatans. Similarly Dottor Gratiano as a mask of the *commedia dell'arte* can be a rich lawyer, a physician or a charlatan always talking off point in convoluted Bolognese dialect and Latin to exhibit his useless knowledge of pagan myths and medieval juridical procedures or medical practices that seem more appropriate to veterinary science than the treatment of humans. Comedy, whether in regular classical drama or the improvised theatre, rejoices in exposing expensive frauds.

In play after play throughout the Cinquecento there reappears in different guises the practitioner of magical arts as sorcerer or witch to introduce the dark side of Renaissance culture in its superstitious reliance on astrology, necromancy, and demonology. Authors of novella collections, sacred dramas, and Latin humanistic comedies had preceded the playwrights of the erudite drama in deriding the claims of rogue magicians and charlatans to perform marvelous feats. Dramatists like Bibbiena in his *Calandria* and Ariosto in *Il Negromante* not only pointed out the falseness of sorcerers but also poked fun at the gullibility of their foolish clients. Agostino Ricchi's comedy *I Tre Tiranni* (1530) shows magic as assisting the three socially tyrannical forces of Love, Gold, and Fortune: the sycophant Listagiro poses as the necromancer Maestro Abraham to rob an elderly miser in the celebration of diabolical rites while the witch-procuress Artemona operates a laboratory to prepare love potions and elixirs for her amorous customers. Bruno's *Il Candelaio* presents the thieving astrologer Scaramuré who exploits the erotic passions of his clients and the swindling alchemist Cencio who extorts high fees for the illusory promise of revealing the secret substance to transmute base metals into gold. In his play *L'Astrologo* Della Porta produced a satire on occultism as practiced by the criminal Albumazar and his rebellious henchmen. The figure of the unscrupulous sorcerer taking advantage of credulous customers passes over into the scenarios of the *commedia dell'arte* as the title character in dramas like *Il Mago*, *Il finto negromante*, and *L'Astrologo del Porta* inspired by Della Porta's comedy.

Renaissance comic drama offers several other character-types that reoccur in the professionally acted plays. The hypocritical priest or friar like Frate Timoteo of *Mandragola* is, however, a type better suited for the relatively liberal first quarter of the Cinquecento before the Catholic Reformation imposed its censureship. The grand courtesan like Aretino's Talanta or the venal go-between who says her prayers while enlisting young women into sexual affairs like Madonna Verdiana of Cecchi's *L'Assiuolo* could retain their vitality into the popular stage. Merrymaking university students, more interested in engaging in adulterous liaisons than in mastering Roman law, would continue to disrupt the bourgeois society in *commedia dell'arte* sketches. The unmasked lovers of the improvised theatre definitely derive from the intrepid heroes and heroines of the erudite comedy: figures like Ferrante di Selvaggia and Ginevra in *Amor Costante* who endured the ordeal of flight from Spain, imprisonment by the Turks, separation and the assumption of false identities until they could be reuinted in a publically acknowledged marriage. With their proper Tuscan speech and elegant dress the *innamorati* or *amorosi* of the *commedia dell'arte* exhibit all the ardor of youth as they defy parents and relatives in the pursuit of romance. Since most of the professional troupes included actresses in their casts instead of the very young men who usually played female parts in the amateur drama, women's roles could enjoy a far wider scope than ever realized in erudite comedy.[19] But in drawing upon the figures of contemporary life, the personages of the novella and Latin humanistic comedy along with the standard types of Plautine and Terentian works, the regular comic theatre of the Renaissance left to the companies of career actors a rich tradition of stage characters.

Erudite comedy also developed numerous plot intrigues that would be

repeated in the scenarios performed by the professional troupes. One of
the principles of construction that prevailed was *contaminatio*: the merg-
ing of plot lines from two or more different sources as Lorenzino de'
Medici had followed in building his *Aridosia* from Terence's *Adelphi* and
Plautus' *Aulularia* and *Mostellaria*. Novel twists in fortune, the discovery of unsuspected relationships, and escape from perilous situations all
provided the delight of variety to heighten the pleasure of viewing long
familiar dramatic tales. Whether unraveling a comedy of strong passions
or constructing a comedy of manners, the classical-style theatre of the Renaissance represented in the constriction of unity of time a tense moment
of turmoil and surprise that would end in the affirmation of a renewed
society.

Cuckolding dramas usually result from the foolishness of an older husband not content with the affections of a young and beautiful wife. Messer
Ambrogio of Cecchi's *L'Assiuolo* exemplifies an erotic fury that drives the
attorney to neglect his lovely wife Oretta to chase after the widow An-
frosina until eventually the handsome youth Giulio entraps Oretta into an
adulterous situation which she discovers to be sexually pleasurable. The
desire to produce an heir to his estate leads Messer Nicia Calfucci of the
Mandragola to participate in a risky enterprise that ends in the romance
between his formerly chaste wife Lucrezia and her devoted admirer Callimaco. Definitely the prototype for the dolt who thinks himself attractive
and irresistible to all women is the arch-simpleton Calandro from Bibbiena's *Calandria*, where the stupidly straying husband allows himself to
be carried off in a chest to a rendezvous only to be stopped by customs
officers as contraband. Calandro's wife Fulvia in the meantime has taken
the Greek youth Lidio as her lover. With his usual originality Beolco
depicted situations of cuckoldry for reasons of separation in times of warfare and famine in his two dialogues in rustic language the *Parlamento
de Ruzante* and the *Bilora*, where in the first play Ruzante loses his wife
not from failing in affection but from her need to avoid starvation and
in the second play the canal boatman Bilora resorts to violence rare in
Renaissance drama by stabbing the old man who has taken his wife Dina
from him. Among the scenarios in Scala's collection *Il vecchio geloso*
shows the downfall of impotent old Pantalone in surrendering his young
wife Isabella to the vigorous rival Orazio who with the aid of the sly
servant Pedrolino tricked the elderly husband into delivering Isabella to
the arms of his competitor. Because of its variety of themes and plot
patterns the *commedia dell'arte* would treat cuckoldry as one element in
its choreography of passion, desire, and deceit.[20]

Boccaccio in the *Decameron*, even more than Plautus and Terence, inspired the comic authors of sixteenth-century Italy. Entire love speeches in plays like *La Calandria* are modeled nearly word for word from romantic declarations in some of the tales of the Florentine masterwork. What appealed to Renaissance dramatists was Boccaccio's theory of love as a right of Nature that must be obeyed or cause disaster to anyone who represses natural desire. Any human institution such as matrimony which opposes the force of love could be swept aside for an adulterous relationship as results in comedies like the *Mandragola* and *L'Assiuolo*. But marriage in Boccaccio's view could represent a crowning moment for romance, and consequently a play of cuckoldry like *La Calandria* would close with plans for a double wedding. In his comedy *L'Anconitana* Beolco fused Boccaccian romance with Petrarchistic amorous tradition in a drama about youths ransomed from Turkish pirates, double disguises by loving females in male attire, a nocturnal assignation between a courtesan and a rich broker in Petrarch's final countryside resting place Arquà, and then double sets of weddings. That transvestite disguise by a woman venturing into hostile neighbourhoods or distant regions to meet her lover distinguishes Fulvia in *La Calandria* and the maiden Lelia in the anonymous comedy *Gl'Ingannati* produced by the Sienese Intronati academy. Among romantic dramas one must include the sub-genre of "serious comedy" often derived from narrative works emphasizing pathetic situations in middle-class settings with the misfortunes of lovers nearly driven to a tragic ending but finally rewarded. Piccolomini's *Amor Costante* early introduced this drama of suffering lovers who display unshakable faith. Della Porta's *La Furiosa* presents two lovers who lose their sanity because of parental opposition to their marriage until in time a physician of genuine medical ability cures them of their mental aberration and love triumphs. The *commedia dell'arte* excelled in putting on plays about distressed lovers who had to overcome obstacles and mutual misunderstandings before they could wed. From the scenario for *Flaminio disperato* there arise multiple rivalries in love: the classic opposition between the father Anselmo and his son Flaminio for Merlino's daughter Isabella, competition for Isabella from Captain Sprofonda who is loved by Anselmo's daughter Cinzia, and conflict for Merlino's maid Ricciolina by Anselmo's servant Spazza and the captain's attendant Coviello. After disguises by Anselmo and the captain as clog-makers and Flaminio as a foreigner the play ends with age giving way again to youth as Flaminio wins Isabella, the captain takes Cinzia, and Spazza receives Ricciolina while the forever hungry Coviello looks forward to a feast. Since comedy is a rite of regeneration, weddings mark a natural conclusion to celebrate a rejuvenated society.[21]

Another plot pattern common to both the erudite comedy and the *commedia dell'arte* is the Boccaccian-inspired victory of intelligence as achieved in a *beffa* against obstructing parties. Here the theme of Fortune, Chance, or Destiny enters as an unpredictable force working to exalt or undermine human endeavor. Although in the twenty-fifth chapter of *Il Principe* Machiavelli concedes the outcome of half of human acts to Fortune, the other half is left to our initiative with an advantage for bold persons over cautious ones. In sixteenth-century classical comedy there is a distinct difference in the presentation of the *beffa* in plays written in the first or second half of the Cinquecento. Earlier authors like Machiavelli and Bibbiena tend to view the *beffa* as a powerful assertion of human wit and courage. The lover Callimaco and his ally the parasite Ligurio in *La Mandragola* devise stratagems to persuade Messer Nicia to make a cuckold of himself, with the aid of the venal priest Frate Timoteo and the lawyer's mother-in-law Sostrata. A knowledge of human motivation permitted the success of the main intrigue in *La Mandragola* that glorifies intelligence and daring. In *La Calandria* the attendant Fessenio demonstrates a diabolical cunning that anticipates that of the Harlequin-figure Truffaldino in Goldoni's *Il servitore di due padroni* except that he has to serve three masters: the young Greek refugee Lidio, Calandro, and the simpleton's intrepid wife Fulvia. Eventually Fessenio delivers the envoi of *La Calandria* since credit goes to him for resolving all the play's complex intrigues. But after the Catholic Reformation ushered in an era of repression and despair in achieving earthly goals, the depiction of the *beffa* by dramatists stressed the futility of human endeavor. Cecchi's comedy *Le Cedole* (c. 1575) represents the repeated failures of the servant Monello to further the amorous pursuits of his young master Emilio: both Monello's hastiness in launching intrigues of impersonation and the intrusion of Chance bring about defeat.[22] It would especially fall to Harlequin to continue the tradition of the *beffa*, sometimes with a Machiavellian wit and bravery but other times with a laughable ineptitude.

Since ancient times the confusion caused by identical twins has created mirthful situations in a continuing comedy of errors. One of the variants introduced by Italian Renaissance playwrights upon the scheme of Plautus' drama of twins the *Menaechmi* is a difference in sex which gives rise to transvestite disguises as occurs in *La Calandria* between Lidio and his sister Santilla. The Intronati comedy *Gl'Ingannati* moves along in a spontaneous and insolent spirit of youthful erotic fury intensified by the disguise of Lelia as the page Fabio courting the maiden Isabella in order to win the affections of Flamminio until Lelia's twin brother Fabrizio arrives in Modena to be mistaken by Isabella for the handsome Fabio. Aretino built the many complications of his comedy *Lo Ipocrito* around the striking resemblance between the twin brothers Liseo and Brizio Rocchetti. A carnivalesque mood of amusement pervades Cecchi's play *La Moglie* on a bewildering day in Florence when the arrival of the long-lost Ricciardo de' Silvani results in a collision between reality and appearance because of the natural confusion for his brother Alfonso de' Silvani. *Commedia dell'arte* scenarios abound with humorous misadventures occasioned by the presence of twins as in *La gelosa Isabella* (with the difference in sex and the sister's impersonation of a man), *Due Flaminie simili* (with twin sisters), *Due Simili* (where Virginio encounters his double "Virginio lo straniero"), and meeting of twin braggart warriors in *Li Duo Capitani simili*. Just as Shakespeare's *The Comedy of Errors* compounds already perplexing situations by adding twin servants for twin masters, so too does the scenario *Li sei simili* with the addition of a third identical pair of brothers. Comedies about identical twins interweave multiple levels of vision in an ambivalent drama that overturns the conventional reality of bourgeois existence.[23]

As plays about twins illustrate, Renaissance comedy frequently resorts to intrigues of impersonation, disguise, and doubling. The necromancer Ruffo in *La Calandria* actually believes a servant's story that Santilla is a hermaphrodite with the ability to appear male or female. Androgynous exchanges of identity intensify a comic spirit of amorous confusion over deceiving appearances. Since the time of action for many dramas is a day during carnival season, characters in plays like *Il Vecchio amoroso* and *L'Assiuolo* enjoy a sense of security in being able to go out on the streets wearing masks. Ariosto constructed *I Suppositi* on the voluntary exchange of identities between the young master Erostrato and his servant Dulippo where the former chose to enter domestic service to be close to a young woman while the latter took his employer's name to attend the University of Ferrara. With his grotesque view of life Giordano Bruno made of *Il Candelaio* a drama of illusion transforming reality with characters appearing on stage wearing false beards and donning the garb of others. Bruno's play advances to a mirror confrontation between the painter Giovan Bernardo and his impostor Bonifacio disguised as the artist in order to meet with a courtesan who turns out to be his own wife in disguise. These stylized costumed masquerades foreshadow the comedy of patterned mannerism in the improvised plays where most of the actors are eternally masked figures in a charade of human doubleness.[24]

Both literary theorists and dramatists of the Renaissance agreed that a stagework should hinge on Aristotle's notion of peripety as a turning around of events, generally through a scene of agnition (recognition) where unsuspected relationships suddenly become known with radical consequences for all the major characters. Sometimes the recognition comes about through the arrival of a *deus ex machina* figure as in Machiavelli's *Clizia* where a gentleman from Naples appears in Florence to claim Clizia as his daughter and thereby makes possible her wedding to Nicomaco's son. Playwrights endeavored to achieve verisimilitude by relating the cause for the separation of families to the political and military events of the period. The fall of Constantinople, the brief Turkish occupation of Otranto in 1480, coastal incursions by the Sultan's commandos who would carry off prisoners, the menace of corsairs across the Mediterranean would all account for the dispersion of parents and children until Chance brought them together years later on a fateful day as happens in plays like *La Calandria*, *I Suppositi*, and Della Porta's *La Carbonaria* among many other comedies. The wars of the Leagues of Cambrai and Cognac form the background for Beolco's plays of peasant hunger and resourcefulness in the devastated Veneto region. Because parents in Renaissance Italy did not expose unwanted infants (especially females) to the elements as was the practice in ancient Roman times, dramatists attributed the disappearance of children to contemporary situations like the sack of Rome in 1527, whose shadow hangs over Aretino's first comedy *La Cortigiana* with its setting in the papal center. Throughout the scenarios of the *commedia dell'arte* parents and children are finally reunited after years of separation, and frequently in both regular and improvised comedies the discovery of family ties removes the danger of an incestuous marriage between father and daughter or brother and sister. While carefully introducing the political vicissitudes of the era as essential forces in their stageworks, the authors of classical-style comedies and the arrangers of scenarios were striving to create a drama of restoration.

Between the erudite comedy of the sixteenth century in Italy and the *commedia dell'arte* one can distinguish the difference between a theatre of text and a theatre of gesture and improvised dialogue. Individual playwrights like Beolco and Calmo early experienced the sometimes conflicting demands of being both dramatists and performers. But in no sense could the professional theatre develop in opposition to the fully scripted erudite comedy.[25] Already in September 1548 a troupe of Italian actors under the patronage of Cardinal Ippolito d'Este presented the *Calandria* at Lyons in honor of the French monarch Henry II and his queen Catherine de' Medici. While the managers of professional companies usually adapted the plots and characters of regular comedies for their scenarios, sometimes a scenario originally based on an erudite play would give rise to the writing of still another drama as when the actor Bernardino Lombardi drafted his play *L'Alchimista* after the sketch derived from Della Porta's *L'Astrologo*.[26] With their classical education and membership in learned societies many of the career actors brought the identical culture of the erudite comedies to their stage productions. Early and continuing sponsorship of the troupes by courts placed the actors together with prominent writers in collaborative relationships as occurred when Torquato Tasso directed the Gelosi company in the premiere performance of his pastoral play *L'Aminta* for the Estense in 1573. While one might very well judge the final supremacy of the improvised theatre over the complete text as an ideological crisis with the actor defeating the author, an objective evaluation must recognize the creative achievements of the *commedia dell'arte*.[27] Authors of regular comedies addressed themselves to limited audiences: the aristocratic circles of courts, the members of academies, and the bourgeois groups associated with *brigate* and confraternities. Frequently the performance of comedies served merely for an adornment of the state as ephemeral *pièces d'occasion* with no hope for future productions. But in time the career actors succeeded in mediating between the demands of aristocratic sponsors and the desire of a broad public for an accessible theatre. The diabolical cunning of Harlequin, the pedantic posturing of Dottor Gratiano, the intrigues of Scapino, and the charming vacuousness of Pulcinella could move with spontaneous freedom in the stageworld of classical unities, types, and plots fully developed by the writers of the erudite comedy. Through the sheer joy of *lazzi* devices, mime, acrobatic agility, and the punctuation-point timing of masterful clowning the career actors of the *commedia dell'arte* adapted erudite comedy for popular expectations and carried its drama of classical inspiration to international audiences from London and Madrid to St. Petersburg and Moscow.

Kent State University

NOTES

1 Pierre Louis Duchartre, *La Commedia dell'Arte*, trans. T. Weaver (1929; New York: Dover Books, 1966) pp. 24–29, affirms direct descent from the Atellan farce. Winnifred Smith, *The Commedia dell'Arte* (1912; New York: Blom, 1964), p. 26, denies the unsubstantiated continuity. Vito Pandolfi, *Il teatro del Rinascimento e la Commedia dell'Arte* (Rome: Lerici, 1969), pp. 151–152,

traces the origins of improvised drama in jesters, buffoons, piazza charlatan medicine acts and perhaps Goliardic performers rather than the amateur actors of erudite comedies. Also on pp. 140–141, Pandolfi posits an intermediate case of semi-professional companies like the group of Jewish actors led by Leone de' Sommi from the 1550s to the 1590s with patronage from the Gonzaga rulers of Mantua. Leone even composed a four-part dialogue on the art of performance with details on acting, make-up, costumes, and lighting.

2 Cf. this observation by Susanne Langer, "The Comic Rhythm," *Comedy: Meaning and Form*, ed. R. Corrigan (San Francisco: Chandler, 1965) p. 124, "Comedy is an art form that arises naturally whenever people are gathered to celebrate life, in spring festivals, triumphs, birthdays, weddings or initiations . . . " Werner Gundersheimer, "Popular Spectacle and the Theatre in Renaissance Ferrara," in *Il teatro italiano del Rinascimento*, ed. M. Lorch (Milan: Comunità, 1980), pp. 25–33 and esp. p. 26, asserts the "anti-democratic" nature of early theatre in northern Italy.

3 Maurice Sand in his text *Masques et Bouffons* of 1860 created the romantic myth of Ruzante. Jackson Cope, *Dramaturgy of the Daemonic* (Baltimore: Johns Hopkins, 1984), pp. 13–34, judges Beolco to be the first creator of a "character" on the modern stage. Pandolfi, *Il teatro*, p. 71, declares that *La Calandria* was in a cultural sense the most important, illustrative, and influential comedy of the Cinquecento for introducing the Boccaccian spirit of love to a courtly stage tradition.

4 Robert Rodini, *Antonfrancesco Grazzini: Poet, Dramatist and Novelliere 1503–1584* (Madison: Univ. Wisconsin, 1970), studies Lasca's many literary talents. D. Radcliff-Umstead, *Carnival Comedy and Sacred Play: the Renaissance Dramas of Giovan Maria Cecchi* (Columbia, MO: Univ. Missouri, 1985), compares Cecchi's comedies modeled on Plautus and Terence, his plays of modern novellistic inspiration, and his religious dramas.

5 Franco Fido, "Il teatro di Andrea Calmo fra cultura, 'natura', e mestiere," in *Il teatro italiano del Rinascimento*, ed. Lorch, pp. 191–215, investigates Calmo's intelligent compromise between the demands of popular theatre and cultural aspirations.

6 Aldo Trionfo, "Appunti su Giordano Bruno e sulla messa in scena del *Candelaio*," in *Il teatro del Cinquecento*, ed. L. Zorzi et al (Florence: Sansoni, 1982), pp. 99–103, considers Bruno to be Italy's greatest playwright, on a level with Elizabethan dramatists. In 1981 Trionfo directed *Il Candelaio* for a national premiere at the Teatro Comunale Metastasio in Prato. Louise George Clubb, *Giambattista Della Porta Dramatist* (Princeton: Princeton Univ., 1965), pp. 302–307, summarizes the arguments on whether or not Della Porta wrote scenarios for the *commedia dell'arte* troupes. Probably his plays served as invaluable sources for new scenarios.

7 Winnifred Smith, *Italian Actors of the Renaissance* (New York: Coward-McCann, 1930), pp. 49–50, mentions Isabella Andreini's classical education

and her academic membership. Florindo Cerreta, "The Entertainments for the Baptism of Eleonora de' Medici in 1568 and a Letter by Girolamo Bargagli," *Italica*, 59, No. 4 (Winter, 1982), pp. 284–295, presents a contemporary description by the Sienese Bargagli of the Florentine festivities that included performances of Lotto del Mazza's comedy *I Fabii* with spectacular intermezzi in the Salone del Cinquecento on February 19, 1568. Coming from a rival city, Bargagli judged the mixed amateur group of Florentine courtiers, merchants and academicians to be almost ridiculously inept actors. Daniele Seragnoli, *Il teatro a Siena nel Cinquecento: "Progetto" e "Modello" drammaturgico nell'Accademia degli Intronati* (Rome: Bulzoni, 1980), investigates the major dramatic projects in Siena.

8 Kathleen M. Lea, *Italian Popular Comedy: A Study in the Commedia dell'Arte, 1560–1620* (1934; rpt. New York: Russell and Russell, 1962), I, pp. 231–232 and 245–251, describes respectively the careers of Cherea and Zuan Polo. Ludovico Zorzi in the introduction to his Italian translation of Beolco's plays, Ruzante, *Teatro* (Turin: Einaudi, 1967), pp. xxxi and lxiv, fn. 39, depicts the activities of the Compagnie della Calza. Siro Ferrone, "Attori, professionisti e dilettanti," in *Il teatro del Cinquecento*, ed. Zorzi, pp. 59–79, surveys the major trends in acting from the end of the Quattrocento to the early seventeenth century, marking 1530 as the year when the humanistic influence in theatre faded away. Ferrone distinguishes between the early buffoons who were at the mercy of noble patrons but relatively independent of other performers from the later collective arrangement of actors in companies where contractual obligations to theatre impresarios by 1580 counted far more importantly than the capricious generosity of a lord.

9 Michele Catalano, *Vita di Ludovico Ariosto* (Geneva: Olschki, 1930–31), I, pp. 122–126 and 580, discusses Ariosto's start as an actor in court plays, his role as supervisor of dramas, and the participation of courtiers as actors in Ariosto's plays. Antonio Piromalli, *La Cultura a Ferrara al tempo di Ludovico Ariosto* (Florence: La Nuova Italia, 1953), pp. 98–103, comments on the ability of the Este to hire painters and sculptors to prepare decorations for public celebrations where the whole city became an embellished theatre space. For Piromalli, pp. 119–122, theatre under the Estense was a form of aristocratic propaganda. Paul Nettl, "Ferrara," *Enciclopedia dello spettacolo* (Rome: Le Maschere, 1958), V, p. 175, remarks how members of the court, pages, writers, university students, and professional actors all took part in the dramas and other festivities of the Este. Although the general public could attend dramas presented first in the ducal palace courtyard and later in a theatre within the building (a theatre destroyed by fire in 1532), seating for the lower classes was greatly limited. Charles Rosenberg, "The Use of Celebrations in Public and Semi-Public Affairs in Fifteenth-Century Ferrara," in Lorch, pp. 521–535, demonstrates how the revival of ancient comedy for performance created a sophisticated image for the Este court.

10 Giulio Ferroni, "La scena, l'autore, il signore nel teatro delle corti padane," in Lorch, pp. 537–570 and esp. p. 553, focuses upon the court setting of *Il Marescalco*. Mario Baratto, *Tre saggi sul teatro* (Venice: Neri Pozza, 1964), pp. 90–91, asserts that the essential intuition of Aretino's Roman play *La Cortigiana* is the street as it coincides with the stage. Marga Cottino-Jones, "Rome and the Theatre in the Renaissance," *Rome in the Renaissance: The City and the Myth*, ed. P. Ramsey (Binghamton: S.U.N.Y., 1982), pp. 237–247, studies the treatment of Rome in comedies by Caro, Aretino, and Francesco Belo (*Il Pedante*).

11 K. M. Lea, *Popular Comedy*, p. 243, describes the insatiable appetite of the Zanni.

12 Daniel Boughner, *The Braggart in Renaissance Comedy* (Minneapolis: Univ. Minnesota, 1954), presents a general study of the *miles gloriosus* in regular comedy. Allardyce Nicoll, *The World of Harlequin, A Critical Study of the Commedia dell'Arte* (Cambridge, Engl: Cambridge Univ., 1963), pp. 97–103, investigates the ambivalence of the Captain in *commedia dell'arte* scenarios. Giacomo Oreglia, *The Commedia dell'Arte*, trans. L. Edwards (New York: Hill and Wang, 1968), pp. 101–111, compares all the masks akin to the Captain. Gérard Luciani, "Un type de dialogue de théâtre: le dialogue schématique de la Commedia dell'Arte," *Essais sur le dialogue*, ed. Jean Lavédrine (Grenoble: Univ. Grenoble, 1980), pp. 21–60, but esp. 29–30, analyzes the Spanish literary influence in the Captain's dialogue with his sidekick valet as an aesthetic of astonishing conceits (*concetti*). Mel Gordon, "Lazzi: the Comic Routines of the Commedia dell'Arte," *Performing Arts and Resources*, 7 (1981), p. 14, remarks that the Captain along with Pantalone is the chief victim of violent *lazzi* routines.

13 Northrop Frye, *Anatomy of Criticism* (1957; rpt. Princeton, N. J: Princeton Univ., 1971), p. 172 refers to the *senex iratus* as a blocking figure or *alazon*.

14 Andrea Calmo specialized in playing the roles of older men. Unicio Violi in a review of Henry Salerno's translation *Scenarios of the Commedia dell'Arte: Flaminio Scala's 'Il teatro delle favole rappresentative'*, in *Italica*, 46, No. 2 (September, 1969), p. 199, stresses the phallic spirit of Pantalone in the scenario *Il Pedante* cavorting with courtesans to the chagrin of his lovely wife Isabella.

15 Slaves of Tartar extraction came to Italy from trade with the Black Sea area. Most of them were females intended as domestic help.

16 Mikhail Bakhtin, *Rabelais and his World*, tr. Helene Iswolsky (Cambridge, MA: Harvard Univ., 1968), p. 317, explores the role of the senses and their immediate gratification as treated by Rabelais. Appetite will lead to regeneration.

17 J. Cope, *Dramaturgy*, pp. 26–27, notes the transformation of the Plautine slave into a servant of rural origin in the character Garbinello of Beolco's comedy *La Piovana* (based on Plautus' *Rudens*), calling him a daemonic plotter of pure appetite. Mel Gordon, "*Lazzi*," pp. 21–23, presents examples of food lazzi about the servants' constant search for nourishment.

18 Antonio Stäuble, "Una ricerca in corso: il personaggio del pedante nella commedia cinquecentesca," in Lorch, pp. 85–101, regards the pedant as an example of a crisis in humanistic culture which had lost general confidence and instead aroused derision. H. Garfein and M. Gordon, "The Adriani *Lazzi* of the Commedia dell'Arte," *TDR*, 22 (1977), pp. 3–12, cite Latin *lazzi* where the parts of pedant and doctor are equally interchanged.

19 Nicoll, p. 112, comments how female lovers were generally bolder than the men, daring to feign insanity or to assume male attire to achieve their desire. Mireille Celse-Blanc, "Du travesti à la folie simulée, ou les jeux du masque dans la comédie siennoise," in *Visages de la Folie*, ed. A. Redondo and A. Rochon (Paris: Sorbonne, 1981), pp. 45–54, shows how within a generation the role of the transvestite (as in the early Sienese comedy *Gl'Ingannati*) gave way to simulated madness, largely due to the influence of the Catholic Reformation.

20 Anna Fontes-Baratto, "Eclairs de la folie dans le théâtre de Ruzante: le *Bilora*," in Redondo and Rochon, pp. 67–80, describes the sense of humiliation that drives the husband to a desperately furious act in Beolco's play. Nicoll, pp. 10–12, summarizes the plot of *Il vecchio geloso*.

21 Marvin T. Herrick, *Italian Comedy in the Renaissance* (Urbana: Univ. Illinois, 1960), pp. 165–166, 205–207, details the features of serious comedy. Nicoll, p. 132, cites the example of *Flaminio disperato* as illustrating improvised comedies of jealousy and amorous despair. Louise G. Clubb, "Italian Renaissance Comedy," *Genre*, 9 (1976–1977), pp. 469–488 and esp. 482–486, declares that "*commedia grave*" was a hybrid development of Italian Renaissance comedy for resembling tragedy except for the happy resolution of the plot, as through revelations in Della Porta's *Gli duoi fratelli rivali*.

22 Salvatore Di Maria, "The *Beffa* as Metaphor in the Italian Renaissance," Diss. Univ. Wisconsin, 1978, investigates the changing nature of the *beffa* across the sixteenth century. M. Gordon, "Lazzi," *Performing Arts*, pp. 51–53, lists trickery *lazzi* with Pulcinella as schemer and Pantalone as dupe.

23 Nicoll, pp. 136–137, describes scenarios dealing with the humorous confusion over identical twins.

24 Cope, *Dramaturgy*, p. 117, cites Harlequin as the expression of human doubleness in our social and appetitive being.

25 Oreglia, p. 3, upholds the essential opposition of scripted versus improvised comedy. I, of course, affirm their closeness.

26 Herrick, pp. 215–216, argues for the process of inspiration from scenario to full text.

27 Zorzi, introduction to Beolco's *Teatro*, pp. xxvi–xxvii, considers the crystalization of masked theatre to be a cultural crisis. Pandolfi, *Teatro*, p. 191, argues that a play like Lombardi's *L'Alchimista* represents a new creative stage transforming the erudite tradition by freeing it from Plautine models. Ferruccio Mariti, "La figura di Flaminio Scala," in *Alle orisini del teatro moderno: La Commedia dell'Arte*, ed. Luciano Mariti (Rome: Bulzoni, 1980), pp. 21–43, in

addition to surveying Scala's career in different troupes, analyzes the poetics of comic theatre in two prologues to Scala's fully scripted play in five acts *Il Finto Marito*, which has a parallel scenario *Il Marito*.

Laurie Detenbeck

Dramatised Madrigals and the *commedia dell'arte* Tradition

In the prologue to *L'Amfiparnaso*, the author Orazio Vecchi wrote:

Although you, illustrious spectators,
Are accustomed to seeing only tragedies
Or comedies embellished in sundry manners,
Do not disdain this our comedy
Which is certainly not graced
With a rich and fancy stage,
But is contrived with double novelty.[1]

That double novelty referred to the two slopes of Parnassus; one devoted to music and the other to comic poetry. Thus the dramatised madrigal was created, during the last decade of the sixteenth century.

These musical comedies were comprised of a series of madrigals, canzonettas, villanellas, and other regional song types, each of which was autonomous, but which were bound by a common theme or dramatic plot. The comic element of the cycles was most often drawn from the highly popular *commedia dell'arte* tradition. Their principal composers were Orazio Vecchi, who served as organ master at the Cathedrals of Correggio and Modena, and his contemporary, Adriano Banchieri, while peripheral contributions appeared by Alessandro Striggio and Giovanni Croce.

The movement began as early as 1567 with Striggio's *Il Cicalamento delle donne al bucato*; however, this style of early madrigal cycle did not contain a proper plot and the songs were bound by unity of subject matter, in this case the idle chatter of women as they do their laundry at the communal washing place.

The genre also appeared in two other incarnations; madrigal cycles whose unity was based solely on the title or on an occasion—for example, Vecchi's *Musical Banquet*—and madrigal cycles which used pastoral themes for their subject. These also contained elements of *commedia dell'arte*; a character called Pantalone sings the first canzonetta in Croce's

Triaca Musicale and later in that same work a character called Dottor Graziano performs. Of particular interest, however, are the later dramatic comedies produced by Vecchi and Banchieri and their close relationship to the *commedia dell'arte.*

Using a *commedia dell'arte* scenario for a musical comedy was not an unreasonable proposition: there had been, from the earliest appearance of improvised comedy, a lively co-existence of music and mime. As Nino Pirrotta has noted, the actor and playwright Andrea Calmo, a pioneer of *commedia dell'arte*, wrote that he and his fellow actors had employed dialect and music in their plays, and particularly the singing of *strambotti*—of *strambotziare musicalmente.*

This verb *strambotziare* brings us into contact with all the poetic and musical literature of the *frottola* of the late 15th and the early 16th centuries, the obscure literary meaning of which, often depending on roguish language and allusions, was certainly completed in the performance by miming and dancing.[2]

Pictorial evidence further indicates the frequent presence of music in *commedia dell'arte* presentations; one need only consult early engravings of the art to support this notion.

In the earliest account of a *commedia dell'arte* style performance, music and comedy are skilfully intertwined by the author, the notable 16th century composer Orlando di Lasso. The description of the entertainment at the Bavarian Court in 1568 reads like the inspiration of the future works of Banchieri and Vecchi:

After the prologue was spoken, Messer Orlando led the singing of a sweet five-part madrigal . . .

This is followed by a scene with the lover Polidoro. In the second scene Pantalone reappears:

From another corner of the stage emerges Messer Orlando, dressed as the Magnifico (Pantalone) in a long surcoat of crimson satin, with scarlet shoes in the Venetian style and a long black gown reaching to the ground. He is wearing a mask, the very sight of which is enough to make the public laugh, and has a lute in his hands. He is playing and singing: "Whoso passes through this street and sighs not, is happy indeed . . . "[3]

Singing and lamenting in this same manner Pantalone enters in the first scene of Banchieri's *La pazzia senile*: "O poor Pantalone, Lauretta is the reason I eat not a bite that tastes good to me . . . "[4] The tradition of musical accompaniment to *commedia dell'arte* performance had been well established by the end of the century. In Vecchi and Banchieri's works, however, the drama accompanied the music, which had become the key mode of performance.

In many respects, dramatised madrigal is a misnomer for this genre; a more appropriate term is "madrigal comedy," since it is not clear if these pieces were accompanied by acting or mime. There is much speculation as to how they might have been performed, and for whose benefit: were they acted out at all? The general consensus is that they were not.[5] Einstein proposes that the comedies were not written for the general public, but rather as social games to be performed at small gatherings, in a nobleman's house, or more likely at a meeting of the local musical academy.[6] It certainly seems clear that Orazio Vecchi did not insist upon the dramatisation of *L'Amfiparnaso*. The prologue contains the following notice:

The city in which this work is presented is the great theatre of the world, for everyone desires to hear it; But meanwhile know that this spectacle of which I speak is seen with the mind, where it enters through the ears and not through the eyes. Therefore be silent and instead of seeing, listen! (p. 17)

Although the work purports to be a comedy accompanied by music, the composer has clearly indicated that the action is subservient to the music. On the other hand, Adriano Banchieri emphasized the importance of the dramatic aspect of the works by providing instructions as to how performance should proceed, as in the following passage taken from the notices to *Il Metamorfosi musicale*: "Before beginning each song, one of the three singers will read aloud all that which is written before the music [that is, the argument of each scene], both to inform the listeners and rehearse the singers."[7] In the preface to the comedy *La saviezza giovanile*, Banchieri "gives directions which indicate that in this work the singers and musicians should be behind the scenes while the actors on the stage mimed their parts."[8] While it cannot here be proven absolutely that they were acted out, this evidence does seem to indicate Banchieri's concern for the integration of the play with the music.

Let us briefly examine these comedies from a dramaturgical viewpoint. Vecchi's comedy *L'Amfiparnaso*, composed in 1597, contains 17 scenes loosely based on a hybrid pastoral-*commedia dell'arte* theme. There are actually three separate plots—two sets of lovers, one happy, one starcrossed, a sub-plot with the stock Spanish captain in love with the principal female lover, and a third *commedia* plot comprised of two elders, Pantalone and Dr. Gratiano, and Pantalone's Bergamasque servant Pedrolino. The dénouement sees the two pairs of lovers happily united and the two

old fools spurned by their respective lovers. This latter sub-argument
providès the comic relief and comments on the main action, which has
a higher moral tone. None of the characters from the principal action
interacts with the *commedia* masks until the final scene, when they all
miraculously, and I might add inexplicably, assemble in the town square
to congratulate the newlyweds. The plots are incomplete and there is little opportunity for character development. Vecchi perhaps anticipated this
criticism and answered in the preface that ". . . this combination of music
and comedy has not been before undertaken, nor perhaps even imagined
by others, and many things may be found whose addition is required to
give it perfection" (p. 15).

   Although the *Amfiparnaso* is central in the development of madrigal
comedy, "there is no need for us to add to the oceans of ink that have
already been spilled" over it.[9] Vecchi's work concerns us less with regard to its relationship to the *commedia* tradition than the works of his
contemporary Adriano Banchieri.

   Banchieri was born at Bologna in 1567. He spent the better part of his
life at the Olivetan monastery of San Michele in Bosco, near Bologna, was
eventually named abbot and died there in 1634. This "renaissance man"
was a poet, a writer, a composer of both sacred and secular music, and an
accomplished musician and theoretician. He founded a music school and
the musical *Accademia de' floridi*. In his spare time he wrote plays in the
erudite comedy tradition as well as four madrigal comedies. Banchieri's
work is usually dismissed by the critics as unimaginatively derivative of
Vecchi. For example, Pirrotta claims:

A pretext is effective only for a time; so Vecchi abstained from repeating it . . . We
cannot praise his admirer and imitator Banchieri for equal moderation, because
he three times repeated his attempt to join the two Parnasses: with *La Pazzia
senile* (1600), with *Il Metamorfosi musicale* (1600), and with *La Saviezza giovanile*
(1608). Although also an author of purely literary comedies, Banchieri did not
change Vecchi's model and proceedings in his musical comedies. The arguments,
characters, and situations of these three works reproduce those of the *Anfiparnaso*
with but small changes.[10]

   While it is true that he modelled his work on Vecchi's, in *La Pazzia
senile* for example Banchieri produced a more dramaturgically refined libretto, creating a coherent plot and characters and dialogue more truly
consistent with the *commedia dell'arte* tradition. The *soggietto* could easily have been extracted from any book of *canovacci*. The central character
Pantalone, an old man from Burano, is told by his servant Burattino that

his daughter Doralice is in love with a certain Signor Fulvio. Enraged, Pantalone decides to marry her to his old friend Dottor Gratiano. Doralice overhears her father's plans and secretly runs off with her lover. Pantalone is further unsuccessful in his pursuit of the local courtesan with whom he is in love, and he and Dottor Gratiano are left alone at the end, deceived and unrequited in their love.

In comparison with Vecchi, Banchieri's cast of characters is economical. He requires only two lovers instead of the five portrayed in *L'Amfiparnaso*. The paradox between the love of the *innamorati* and the foolish old men becomes more pointed through Banchieri's thoughtful juxtaposition of scenes, alternated with *intermedi* which comment ironically on the central action, often with erotic overtones and *double entendre*.

The structure resembles that of a typical *commedia dell'arte* performance such as the following described by Oreglia: "Before the curtain rose, an actor spoke the prologue, which usually had no direct relation to the subject of the performance; in the intervals between the acts it was the custom to present brief intermezzos, often delightfully burlesque character sketches . . . "[11] Banchieri's comedy opens with an introduction sung by the author in which he informs the audience that the work has been composed in order to defeat melancholy and for pleasure.[12] Immediately following are two *intermedi* (as found in the earliest edition of 1598): a pastoral song of three nymphs which establishes the love theme of the comedy, succeeded by the interlude of the matchvendors. "Bizzarre Humour" enters to deliver the prologue, in which he presents the first concrete evidence that the piece was intended for performance before an audience: "Illustrious spectators, I have come out here into your presence to make reverence to you . . . " He tells who he is and then bids silence "because I see Pantalone who humbly approaches, to begin this Senile Madness" (p. 5). Banchieri has included implicit stage directions in the text in the manner typically used by Renaissance playwrights.

Pantalone begins Act I with a monologue. In his native Venetian dialect he expresses his love for Lauretta, the courtesan. The language here, as often throughout this comedy, is coarse, with frequent reference to eating and bodily functions. Vecchi's dialogue is refined in comparison. In scene 2 a new character joins Pantalone, his servant Burattino, one of the many manifestations of the Arlecchino mask. He introduces in Bergamasque dialect the first intrigue of the play: Doralice has been seen consorting with Fulvio from her balcony. An angry Pantalone vows to marry her to Dottor Gratiano in order to save the family honour and the two characters leave the stage, making way for the said Signor Fulvio. In almost perfect Tuscan Italian, he sings a beautiful madrigaletto in praise of Doralice's hair.

Re-enter, in scene 4, Pantalone in the company of Dr. Gratiano, and the marriage contract is confirmed. Banchieri here exhibits his comedic skills in the misunderstandings of dialect and confusion of vocabulary of the Bolognese pedant. Pantalone must decipher the good doctor's speech for the audience. Gratiano wishes to make a present to Doralice of "una gallana e du pugn'in ti dent," that is, a hen and two fists in the teeth (p. 7). He actually means, as Pantalone tells us, "una collana e due pendenti," a necklace and earrings. The act ends with a lively *intermedio* replete with licentious overtones.

Act 2 rediscovers Pantalone and Burattino, whose mind is, as usual, on food. The master tenders a list of wedding invitees to Burattino and commands the servant to seek them out. In a familiar *commedia dell'arte* dialogue, Pantalone enumerates the guests while the servant comments crudely on the selection in asides to the audience. This scene indicates another implicit stage direction: Doralice must appear at a window or in a doorway, unseen by the two characters on stage, in order to overhear their conversation. She laments her destiny in a touching song reminiscent in content of a pastoral monologue. Juxtaposed against this profession of pure love, Gratiano and Pantalone express their ridiculous affections in the third and fourth scenes, Gratiano to Doralice and Pantalone to the courtesan Lauretta. Although Doralice does not respond to her admirer, in the parodic scene Lauretta scorns Pantalone and his serenade ends comically in mutual verbal abuse. A bawdy interlude on the "death of my cricket" followed by the dance of the chimneysweeps draws Act 2 to a close.

Banchieri begins Act 3 with one of his most clever parodies: Gratiano serenades his beloved with a mutilated version of Palestrina's famous pastoral madrigal "Vestiva i colli." In his muddled way, rather than "the spring clothing the hills and fields in new love," in Gratiano's version "the horns and chestnuts are baking in the oven, emanating new odours" (p. 9)[13] The music provided for this mutation is charming, but the words are senseless. Poor Gratiano! Fulvio and Doralice reaffirm their love in the following scenes and run off to be secretly joined in wedlock. Pantalone reappears, bewailing his spurned love, followed by Bizzarre Humour who enters in order to summarize the dénouement for the audience. The cycle ends with a lively dance and song recapsulizing the substance of the text.

Banchieri's other two major comedies, *Il Metamorfosi musicale* (1600) and *La Saviezza giovanile* (1607; revised by Banchieri in 1628), have essentially the same plots as *La Pazzia senile*, based on *commedia dell'arte* scenarios, but with different character names and places. *Il Metamorfosi musicale* is set in Pisa. Pantalone has become Stefanello Battarga, a fig merchant, and Dottor Gratiano is now Dottor Partigiana. There are three acts, the first preceded by a Prologue called Chromatic Humour. Once again Dottor Partigiana wishes to marry the merchant's daughter and Stefanello himself is in love with a maiden. However both of the ladies already have young lovers. The marriage plans of the two old men are thwarted, the two pairs of lovers wed with the help of Zanni and the play ends with the customary dance.

L'Amfiparnaso is described by critics as the most perfect, consummate madrigal comedy. Given that the major contribution of criticism originates from scholars of musicology, these accolades may be attributable to the superior quality of the music over that composed by Banchieri for his comedies.[14] Vecchi wrote madrigals and adapted regional songs for five voices, thereby creating a more elaborate sound. Banchieri reduced his music to three part singing. In fact, in *Studio dilettevole fiorito dal Anfiparnaso*, he consciously reworked Vecchi's composition using only three voices. In his dialogues one voice sings the role of the first character while the other two voices take on the second. Musical sophistication may not exemplify Banchieri's comedies; however, from a strictly dramaturgical viewpoint, the simpler style facilitates the action, rendering the plot more easily comprehensible to the audience and permitting comedic interpretation of the music by the actors or singers. It is probable that the popular tradition of the *commedia dell'arte* also avoided complicated music so that the action would be continually lively and progressive and not bogged down in elaborate musical compositions.

This returns us to the question of performance. The comedies of Banchieri permit staging. He provided some ideas himself in the preface to *La Saviezza giovanile*.[15] Various other possibilities have been suggested: "the music should be performed behind the set and pantomimed by actors in front; each role should be performed by an appropriate singer accompanied by the others from behind the set; the singers themselves should be in front of the set and perform the action; or the action should be delegated to puppets with all singers behind the set."[16] An enterprising director could easily expand the bare structure of the plot with improvisation and mime. It may even have been feasible to engage a *commedia* troupe to perform the comedies. There is evidence of both the musical and acting capabilities of the *comici*.[17]

It has been noted how Banchieri incorporated stage directions into his text and provided possibilities for performance; indeed, it is almost necessary to accept the proposal that the works were sung by one group of musicians and mimed by a second group of actors or singers taking on specific roles. The objection to acted performances seems to stem from two principal sources: firstly, that contemporary recitals have generally failed in their efforts to act out the comedies and, secondly, that Vecchi condemned such efforts in his defence of *L'Amfiparnaso.*

The action is more succinct than it should be, since, bare speech being more brief than words united with music, it was well not to go into some of the details in order not to tire one's ears before the end. Moreover, the music is not interspersed with such pleasures for the sight as might relieve the one sense by the attentiveness of the other. (p. 15)

Clearly Vecchi was emphasizing the importance of the musical aspect of his work over the dramatic. However, in worrying that any visual activity might diminish attention to the music, he does an injustice to his intended audience, most of whom would be accustomed to watching erudite comedies with intricate plots, whose performances were often punctuated by elaborate *intermezzi.* Perhaps he wished to detract attention from his weakness as a playwright. On the other hand, Banchieri's scenarios invite physical activity on the stage, adding to the pleasure and delight of the audience.

One cannot deny the excellent quality of Vecchi's music or the importance of his work as inspiration for Banchieri; however, the latter's comedies approach the spirit of the *commedia dell'arte* tradition with an open mind and a lively sense of fun. The dramatic qualities exhibit Banchieri's greater skill as a playwright; the works each contain an introduction, development of plot and a fitting dénouement in true comedic style.

Neither should these works be viewed as precursors of *opera buffa* or *opera seria,* forms which were progressing under the hands of Monteverdi and his followers. It is generally acknowledged that this short-lived genre, which flourished for a brief 30-year period, was attached to the madrigal tradition and was a fitting culmination of that form.[18] Incorporating the popular traditions of the stage and the music chamber of the sixteenth century, they remain a unique development in the history of both *commedia dell'arte* and renaissance/mannerist music and may still be enjoyed today for their clever coupling of the two slopes of Parnassus.

University of Toronto

NOTES

1 Orazio Vecchi, *L'Amfiparnaso: A New Edition of the Music with Historical and Analytical Essays*, transcribed, translated and edited by Cecil Adkins (Chapel Hill: University of North Carolina Press, 1977) 17. All further references to *L'Amfiparnaso* will be to this edition.

2 Nino Pirotta, "Commedia dell'Arte and Opera," *Musical Quarterly* 41 (1955) 309–310.

3 Giacomo Oreglia, *The Commedia dell'Arte*, trans. by Lovett F. Edwards (London: Methuen & Co. Ltd., 1968). The Italian version of the episode may also be found in Vito Pandolfi, *La Commedia dell'Arte, storia e testo*, 5 vols. (Firenze: Edizioni Sansoni Antiquariato, 1957–61) 2:79–83.

4 Bonaventura Somma, ed., *Capolavori polifonici del secolo XVI* 12 vols. (Rome, Edizioni A. De Santis, 1956–1971) 6:5. This series of *libretti* contains most of the existing madrigal comedies, including Vecchi's *L'Amfiparnaso*, Striggio's *Il cicalamento delle donne al bucato* and Adriano Banchieri's *La Pazzia senile*. All further references to *La Pazzia senile* will be taken from this edition. The translations are my own.

5 For example, see Edward Dent's comments contained in Vecchi 102 and those of Alfred Einstein, *The Italian Madrigal*, 3 vols. (Princeton, NJ: Princeton University Press, 1949) 794–5.

6 For the complete discussion see Einstein 755ff.

7 "Avanti si dia principio, di canto in canto, uno de gli tre cantori legga forte tutto quello che sarà scritto avanti la musica, e questo per avertire gli auditori, e pratticar gli cantori." *Antiquae Musicae Italicae Monumenta Bononiensia*; vol. 12, *Adriani Banchieri, Opera Omnia* Joseph Vecchi, ed. (Bologna: Università degli Studi di Bologna, 1963) pt. 1, fasc. 2:XII.

8 Donald Jay Grout, *A Short History of Opera*, 2nd ed. (New York: Columbia University Press, 1965) 33. I am relying on Grout's comments in this matter, as I have been unable to procure a copy of *La Saviezza giovanile*.

9 Einstein 794.

10 Pirotta 311–312.

11 Oreglia 12. One might note that this was also the practice among authors of sixteenth century erudite comedies. For example, according to Castiglione, the first production of Bibbiena's *La Calandria*, which took place at the Court of Urbino in 1513, contained elaborate *intermezzi* between the acts. Also, the prologue written by Bibbiena's bears little or no relation to the plot of his play.

12   L'altra estate per bizzarria
      E passar malinconia,
      Per fuggir i caldi estivi
      Che per l'otio son nocivi,
      Secondando il mio parere
      Ho composto per piacere

Con dolcissimi concenti
Questi miei ragionamenti. (*La Pazzia senile* 5.)
This purpose is in direct contrast to Vecchi's which purported to present "a mirror of human life, its aim being utility as much as pleasure, not merely the arousal of laughter," a properly Horatian sentiment (Vecchi 15).

13 Palestrina's original text (following) is recorded in the text parallel to Gratiano's version by Banchieri:

   Madrigale antico
   Vestiva i colli e le campagne intorno
   La primavera di novelli amori,
   E spiravan soave arabi odori
   Cinti d'erbe, e di frondi il crine adorno.

   Trasmutazione di Gratiano
   Rostiva i corni, e le castagne in forno,
   Il prim'havea de i novelli humori,
   Sospiravan le rane arbori e mori
   Cinti d'erbe, e di trombe in fin al corno. (*La Pazzia senile* 9)

14 See, for example, the comments of Edward J. Dent, Carlo Perinello, Ernest Newman and others in Vecchi 100–105.

15 As well as Grout's comments (note 8), there is an expanded discussion in Vecchi 9.

16 Vecchi 9.

17 In a well-known episode of the performance of Monteverdi's *Arianna* in 1608 "the singer for whom the role of Arianna had been intended had died and the part was entrusted to an actress of the *Comici Fedeli* troupe, who not only was able to learn it in a few days, but sang it, according to reports of the time, in such a way that she made all the ladies present weep." Pirotta 317.

18 See for example, Edward J. Dent in Vecchi 102.

Guido Pugliese

Commedia dell' arte Elements in Boccaccio's Decameron

The *Decameron* served as a frequent source for the *commedia dell' arte*.[1] Some *novelle* provided scenarios which underwent only slight modifications. For instance, the ninth novella of the second day, dealing with the vicissitudes of the innocent wife of Bernabò da Genova, will become *L'innocentia ri[n]venuta* (Innocence restored); the central incident of Flaminio Scala's *Cavadenti* (The Tooth-extractor) seems to have been suggested by Lydia's orthodontic skills practiced on her husband as described in *Decameron*, VII, 9. Calandrino's allegedly magic stone, the heliotrope, was utilized as the basis not just for one but for three scenarios: *Trappolino invisibile, Pantalone innamorato*, and *Pietra incantata*—naturally with an even greater degree of mock invisibility and pelting. It is also surmised on good grounds that many fables of conjugal squabbles were derived from Boccaccio.[2] But the *Decameron* was raided not only for plots, themes, and incidental notions, but also for outright performing material. For instance, in the comedy scenario *Il vecchio geloso*, one of the characters, Dr. Graziano, invited by the company, tells them a story from Boccaccio's *Centonovelle*. The practice must have been fairly widespread if Ben Jonson's Volpone can make the following sneering remark about a troupe of 'commedianti': "I cannot endure to see the rabble of these ground *ciarlatani* that spread their cloaks on the pavement as if they meant to do feats of activity, and then come in lamely with their mouldy tales out of Boccaccio."[3]

It is obvious from all this that professional actors, whose business it was to entertain for a livelihood, considered Boccaccio a kindred spirit and a master of revelry.

My aim in this paper will be to demonstrate the correctness of this view by showing that the *Decameron* contains all of the distinguishing features of the Italian popular theatre. The value of such a critical exercise, if sound, should be two-fold: to bring to the fore a dimension of Boccaccio's masterpiece, hitherto unemphasized—a dimension which will necessarily colour our total evaluation of the work, and secondly, to suggest that the import of the *commedia dell'arte* was weightier than it is generally made out to be.

As is well known, the elements that typify the "commedia a soggetto" were characteristically few; they included first and foremost improvisation, the partial use of masks, the use of *lazzi*, or comic tricks, and a plot outline that normally revolved around the theme of love. Improvisation was considered the first requirement because the play was conceived as a performance and not a text proposed for meditation. As a performance, it had to have all the marks of a living essence but of course in theatrical terms. The people best qualified to achieve this illusion of life, or better, to give life to this illusion, were considered to be the actors themselves. Flaminio Scala, who perhaps embodies the spirit of the *commedia dell'arte* in its most characteristic form, justified his right to compose scenarios on the grounds that he was an actor. As he says, "l'arte vera del ben fare le commedie, credo io che sia di chi ben le rappresenta . . . "[4] . (I believe that the art of constructing good plays is best practiced by those who perform them). It is true that improvisation did not start *ex nihilo*: the skeleton plot, the promptbooks (*generici*) which were prepared beforehand by the actors themselves or by other professionals, and the masks: all of these provided materials and served as clear points of reference for the performer. But it should be remembered that this stock-in-trade could never be used mechanically or without reference to the requirements of the action at any given moment. In the final analysis, therefore, even if the actor possessed a generic identity through his mask and could draw on a variety of set speeches, it was he who created the specifics of his role. In other words, in the improvised play the actor is his own author. Before the action, he is a phantom, a something in potency that only the action can actualize. The literal immortality of these characters is proof of the special ontological status of the individualized type.

The illusion of characters as architects of their own coming into being is equally the first trait of the *Decameron*. To begin with, the narrative is cast in theatrical terms. The tales are given as generated by ten narrators who perform over a period of ten days. Moreover, the frame characters act in turn as actants, authors, and audience as the roles are assumed by them in turn.

But the impression of self-generating characters, both for the frame and actual tales, is achieved even more through a form of characterization that is analogous to the use of the mask in the *commedia dell'arte*. The mask, as already mentioned, gave the character, among other things, a generic identity which the performer had to actualize in every performance. The same can be said of the *Decameron* characters. With the exception of Ser Ciappelletto, friar Cipolla, and Guccio Imbratta, the protagonists are identified with only generic epithets and strictly in relation to the theme of the story. It may be then that we are given an indication of age, social rank, physical appearance, economic status, or other qualifier, but never a psychological profile or a full-length portrait. Of Andreuccio da Perugia we are told that he was a young horse-dealer who had never been out of his city; of Ghismunda that "in face and body she was most beautiful, and young and merry and perhaps cleverer than a woman should be"[5] ; of Calandrino that he was an ingenuous man of eccentric character. Of Griselda, who is the last figure we meet in the book, we are given no personal details at all: only that she blushed when Gualtieri called her name and that she was the daughter of a peasant. And the same method is adopted for all the other figures.

This representational mode has caused one critic to comment aptly that the *Decameron* characters are so many "voyageurs sans bagage."[6] Yet this initial lack of character individuation has not lessened the aesthetic identity of the personages. This because the characters are fully actualized through the action: like characters of the *commedia dell'arte* they create their own being in the course of events. Because we know so little about them at first meeting, we are left with the feeling that they are improvising as they face the various contingencies of life. The non-scripted impression is so strong that the reader is hard-pressed to predict how the characters would behave in similar situations again, except to say that they would conduct themselves in conformity with their general identity but in unforeseeable ways with regard to specifics.

Turning to the *commedia dell'arte*, we have seen how improvisation was made into a primary requisite. But the necessary support for improvisation had necessarily to be great presence and suppleness of mind, that faculty which Scala calls "inventare" and which he considers "l'anima e il tutto nelle commedie"[7] (the very soul of comedy). However, if on the one hand this inventiveness was the fruit of a lively imagination, on the other it had to have method even in its most surreal flights, cleverness and ingenuity in its verbal pyrotechnics, some semblance of order in its confusion or at least consistent inconsistency. A foremost authority on the improvised comedy of his time, Andrea Perrucci, maintained that the right kind of inventiveness could be mastered only by those well versed in language, in "figure rettoriche, tropi e tutta l'arte rettorica, avendo da far all'improvviso ciò che premeditato fa il poeta"[8] (figures of speech, tropes and the whole of the rhetorical art since he has to do impromptu what the poet does after long meditation). In accordance with the critical speculation of the mannerist and Baroque period, the figures of speech that were given pride of place were the extended metaphor and the conceit (although the entire arsenal could be used). Of course the better actors developed their own treasury of set passages; for the less imaginative this need was fulfilled by professional writers. As an example of this type of speaking, Giraldi Cinzio cites the following passage, by an unknown author:

Edificato ho il muro delle mie speranze su la ferma pietra della mia fede, e con gli chiovi della servitù fissi nelle travi del desiderio, ho edificata una stanza al mio cuore nel soave piano delle vostre bellezze: e alle finestre del discorso, giorno e notte lo miro e contemplo.[9]
(I have erected the walls of my hopes on the solid rock of my faith, and with the nails of my devotion anchored to the beams of my desire, I have built a room for my heart in the sweet abode of your beauties: and I gaze at and contemplate it day and night through the windows of speech.)

To the classically minded Cinzio such extravagance should have no place in the well-made play; but to someone free of normative canons, the speech could appear as the creation of a Salvador Dalì after he had read Emanuele Tesauro.

At the level of the plot, inventiveness entails the devising of a story that generally poses a seemingly insoluble problem. In *L'innocentia ri[n]venuta*, for example, the action is set in motion by the need to find a cure for the gout that afflicts the wife of the main authority figure in the play, a duke. An oracle is consulted and the following reply is received: "a woman who is married, widowed and yet a virgin shall free her."[10]

A glance at the plot-summaries provided at the beginning of the *Decameron* tales quickly reveals that for the most part they have the same structure. The very first tale records an apparently impossible occurrence: the canonization of the most wicked man that ever was. Others are no less unbelievable: Masetto da Lamporecchio pretends to be deaf and dumb in order to become a gardener to a convent of nuns, where all the women eagerly lie with him (III, 1); Ferondo eats a certain powder and is buried as if dead. The abbot, who is in love with his wife, takes Ferondo out of the grave and makes him believe he is in Purgatory. He is resurrected and brings up as his own a child begotten by his wife and the abbot (III, 8). Two Sienese are in love with the same woman and one of them is godfather to her child. The godfather dies and, as he had promised, his spirit returns to his friend and tells him his state in the next world (VI, 10); master Simone, egged on by Bruno, Buffalmacco and Nello, makes Calandrino think that he is pregnant. He gives them capons and money to prepare medicine and is cured without having a child, and so on.

As to the aforementioned *commedia dell'arte* requirement of verbal bravura, the denizens of the *Decameron* do not fare any worse; indeed, it might be said that more than heroes of the sword, they are champions of the word. Thanks to his brilliant manipulation of the logos, Ser Ciappelletto creates a reality which is the complete opposite of the true situation. A person who might be called his country cousin, friar Cipolla, more than lives up to the reputation of being an orator equal to Quintilian and Cicero—but as these might have been seen through a *commedia dell'arte* perspective. His speech, by necessity impromptu, since his friends have replaced without his knowing the allegedly holy feather of the angel Gabriel with common pieces of charcoal, is solemn nonsense but it has the semblance of true solemnity. This because it is constructed according to the popular narratives of voyages to the Holy Land and makes skilful use of religious language.

After a seemingly interminable voyage, the friar says that he reached Jerusalem where the Patriarch showed his numerous relics:

First of all he showed me the finger of the Holy Ghost, as entire and sound as it ever was, and the forelock of the Seraph which appeared to St. Francis, and a nail of one of the Cherubim, and a rib of the Verbum Caro made at the factory, and clothes of the Catholic faith, and some of the rays of the star which appeared to the wise men in the east, and a phial of St. Michael's sweat when he fought with the devil, and the jaw-bones of St. Lazarus, and many others.

After this accumulation of marvels, it is little wonder that the charcoal pieces would be accepted as those "over which the most blessed martyr St. Lorenzo was roasted."[11]

Similarly clever extravagant speeches are uttered by other personages including Alatiel and Maso del Saggio.

Another essential requirement demanded by the *commedia dell'arte* was of course the creation of laughter. The question naturally arises as to what kind of laughter was sought and how this laughter was to be created. Among those who were experts in the theatrical realm and were endowed with great performing skills, the laughter requirement was seen as subservient to the whole piece and as the fruit of ingenuity, craft, and intelligence rather than exaggeration, grossness, or absurdity. As Allardyce Nicoll observes, "Pier Maria Cecchin, who created the role of Fritellino, declared that laughter in these performances should be like salt with food and that the aim should be to produce a 'commedia' not a 'buffoneria'."[12] Similarly, Niccolò Barbieri maintained that the true *commedia* is not a piece of buffoonery but a tasteful entertainment "well-balanced and sober, witty and not full of impertinent trivialities . . . The comedian produces laughter as the sauce to his skilful speeches; the stupid buffoon makes it the be-all and end-all of his display."[13]

If the more gifted performers were able to achieve this almost classical balance, it cannot be said that as a whole moderation and decorum were the hallmarks of the popular theatre. To be sure, the verbal luxuriance, which we have already illustrated, was not only demanded to create the reality of the unscripted action, but also to arouse laughter—a laughter born of the intellectual recognition on the part of the spectator that the performer was devilishly clever. The kind of laughter, for instance, provoked by the captain's "outlandish bombast," the improbably lyrical ecstasies of the lovers, the mouldy saws put in the mouth of Dr. Graziano or the type of surrealistic routine described by Casanova, perhaps referring to the actor Antonio Sacchi in the role of Harlequin. "The substance of his witty speeches," he wrote, "always fresh and spontaneous, is so disjointed and confused . . . so replete with divers ridiculous metaphors, that it would seem as though the whole must prove but a formless chaos . . . This actor has the unique and immutable gift of being able to make his audience share in the entanglement of those speeches: he plunges in and emerges with the wittiest confusions of intricate rhetoric, boldly he goes on, appears so lost that he cannot get out again, then in a moment wriggles out of his predicament . . . no one can refrain from laughing, confronted by this constant bubbling up of images enlivened by a sublime genius."[14]

But perhaps even more than poking fun at men with loads of learned lumber in their heads and creating word arabesques to arouse laughter, considerable reliance was placed on beatings, flytings, erotic double entendres, scatological instruments and functions. The chamberpot was never too invisible and the satisfaction of hunger was often the principal aspiration. The ecclesiastical authorities regarded these performances, which in their words were full of "sozzi maliziosi equivoci" (obscene double entendres) and "sconcie scurrilità" (lewd surrilities)[15] as instruments of private and public immorality.

A milder but analogous reaction greeted Boccaccio's tales.[16] Boccaccio made light of the charge but he nonetheless took care to answer his critics, at the beginning of the fourth day and at the conclusion.

The critics, it must be admitted, as spokesmen of the official asexual and conventionalized cultural ideology of the time, were not wrong: the *Decameron* does use many of the *commedia dell'arte* materials and tactics to construct its image of the human condition. It will be recalled that the tales are intended for the amusement and recreation of ladies in love. The pleasure principle underlying the narratives is stated on more than one occasion by Dioneo and is repeated by the author himself at the conclusion of the work. But if a good portion of the entertainment consists of the celebration of exquisite manners, fine feelings, human intelligence and initiative in all their manifestations, an even greater number of stories entertain through the use of socially prohibited themes, attitudes and values. A conservative estimate would fix the number of tales of illicitly erotic love at about thirty—and these are the ones that unfailingly arouse side-splitting laughter. An approximately equal number contain beatings, cheating, killings, betrayals and the like. Nor are the victims necessarily deserving of their fate. Peronella's husband is cuckolded, so to speak, in his own presence for no other reason than the fact that he returned home at the wrong time; Madonna Filippa commits adultery simply because she has too much to give; Madonna Beatrice (the *new* Beatrice) not only betrays her longtime husband, but she has him beaten up for good measure. And the list could be lengthened substantially.

Yet the young people of the frame laugh. And we laugh. Why? In the first place, because Boccaccio has used language, surface characterization, and rapid action, just as the *commedia dell'arte* used masks and a quick tempo, to achieve a necessary condition posited for laughter by Bergson: absence of feeling.[17]

More importantly, however, I believe, we laugh, not because Boccaccio is realistic and the *commedia dell'arte* fantastic—Boccaccio himself, in the very first tale, dramatizes the fact that literature cannot make truth claims—we laugh because both fictions satisfy the darkly selfish reasons indicated by Freud or because, as Bacon might have expressed it, both fictions are the kind of "feigned history [devised] to give some shadow of satisfaction to the mind of man in those points wherein the nature of things doth deny it."[18]

University of Toronto

NOTES

1 See Winnifred Smith, *The Commedia dell'Arte* (New York: Blom, 1964; 1st ed. 1912), pp. 13, 54, 85, 189 and K. M. Lea, *Italian Popular Comedy* (New

York: Russell and Russell, 1962; 1st ed. 1934), Vol. I, pp. 137, 157, 242; Vol. II, p. 403.

2 Lea, I, 242.

3 Ben Jonson, *Volpone*, Act II, sc. 1.

4 Flaminio Scala, *Il finto marito*, in *Commedie dei Comici dell'Arte*, ed. Laura Falavolti (Turin: UTET, 1982), p. 231.

5 Giovanni Boccaccio, *The Decameron*, trans. Richard Aldington, (New York: Dell, 1962; 1st ed. 1930), p. 22. All the passages from the *Decameron* are taken from this edition.

6 Guido Almansi, *The Writer as Liar: Narrative Technique in the Decameron* (London & Boston: Routledge & Kegan Paul, 1975), p. 33.

7 Scala, p. 230.

8 Included in Roberto Tessari, *Commedia dell'Arte: La maschera e l'ombra* (Milan: Mursia, 1981), p. 140.

9 G. B. Giraldi Cinzio, "Discorso intorno al comporre delle commedie a delle tragedie," in *Saggi critici* (Milan: Marzorati, 1973) p. 214. Cited by Tessari, p. 90.

10 Cited by Lea, II, 574.

11 Boccaccio, p. 392.

12 Allardyce Nicoll, *The World of Harlequin* (Cambridge: Cambridge University Press, 1963), p. 15.

13 Nicoll, p. 15.

14 Cited more fully by Nicoll, p. 16.

15 L. Tragiense (G. A. Bianchi), *De i vizi, e de i difetti del moderno teatro. . . .* (Rome: Pallade, 1753). Cited by Tessari, p. 18. Bianchi expressed the typical ecclesiastical position: cf. Tessari, pp. 15–47 and the study, complemented with numerous selections from various clerical writers, by Ferdinando Taviani, *La Commedia del'Arte e la società barocca: la fascinazione del teatro* (Rome: Bulzoni, 1969).

16 Cf. Vittore Branca, *Boccaccio medievale*, 5th ed. (Florence: Sansoni, 1984), p. 7 and *passim*.

17 Henri Bergson, "Laughter," in *Comedy*, ed. Wilie Sypher, (Garden City, N.Y.: Doubleday Anchor Books, 1956), p. 63.

18 Francis Bacon, *The Advancement of Learning*, ed. W. A. Wright, Book II, iv, 2. (Oxford: Clarendon Press, 1876), p. 101.

Hannibal S. Noce

Aspirations for an Italian National Theatre and the *commedia dell' arte*

The aspiration for a national theatre is one of the manifestations of the emergence of an Italian national sentiment in cultural and intellectual endeavours during the Arcadian period.[1]

Among the more significant contributions to this aspiration in the first decades of the 18th century are those of Scipione Maffei, erudite Veronese aristocrat, and of Pier Jacopo Martello, Bolognese professor of humane letters and civil servant. Protagonists in one of the lesser controversies of the age,[2] the rivalry between them was, on the whole, literary and particularly referred to dramatic forms. Their common concern was the defense of the theatre against the criticism coming from France that Italy had no tragedies or comedies worthy of the name. Determined to remedy this situation, each in his own manner and according to his own talents, attacked the problem on two levels, practically by composing plays, and theoretically in treatises dealing with various aspects of dramaturgy.

Through the analysis of the critical literature, perforce restricted by the exigencies of space and time to an examination of comedy, I shall attempt to define the role attributed by each to improvised comedy and to indicate at the same time how their evaluation of this type of theatrical activity is a relevant aspect of their efforts to improve at the doctrinal and practical level, by example and by reform, the conditions of the Italian stage.

The necessity of a reform of dramatic poetry had already been discussed by Lodovico Antonio Muratori whose work was well known to Martello, a close friend, and to Maffei. Since some of Muratori's thought on the comic theatre is reflected in their treatises, we must briefly recall its salient points.

Muratori had first turned his attention to critical dramatic problems in his biography of Carlo Maria Maggi (Milano, 1700).[3] In appraising the Milanese poet's career as a dramatist, he significantly asserts that Maggi had devised a plan to divert his fellow citizens from the profanities of the

theatre by composing comedies in the Milanese dialect. In these, by es-
chewing the boisterous intrigues, equivocations and passions that lack any
semblance of verisimilitude, the author had imitated human actions and
had portrayed them naturally. The Milanese comedies, moreover, were
interspersed with moral maxims, relevant components in balancing comic
effects and ethical aims (a statement that expresses Muratori's conviction
that comedy is the art which *castigat ridendo mores*).

Some of the themes found in Maggi's biography as well as a more
expanded statement on the situation of the theatre are dealt with in the
third book of *Della perfetta poesia italiana* (Modena, 1706).[4]

In reference to comedy, Muratori deplores the fact that in their composition verse has been replaced by prose; but even this could be tolerated if
only the rules that govern good dramaturgy were not so grossly violated.
Most comedies, he maintains, consist in stage tricks, indecent intrigues,
or rather in a confusion of ridiculous actions in which a crumb of the
verisimilar, so necessary to the plot of a play, is not to be found. The
theatre has fallen into the hands of ignorant persons who, scornful of any
restraint that good taste might dictate, are primarily concerned in reducing
the audience to laughter. To achieve this end they have recourse to scurrilous and witless equivocations, facetious gestures, mockery, disguises,
and similar buffooneries known as *lazzi* which, in most cases, are trite,
vulgar, nonsensical, largely deprived of any probability, a conglomeration
of unrelated actions of the kind that could never realistically occur. Humour produced by such means is unworthy fare for a civilized person, and
amuses only the uncouth.

To correct the faults and abuses that vitiate the theatre Muratori proposes that it be returned to the poets, that is, to men of culture who by
following the precepts of sound poetics in the light of moral philosophy
will be able to restore its prestige and make of it a pleasant school of
behaviour.

At the doctrinal level Scipione Maffei's ideas on the theatre reflect
intellectual tendencies very close to those illustrated by Muratori.

One of Maffei's earliest statements on the condition of the theatre is
found in an essay on Corneille's *Rodogune*, written in 1700 after attending
a performance of the play in an Italian version.[5] He asserts that French
tragedies are admired and appear sublime when compared to the madness
(*pazzie*) perpetrated on the Italian stage by the comedians. Categorically
he attributes the origins of such decadence to the introduction of the masks
and the use of dialects, with the eventual result that verse was no longer
employed. Once verse was removed, the comedians themselves, or per-

sons of an equally limited literary background, began to write plays. With time, the best literary drama was no longer performed and was completely forgotten.

To demonstrate that Italy indeed had dramatic poetry artistically and theatrically valid Maffei edited a collection of twelve Italian tragedies—from Trissino's *Sofonisba* to Delfino's *Cleopatra*—with suggestions on how they could be adapted for the modern stage, and he gives the collection the title *Teatro italiano*,[6] claiming that it is eminently suitable since outside of Italy (read France) it has been derisively used to designate books containing nothing more than "the jests and beatings of Truffaldino."[7]

In the prefatory essay to the collection he restates some themes from his earlier work and extends them into a historical survey of the development—in all of its forms—of Italian dramatic poetry.

While in the 16th century both verse and prose comedies were written and performed, in the following, the comedians, taking pleasure in the use of common speech, enjoying the freedom of not being tied to a written text, and of being able to perform with less application, abandon verse completely; abetted in this by the fact that the practices of modern comedy required the hiring of actors who were incapable of properly reciting verse. Their predilection for prose was further enhanced by their marvelous ability at improvisation—a talent, Maffei asserts, totally unknown to actors of other nations, ancient or modern.

Maffei recognizes that improvised comedy can be graceful, well-turned, lively in its wit, natural in expressing feeling, nimble in repartee, all qualities which an author would be hard put to achieve. And these qualities the *commedia* possessed in its initial period when members of the various troupes were more learned, intellectually better prepared. But during the 17th century such a deterioration had ensued in the intelligence and cultural preparation of the comedians that Maffei ascribes the principal cause for the abolition of verse from the stage to their ignorance. Once verse plays had become disreputable, it followed that poets ceased to compose them, with the eventual result that written or published plays were eliminated. To fill this void, comedians drew up their scenarios consisting of material indiscriminately chosen and which could only generate confused theatrical actions without order or form. With the consequence that the eight or ten troupes circulating throughout Italy offered the public dramatic pastiches which by no stretch of the imagination could be classified as tragedies or comedies.

Before an improvement in the conditions of the theatre could be affected both actors and the public needed to be educated. Hence in the

closing pages of the essay Maffei offers these practical suggestions to actors: choose a director; learn to speak your lines effectively; understand
what you are saying; rehearse; memorize. As for the public, it must be
instructed to identify the proper pleasure induced by a well conceived
dramatic production, and must be encouraged to patronize this kind of
theatre.

A final admonition: "But to insure propriety in the theatre and to restore
its nobility and decorum, it is enough for it to become learned, regular,
intelligent, for it is certain that in the past century obscenity did not enter
our scenes if not through ignorance."[8]

Maffei's contribution to the definition of the basic aspects of a national theatre are not limited to the formulation of principles contained in
his theoretical writings, but is also expressed in an active participation in
contemporary theatrical life. Evidence of this practical interest is provided
by the inducements given to Riccoboni and his troupe for the performance
of modern and classical tragedies; by his sponsoring and endowment of
the Teatro Filarmonico in his native city, opened in 1732 with his pastoral
drama *La fida ninfa* set to music by Vivaldi; by the invitation and encouragement extended to his contemporaries (e.g. Gian Vicenzo Gravina) to
write for the stage; and, of course, by his own plays, in addition to the
pastoral drama, two comedies, and the much-edited and much-performed
Merope.

Martello's dramaturgical activities are similarly characterized by practical and theoretical interests. Like Maffei, and for the same reasons, he
too takes pride in the encouragement given to others, as the following
words attest: "Above all things my satisfaction is to have awakened an
interest in writing tragedies among the Italians, by means of which I hope
that with time, but be patient, with time we will surpass the French."[9]

One of the means to stimulate this interest was to set an example.
Fifteen of the thirty-five plays contained in his theatre are tragedies, the
remainder pertain to other dramatic forms since he was resolved to include
all types of dramatic actions suited for the stage. With one exception:
deliberately Martello excluded any type of dramatic text which might serve
as a scenario for the *commedia dell'arte*. The reasons he gives for the
exclusion are that (1) he is incapable of handling the dialects it requires;
(2) the *commedia* can be performed with pleasure, but it can only be read
with nausea; (3) should one wish to print it, since its effects are mainly
dependent on mime, one would have to devise some means to indicate the
stage tricks and the curious, facetious, phallic and unbecoming gestures
which it employs, an impossibility, as well as contrary to modesty and

morals.

The poetics of dramatic language in its broader articulations form one of Martello's main theoretical interests. A treatise on tragic verse serves as a preface to the first edition of his plays (1709).[10] The essay examines classical and French prosody, and the author analyzes in more detail the metrical structure of Italian tragedies, in order to justify the introduction and adaptation of a fourteen syllable rhymed line. A more extensive treatment of practical and theoretical dramatic problems is contained in the dialogues on ancient and modern tragedy (1714).[11] Significant dramaturgic information is also included in the dedicatory letters and proems to the individual plays.

In one of these, the dedication of the comedy *Che bei pazzi* to the Venetian nobleman G. B. Recanati,[12] Martello discusses at some length the nature of comedy.

A staging of Ariosto's *Scolastica* in Venice (1716) was whistled off the stage. Apprised of this by Recanati, who had been one of the promoters of the production, Martello became apprehensive since he had just finished his own comedy using Ariosto's verse form, and his first impulse was to destroy his work. Mindful, however, of the care and labor he had expended, he began to search for reasons for its preservation. One that occurred to him was that while Ariosto had imitated Plautus and Terence who ridicule errors of the will, he had followed Aristophanes, whose ridicule is less venomous in that it is concerned with errors of the intellect. He next consulted authors[13] who had critically examined the art and technique of comedy and found that he had followed their precepts.

But surely Ariosto had pondered the great comic masterpieces of antiquity, and in his work had essayed all the means to create a comic structure amply suitable to captivate a modern audience. How then account for the fact that the *Scolastica* had failed in Venice?

Martello's reply is that Ariosto's comedy would have been applauded if it had been acted before a select audience, for it is always a mistake to perform a verse comedy before the mob (*popolaccio*). Comic actors, as he all too well knows, are venal and are convinced that when petty artisans and gondoliers go to the theatre to be amused thay expect to find there the Doctor, Pantaloon, Harlequin and Finocchio, rather than characters activating a learned comedy. Still it must be recognized that, according to Martello, there is no comedy, be it ever so wise, brilliant, vivacious, and containing all the canons of propriety, that can match the *commedia dell'arte*; nor is there a language in the world, or a nation where it is possible to find "an invention of the ugly without harm"[14] that can be compared with it. Does not a Spanish audience, so proud of its theatre, or a French audience, so enamoured of Molière, leave vacant its theatres in order to frequent Italian improvised comedy?

In a remarkable passage[15] devoted to a vivid, admiring, enthusiastic description and characterizaton of the masked and unmasked members of a troupe, Martello becomes so enraptured with his subject to the point of admitting that he would willingly forego Sophocles' *Oedipus* or Plautus' *Amphytrion* to be present at a performance of the *commedia dell'arte* staged by competent actors.

When Martello refers to "mob" "petty artisans" "gondoliers" it might be surmised that he is expressing a negative judgment on the *commedia*, were it not for the fact that in the development of his argument and in the exhaltation of the masks referred to above, he is in fact making a new statement, at least by implication. An art so supple as to become an instrument of amusement on a scale sociologically so extended as to move indiscriminately kings and gondoliers acquires a dimension of universality undeniably valid.

The views on the *commedia dell'arte* which we have—all too cursorily I am aware—surveyed may be considered in their totality a critical body of remarkable relevance because of its relationship with the critical tradition of the past, and because it adheres to the new directives of the Arcadian culture which, for the theatre, reintroduces and emphasizes the principle of verisimilitude.

Muratori's approach to the *commedia* is indisputably novel when it no longer considers it as detrimental to morals, as "a dangerous excrescence emanating from the body of society,"[16] but rather as a cultural phenomenon that can be corrected and improved through reform, and thus become an effective instrument for the amelioration of society.

Sharing Muratori's ethical and sociological concerns, Maffei and Martello in their theoretical writings, and as playwrights, add new insights.

In his attitude towards the *commedia* Maffei stresses its abuses and excesses. His recognition of the achievements of the *commedia* in its initial stages serves only to underline the extent of its deterioration and the need for reform that will only be fully realized when actors and the public alike are re-educated. Characteristic of Maffei's practical approach are the instructions he gives to the comedians for their professional improvement.

Martello has a deeper appreciation of the potentials of the *commedia dell'arte*, perceiving it as a form endowed with incredible vitality in the living theatre. He clearly distinguishes between the specific, and limited, appeal of literary comedy, and the allure of the theatrical modes created and perfected by improvised comedy. He recognizes that the essence of the art of comedy may be attained not only through a comic structure destined for a learned audience, but also by the *commedia*, a dramatic unit composed of a series of elements which, at their best, can be highly effective in entertaining a broader and more heterogenous public.

In their aspirations for a national theatre Maffei and Martello, in theory and in practice, were primarily concerned with the re-vitalization of tragedy as a means of restoring prestige and decorum to the Italian stage. Their speculations on the *commedia dell' arte* became a source of ideas to be utilized in their plans for a reform of the Italian theatre and, particularly with Martello, in formulating profound and original conclusions on the essential and universal character of comic theatre.

University of Toronto

NOTES

1 See Aldo Andreoli, *Nel mondo di Lodovico Antonio Muratori* (Bologna: Il Mulino, 1972) especially the essay "Voci italiane nel tempo del Muratori," 197–227.

2 See Vincenzo Placella, "La polemica settecentesca della *Merope*" in *Filologia e Letteratura* XIII (1967), 309–336 and 394–447. The Maffei-Martello controversy is examined in 327–336 and *passim*.

3 Lodovico Antonio Muratori, *Vita di Carlo Maro Maggi* (Milano: Giuseppe Pandolfo Malatesta, 1700).

4 Lodovico Antonio Muratori, *Della perfetta poesia italiana* was first published in Modena: Soliani, 1706. I have used the second edition (Venezia: Coleti, 1724) preferred by the author, with the critical annotations of Anton Maria Salvini, instead of the most recent one edited by Ada Ruschioni (Milano: Marzorati-Editore, 1971) which does not reproduce Salvini's notes.

5 With the title *Osservazioni sopra la Rodoguna tragedia francese* and dedicated *Al signor NN nell' anno 1700*, the essay is included in the volume *Rime e Prose del Signor Marchese Scipione Maffei, parte raccolte da varj libri, e parte non più stampate* (Venezia: Sebastiano Coleti, 1719), 165–185.

6 *Teatro italiano, o sia scelta di tragedie per uso della scena (. . .) premessa un'istoria del Teatro e difesa di esso* (Verona: Jacopo Vallarsi, 1723–1725, 3 vols.). The prefatory essay is contained in I, 1–xliv. Many of its themes are later elaborated in the treatise *De' teatri antichi e moderni, trattato in cui diversi punti morali appartenenti a teatro si mettono del tutto in chiaro* (Verona: Agostino Carattoni, 1753). Maffei's theoretical ideas on the theatre are remarkably constant over a period of fifty-three years, from his essay on the *Rodogune* written when he was twenty-five to the treatise composed in his seventy-seventh year.

It should be noted that the title *teatro italiano* had been used by Martello eight years earlier (in the 1715 edition of his theatre) and he therefore felt justifiably piqued when Maffei implied that he was the first to introduce it.

7 *Teatro italiano*, I, xv, "(. . .) i motti e le bastonate di Truffaldino."

8 *Ibid.*, I, xxxiii, "Ma per rendere onesto il teatro sicuramente, e per ritornarlo a nobiltà e decoro, basta renderlo dotto, e regolato, e ingegnoso, poichè egli è certo che non entrò nel passato secolo l'oscenità su le nostre scene se non con l'ignoranza."

9 *Lettere di Pier Jacopo Martello a Lodovico Antonio Muratori*, ed. H. S. Noce (Modena: Aedes Muratoriana, 1955), 61. "Sopratutto il mio godimento è di avere svegliata l'emulazione tragica negli Italiani, mediante la quale spero che col tempo, ma abbiate pazienza, col tempo supereremo i Franzesi."

10 *Del verso tragico* in: P. J. Martello, *Scritti critici e satirici*, ed. H. S. Noce (Bari: Laterza, 1963), 151–186.

11 *Della tragedia antica e moderna*, in: *Scritti critici e satirici*, 187–316.

12 P. J. Martello, *Teatro*, ed. H. S. Noce, I (Roma-Bari: Laterza, 1980), 227–332. The dedication reads: All'Eccellenza di Giovanbattista Recanati, nobile veneto fra gli Arcadi Teleste Ciparissiano.

13 Those mentioned are Antonio Riccoboni (*Ars comica*) and Tarquinio Galluzzi (*Commentario della commedia*).

14 *Teatro*, I, 235, "(. . .) un'invenzione di turpezza senza dolore." This definition of the ridiculous is practically a translation of that formulated by Aristotle (*Poet.*, 1448, b, 31): "The Ridiculous may be defined as a mistake or deformity not productive of pain or harm to others." See: *Introduction to Aristotle*, ed. R. McKeon (New York: The Modern Library, 1947), 630.

15 *Teatro*, I, 235–236. The passage is quoted in full by Ferdinando Taviani, *La commedia dell'arte e la società barroca. La fascinazione del teatro* (Roma: Bulzoni Editore, 1969), cxix–cxx. An English paraphrase is found in Allardyce Nicoll, *The World of Harlequin* (Cambridge: The University Press, 1963), 116.

16 Taviani, cxii, "(. . .) una pericolosa escrescenza dal corpo della società."

Krystyna Piechura

Not only *Théâtre Italien*

It is commonplace to say that throughout the eighteenth century, west-European theatre had a profound impact on Polish drama. Nevertheless, there is no comprehensive analysis either of the Italian repertoire presented to the Polish public, or its influence on Polish writing. Recent archival discoveries suggest that the development of Italian troupes in the Republic should be divided into three stages, corresponding to the three periods in the evolution of drama in Poland-Lithuania.

During the first period, covering the reign of Augustus II, elector of Saxony and King of Poland-Lithuania (1698–1733), now little-known repertoires of *commedia dell'arte* were staged in the royal theatre in Warsaw not only by the famous Italian troupes of Gennaro Sacco (1698), Angelo Costantini (1699) and Tomasso Ristori (1718, 1725–1730), but also by lesser-known Italian troupes in Polish magnate theatres.[1]

For the second period, which began with the election of Augustus III to the Polish throne in 1734, and ended in 1756 with the outbreak of the Seven Years War, more documentation is available, and it includes Hofkaländer, Hofjournal, as well as numerous arguments and scenarios. During this period, the Polish public could enjoy excellent staged opera (e.g. Metastasio performed by the Dresden opera), French comedy of characters, *comédie noble*, *comédie larmoyante*, and *drame bourgeois* (e.g. Molière, Regnard, Destouches, Dancourt, La Chaussée and Diderot presented by Albani's French troupe) and Italian *commedia dell'arte* interpreted by Bertoldi's troupe, and the private, professional troupes of P. Hilverding (1741), M. Leppert (1754) and A. Ackerman (1754). Betwen 1754 and 1765, presumably no *commedia dell'arte* royal troupe performed in Warsaw because of the Seven Years War (1756–1763), Augustus III's illness and death, and the election of Stanislas Augustus Poniatowski to the throne (1764).[2]

Bertoldi's troupe was regarded as one of the best in Europe, and had among its members Cesare D'Arbes, Andrea and Antonio Bertoldi, Camillo Canzachi, Bernardo Vulcano, Mathe Bastona-Focher, Giovanna

Casanova, and Paola Falchi. It has been suggested that, because this troupe accompanied Augustus III during his stays in Poland, both the Dresden and Warsaw public had a chance to enjoy the same *commedia dell' arte* repertoire. However, archival sources suggest that the Warsaw public was familiar with only a part of the troupe's repertoire, as before 1756 the King rarely travelled to Poland. It seems that *comici italiani* performed in Dresden in the years 1734–36, 1740, 1742–44, 1746–56, while in Warsaw only in 1738–40, 1748–49, and 1754. We have over one hundred Dresden and twenty-five Warsaw arguments and scenarios. Comedies staged during the 1735–36 season belonged to the Neapolitan tradition. Those put on between 1740 and 1748 were either entirely or in part improvised imitations or adaptations of traditional comedies performed by the *Théâtre Italien* till the beginning of the eighteenth century, when the Italian language and repertoire still dominated that stage. The performances given during the years 1748–1756 included not only entirely and partly improvised seventeenth-century comedies but also eighteenth-century plays, by such writers as Goldoni, Giacomo Casanova, Camilo Canzachi, Girolamo Focher (Focari) and Cesare D'Arbes. Among the six plays of Goldoni staged during the 1748–49 season, there is the almost entirely improvised *Trenta tre disgracie ridicole d'Arlechino*, as well as his first written comedy, *La donna di garbo*. Between 1750 and 1756, the best eleven of Goldoni's comedies were put on—most of them only a few years after their première performances. The arguments and scenarios referred to above either provide only the beginning of a plot, then interrupt the narrative which is supposed to be presented on stage; or they include a full summary of the plot but the *lazzi* are omitted; or they consist of nothing more than ten or twenty-page handwritten summaries of scenes or acts.[3]

The third period began in 1765 with the establishment of the National Theatre, the first professional and public theatre in the Republic, and ended in the 1780s, when *commedia dell' arte* disappeared from the Polish repertoire and was replaced by French *comédie noble, comédie larmoyante, drame bourgeois* and *opera buffa*. The National Theatre followed the latest west European models, and it was intended to be an *école du monde* propagating Enlightenment ideas. The Theatre did not perform between the beginning of the Confederation of Bar in 1767 and the first partition of Poland-Lithuania in 1773. When the Theatre reopened in 1774, the staging of Italian *opera buffa* led to the emergence of the first Polish opera and the decline of the anti-buffonistes who favoured French *tragédie lyrique*. The early 1780s witnessed a revival of the indirect influence of *commedia dell'arte* on Polish drama, when the National Theatre produced several excellent Polish comedies of manners based on the repertoire of the *Théâtre Italien*.[4]

Recently discovered sources indicate that traditional and reformed *commedia dell'arte* were much better known to Polish writers than hitherto supposed. This points to a need for thorough re-examination of the influence of this literary genre on the development of Polish modern comedy, born in the eighteenth centry. An example of this influence is found in the plays and librettos by Franciszek Bohomolec, the first Polish Enlightenment writer to adapt European masterpieces to Polish school and national theatres. The author of the first eighteenth-century Polish comedy and opera, Bohomolec played a central role in royal cultural policy, and his talent contributed to the triumph of comedy and not tragedy on the Polish Enlightenment stage.

Bohomolec's dramatical texts are usually divided into three groups. The first consists of twenty-five school comedies which became the basic repertoire of the reformed Jesuit theatre. They were performed between 1753 and 1760 in the *Collegium Nobilium*, and published between 1755 and 1760. This five volume set of school comedies was the first small-format edition of Polish eighteenth-century plays, and was later imitated by the best publishers when they prepared editions of the collected works of other Polish playwrights. The second group consists of nine comedies called *na teatrum*, as they were written for and performed by the National Theatre after its establishment in 1765, and again after its reopening in 1774. They were published in separate editions, usually after their first performances. The third group is composed of two librettos, *Nędza uszczęsliwiona* (*Misery made happy*, 1770; revised by W. Boguslawksi, 1778) and *Prostota cnotliwa* (*Virtuous simplicity*, 1779) which, accompanied by M. Kamieński's music, were the first Polish operas, staged and published in 1778 and 1779 respectively. Very popular in the second half of the century, his comedies and librettos were reprinted several times between 1755 and the 1780s. Almost forgotten for over a century, only some of them were reprinted in 1959–60. None of the recent studies on Bohomolec centers on his theatre, a subject that deserves a comprehensive monograph.[5]

Bohomolec's school comedies were written, performed, and published towards the end of the second-mentioned period and throughout the following intermediate period when presumably no *commedia dell'arte* troupe performed in Warsaw. Bohomolec's *na teatrum* comedies and librettos were written, staged and printed during the third period of the development of *commedia dell'arte* troupes in the Republic. How important were the *commedia dell'arte* elements in Bohomolec's writings and what were his major sources of information about this genre? I will limit my considerations to a short analysis of the *commedia dell'arte* elements in the strucutre, plot, humour, language, fantasy, realism and characters of Bohomolec's comedies and librettos.

In spite of its frequent references to Aristotle's poetics, early eighteenth-century Polish school drama mixed freely literary genres. A more strict generic division of theatrical texts, based on classical models, was introduced by S. Konarski, the foremost reformer of the Piarist colleges. Bohomolec was the first Polish playwright to compose generically uniform comedies, though it was not until 1765 that the rigorous classical differentiation between tragedy and comedy was generally approved. In 1766, the *Monitor*, co-edited by Bohomolec, stated that the presence of the three classical unities of action, time and place in tragedy and comedy distinguished them from other genres but that comedy enjoyed special privileges. Specifically, it did not have to respect these unities rigorously; its division into acts and scenes did not strictly follow classical schemes; its protagonists were not "prominent personalities" but "common people"; and its plots did not concern "great and serious undertakings" but "common" events. Moreover, it was noted that in a comic text, "high" style should be replaced by "ordinary style" because, unlike tragedy which should arouse "pity," comedy "excites laughter and arouses a disgust for faults."[6]

Bohomolec's school comedies followed the most common schemes as, with the exception of one one-act play, they were divided into five or three acts. The comedies *na theatrum* were three-act plays, with the exception of the *Monitor* which had only one act. Thus, in the course of time, Bohomolec rejected the rigorous classical five-act structure of comedy favoured by his Jesuit masters. Much more important is another structural difference between his school and *na theatrum* comedies: only the first were preceded by arguments. Like some of the arguments of *commedia dell'arte* presented in Warsaw between 1748 and 1756, Bohomolec's arguments gave a full summary of the plot. However, unlike the *commedia dell'arte* texts, Bohomolec's arguments explained also what moral lessons were to be drawn from his plays: aware of his young viewers' lack of experience, he helped them understand and interpret his plays. The comedies *na theatrum* were not preceded by arguments, as they were addressed to a much more demanding and refined audience whose relativist aesthetics and ideology would neither require, nor even accept a statement summarizing the plots or explaining the moral meaning of plays. Several of Boholomec's school comedies not only followed the classical division into acts, scenes and dialogues, but their five-act division corresponded to the five-part dramatic structure: one act of exposition, one of rising action, one of climax, one of falling action and one of dénouement. However, combining certain characteristics of reformed *commedia dell'arte* and of French comedy, as well as of Polish popular tradition, Bohomolec usually rendered the plots simple, realistic, and freely structured: they depicted virtue and innocence opposed to meanness, evil and treachery. It has been accepted that his indebtedness to his foreign sources included free translations, adaptations and minor borrowings. However, even in his first, least original comedies, he espoused the principle, widely accepted in those days, that a good translation should be faithful to the "circumstances of place and time." This was for ideological and theoretical reasons. He had to remember that colleges disposed of relatively modest technical equipment. He intended to stress the moral and didactic value of his texts, as well as to make them understandable to his young viewers and acceptable to his Jesuit patrons. The slightly reformed but still obligatory *ratio studiorum* imposed on him numerous rules that his original texts ignored, the most important being the necessity to remove all the female roles. Critics have stressed how in the first two volumes of his comedies, plots were centred on the competition for financial, professional or social rewards as, when adapting his French and Italian sources, Bohomolec replaced affection between young lovers by competition for dowries, paternal or fraternal love. Only in the third volume of his school comedies did Bohomolec mention love, as he evidently did not consider the topic to be dangerous any longer.

Although in all of Bohomolec's comedies the arrangement of incidents did constitute a whole, there were numerous episodic subplots which were not related to the main plot by a logic of necessity. Some actions could even have been removed from a text and its plot would not have been changed, as causality was not a key element in these plays. As in traditional and reformed *commedia dell'arte*, the actions of these plays were often manipulated by one or more protagonists: Harlequin, or a character replacing him, was responsible for the development of plots and subplots. He not only determined the structure of the incidents on stage, but he also interrupted the action to offer important critical observations about the protagonists—the comic intrusions and low buffoonery of *commedia dell'arte* were frequently replaced by comical and witty commentaries.[7]

In some *na theatrum* comedies, Bohomolec moved away from this *com-*

media dell'arte scheme: the *Monitor* (1767) and the *Autor comedii* (*Author of comedy*, 1779), were entirely original and innovative propaganda plays almost without plot. In the former, the protagonist impersonated Bohomolec and discussed matters dealt with by the journal the *Monitor*; in the latter the main character played Bohomolec and defended his comedies against admirers of *comédie larmoyante*. These texts were stylistically very close to Bohomolec's journalism and to the future Polish novel. Our discussion suggests that the plots of his comedies were often close to *commedia dell'arte* and only a few of the *na theatrum* comedies evolved towards dramatized dialogue, imitating Molière's *Critique de L'École des femmes*, what in Polish is called *komedie dyskusyjne*.

Following French and English writers, Polish critics spilled much ink in debates concerning the definition of humour. This definition was supposed to help playwrights combine moral and artistic values, establish the generic differences between tragedy and comedy, and protect the latter against encroachments by such generic hybrids as *drame bourgeois* and *comédie larmoyante*. As the editor of the *Monitor* and a major playwright, Bohomolec strongly opposed the latter genres which, he wrote, did not respect even the most basic theatrical rules. This point of view was accepted by most Polish literary critics who usually distinguished only three categories of comedy: comedy of intrigue, comedy of characters, and *komedie dyskusynjne*. Another classification, based on a division of humour into "low" and "high," distinguished "high comedies" addressed to "the enlightened" and "low comedies" oriented towards "commoners." Bohomolec did not accept this classification, and in his *Autor komedii* he simply divided humour into "excessive" and "measured and wise."[8]

Consequently, one finds in his comedies and librettos elements of both low and high comedy. In the first case, the humour of his comedies often stemmed from techinques common to farce, interlude, and traditional reformed *commedia dell'arte*. Humorous scenes, ridiculous incidents, and incongruous situations were frequent; so were plots within plots, disguise, mistaken identities, unexpected meetings, extraordinary happenings, and repetitions of mistakes. Stressing the importance of the non-literary value of drama, his texts required that gesture, movement, body expression, voice and physical actions become theatrical techniques. Hence, even in his comedies *na theatrum*, Bohomolec did not avoid primitive and vulgar scenes in which the protagonists fought with each other or were beaten soundly. Foolish gestures, *contrasto*, and free-for-alls also abounded. One of his comedies, *Fijacy* (*Drunkards*, 1767), was devoted to a sarcastic description of the behaviour of drunken men and women. According to

Bohomolec's explanations, the comedy was to educate by mocking improper conduct. Nevertheless, the comedy was severely criticised both by the audience and the critics, who required that positive, "enlightened" examples be shown on the stage of the National Theatre. However, alongside buffoonery and grotesque humour, Bohomolec's comedies were rich in sophisticated double-edged satire typical of French comedy of manners and comedy of types. As in the latter genre, comic interest in his plays derived largely from opposing protagonists whose conduct was determined by a single character trait. Since Bohomolec did not try to hide theatrical illusion, and exploited it for satiric and didactical purposes, there was no realistic study of personalities: their speech, dialogues, and intrusions were supposed to provide relief from moralizing, but at the same time to enrich and deepen it.[9]

During Bohomolec's lifetime, style and language were seldom discussed by Polish critics who usually limited their observations to two issues. They emphasized the necessity to avoid moralizing soliloquies and the transformation of characters into the authors' mouthpieces, and they argued that comedy should be written in "common language" more suitable to express the emotions felt by the representatives of different social, ethical and cultural groups. Bohomolec's scientific works were written in heavy, baroque style; only in his dramatic texts did he use simple syntax, precise and short arguments, and figurative comparisons. In his plays, he consciously questioned not only the classical rules of composition, but also rejected high style, rhythms and rhymes. His talent was at its best in light and vivid dialogue which he filled with both "high" and "low" humour. As in traditional and reformed *commedia dell'arte*, the dialogue of his plays and librettos was individualized. He introduced to the stage dialectal jargon, and borrowings from French, Italian, German and Latin. He realized that the *style noble* limited satiric expression which required strong words, abuse, invective, boasts, brags, swaggering, big words, as well as sayings, proverbs, and witticism. He mocked the high style both in its baroque and Enlightenment versions, their unnecessary foreign borrowings, long and unclear sentences, and quotations made out of context and incorrectly. His positive characters spoke eighteenth-century colloquial Polish: their dialogues were quick, witty, finished, intensive and intellectual rather than imaginative; their short and clear sentences expressed Enlightenment ideas simply but cautiously. One finds in Bohomolec's comedies character types rather than marionettes, primarily due to the individualization of their language, which also helped these excessively didactic plays and sentimental librettos to preserve their humour.[10]

Being derivative, Bohomolec's comedies can be classified as belonging to the literature of ideas rather than to imaginative writing. The most important fantastic and exotic elements, evident in setting, characters and intrigue, were borrowed from traditional and reformed *commedia dell'arte*. These elements were particularly numerous in Bohomolec's early comedies, like *Arlekin na świat urażony* (*Harlequin with a grudge against the world*), which is recognized as the first Polish *commedia dell'arte*, the text of which was fully written and followed the formal scheme of a dramatic division into dialogues, scenes and acts.[11]

However, as in reformed *commedia dell'arte*, Bohomolec limited fantasy in favour of realism in his later plays. As might be expected, he became less dependent on his sources in the course of time, and his initially cosmopolitan comedies evolved into clearly Polish national plays, as he was the first playwright to show on stage details of every-day life in the eighteenth-century Republic. He was also one of the first literary critics to stress that, unlike tragedy, comedy aimed to educate by deriding the negative aspects of contemporary local customs, manners, and mentality. Bohomolec's references to the Republic rendered stock characters closer to the viewer, thus encouraging the audience to reflection. Having the skill of a journalist, with an eye for detail and a knack for social satire and literary parody, Bohomolec instructed as well as amused a status-conscious society. Indulgent towards the peasantry and lower bourgeoisie, but ready to criticise the nobility and upper bourgeoisie, he mocked both the backwardness of the provinces and the pseudo-cosmopolitanism of the capital. This two-fold criticism was to become the most important issue of the reform program launched under Stanislas August Poniatowski: a clear rejection both of reactionary "sarmatism" and the uncritical acceptance of foreign models. Bohomolec's later comedies and librettos were full of humanitarianism, moralizing, and idealism, as they opposed a centrally administered land reform and favoured the introduction of written contracts between individual peasants and land owners. Thus he was neither politically nor socially radical, but was one of the most "enlightened" writers of the first half of the eighteenth-century.

As in reformed *commedia dell'arte*, the schematism of comic scenes in Bohomolec's plays was enriched by realist details observed in a street, a salon, a shop or in a school. One could see all the main social groups: the nobility, bourgeoisie, peasantry and the "masterless men" of the workshops in his comedies and librettos. Bohomolec was not only the first to introduce the two latter groups into eighteenth-century Polish theatre, but also to speak out in their defence. He situated his plots in villages, small towns, and in Warsaw, thus depicting the fierce competition between the workshop and the farm, one of the most significant social characteristics of the pre-industrial Republic. In his later comedies and librettos, both the physical and spiritual background were very clearly indicated: the time and place in which an action developed was eighteenth-century Poland-Lithuania; the characters' occupations and manners, as well as the political, moral, social and religious values they represented, were typically Polish. The growing realism of his dramatical texts reflected the development of Polish comedy in general, which evolved from very incompetent translations of foreign plays into fully original texts dealing with eighteenth-century Polish subjects. Bohomolec's plays and librettos, as well as theoretical considerations, paved the way for this transformation.[12]

The construction and presentation of comic protagonists were frequently discussed by Polish playwrights who stressed the differences between tragic and comic characters. The first were supposed to represent the general, permanent values of human nature, while the second were to combine both universal "types" and traits characteristic of particular national, social, or professional groups. Comedy was to conform to the classical notion of the immutability of human nature, and to mock its weaknesses. The satirical and moral functions of comedy were to be strengthened by an exaggerated accumulation of faults and their association with a particular group. Humour was to be directed against generally recognized negative values, not against individuals.[13]

All these principles were fully espoused by Bohomolec who professed the values of the cautiously progressive Polish bourgeoisie, and whose objective was to mock anything that did not conform with the Enlightenment conventions. According to the principles of Enlightenment comedy of manners and comedy of morals, the comportment, mentality, and personalities of Bohomolec's characters were used to symbolize the faults of Polish society. Borrowed from ancient, medieval, seventeenth-century and eighteenth-century texts, his gallery of types was rich. However, several of his best protagonists were derived from *commedia dell'arte*, as well as from Polish farce, interlude, and minstrel comedy. This double heritage determined a certain schematism of these characters, as they can be reduced to a number of stock parts, which Bohomolec introduced into his plays with slight alterations or even without any changes. Instead of masks, he granted them meaningful names (like Mr. Good, Mr. Stupid) which he sometimes repeated in several comedies.[14]

As in reformed *commedia dell'arte*, these stock parts were enriched by new elements based on Bohomolec's own observations and experiences: his characters were undoubtedly eighteenth-century Poles. Very often, they were typical noblemen and their servants, whom he reproached for their "backward," "uncivilized," provincial, and traditional mentality, manners, costumes, and way of life, and whom he depicted with rough and coarse language in scandalous situations. However, always didactic in intention, Bohomolec contrasted these scandalous protagonists and scenes with demonstrations of sensible good taste and elegance that demanded discretion and forbade expressions of one's feelings in an idiosyncratic or impulsive way. Gentler than his Polish predecessors, he gave those characters a certain delicacy and subtlety. Following French Jesuit models, he used not only contrasting characters but also made them engage in *disputationes* (debates for and against a given statement or observation). The protagonists conformed to a general schema and never evolved into individuals. As in farce, *commedia dell'arte*, minstrel comedy, and interlude, the most significant, sarcastic or humorous observations were often pronounced by characters of humble social origin.[15]

In time, Bohomolec's types evolved: from faintly sketched, conventional, young dandies, they turned into better characterized, high-ranking nobility and rich bourgeoisie; from Harlequins full of vivacity, indocility and good ideas, they became servants, clever and outspoken, but deprived of imagination. Readier to see the faults of the privileged, Bohomolec became more direct in his aggressiveness, stressing that it was easier to excuse a youth for his faults than an allegedly respectable adult. As required by the *ratio studiorum*, Bohomolec had to eliminate feminine parts from his school comedies, but this gap was filled in the *na theatrum* comedies in which Polish public had a chance to observe women of different social origin. Bohomolec created the first modern Polish prototypes of masculine and feminine characters, an accomplishment that facilitated the triumph of comedy in Polish Enlightenment literature.[16]

Much of the research on the decline of *commedia dell'arte* focuses on its integration with eighteenth-century French comedy. The influence of *commedia dell'arte* on Polish drama is too often associated with French writers of the *Théâtre Italien*. The best article on the subject concludes as follows:

Par l'intermédiarie du Théâtre Italien de Paris, les invensions caractéristiques de la comédie dell'arte ont pu filtrer dans le théâtre polonais .. . .C'était ainsi une influence fructueuse, bien qu'elle se soit exercée non directement, mais par l'intermédiaire des écrivains français.[17]

In light of the available sources, the accuracy of this statement may be challenged. The plays of Bohomolec give us evidence that the interest of eighteenth-century Polish writers in *commedia dell'arte* was stimulated by French, Italian and Polish sources. The impact of French writers on Bohomolec's plays was discussed several times at the beginning of this century. The most comprehensive Polish article on the subject traced Bohomolec's indebtedness to Molière in twenty comedies: five were classified as free translations, three as adaptations, twelve were said to contain minor borrowings. The author denied any possibility that Bohomolec borrowed directly from Italian. This conclusion was corrected in 1923 by A. Stender-Petersen who pointed to Bohomolec's indebtedness to Goldoni and to the traditional *commedia dell'arte*, but was unable to specify the sources of the latter borrowings. Since no research on the subject was carried out afterwards, in his introduction to the 1959–60 edition of Bohomolec's selected comedies, J. Kott stated that among the already meticulously examined sources one should include *"commedia dell'arte,* taken up most likely from French adaptations from the end of the seventeenth century, but maybe also directly, and of course Goldoni." As mentioned above, the excellent performances by the famous Italian troupes at the royal theatre in Warsaw included old Italian scenarios and arguments. A detailed comparative analysis of these texts and of Bohomolec's comedies might cast some new light upon what his *commedia dell'arte* sources were.[18]

Bohomolec was deeply interested in the most prominent writer of the reformed *commedia dell'arte*: not only did he derive several of his comedies from Goldoni but he also popularized his plays in the Republic. It was not coincidental that for two years after the establishment of the National Theatre, Goldoni's and Bohomolec's plays constituted its basic repertoire. Prefect of the Royal Printing-house, the second most important editor of the *Monitor*, a famous playwright and stage manager, Bohomolec was one of the main inspirations and executors of royal cultural policy. He certainly was one of those who influenced the repertoire of the Theatre, as the King's very modern concept of propaganda was based on the idea that both print and stage should be used to disseminate his programme of reforms. When the Theatre reopened in 1774, the comedies of these two playwrights appeared on its playbills for only a short period of time, but neither of these moderate bourgeois reformers satisfied the demands of the more progressive Polish intellectual elite who wished to use fiction as a vehicle to propagate their social and political beliefs.[19]

Both formally and ideologically these two bourgeois playwrights were close to each other: they were interested in the modernizing of their respective national theatres by the cautious implementation of Enlightenment ideas and by progressive changes in the structure of texts and theatrical techniques. Their dramatical texts developed from Latin, French and popular drama; their plots were based on contrasts of character, as well as on melodramatic or romantic incidents. They depicted numerous social, professional and ethnic groups, and alluded to their manners, customs, habits, dialects or languages. These texts were more critical of upper than lower social groups; they abounded in realism, moralism, sentimentalism. Their stock characters evolved from stereotyped buffoons into "enlightened" citizens of the two respective capitals. These similarities led to both authors being rejected by the new Polish elite which was pleased neither with the form, nor with the content of their comedies. From the point of view of the new requirements, Bohomolec's and Goldoni's characters were insufficiently individual, their understanding of contemporary reality was too simple, their description of Enlightenment bourgeois manners was too imprecise. Though their comedies enjoyed remarkable success with audiences, they were replaced by more modern, more restrained and refined, but also less spontaneous Polish comedies of morals, based on *comédie noble* and *comédie larmoyante*. Bohomolec's example was followed by several other Polish writers who translated or adapted Goldoni's plays, but who did not exercise an important influence on Polish comedy of that time.[20]

However, both Goldoni and Bohomolec continued to set an example for Polish artists—their librettos, strongly tinged by *commedia dell'arte*, contributed to the enormous success of opera in the Republic. Once more, Bohomolec's theatrical writing was to pave the way for the future evolution of a literary genre in Poland-Lithuania: he was the author of the first Polish libretto which, accompanied by Boguslawski's music, was staged in 1778 as the first Polish opera. Bohomolec's two librettos, *Nędza uszcsęśliwiona* and *Prostota cnotliwa*, derived not only from *commedia dell'arte*, but also from the Italian interlude and Italian *opera buffa*. Their indebtedness to French *comédie larmoyante* was secondary. Due to their didacticism, peasant subject matter and Enlightenment propaganda both librettos were later frequently imitated, and their popularity helped Polish buffonists win polemics with antibuffonists, thus determining that Polish opera would follow Italian *opera buffa* more closely than it would French *tragédie lyrique*.[21]

Least known to us and most difficult to analyze due to the limited archival material is the third, Polish group of Bohomolec's sources of information about *commedia dell'arte*. His indebtedness to Polish interlude and minstrel comedy has been already mentioned, but it has been seen only as a proof of his familiarity with the Polish theatrical tradition. However, recent studies on the eighteenth-century Polish school and magnate theatre, and on the *commedia dell'arte* staged in the Republic, suggest that the Polish tradition was itself influenced by *commedia dell'arte* and in turn aroused Bohomolec's interest in this literary genre. These publications establish the presence of elements of *commedia dell'arte* in Polish interlude and minstrel comedy. The latter flourished in the Republic until the 1630s, and became the direct predecessor of Enlightenment comedy. Besides, during the first half of the eighteenth century, low comic relief was incorporated into dramas performed at Jesuit schools. Polish tradition undoubtedly shaped Bohomolec's choice of foreign models: his taste for low comedy determined that his plays would follow closely French and Italian texts that either belonged to or were tinged by *commedia dell'arte*, interlude and minstrel comedy, while he rejected *comédie larmoynate* and *drame bourgeois*.[22]

I have argued that the impact of *commedia dell'arte* on eighteenth-century Polish drama is too often associated primarily with the francophone repertoire of the *Théâtre Italien*. Bohomolec's writings suggest that more attention should be given to *commedia dell'arte* borrowings from Italian and Polish theatrical traditions. Recent discoveries concerning the performances given by *comici italiani* in the Republic point to the need for a comprehensive analysis of the *commedia dell'arte* tradition in Poland-Lithuania.

University of Toronto

NOTES

1 M. Wierzbicka-Michalska, *Teatr warszawski za Sasów* (Warszawa: Instytut Sztuki PAN, 1964), pp. 7–75; M. Klimowicz, "Commedia dell'arte à Varsovie et son influence sur le développement du théâtre national polonais," in *Italia, Venezia e Polonia tra Illuminismo e Romanticismo*, ed. V. Branca (Firenze: Fundazione G. Cini, 1973), pp. 151–74; M. Wierzbicka-Michalska, *Teatr w Polsce w XVIII wieku* (Warszawa: Instytut Sztuki PAN, 1977), pp. 22–23.

2 B. Korzeniewski, "Komedia dell'arte w Warszawie," *Pamiętnik Teatralny* 3–4 (1954), pp. 29–31; M. Klimowicz, "Teatr Augusta III w Warszawie," *Pamiętnik Teatralny* 2 (1954), pp. 22–43; B. Korzeniewski, "Teatr francuski w Warszawie za Augusta III," *Pamiętnik Teatralny* 1 (1956), pp. 95–101; M. Brahmer, "Venezia nella vita teatrale polacca del Settecento," *Lettere italiane* 3 (1963), pp. 280–281; Z. Raszewski, "Za króla Sasa," *Pamiętnik Teatralny* 1 (1965), pp. 94–101; M.Klimowicz, "Wstęp," in C. Goldoni, *Uczciwa dziewczyna; Pan*

Teodor zrzęda (Wroclaw: Ossolineum, 1971), pp. XXV-XXVII.

3 M. Klimowicz, "Komedia dell'arte w Warszawie. Trzy nieznane argumenty warszawskie," *Pamiętnik Teatralny* 1 (1965), pp. 77–82; J. Lewański, "Komedia dell'arte w Warszawie. Pięć nieznanych argumentów warszawskich," *Pamiętnik Teatralny* 1 (1965), pp. 62–76; Z. Raszewski, "Za króla Sasa;" Redakcja, "Komedia dell'arte w Warszawie. Zestawienie odszukanych argumentów," *Pamiętnik Teatralny* 1 (1965), pp. 57–82.

4 M. Brahmer, "Goldoni in Polonia," *Studi Goldoniani, Civiltà Veneziana*, vol. 2, ed. V. Branca and N. Mangini (Venezia-Roma: Istituto per la collaborazione culturale, 1960), pp. 239–40; N. Mangini, "Goldoni e la Polonia," in *Venezia e la Polonia nei secoli dal XVII al XIX*, ed. L. Cini (Venezia-Roma: Istituto per la collaborazione culturale, 1968), p. 209.

5 *Komedie*, 5 vols. (Warszawa: Drukarnia J. K. Mci i Rzeczypospolitef, 1755–60); *Komedie*, 3 vols. (Lublin: Societatis Jesu, 1757–58); *Komedie*, 3 vols. (Lwów, 1768); *Komedie*, 5 vols. (Warszawa: Drukarnia J. K. Mci i Rzeczypospolitej, 1772–75); *Komedie konwiktowe*, ed. and introd. J. Kott (Warszawa: PIW, 1959); *Komedie na teatrum*, ed. and introd. J. Kott (Warszawa: PIW, 1960). Concerning Bohomolec's writings see in particular A. Stender-Petersen, *Die Schulkomödien des Paters F. Bohomolec S. J.* (Heidelberg: C. Winter's Universitätsbuchhandlung, 1923) and B. Kryda, *Szkolna i literacka dzialalność F. Bohomolca*.

6 Z. Woloszyńska, "Komedia," in *Slownik literatury polskiego Oświecenia*, ed. T. Kostkiewiczowa (Wroclaw-Warszawa: Ossolineum, 1977), p. 267.

7 *Pan Dobry* (1767), Act 1, scs. 1, 4, 7, 9, Act 2, scs. 3, 13, 14.

8 *Autor komedii*, Act 3, sc. 4; Z. Woloszyńska, "Komedia," pp. 270–71.

9 Bywalski, Glupski (*Urazający się niesłusznie o przymówki [1755]*); Arlekin, Jodelet, Pantalon, Polion (Arlekin na świat urażony [1756]); Bywalska, Ernest, Marnotrawski, Staruszkiewicz (*Molzeństwo z kalendarza [1766]*).

10 *Paryżanin polski* (I, 1757), Act 1, scs. 1, 3, 4, Act 2, scs. 1, 3; *Monitor* (1767), Act 1, scs. 1–3; *Czary* (1774), Act 3, scs. 3–4; J. Węgier, "Stylizacja parodiująca w komediach F. Bohomolca," *Zeszyty Naukowe* (Szczecin: Wyzsza Szkola Nauczycielska, 2 (1970), pp. 83–96; idem, *Jęzuk F. Bohomoloca* (Poznań, 1972), pp. 115–16; idem, "Wplywy obce w jęzkku F. Bohomolca," *Zeszyty Naukowe* (Szczecin: Wyzsza Szkola Nauczycielska, 15 (1976), pp. 23–52.

11 *Arlekin na świat urażony* is said to refer to a conflict between the famous commedia dell'arte actor D'Arbes and Warsaw audiences (A. Stender-Petersen, *Die Schulkomödien*, pp. 252–53).

12 *Pan Dobry*, Act 3, sc. 10; *Monitor*, Act 1, scs. 1–3; *Czary*, Act 3, scs. 3–4; M. Piszczkowski, *Zagadnienia wiejskie w literaturze polskiego Oświecenia*, vol. 1 (Kraków, 1960), pp. 31–48.

13 M. Terter, *Sylwetki portretowe z czasów Stanislawa Augusta* (Lwów, 1923); S. Reczek, "O nazwiskkach bohaterów komedii XVIII wieku," *Pamiętnik Lit-*

eracki 3–4 (1953), pp. 217–37.

14 *Autor komedii*, Act 1, sc. 2; Bogacki (*Paryżanin polski* [I, 1757], *Paryżanin polski* [II, 1771]); Bywalska (*Małżeństwo z kalendarza, Staruszkiewicz*, [1766]; J. Węgier, *Język F. Bohomolca*, pp. 59–60.

15 Frantocki, Glupski (*Urażający się nieslusznie o przymówki*, [1755]); Umizgalska (*Staruszka mloda* [1766]); Pijakiewicz, Pijakiewiczowa, lykaczewski, Ebriacki, Sobrecki (*Pijacy* [1767]).

16 Arlekin (*Arlekin na świat urażony*); Figalcki (*Staruszka mloda; Figlacki, polityk teraźniejszej mody [1]; Figlacki, polityk teraźniejszej mody [II]*); Agata, Chudziński, Maciek, Wagusewicz, Wawrek (*Pan Dobry*); Bartek, Jaga, Ochotnicki, Wawrek, Wiernicki, (*Monitor*); Nastka (*Czary*).

17 M. Klimowicz, "Commedia dell'arte," p. 167.

18 W. Strusiński, "Komedie X. Franciszka Bohomolca w zależnósci od teatru francuskiego i wloskiego," *Pamiętnik Literacki* 4 (1905), pp. 246–60; J. Goląbek, *Komedie knowiktowe ks. Franciszka Bohomolca w zależnosci od Moliera* (Kraków: PAU, 1922), chapters 2 and 3; A. Stender-Petersen, *Die Schulkomödien*, pp. 131–91.

19 W. Strusiński, "Komedie X. F. Bohomolca," pp. 247–49; A. Stender-Petersen, *Die Schulkomödien*, pp. 132–33, 141–43, 204–205, 228–29, 234–37; M. Brahmer, "Goldoni in Polonia," pp. 239–41; N. Mangini, "Goldoni e la Polonia," pp. 208–209.

20 K. Wierzbicka-Michalska, *Sześć Studiów o teatrze stanislawowskim* (Wroclaw-Warszawa: Instytut Sztuki PAN, 1967), p. 115; M. Brahmer, "Wstęp," in C. Goldoni, *Kawiarenka wenecka, Mirandolina*, ed. M. Brahmer, trans. Z. Jachimecka (Wroclaw: Ossolineum, 1972), pp. III-XX; K. Zaboklicki, *Carlo Goldoni* (Warszawa: PWN, 1984), pp. 452–56.

21 J. Kott, "Wstęp," pp. 73–5; M. Piszczkowski, *Zagadnienia wiejskie*, pp. 41–47; K. Zaboklicki, *Carlo Goldoni*, p. 458.

22 St. Windakiewicz, *Teatr Kolegiów jezuickich w dawnej Polsce* (Kraków: 1922), pp. 35–47; M. Brahmer, "La commedia dell'arte in Polonia," *Ricerche Slavistiche* 3 (1954), pp. 184–195; J. Lewański, "Faust i Arlekin. Niezwykle przedstawienie na secenie leszczyńskiej w roku 1647," *Pamiętnik Teatralny* 1 (1957), pp. 76–93; J. Popolatek, *Studia z dziejów jezuickiego teatru szkolnego w Polsce* (Wroclaw: Ossolineum, 1957), pp. 8–10; Z. Raszewski, "Porcelanowa Arlekinada," *Pamiętnik Teatralny* 1 (1957), pp. 121–23; W. Roszkowska, *Wloski rodowód komedii St. H. Lubomirskiego* (Wroclaw: Ossolineum, 1960), pp. 112–142, 161–179; W. Roszkowska, "Le componenti italiane nella cultura teatrale della corte polacca nel Seicento (La commedia all'improvviso)," in *Barocco fra Italia e Polonia*, ed. J. Slaski (Warszawa: Accademia Polacca delle Scienze, Comitato degli Studi sull'Arte, 1977), pp. 294–95.

David Trott

A Clash of Styles: Louis Fuzelier and the "New Italian Comedy"

Theatrical performance and writing do not mix well. *Commedia dell'arte* is primarily performance. This fact has bothered many French theatre historians and theorists in their attempts to describe the importance of *commedia* in the dramatic works of a given playwright or period in France. Be it François Moureau's evocation of "an Italian-style spectacle" in the late seventeenth century,[1] or Patrice Pavis's theoretical reconstitution of the underlying principles of a *Comédie Italienne* performance around the 1720's,[2] we are invariably confronted with the fundamental elusiveness of the theatrical fact.

It is generally agreed that the fate of the *commedia dell'arte* in France was to be assimilated into French, or more specifically, Parisian forms and traditions. According to Gustave Attinger, some theatre critics go farther, by refusing even to consider Italian theatre in France as true *commedia*,[3] and, indeed, it is extremely difficult to isolate the specificity of so-called French and *commedia dell'arte* forms. On a theoretical plane at least, it is obvious that the blending of two entities, French theatre and *commedia*— themselves composed not only of a measurable corpus of written scripts and technical documents, but also of an immense set of unwritten "adjuncts" which most dramatologists consider to be the very essence of theatre—cannot result in the total absorption of one entity by the other. Transformed elements of both linger on in the new compound which, although it may retain the label of one of its original components, is in fact something quite different. Instead of absorption, with its implied suppression of one constituent entity, it would perhaps be preferable to speak of "fusion."

An analysis of the theoretical combinatory process of a fusion of styles is, however, further complicated by historical fluctuations of the idea of *commedia dell'arte* in France. Already inherently evasive, as we have seen, *Comédie Italienne* as perceived by the French was further clouded as a notion by the sporadicity of its physical presence in Paris.[4] In fact, rather than a single, describable, unbroken tradition, we have to cope with a variety of "moments" of that tradition, suddenly separated from their Italian base, and re-interpreted for Parisian audiences through the often differing views of their art held by individual *commedia* practitioners: Dominique Locatelli played Trivelin in an Arlequin costume, minus the slapstick or bat; Angelo Constantini was noted for an Arlequin without mask; Luigi Riccoboni came to Paris with a vastly over-ambitious vision of his mission, only to be pulled back to reality by the less-elevated tastes of Parisian theatregoers.

The frequent physical departures of Italian theatrical companies from Paris, particularly in 1697,[5] when Louis XIV banished them and locked their theatre, did not mean the abrupt cessation of *commedia* influence on the French repertory. Molière's celebrated though fleeting collaboration with Tiberio Fiorilli when the fledgling *Troupe de Monsieur* shared the *Théâtre du Petit Bourbon* with the successors of Mazarin's Italian Players, and Dufresney's more prolonged collaboration with what I shall call the "Old" *Comédie Italienne*[6] later in the seventeenth century, left a lasting impression on both French playwrights; an impression that Gustave Attinger calls in his study of Italian influences on French theatre, the "spirit" of *commedia dell' arte*.[7]

Given the fact that this section of our conference is devoted to "The National Theatres of Europe," it might appear appropriate to present an article of the scope of Attinger's vast survey. However, the space available for a consideration of *commedia* fortunes in pre-revolutionary France demands something distinctly more succinct. That is why I have chosen to focus on a specific meeting of theatrical styles during the early eighteenth century in France, prior to the successful blending of French and Italian brands of theatre in the plays that Marivaux worte for the "New" *Comédie Italienne* of Luigi Riccoboni. During the period that runs roughly from 1700 to 1730, Parisian audiences were torn between the desire to pursue Louis XIV's dream of a single "National Theatre,"[8] and an insatiable desire for more, and more varied theatre fare. On the surface, the banishment from the French capital of Evariste Gherardi's "Old" *Comédie Italienne* in 1697 left the *Comédie Française* with the monopoly on spoken dramatic performances that it had always wanted. This apparent monopoly was to last until 1716, the year after Louis XIV's death, when the Regent officially recalled Italian theatre to Paris in the form of Riccoboni's "New" *Comédie Italienne*. In fact, however, Italian-style theatre during the twenty-year interval of its banishment had simply gone underground where it flourished and evolved at the two annual Paris Fairs, *La Foire St. Germain* and *La Foire St. Laurent*, in the form of numerous adaptations.[9] This gives us an elaborate pattern of transmigrations that exemplify the larger problem of the meeting of *commedia dell'arte* and French theatre. Accordingly, the seemingly fresh infusion of Riccoboni's "New" Italian Theatre into a Parisian context in 1716 must be viewed in the much wider context of an already highly involved interlacing of French and Italian styles.

* * * * *

Gustave Attinger tells us that Riccoboni arrived in Paris with dreams of theatrical reform.[10] He possessed a repertory of serious works, including many tragi-comedies of his own composition and tragedies by others, which he made persistent attempts to perform.[11] The Parisian public, on the other hand, seeking amusement over edification, demanded regularly that he revert to improvisational sketches, stock characters and masks. By 1718, after the novelty of an Italian theatrical company had worn off,[12] Riccoboni and his colleagues were obliged to resort to the use of French in their performances if they wished to survive.

By the end of the decade that followed, culminating roughly with the withdrawal of a disillusioned Riccoboni from the *Comédie Italienne* in 1729,[13] and the first performance of Marivaux's masterpiece *Le Jeu de l'amour et du hasard* in 1730, the "New" Italian Players had searched in a variety of directions for a formula for success. One of the people to whom they turned for help was Louis Fuzelier. Fuzelier, the little-known author or co-author of some 237 plays and opera libretti,[14] provided 27 scripts for Riccoboni's actors between 1718 and 1732. His production, which remains largely unrecognized, falls into three main, and frequently overlapping categories: (i) early attempts at collaboration which included popular successes like *La Méridienne*; (ii) theatrical parodies, one of the better-known of which was *Le Serdeau des Théâtres*; (iii) plays bearing the unmistakable hallmark of *théâtre forain*. Although the collaboration between Fuzelier and Riccoboni's company did not produce any lasting literary monuments, it can nevertheless serve to reveal the processes by which theatrical cross-fertilization occurs.

* * * * *

During the first two seasons of Fuzelier's collaboration with the Italians, the French author wrote six plays for the company.[15] Because they cover the period during which Riccoboni and his colleagues were making the difficult transition from Italian to French, it is not surprising to see them incorporating the problems of translation into their plots. Since his days at the early Paris Fairs when he had to produce written scripts for unspoken, mimed performances (the famous *pièces à la muette* of 1711), Fuzelier had become recognized as a gifted "theatrical translator" who could facilitate the move from one theatrical medium, or language, such as stage dialogue, to another, such as pantomime.

It is therefore fitting that Fuzelier's first play for the "New" Italian Players should be *Love the Language Teacher, L'Amour maître de langue*.[16] The work contains several scenes of dialogue which, although written in French, were intended to be performed in Italian. This fact opens the whole question of the relationship between an author's text and the live interpretation of it by an actor; clearly here, the actors improvised in Italian, using the French version as a mere springboard. This of course was standard *commedia* practice. In addition, the split between "languages" and their status points to another typical *commedia* trait which Patrice Pavis has described as the organization of performances around a succession of set pieces highlighting individual actors and their specialities.[17] Act I of *L'Amour maître de langue* contains three distinct parts: in the opening scenes, the servant types, Arlequin, Scaramouche, Scapin, performed in Italian punctuated with much gesture and stage business; their masters followed, performing in French and presenting the plot line; the act closed with a Fuzelier set piece which was the on-stage portrayal of his own world of writers, composers and authors.

Gustave Attinger reflects a still-current disdain for Fuzelier's writings by referring to "quelques piècettes de Fuzelier,"[18] and by naming only two of his texts. He seems to cite *L'Amour maître de langue* only in order to quote extensively from a negative review of Fuzelier's day.[19]

In 1719, Fuzelier's collaboration with the Italians met with slightly more success. The May issue of the journal, *Le Mercure*, is quoted as considering the show written by him to be a "spectacle d'un genre tout nouveau."[20] It was referring to the fact that three distinct one-act plays, *La Mode, La Méridienne* and *Le May*, had been combined to form a single program called an *ambigu comique*, or mixture of separate plays, each with their own titles.[21] *La Mode* is a review play, structured around an alignment of otherwise unrelated set pieces. The marchpast of characters includes the publisher M. Brochure and M. De l'Entrechat, dancing master, who launches into a criticism of the opera *Les Ages*, of which, it should be noted, Fuzelier was also the librettist. Fuzelier's penchant for self-representation and self-parody, another trait he shared with *commedia dell'arte*, was in later years, as we shall see, to assume enormous proportions. *La Méridienne*, a fast-moving, truly bilingual comedy of intrigue and ironic asides, pits Pantalon against his niece Silvia's lover with the predictable result. It is an excellent example of the way in which Fuzelier moulded his texts on situations leading to a sliding between different languages; not only from French script to improvised Italian dialogue, but from discourse to gesture and back again. In a famous study of Molière, W. G. Moore saw this elusive blending of different stage languages as a subordination of words to mime which, "were it still available, might give us the most living and 'dramatic' form of diction possible."[22]

Patrice Pavis sees it as a fusion of word and gesture.[23] In addition, self-conscious winks at the audience with attendant shifts between "straight" and ironic registers further heighten the overall impression of movement in this play.

Following the completion of what must have been a two-year trial period, two, more specific types of collaboration were attempted: Fuzelier was to provide a steady supply of parodies commencing in July 1719, even before the stock of early works had been exhausted, and, after 1721, he became involved in a desperate attempt by the Italians to compete directly with the Paris Fair theatres in both their style and location.

* * * * *

Recourse by the *Comédie Italienne* to parody was established in the seventeenth century. As an actor's weapon in the struggle to win audiences, it took the form of comic imitation of the gestures, diction and/or general stage comportment of other actors in rival companies. The shift from an actor-centred spectacle to one in which authors' texts played a greater role had as a corollary the development of "text" parodies in which the entire play—or more frequently, opera or ballet—of rival troupes was parodied in place of the individual performances. Alvin Eustis already attributes Molière's use of parody to *commedia dell'arte* influence.[24] Dufresney and Regnard wrote parodies for the "Old Italian Players." Fuzelier in turn acknowledges the "New Italian Theatre's" debt to what he calls an established Italian tradition in the prologue to his parody, *Hercule filant*:

. . . lisez les Annales de la Comédie Italienne, vous verrez que nos ancêtres comiques ont chanté d'après . . . Dumenil . . . ; ne devez-vous pas sçavoir qu'Armide, ce chef-d'oeuvre du fameux Lully, a été fredonné par un gosier Arlequinique?[25]

By turning once again to Fuzelier, this time for parodies of the then-current operatic or dramatic successes, Riccoboni was appealing to the pioneer who kept the tradition alive during the days betwen the "Old" and "New" *Comédies Italiennes*.

Between 1719 and 1732, Fuzelier wrote or rewrote some twelve parodies for the Italians. His contributions in this genre were probably the most important part of his collaboration with Riccoboni. They were primarily inspired by productions at the Paris Opera, and by far the most "victimized" author was Houdard de La Motte, whose written or even anticipated works were targetted in five different Fuzelier texts. *La Rupture du Carnaval et de la Folie* takes aim at the overly-affected style of La Motte's ballet *Le Carnaval et la Folie.*[26] Opening with Folie's attack on "la Métaphysique à l'Opéra," Fuzelier's one-act takeoff on La Motte moves to an evocation of the expressiveness through gesture that was—and still is—a *commedia dell'arte* hallmark:

L'AMOUR
. . . mais si je parle moins, je gesticule davantage.

LA FOLIE
Vous ne pouvez gesticuler qu'avec grace: gesticulez charmant Amour, gesticulez.

L'AMOUR
Peste! vous vous connaissez en style! vous sçavez que les gestes sont moins trompeurs que les paroles . . .[27]

Marivaux, who was to have his first play with the Italians performed the following year, would appear to be referring to the same practice of having gesture supplant verbal expression in his prologue to *L'Amour et la Vérité.*[28]

Fuzelier's second "Italian" parody, of another La Motte opera, *Omphale*, was staged by Riccoboni's actors in May 1721. Entitled *Hercule filant*, it represents a significant advance through the explicit way in which it attempts to present a rudimentary theory of parody at the same time as it seeks to justify the use of familiar Paris Fair techniques. One of these, the use of popular tunes of the day, or vaudevilles, is called ". . . un pot-pourri de 'Vous m'entendez-bien' [et] de 'Flon-flon'."[29] A character named Le Connoisseur objects to the debasing of the "Italians'" repertory through the use of such tunes: "Eh, morbleu, laissez à la Foire le soin de ridiculiser les Héros en bémol; c'est-là son métier."

The character Trivelin points out that, whereas French tragedy could easily be ridiculed at the level of an individual actor's diction, presumably with little or no alteration of the lines being spoken, opera parodies require the substitution of inappropriate music, such as the abovementioned popular tunes, for the more formal notes of the operatic musician's score:

La Tragedie Françoise reçoit dans la Parodie un comique qui peut être rendu par la déclamation, mais le Poème Lirique ne peut se présenter sur le théâtre de la Comédie Italienne sans le passe-port du Vaudeville.

Fuzelier seems to be grappling once again with the transposition of one medium into another.

Every aspect of La Motte's text is ridiculed in *Hercule filant*: the manner in which Opera actors walk on stage; the setting in Omphale's palace which is downgraded to the palace kitchen; and the illogicality of set changes. On the level of auto-representation, the wearing of Arlequin's mask is made textually explicit through the same epithet *brunet* that Marivaux had used nine months earlier to characterize him in *Arlequin poli par l'amour*.[30]

That *Hercule filant* represented an obvious shift by Riccoboni's company in the direction of the "comic-opera" style made famous by the Paris Fairs was futher underlined by a brief notice of the parody in *Le Mercure*.[31]

In the nine parodies that followed,[32] Fuzelier embarked with Riccoboni's company on a veritable spree of intertextuality. In *Arlequin Persée*, a list of virtually every major city in Europe, placed at the end of an advertisement for a recently-published poem, is transformed into two full pages of riming verse and set to the popular tune "Que n'aimez-vous, coeurs insensibles." Fuzelier's *Serdeau des Théâtres* (translated very freely: theatrical smorgasbord) transforms four works from the other Paris theatres into a parodic *ambigu comique*. In addition to referring to itself, Fuzelier's next parody, called *Parodie*, bristles with textual fragments from Corneille's *Le Cid, Cinna, Rodogune*, Racine's *Andromaque, Mithridate, Phèdre* and *Bajazet*, La Motte's *Inès de Castro*, and Danchet's *Nitétis*. Fuzelier's *Saturnales*, about which I have written elsewhere,[33] was the seventh of eight different versions of a subject that Fuzelier spent much of 1723 writing and rewriting. *L'Italienne Française*, on which Fuzelier collaborated, was the Italians' response to a *Comédie Française* play, *La Française Italienne*, in which the French actors parodied Arlequin whom they had one of their actresses portray. Fuzelier's *Bague magique*, which was written in anticipation of La Motte's *Le Talisman*, was performed and withdrawn

eleven days before La Motte's play was even put on.[34]
That parody is an essential element of *commedia dell' arte* is revealed by
its long history in *Comédie Italienne* annals, by the proportion of Fuzelier's
efforts for the Italians that it took up, and by the fact that four volumes of
parodies were published to supplement the plays in *Le Nouveau Théâtre
italien*. It is also demonstrated by the fact that the Italians themselves
went on to make parody one of their mainstays.

* * * * *

Much less prolonged and clear-cut was Fuzelier's role as a writer who
attempted to steer Riccoboni's theatre in the direction of the Paris Fairs.
And yet, when critics even deign to mention Fuzelier, it is usually to blame
him for degrading Italian-style theatre with Paris Fair scripts.[35] Between
1722 and 1726, Fuzelier produced nine plays in the *forain* category. Only
three appear to have been written by him alone, and, with the exception
of some fragments in manuscript, all these have disappeared.
What *is* known more clearly is that Riccoboni leased the famous Pellegrin theatre for three seasons (1721–1723) at the *Foire St. Laurent*.[36] This
physical relocation of the *Comédie Italienne* can be seen not only as a
quest for better gate receipts, but on a deeper level as a collective identity
crisis on the part of the Italians. An impression of the company's dis-
orientation is heightened further when one discovers that the author who
provided the bulk of the plays they performed during their first season at
the Fair was the *Comédie Française* playwright and actor, Marc-Antoine
Legrand, probably lent with his company's blessing as part of a temporary
alliance with the Italians.[37]
This system of alliances and counter-alliances intensified in 1722 when
the Fair companies lost their franchise to stage live theatre, and Fuzelier,
this time in association with Lesage and d'Orneval, moved again to the
Italians. Their first play was the three-act *Jeune Vieillard* which clearly
subordinated its actors to the stage machinery of Pellegrin's theatre. Although this change in focus appears to represent a significant departure
from *commedia*-type performance, Marcello Spaziani, who studies it from
the opposite perspective of *théâtre forain*, detects some slight concessions
to the Italians:

. . . in questa *pièce italienne* domina il movimento, ma la buffoneria è abbastanza
contenuta, né avvertiamo il disagio degli autori costretti a rinunciare a qualche
pezzo del loro repertorio abituale.[38]

The following month, on August 8, Fuzelier and his collaborators provided the Italians with a second program, another *ambigu comique*. *Le Dieu du hasard* is a prologue which provides an avowedly tenuous link between the two works following it. The god of Chance simply has the Italians draw numbered titles from an urn. Arlequin picks ticket number 419, *La Force de l'amour* and Pantalon, number 740, *La Foire de fées*, which leads to a discussion about the relative merits of *ambigus comiques* over more unified three-act plays.[39] Thalie presents a defense of varied programs which appears to assuage the Italians' fears of adopting a Paris Fair recipe for success:

Une comédie de trois Actes n'est qu'un plat, après tout; si on trouve ce plat mauvais, serviteur au festin. (. . .) Au lieu que des Morceaux détachez font des ragoûts différens, dont l'un peut suppléer à l'autre. (. . .) . . . il faut de la variété dans les mets, pour contenter la diversité des goûts.

(scene 3)

La Force de l'amour, following *Le Dieu du hasard*, contains hidden within a complicated plot [40] several of the elements that Marivaux would re-combine later in his *Jeu de l'amour et du hasard*. Otherwise, the play seems little more than an arbitrary assemblage of theatrical tricks.

The period after August 1722 is characterized by a fragmentation of the evidence concerning Fuzelier's collaboration with Riccoboni's company. A September 16 *ambigu comique*[41] has disappeared, except for a manuscript of its prologue. In 1723, the year of the "scattergun" parodies (*Serdeau* and *Parodie*) and of his "re-writing" odyssey (*Les Saturnales*), the reference to a play purportedly performed the same evening as a 3-act version of *Les Saturnales* remains a mystery in the absence of both texts. In summing up Fuzelier's alleged impact as a corrupting Paris Fair influence on *La Comédie Italienne*, it would appear to be less demonstrable than the more positive instances of collaboration that were detected earlier in the trial period and in the parodies.

* * * * *

Louis Fuzelier or "New Italian Comedy"? "Clash" of styles or "fusion" of styles? Where lies *commedia dell'arte* in this maze of entities and of possible relationships between them? At the end of the brief survey just presented of Fuzelier's work for the "New" Italian Theatre in Paris, it must be pointed out that in whatever category he wrote, his successes, when they occurred, were short-lived. The Italians themselves carried dramatic parody to far greater heights than Fuzelier's literary spoofs. Of the early works, only *La Méridienne* seems worthy of interest now. Sporadic flashes of potential brilliance, as in *Le Dieu du hasard* and *La Force de l'amour*, remained for Marivaux to extract from among the obscurities and clumsiness of Fuzelier's numerous and rapidly-written texts. This all appears to confirm the impression of many theatre historians that Fuzelier was merely a second-rate hack, deserving of the oblivion to which he has perhaps too hastily been condemned.

However, Riccoboni also was to fail. In his dream of theatrical reform, at least on the level of acting and directing a company of live actors,[42] his attempts to include elevated drama in the repertory of the New *Comédie Italienne* were blocked by the tastes of Parisians who remained haunted by a vision of the *commedia dell'arte* that Fuzelier as a Paris Fair stalwart had nourished for so long. After Riccoboni's withdrawal from the theatre for a career as a writer, the Italian Players mounted a repertory that consisted of massive doses of ballet, parodies and pyrotechnics, all now, like the latter—and like Fuzelier's plays—, gone up in smoke. The only lasting, palpable monument of the Italians in Paris is, of course, the body of plays written for them by Marivaux; Marivaux, whose reputation diminished as the tradition on which it was based declined, and whose emergence in our generation as the most-frequently performed French playwright in France[43] is, I suspect, not unrelated to our renewed interest in *commedia*.

I said at the outset of this paper that the product of a fusion of styles, even though it may retain the name of one of its constituent ingredients, is not identical to any of its parts. It is clear, for example, that Marivaux's theatre may be considered as such a "product." Among its components, we must place both *commedia dell'arte* as interpreted by the "New Italian Players" and *commedia dell'arte* as interpreted by Fuzelier. Indeed, the record we have been able to reconstruct of Fuzelier's involvement with Italian theatre shows an affinity with the spirit of *commedia dell'arte* in France that in some ways may have been deeper than Riccoboni's.

Certainly this may be said of the manner in which the fluidity of certain of his texts calls forth the idea of improvisation. Fuzelier's failure to publish many of his plays was seen by his detractors as proof of their low worth—at least as books. Might it not also attest to their "theatricality," by which term I mean their closeness to the changing, volatile nature of performance? In the case of *Les Saturnales*, this meant the shifting form of repeated re-writings. We have seen how dialogue in *La Méridienne* functioned less as a constraint on the Italian-speaking actors than as a point of departure from which they invented their own words. The French dialogue became a scenario instead of a closed, fixed text, triggering not servile imitation, but rather verbal inventiveness on the part of the actors. A similarly dynamic relationship is established in the case of Fuzelier's parodies which generate a ceaseless *mouvement* between the target text and the parody; a *mouvement* that accelerates as the number of theatre languages (music, dialogue, decor, gesture) grows, as in *Hercule filant* or as the number of targets proliferates, as it did in the case of *Parodie*. Ultimately, the fusion of different theatre languages in Fuzelier's works may be equated with the fusion of language and gesture in *commedia dell'arte*.

On the other hand, *commedia dell'arte* is not necessarily tied to Italian actors. When the *Comédie Italienne* was banished from Paris in 1697, theatre historians were at a loss to decide whether the departure of the Italians meant the disappearance of the art equated with them. In this particular instance, the removal of the Italians seems paradoxically to have led to a resurrection of *commedia dell'arte*. The closing of the Hôtel de Bourgogne brought about a relocation of *commedia* to the flimsy boards of the *St. Laurent* and *St. Germain* Fairs. It was there, and not in the quasi-institutional setting of a permanent theatre that a re-creation of conditions like those which gave birth to *commedia dell'arte* as a popular art form, occurred: ". . . en ramenant le genre italien aux tréteaux qui le virent naître, elles[44] retrouvent assez naturellement l'esprit de la fameuse *commedia*."[45]

The conditions re-created at the Fairs combined harsh adversity, rudimentary theatres, and an audience united by an unabashed quest for entertainment. The result was an ever-tense atmosphere which required of those Fair practitioners who survived unending creativity, inventiveness and resourcefulness. The decision by the "New Italian Players" to return to the *St. Laurent* Fair in 1721 may thus be viewed as an unconsciously symbolic pilgrimage to their mythical place of origin. The essence of *commedia dell'arte* ceases to derive from a necessary link with Italianism and becomes instead the placing of *commedia* characteristics within a popular framework.

The clash of styles which took place between Fuzelier and Riccoboni was therefore not as simple as the mere incompatibility of Parisian and "Italian" (ie. *commedia*) theatre. It was rather a clash between an Italian who, in one sense, betrayed *commedia dell'arte*, to become, in the words of Patrice Pavis, "plus Français que les Français,"[46] and a Frenchman who was unwilling or unable to espouse a view of theatre as anything

other than live—and therefore ceaselessly changing—performance. Those
who placed writing above performance (Riccoboni, Marivaux) have left
a clear mark through their texts. Those who did not (Fuzelier, the collective creators of *commedia dell'arte*) suffered the fate of all makers of
performance: an image that is blurred. . . .

University of Toronto

NOTES

1 "Un spectacle à l'italienne," in François Moureau, *Dufresny, Auteur dramatique
   (1657–1724)*, (Paris: Klincksieck, 1979), pp.125–60.
2 "Les Conditions de la Représentation à la Comédie-Italienne," tome I, pp. 168–
   279, in Patrice Pavis, "Marivaux: L'Epreuve de la scène contemporaine" Thèse
   pour le doctorat d'Etat, Université de la Sorbonne Nouvelle, Paris III, 1983, 3
   vols.
3 "La critique littéraire d'aujourd-hui—particulièrement les savants italiens—
   refuse à cette comédie italienne de France le nom de véritable *commedia
   dell'arte.*" Gustave Attinger, *L'Esprit de la "Commedia dell'arte" dans le
   théâtre français*, (Paris: Librairie théâtrale, 1950), p. 358.
4 Companies of *commedia* actors came to the French capital in waves from the
   sixteenth century to the eighteenth: *I Gelosi* in 1577, and again in 1588, the
   Comici Confidenti in 1584, the *Fedeli* in 1613, a company which may have included Tiberio Fiorilli—Scaramouche—in 1639, a *troupe* including Dominique
   Biancolelli—Dominique—in 1661, and the actor Luigi Riccoboni in 1716.
5 Louis XIV banished the Italian players of Evariste Gherardi when they attempted to put on a play entitled *La Fausse Prude*.
6 In fact, after the death of Dominique (Arlequin), the "Old Italian Players" were
   led by Angelo and Jean Baptiste Constantini (Mezzetin and Octave respectively). Gherardi replaced Dominique in the role of Arlequin, and it is he who
   published many of the company's plays—including several by Dufresny—in *Le
   Théâtre Italien, ou le recueil général de toutes les comédies et scènes françaises
   jouées par les comédiens italiens du Roi*, (Paris: 1694–1700), 6 vols.
7 Attinger, see note 3.
8 The *Comédie Française*, founded by Louis XIV in 1680.
9 "Les troupes (. . .) puisent sans scrupule leur répertoire dans celui du théâtre
   qui n'est plus.," Xavier de Courville, *Un Apôtre de l'art du théâtre au XVIIIe
   siècle. Luigi Riccoboni, dit Lélio*, Tome II, "L'Expérience française," (Paris:
   E. Droz, 1943), p. 10.
10 For a detailed study of Riccoboni's program of theatrical reform in Italy, prior
   to his arrival in Paris, see Xavier de Courville, *Luigi Riccoboni, dit Lélio*, Tome
   I, "L'Expérience italienne."
11 He staged Maffei's *Mérope* in January and March 1717. In 1725, he and his
   wife, Flaminia, actually staged Racine's *Andromaque*, in Italian.

12 This was the same dilemma faced a generation earlier by Gherardi's troupe: "Une compagnie étrangère ne peut appuyer indéfiniment ses succès sur cet attrait de curiosité, de surprise ou de scandale que lui prêtent à ses débuts son accent, son costume et son style." Courville, Tome II, p. 5.

13 The ". . . orientation du répertoire vers la Foire ne correspondait certes pas aux intentions et aux espoirs de Lélio [Riccoboni] . . . il prit sa retraite en avril 1729." Attinger, p. 340. Riccoboni's retirement from directing the *Comédie Italienne* opened the way for his subsequent historical and theoretical writings on the theatre.

14 See my article "Louis Fuzelier et le théâtre: vers un état présent," *Revue d'Histoire Littéraire de la France*, vol. 83, no. 4, pp. 604–17.

15 Evidence suggests that a package of at least four, and possibly six scripts, running the gamut of genres, lengths and styles, were handed over to Riccoboni as a package on August 1, 1718. A receipt signed by Fuzelier and Riccoboni specifies that *L'Amour maître de langue*, *La Mode*, *La Méridienne* and *Le May* were delivered to the Italians well before they were performed.

16 First performed on September 18, 1718, at the Hôtel de Bourgogne, after a prologue entitled *La Mode*, *L'Amour maître de langue* was not published. A summary appears in J. -A. J. Desboulmiers' *Histoire anecdotique et raisonnée du Théâtre Italien*, (Genève: Slatkine Reprints, 1968), tome 1, pp. 68–69. In this paper, references are based on the manuscript, BN f.fr. 9332, fol. 135–229.

17 ". . . les postures et les lazzis forment encore [ie. before the middle of the eighteenth century] des points de focalisation très forts et . . . la structure *épique*—successive et désillusionnante—de la présentation imposait une suite de numéros (postures, lazzis) assez indépendants . . . ," Pavis I, p. 234.

18 Attinger, p. 337.

19 ". . . il était aisé de voir que cette pièce avait été faite pour un autre spectacle . . . elle se ressentait du lieu de sa destination: aussi jugea-t-on d'abord qu'elle partait d'un auteur de la Foire qui n'avait point encore dégorgé." (This quotation comes from N. Boindin's fourth letter on the Italian theatre. See Attinger, p. 337).

20 Courville, Tome II, p. 138.

21 The combining of short plays to fill a program was an old *forain* trick with which Fuzelier was quite familiar. The three plays in question here were performed on May 23, 1719, at the Hôtel de Bourgogne. Résumés of all three have been published in Desboulmiers, *Histoire anecdotique*, tome I, pp. 87–94. A brief summary of *La Mode* is to be found also in *Le Nouveau Théâtre Italien*, (Paris: Briasson, 1729) tome I, pp. 112–116. Complete manuscripts are to be found in BN f.fr. 9332, fol. 232–92.

22 W. G. Moore, *Molière, a New Criticism* (Oxford: 1949) p. 54.

23 Pavis, tome I, p. 227.

24 Alvin Eustis, *Molière as Ironic Contemplator*, (The Hague: Mouton, 1973).

25 In *Les Parodies du Nouveau Théâtre Italien*, tome II, (Paris: Briasson, 1738).

26 *La Rupture du Carnaval et de la Folie* was produced on July 6, 1719, at the Hôtel de Bourgogne.

27 *La Rupture du Carnaval et de la Folie*, in *Parodies du Nouveau Théâtre Italien*, tome II.

28 "L'AMOUR.- Enfin Madame, ces tendres et tremblants aveux d'une passion, ces dépits délicats, ces transports d'amour d'après les plus innocentes faveurs, d'après mille petits riens précieux, tout cela disparut. L'un ouvrit sa bourse, l'autre gesticulait insolemment auprès d'une femme, et cela s'appelait une déclaration." Marivaux, *Théâtre complet*, éd. F. Deloffre, (Paris: Garnier, 1968). All subsequent quotations of Marivaux's plays will be based on this edition.

29 Produced for the first time on May 15, 1721, *Hercule filant* was published in *Parodies du Nouveau Théâtre Italien*, tome II, 1737. All subsequent quotations from the play are based on this text.

30 "Beau brunet, l'Amour vous appelle" is repeated three times in the musical interlude that opens scene 3. The reference in Omphale's song in scene 3 of *Hercule filant*: "Qu'il est poli!/Qu'il est joli!" also hark back to the title of Marivaux's *Arlequin poli*, as well as to the numerous references to Arlequin's physical attractiveness: "TRIVELIN.- . . . un beau brun, bien fait; c'est la figure la plus charmante du monde" (scene première); "SILVIA.- . . . Ah mon Dieu le beau garçon!" (scene 5); "SILVIA.- Vous êtes joli aussi, vous." (scene 5).

31 "*Hercule filant*. Pièce d'un Acte avec un Prologue dans le goût des pièces de l'Opéra Comique. . . " (*Le Mercure*, juin & juillet 1721, 2e vol. p. 21.)

32 *Le Serdeau des théâtres* (1723), *Parodie* (1723), *Les Saturnales* (1723), *Les Debris des Saturnales* (1723), *Amadis le cadet* (1724), *Momus exilé* (1725), *L'Italienne française* (1725), *La Bague magique* (1726), *Arlequin au Parnasse* (1732).

33 "Textes et réécritures de textes: le cas des *Fêtes grecques et romaines* de Louis Fuzelier," in *Man and Nature*, III, 1984, pp. 77–88.

34 *Le Talisman* was performed on March 27, 1726; Fuzelier's play, on March 16.

35 *Le Serdeau des Théâtres* "est une pièce dans le goût de celles de l'opera comique" (*Le Mercure*, février 1723, p. 336); *Parodie* "est une échappée de la foire" (*Le Mercure*, mai 1723, p. 970); see also above Attinger's quote of Boindin.

36 "Le 13 juillet, les Comédiens abandonnèrent leur maison, et se transportèrent avec armes et bagages dans la belle loge que leur louait le sieur Pellegrin. (. . .) La scène de Pellegrin était riche en ressources décoratives, et l'on admirait surtout la machine qui pouvait en un quart d'heure transformer le théâtre en une salle de bal." (Xavier de Courville, tome II, p. 144).

37 "La politique habituelle de la Comédie [Française] était de faire tout son possible pour empêcher et les forains et les Italiens d'atteindre à trop de popularité; elle se servait constamment des uns pour faire échec aux autres." (Mary

Scott Burnet, *Marc-Antoine Legrand, acteur et auteur comique (1673–1728)*, (Genève: Slatkine Reprints, 1977), p. 118.

38 Marcello Spaziani, *Il Teatro minore di Lesage*, (Rome: Studi e Ricerche, 1957) p. 134.

39 The god of Chance unequivocally opts for chaos: "Je me moque de l'ordre, moi, (. . .) Je me soucie de la raison, de la justice & du bon goût, comme de cela." (*Le Dieu du hasard*, scene 2, in *Le Théâtre de la foire, ou l'opéra comique*, tome V, (Amsterdam: Chez Zacharie Chatelain, 1726).

40 "Macchinosa commedia di evidente origine spagnola: travestimenti, riconoscimento finale, pletora di personnaggi, lentezza nell'andamento. . ." (Spaziani, p. 134).

41 The program included a prologue, *Les Noces de Gamache* and *Le Vieux Monde, ou Arlequin Somnambule*.

42 After 1729, he turned to writing about the theatre rather than practising it. He intensified the editing of his company's repertory (*Le Nouveau Théâtre Italien*), and then went on to write works such as *Pensées sur la déclamation* (1738) and *De la Réformation du théâtre* (1743).

43 "Marivaux est devenu en France l'auteur dramatique le plus joué de notre répertoire." (Michel Cournot, "Marivaux et l'inconnu de Lyon," *Le Monde*, 14 mars 1985, p. 13).

44 It should be noted that they first attempted to replace the Italians *in their own theatre*, but they were quickly expelled by the authorities.

45 X. de Courville, tome II, p. 10.

46 "N'est-il pas affligeant de lire leur condamnation [the condemnation of *lazzis*] sous la plume de Lélio, plus Français que les Français, et qui trouve que les lazzis ne sont 'que des épouvantes et des badineries étrangères au sujet de la matière que l'on traite,' et que des 'inutilités' " (Patrice Pavis, "Marivaux: L'Epreuve de la scène contemporaine," tome I, p. 218).

J. Douglas Clayton

From Gozzi to Hoffmann: German Sources for *commedia dell'arte* in Russian Avant-Garde Theatre

There exists no comprehensive history of *commedia dell'arte* in Russia. The reader looking for information on this topic must turn to such sources as the article by Ettore lo Gatto, which concentrates on the theoretical polemics surrounding the genre in Soviet Russia in the 1920s, and to studies devoted to individual topics, such as the article by Virginia Bennett on Aleksandr Blok's play *The Fair-Ground Booth*, and Olle Hildebrand's study of the theatrical aesthetics of Nikolai Evreinov.[1] It is beyond the scope of this paper to survey the entire question; rather its aim is to throw some light on the importance of German models and sources for Russian experiments in *commedia dell'arte* during the first quarter of the twentieth century.

As lo Gatto and others have pointed out, the first acquaintance of the Russians with *commedia dell'arte* goes back to 1733, when a troupe of Italian actors under Tomaso Ristori visited St. Petersburg and put on a number of plays. However, their first visit was short-lived and did not have a deep impact, although Russian folk theatre, traditionally performed at Shrovetide and active throughout the nineteenth century, did have its Petrushka, and so a kind of Russian Punch and Judy did exist. This tradition was drawn upon by Stravinskii in his ballet *Petrushka* (1910). Interest in this native variant of *commedia dell'arte* was a manifestation of the desire of avant-garde artists in Russia (whether in the visual arts, literature, or music) to inject the vitality of primitive culture into their work, and draw upon Russian popular roots.

However, the major stimuli toward the use of *commedia dell'arte* in Russia in the early twentieth century came from abroad, for native sources did not offer the rich variety of motifs, plots, images and masks that could be found elsewhere. A foretaste of this wealth was Leoncavallo's *I*

Pagliacci, which was performed in Russia for the first time on November 11, 1893 at the Bolshoi Theatre, and hardly left the Russian lyric stage thereafter.[2] *I Pagliacci* was one of the first manifestations of the Europe-wide popularity of *commedia dell'arte* motifs in the theatre, poetry, and the visual arts in *fin-de-siècle* culture. In the visual arts, as Bennett points out, the popularity among the World of Art group of Aubrey Beardsley's drawings of Pierrot played an important role, while in poetry it was the influence of the French Romantics that was most significant. In the early 1900s these influences began to flood into the country, and the modern story of *commedia dell'arte* in Russia began.

The main branch of the arts in Russia to be affected by the *commedia dell'arte* was, naturally, the theatre, for which the main source was neither France nor England, but Germany, a fact that no researcher has stressed sufficiently. This phenomenon may be attributed in part to the fact that the leading figure in the incorporation of *commedia dell'arte* into Russian theatrical practice was the director Vsevolod Meyerhold. Meyerhold, we recall, was ethnically German, and he seems to have followed closely developments in German theatre. Thus, his first appearance in a *commedia dell'arte*-like role was as the aging clown Landowsky in a play by the Austrian playwright Franz von Schönthan entitled *Cirkusleute* (1902).[3] Meyerhold translated this play into Russian as *Akrobaty* and produced it in 1903, shortly after his break with Stanislavskii. It is memorable chiefly for the last act, which is set backstage in a circus, where the aging clown must face up to the fact that his career is at an end. The play is a facile and sentimental tear-jerker, and has apparently not been produced in Russia since. However, the pathos of the role of Landowsky had intimations of the pierrotic, and it seems to have served the crucial purpose of attracting Meyerhold to the image of the Pierrot or clown.

The promise of this play bore fruit in one of the most important productions in the history of Russian theatre, Meyerhold's *mise-en-scène* of Aleksandr Blok's *The Fair-Ground Booth* (*Balaganchik*, 1906), with which Russian theatre made the transition from derivative symbolist productions inspired by Maeterlinck into what Wylie Sypher has called cubist theatre. Blok's play was a *tour-de-force* incorporating and synthesizing *commedia dell'arte* motifs that had already been present in his poetry. Central to the play is the image of Pierrot, clearly a transcription of the poet onto the stage, and the love triangle involving Pierrot, Columbine, and Harlequin was only too transparent a mask for Blok's relationship with his wife, Liubov' Mendeleeva, and the poet Aleksandr Belyi.

Structurally the play incorporated meta-theatre, or the theatre-within-the-theatre. Onstage was a small fair-ground booth of the kind to be found in Russian folk fairs. The action in the first half of the play took place in this booth, which was hoisted up for the second half, leaving the stage empty. Moreover, the action is interrupted a number of times by the intervention of the "author," who protests at the perversion of his realist script, and is unceremoniously pulled back into the wings by his coat-tails. This satirical attack on the conventions of the theatre is matched by a sarcastic image of a group of mystics, represented as card-board figures with holes through which the actors stuck their faces and hands, who, unlike Pierrot, perceive Columbine not as a beautiful maiden, but as Death.[4] This was a theatrical realization of the ambiguity of the Russian word *kosa*, which can mean both a lock of hair and a scythe. By mocking the mystics in this way Blok was parting company publicly with his fellow Symbolist poets.

Most probably Blok found a precedent for his use of the theatre-within-the-theatre in Ludwig Tieck's plays *Der gestiefelte Kater* (*Puss-in-Boots*), and *Die verkehrte Welt* (*The Topsy-Turvy World*).[5] Both of Tieck's plays foreground theatrical convention, using such characters as the poet, the director, a mock audience, a prompter, and so on, and both contain ironic references to the script that is either unfulfilled, or only partially performed. In particular, Tieck's theatrical satire was directed at the realist expectations of the audience (and their fulfullment by certain playwrights, e.g., Kotzebue). Blok's play likewise uses metatheatrical characters; the satire of the author's complaints at the fact that his script is being ignored is directed against Stanislavskii's theatrical realism, while the Mystics function in a way that closely parallels Tieck's use of members of the "audience," whose banal tastes are held up to ridicule. Most important, Tieck was *the* Romantic transformer of *commedia dell'arte*, building on Gozzi's idea of combining *commedia dell'arte* with the folk tale, and manipulating *commedia dell'arte* characters—Pierrot, Scaramuccio, Harlequin, and Pantalone—as quotations from theatrical tradition, to create ironic effects. The relationship between Gozzi and Tieck will be discussed further below.

Blok's play, and Meyerhold's production of it, opened the path to a whole new concept of theatre in Russia. Thereafter, Meyerhold's notions of theatricality became intimately bound up with his experimentations in *commedia dell'arte* in various cabaret and studio settings. On the practical level this interest was almost certainly inspired initially by Max Reinhardt's experiments with *commedia dell'arte* in the cabaret "Schall und Rauch," which presented "satirical sketches, songs and dances, its attendants all dressed like pierrot."[6] Indeed, the early career of Meyerhold had many parallels to that of Reinhardt, right down to the choice of repertoire. However, the Russian went further along this path than his German mentor, and we can consider *commedia dell'arte* one of the main sources of Meyerhold's unique theatrical experiments.

On the theoretical level these experiments were inspired to a considerable extent by German work on the renewal of the theatre, especially Georg Fuchs's *Revolution in the Theatre*.[7] Fuchs's advocacy of popular forms of spectacle, of which *commedia dell'arte* was one, as a source of renewal for the theatre have a prophetic ring when we consider the subsequent evolution of the Russian avant-garde theatre:

The variety, or vaudeville stage is the place where drama in its simpler outlines is cultivated today in the form of dancing, acrobatics, juggling, sleight-of-hand, boxing, and wrestling, exhibition of trained animals, musical dialogues (chanson), and what not. (138)

Meyerhold's insistence on the training of actors in acrobatics and juggling, Radlov's post-1917 experiments with circus performers in the theatre, and Eisenstein's introduction of a boxing match into the theatre in his production of *Meksikanets* (*The Mexican*) based on a novel by Jack London, can be seen to have their theoretical basis in Fuchs's book. In theoretical writings that Meyerhold published before 1917, Meyerhold echoed Fuchs and Wagner in expressing his revulsion at the stultification of nineteenth-century theatre. Like Fuchs, Meyerhold lays the blame at the feet of literature:

In the contemporary theatre the comedian has been replaced by the "educated reader." "The play will be read in costume and make-up" might as well be the announcement on playbills today. The new actor manages without the mask and technique of the juggler. The mask has been replaced by make-up and the technique of the exact representation of every feature of the face as it is observed in real life. The actor has no need of the juggler's art, because he no longer "plays" but simply "lives" on stage.[8]

Before the revolution, Meyerhold led a double life, being a director in the state theatres in Petersburg while working in studio productions under a pseudonym Dr. Dapertutto. This is the name of a diabolical character in E.T.A. Hoffmann's *Die Abenteuer der Silvesternacht* who is instrumental in the character Erasmus giving up his reflection in the mirror. The grotesque and mysterious figure of Dapertutto—and the way he manipulates the fate of Erasmus—evidently offered an attractive persona to Meyerhold (one which was reinforced when in 1916 he played Dorian Gray in the film based on Wilde's novel—the hoffmannesque aspects of which are self-evident). Moreover, a further association is implied by the mention of Hoffmann, for in the subtitle to *Die Prinzessin Brambilla*, "A Capriccio in the Style of Jaques Callot," Hoffmann invokes the name of an artist—Jacques Callot (ca. 1592–1635)—whose etchings of *commedia dell'arte* characters (Balli di Sfessania) were famous. The reference to Hoffmann was thus not a chance one, for it was in Hoffmann's grotesque fantasies and Callot's equally extraordinary drawings that Meyerhold found the inspiration for his notion of *commedia dell'arte*.

His next important *commedia dell'arte* production was in the guise of Dr. Dapertutto. The play was his adaptation of Arthur Schnitzler and Ernst von Dohnányi's pantomime *Der Schleier der Pierrette* (*Sharf Kolombiny* [*Columbine's Scarf*]; premiere: October 9, 1910). Significantly, Meyerhold's production at the "House of Interludes" preceded the Viennese premiere of this work (which took place on September 20, 1911).[9] Schnitzler's pantomime in dialogue was turned by Meyerhold into a grotesque fantasy, as one critic—M.M. Bonch-Tomasheviskii—remembered:

When I recall the nightmarish polka that the comic musicians played on broken instruments, under the direction of a one-eyed, diabolically unhappy Kapellmeister, when I recall that nightmarish whirlwind of brightly-coloured and loutish bodies that whirled, embracing in their circle Gigolo, the diminutive dancing master, with his hair puffed up like a cox-comb . . . I can feel that shiver that ran up my spine as I sat in the audience. And I understand what the external, apparently empty and laughable form means for *commedia dell'arte*, for behind it lurks the face of Eternity. I understand how it is possible to laugh and at the same time to feel all the abyss of horror, all the blackness of desperation. . . .[10]

The reference to the Kapellmeister was interpreted by aware readers as a reference to Hoffmann himself. Thus, in a review of Hoffmann's tale *Princess Brambilla* D. Filosofov recalls:

Just as in 1841 Annenkov visited the Berlin tavern of Luther and Wegener where Hoffmann and Devrient caroused, so fifty years after Annenkov Aleksandr Benois dragged me there. We too asked for some Johannisberger and recalled the wizard Kapellmeister. . . . We were attracted not only by the writer Hoffmann, but by his multifarious artistic personality, his "musical soul," his many-facetted dilettantism, his understanding of the theatre. The director and the Kapellmeister were for Hoffmann not just "talented" technicians, but the masters of a whole world, wizards who make fools of philistines and carry pure, naive, musical souls into a world of fantastic but authentic reality. In almost all his works there is such a wizard director. . . . They are all variants of that same Hoffmann, that same Hoffmann that he would like to be, that same enthusiastic Kapellmeister improvising in life and onstage. The fantastic theatre seemed to Hoffmann much more real than bourgeois drama, the conventional realism of Goldoni. It is not surprising that in the World of Art circle which gave birth to so many successful theatrical undertakings, Hoffmann was "our" man.[11]

The sinister, the macabre, and the hoffmannesque were thus a characteristic of Meyerhold's early experiments with *commedia dell' arte*.

Another version of Schnitzler's pantomime (this time translated as *Pokryvalo P'erretty [Pierrette's Veil]* was directed by Tairov at the Free Theatre, Moscow, 1913, and revived in 1916 when Tairov had his own theatre, the Kamernyi.[12] As in Meyerhold's production in Petersburg, the ball scene was central, as Markov recollects: "The core of the pantomime was the ball scene, enacted against a background of silver columns created by the artist Arapov. In the unexpected combination of Alisa Koonen's lyricism and the tragic grotesque of Chabrov as Harlequin the mysterious appearance of Pierrot and even the theme of death came across in a theatrically festive way, without any mystical colouring."[13] Markov's comments are somewhat belied by Baltrusajtis's "Prologue" to the production, which was not the traditional monologue by one of the masks. Rather, it took the form of a somewhat heavy-handed dialogue, reminiscent of Goethe's *Faust*, between a sibyl and the characters Pierrot and Pierrette (who are, it should be recalled, silent in the pantomime itself). At their insistence, the sibyl reveals to Pierrot and Pierrette what their fate will be in the course of the play. The prologue is a conceit on the "life's a dream" or *theatrum mundi* idea that recurs in metatheatrical drama. The two will forget their encounter with the sibyl, and will enact their fate as she has foretold it: "Go off into your dream, your brief and troubled delusion, and you will remember this reality, which is not false, having learned what is known to those who sleep in their graves. Go off then into reality, to that gloomy golgotha, and you will have to bear this dream deep in your breast, like a vague presentiment with which you, a chosen one, will wend your weary and thorny way through your days."[14] The prologue has the effect of strengthening the metaphysical connotations of the play, and stresses the role of fate in a way rather typical of Russian literature. It also places the events of the play, which are, in Schnitzler's original, specific as to time and place, in a timeless context, suggested by the ancient, mythical figure of the sibyl.

Tairov, in his own memoirs, recalled the incantatory power of Dohnányi's music, and described his own work in the production as the search for pantomimic gestures and movements adequate to express its emotive content:

. . . how fascinating was our ignorance when we gave ourselves up hour after hour to the music of Dohnányi; in limitless, fantastic spaces the speechless figure of Pierrot glided before us, with the senseless Pierrette, her wedding veil lost, sweeping after him in a vortex of harmony. And then there was Harlequin, with his mighty swellings of brass resounding over the whole world, and his guests, the obsequious issue of his power and fantasy—all these suddenly died away when Columbine appeared to the rising strains of the harp. The rising fury of the *schnell-polka* crowned the phantasmal revelry of Harlequin, and in the quavering expirations of the flutes, the light of reason flew out from the enfeebled body of Pierrette. (quoted in Torda, 164)

In 1919 this production travelled to Petrograd. Although the critic Andrei Levinson appreciated the coordination of music and gesture, he was merciless about Dohnányi's music with its "multitude of longueurs, insertions, dances in the style of the elder Strauss," and concluded "To cut *The Veil* three times would be to intensify the impression that much" (*Zhizn' iskusstva*, No. 97 [Friday, 14 March 1919], 3).

Most telling is Levinson's comparison of Tairov's production with that of Meyerhold:

This [cutting] was the path taken by Meyerhold in his time in *Columbine's Scarf*. He took the risk of throwing out Dohnányi's music and taking different music. The action developed with somnambulistic rapidity; not one grouping or gesture was repeated; each was final. The ball in *Columbine's Scarf* was not a party in good old Vienna, but a masquerade of fearful and lascivious masks, visions of Columbine's obsessive nightmare. In the ironic twist of the spine of Harlequin, who seemed to have stepped out of the transparent canvas of Picasso, all his demonic image was captured. In *Columbine's Scarf* the music was only the emotional background. . . . In Tairov's production the psychological detailing and the abundant pictorial effects based on the music and in the milieu of a historical style were paramount. In Meyerhold's there was the extreme laconicness of the symbolic gesture in the atmosphere of the grotesque; in the first—the expressiveness of faces, in the second the allegory of masks. (ibid.)

In 1914 Meyerhold, encouraged by the success of his experiments, started a studio school for the systematic implantation of *commedia dell' arte* techniques, and along with it published his journal *Love for Three Oranges*, the opening number of which contained a translation of Gozzi's play of that name by Meyerhold and Solov'ev. Placing the name of Gozzi's play on the masthead next to the name of a character from Hoffmann was in the nature of a manifesto, for, along with Tieck, whom they, as it were, bracketed, these two were felt by Meyerhold and his collaborators, expecially Vladimir Solov'ev, to be the true continuators of the popular *commedia dell'arte* tradition.[15] Goldoni and Schiller (who adapted *Turandot*, turning it into an impassioned plea for women's emancipation) were their *bêtes noires* as perpetrators of the *embourgeoisement* of *commedia dell'arte*.

The journal *Love for Three Oranges* served as an important outlet for Russian research and theoretical articles on *commedia dell'arte*, publishing material by Konstantin Miklashevskii and Vladimir Solov'ev, as well as translations of plays and scenarios (including Tieck's *Der gestiefelte Kater*—see above). In addition, the journal contained a regular feature entitled "Hoffmaniana" by Vladimir Kniazhnin and others, which contained research and notes on such questions as the reception of E.T.A. Hoffmann in Russia—testimony to the importance that Meyerhold's circle attached to Hoffmann *in the context of commedia dell'arte*.

In this section there is an interesting note entitled "E.T.A. Hoffmann on the stage" by Sergei Ignatov. This is a discussion of the unfinished dramatic work by that author entitled "Princess Blandina." Ignatov considers that in Hoffmann's work "Callot blended with Gozzi" and sees in the play "the possibility of a scenic creation 'in the manner of Callot,' in which the director would need the techniques of Gozzi, for in this dramatic fragment Hoffmann is so close to the Italian fabulist" (*Liubov'k trem apel'sinam*, 1915, Nos. 4–7, 179–82). Specifically, Ignatov thinks that the grotesque poses of the figures on the forestage at the beginning of the fragment should remind one of such pieces by Callot as "The Fan," "The Tournament in Florence," or "Primo intermedio." He continues: "Meanwhile on the illuminated stage the action unfolds, the characteristic features of which are a very rapid tempo, convention-foregrounding [*uslovnost'*] in the style of *commedia dell'arte*, rhythmical movements and a sharply expressive mimicry. In the performance one should avoid the coarseness characteristic of *commedia dell'arte*, remembering that we have to do not with an exaggerated parody, but with a light irony which must be carefully conveyed. We should also not forget the character of that theatricality that Hoffmann had in mind." (ibid., 181). It is evident from the closeness with which he follows Meyerhold's "line" that Ignatov was one of his students. Apparently this production, for which the note reads like a preliminary director's sketch, never took place.

Ignatov's note is followed by an unsigned review of a translation of Hoffmann's *Princess Brambilla*. The reviewer remarks approvingly: "This is not only one of Hoffmann's most resplendent and harmonious achievements, in which he attains a complete and graceful immersion in Callot and Gozzi, but it is a work that is particularly close to the Russian reader" (ibid., 183).

The journal also published a seminal article by Viktor Zhirmunskii on the German sources for Russian *commedia dell' arte* entitled "The Comedy of Pure Joy."[16] This was a discussion of Ludwig Tieck's *Der gestiefelte Kater* and its links with Carlo Gozzi's comedies. Zhirmunskii begins his paper with a description of the discovery of Gozzi's comedies by the German Romantics, especially Schlegel and Novalis, who found in them "a splendid joy" of pure play, free of any didacticism, and were carried away by them into a "world of another order, more exalted, joyful, and resplendent than the one that surrounds us" (86). What fascinated the romantics, according to Zhirmunskii, was the irony that coexisted with this lyrical vision, and which had its source in the play of the masks:

In their conscious comic play, their reflection of what is said by the heroes, they accompany all they do and say. They are onlookers, ideal comic mirrors of differing curvature that distort in varying ways the development of the poetic action. By their comments on the action, their remarks addressed to the audience, their mentions of the phenomena of everyday, non-theatrical reality, they disrupt the scenic illusion of the main, lyrically significant action, or rather, they reveal the illusoriness of everything that happens on stage . . . what is depicted on the stage is not solid, material reality, but only a merry game, only a spectacle invented to amuse the spectators. (ibid., 86–87)

Here, Zhirmunskii suggests, the Romantics found the precursor of Tieck's use of metatheatrical characters as commentators on the action and exposers of its illusory nature.

This was not to say that Tieck had the same objectives or that he achieved the same results as Gozzi:

Thus the participation of the denizens of the parterre in the action permitted Tieck to develop the element of comic reflection that in Gozzi had been borne by the masks. This element is developed there into a separate plot—the "action in the parterre," the characters of which are the spectators. It could be called "the story of how a romantic comedy/fable was received by the enlightened public." In this connection the disruption of the scenic illusion also assumes completely new and exclusive forms. The presence of a public onstage, the participation of an author and a theatre technician who converse with the audience—all this gives the fairy-tale plot the character of something illusory, unreal, a merry game, a fair-ground spectacle, not serious reality. (88)

Zhirmunskii goes on to argue that the development of the metatheatrical aspect of the play gives Tieck's plays different qualities from those of Gozzi, qualities that are especially relevant for the contemporary Russian stage:

The poetic content of the children's fairy-tale is as it were totally absorbed by the comedy of the artistic form. The dramatis personae of "Puss in Boots" are in a sort of contemporary and pointedly trivial travesty. In the fairy-tale plot everything reminds us of our time and our every-day life, so that it by the same token loses that fairy-tale perspective, that temporal and spatial distance from us that is necessary for the sympathetic reception of the fantastic and miraculous images and events. (ibid., 88)

The unreality of the action reminds Zhirmunskii of Hoffmann's comment that the best theatre for Gozzi's plays would be the marionette theatre. Zhirmunskii's final observation is one of the most important, namely that Tieck's satirical portrayal of the audience and its expectations—realism, everyday detail, and didacticism—corresponded closely to that found in recent Russian plays: in particular he mentions Blok's *The Fair-Ground Booth*. His conclusion explains why such theatrical activists as Meyerhold found Gozzi and Tieck interesting: "not only in the general feeling of life, but in many details of the development of artistic forms our contemporary Symbolism (or Neo-Romanticism) holds astonishing analogies with the Romanticism of the end of the eighteenth and the beginning of the nineteenth centuries" (91).

The theoretical work of Meyerhold and his group on *commedia dell'arte* was paralleled in Russian theatrical practice. A harbinger of this trend was *Turandot*, which was produced by Fedor Komissarzhevskii in Moscow in 1912. (Curiously, Meyerhold never directed any of Gozzi's or Tieck's plays himself.) Komissarzhevskii's production seems to have been suggested by Reinhardt's *mise-en-scène* of the same play at the Deutsches Theater in 1911.[17] Acccording to Solov'ev the text was not the original one by Gozzi but a translation of the Schiller version:

In Schiller's version Gozzi's ironic smile disappeared, to be replaced by *psychological motivation*. Gozzi's theatre of wonders was sacrificed to versimilitude and poetry. For the orthodox representative of *Sturm und Drang*, Princess Turandot is a woman whose cruelty can be explained by the desire for limitless freedom and by a feeling of revenge towards men for the many years of female enslavement. For Gozzi Turandot is a fabulous sphinx, driven one knows not where by a secret and vague instinct, a sphinx that loses its wisdom and power as soon as the three riddles are solved. (*Liubov' k trem apel'sinam*, 1914, No. 2, 47)

Reinhardt had used a new adaptation of Gozzi's text by Karl Vollmoeller. Komissarzhevskii's production was distinguished mainly as a colourful spectacle. One reviewer—Sakhnovskii—was delighted by the colourful effects and the music of the production, speaking of an "elegant mannerism."[18] The purist Solov'ev was less appreciative, criticizing the acting of the masks and the un-Gozzian effect of the music by Rameau.

November 1917 saw another production of a German play in the *commedia dell'arte* genre: Tairov's constructivist version of the Austrian playwright Rudolf Lothar's *König Harlekin* (*Korol' Arlekin*). This play had an enormous success throughout Europe at the beginning of the century, being banned in several countries, and was one of the first plays to be introduced into the Russian repertoire after 1917. In the artist Ferdinandov's geometrical shapes that made up the set Russian *commedia dell'arte* made the transition from the World of Art impressionist style into the radical abstraction of the constructivist movement. Critics admired the freshness and plasticity of the actors' technique and their acrobatic agility. Evidently Tairov had paid attention to the theoretical as well as the practical work of Meyerhold. Another more conventional and less distinguished production of the play by Zvantsev ran simultaneously at the private Nezlobin Theatre, also in Moscow, and the play was produced at the Akvarium in Petrograd in 1918 as well—more evidence of the popularity of German *commedia dell'arte* plays in Russia.[19]

Of even more interest to us in this context was Tairov's production of a stage version of Hoffmann's *Die Prinzessin Brambilla* (*Printsessa Brambilla*; premiere 4 May, 1920). Here Tairov's attempts to put into practice the theories of Meyerhold and his school were crowned with remarkable success. In this "cappriccio of the Kamernyi Theatre" the spirit of Gozzi, Callot, and Hoffmann found its finest incarnation on the Russian stage. The dramatisation of the tale was by L. Krasovskii, and took the form of a short scenario with a verse epilogue by Pavel Antokolskii.[20] Tairov described his objective as being not to give a "correct interpretation" of Hoffmann, but to "unite the new discrete elements of harlequinade, tragedy, operetta, pantomime, and circus, and . . . refract them through the modern soul of the actor and the creative rhythm allied to it" (quoted in Torda, 148). The results combined *commedia dell'arte* with Hoffmann's grotesque in a remarkable way that Torda describes as "expressionist theatre." He writes: "One example of Tairov's dramatic orchestration in *Printessa Brambilla* was in the second act, where a fifteen-minute *commedia dell'arte* pantomime was integrated into the action of the play. Harlequin is transformed into a scarecrow, cut up into pieces by the Doctor, and his members scattered about the stage to be reassembled 'by magic' into the living, dancing Harlequin" (312–13). In one way, however, the production seemed atypical of Meyerholdian thinking about the harlequinade, and more in the tradition of Reinhardt and Komissarzhevskii, namely in that the metatheatrical aspects seem not to have been paramount, but to have ceded to the play as spectacle.

After the Revolution the function of *commedia dell'arte* changed somewhat. Then the subversive and popular nature of the genre was seen to be in keeping with the times, at least by the avant-garde wing of leftist art—Meyerhold, Radlov, Maiakovskii, even Eisenstein. As a result, *commedia dell'arte* became much more integrated with other popular forms, especially the circus, as we have seen in *Printsessa Brambilla*, in an effort to create new theatrical forms. The purist, stylized versions of *commedia dell'arte* as museum-pieces that had been tried in the experimental theatre before the revolution gradually disappeared. But the legacy of the experimentation and theoretical writings on the subject remained—in the popularity of such devices as meta-theatre, the play-within-the-play, the montage of styles, rupture of the illusion (*illusionsbruch*), and interaction with the audience. This movement prevailed as long as the hegemony of the avant-garde in Soviet theatre lasted—that is to say, until the onset of NEP in 1921 and the state requirement that theatres operate without subsidy. By 1922 the experimentation with *commedia dell'arte* was passé, although occasional examples continued to appear.

In this context Vakhtangov's 1922 production of *Turandot* assumes a prime importance, as the last and the greatest Soviet production in the *commedia dell'arte* tradition. The production began as a student exercise with a Russian translation of the text by Schiller. Gradually the need was felt to go back to the original text by Gozzi, and a new version was produced. No doubt Vakhtangov was influenced, in this, as in other matters, by the debate that had been provoked by Komissarzhevskii's 1912 production, and expecially Solov'ev's review in *Love for Three Oranges*. Original music was written for the production, fantastic constructivist sets were prepared and a book was published with the text, reproductions of the set design, photographs, and even the score of the music.[21] As the last production of the dying director, *Turandot* has entered the legends of Soviet theatre history.

It was the director's concern to distance himself from Stanislavskii's naturalistic theatre, and yet avoid the excesses that had tended to discredit avant-garde experiments. Thus Matskin tells us that "he recommended [to his actors] that they act, not Gozzi's fantastic characters, but the totally real Italian actors that had once played the characters . . . but each mask in *Turandot* had a third face, the face of the contemporary actor."[22] By placing the acting of the roles within these double quotes Vakhtangov attempted a new solution of the problem of the reconstruction of a past theatrical style. Yet he insisted that the actors "lift the quotes" at crucial moments, and thus elicit the audience's involvement. It seems that this interplay of irony and sympathy, laughter at and identification with the characters was central to the production.

By the 1920s the lessons of *commedia dell'arte* and the avant-garde theatre in general had been absorbed by Russian playwrights. A number of plays appeared that exploited Tieck's devices of metatheatre or the play-within-the-play. Tieck's importance for contemporary playwrights as an innovator before his time is illustrated by the remark which Nikolai Evreinov puts in the mouth of Hoffmann: "Yet, long before the 'discoveries' of your much-praised theatrical performers, Tieck had laid bare the defects and shortcomings of the contemporary public theatre . . . for his ideas are just as fresh today as they were a century ago. . . . Thus, Tieck regarded the sharp division between the stage and the audience as essentially anti-artistic; the theatre looks like a building a part of which has been chopped off."[23]

Nikolai Evreinov's most ambitious harlequinade *The Main Thing* (*Samoe glavnoe*; premiere February 1921) enjoyed wide success in Russia, with more than 125 performances at the Free Comedy in Petrograd from its premiere in 1922 until that theatre was closed in 1925 and Evreinov left Russia.[24] In it, Evreinov gave the fullest expression to his vision of reality—and hence also of theatre—as a palimpsest of illusion upon illusion, a world of multi-layered deception, and developed the image of Harlequin as a sort of saviour of humanity, and the *commedia dell'arte* as a programme for the use of theatre as a solver of the problems of life. The play is strongly reminiscent of Tieck's experiments in metatheatre, especially *Die verkehrte Welt*, deploying such metatheatrical characters as the director, the prompter, and the electrician; in it the play-within-the-play takes the form of a dress rehearsal of a provincial production of *Quo Vadis* in a way that is strongly reminiscent of Pirandello's *Sei personaggi in cerca d'autore*. Another device that owes much to Tieck is the way the characters slip out of their roles. As in *A Merry Death*, in *The Main Thing* there is a serious message, expressed by the central character Dr. Fregoli, who peddles the idea of theatre as a "market-place of illusions." The overlay of play upon play reaches its most intricate in the final act, in which we see the actors who have appeared in various guises in the previous acts now dressed in *commedia dell'arte* costume for Shrovetide. The structural intricacy of the play, with its different characters and plots, reaches its logical conclusion in Paraclete's (Fregoli's) monologue to the audience in which he offers them a range of possible endings.

In the Pirandelloesque comedy *The Apes are Coming!* (1923) by Lev
Lunts, a character called the Fool, who is the only character who is aware
that he is in a play, engages in repartee with the audience, and tries to
impose order on the chaotic events onstage. The intended play—*In Ser-
ried Ranks*—degenerates into a near-riot as the enemy approaches the city
and the set is torn up to build defences. A better-known play of this
type is Mikhail Bulgakov's *The Crimson Island* (*Bagrovyi ostrov*, 1928).
Reminiscent of Tieck's *Puss in Boots*, this play takes the form of a dress
rehearsal of a play in which slipping out of role is a prominent device.
Among the metatheatrical characters is a newcomer, the censor Savva
Lukich, who must be persuaded of the play's suitability before it can go
on. Bulgakov uses his play as a vehicle to satirize the tastes of both the
Soviet theatre-going public and the Soviet censor. The lessons of *commedia dell'arte* are also discernable in Maiakovskii's plays, especially *A
Mystery-Bouffe* (*Misteriia-Buff*) and *The Bath-House* (*Bania*, 1929) which
includes a whole act of meta-theatre in which the characters discuss the
play they are performing with Soviet bureaucrats who are members of the
"audience."

Commedia dell'arte, then, was intimately bound up with the history of
the theatrical avant-garde in Russia, but it was, as I have tried to show,
a phenomenon that owed much to German intermediaries and interpretations. Coloured with the grotesque visions of Callot, Gozzi, Tieck and
Hoffmann, it served as a source of inspiration for the post-Stanislavskian
generation of Russian directors such as Nikolai Evreinov, Vsevolod Meyerhold, Tairov, Vakhtangov, and Komissarzhevskii.

Like most other aspects of modernist art, the theatrical avant-garde was
superseded in the 1930s by Socialist Realism, which turned out to mean a
recrudescence of the theatre of Stanislavskii. To use Bakhtin's terminology, the "dialogic" world of the *commedia dell'arte*, with its linguistic,
stylistic, and social "heteroglossia" and its ironical, anti-realist, deform-
ing aesthetic of the grotesque was replaced by a "monologic" theatre in
which all the characters spoke the same, dressed the same, and lived in
a "realistic" world from which all fantasy and play were banished. The
experiments in *commedia dell'arte* disappeared almost without trace, and
were only revived indirectly in the 1960s and 1970s when the Liubimov
experimented with the techniques of Meyerhold. His work had its theoretical equivalent in the call by Andrei Siniavskii, in his essay "What is
Socialist Realism," for a new poetic of the grotesque, which sounds very
much like the cult of Hoffmann in Russian avant-garde culture of the teens
and twenties of this century.

At the present time the subject of *commedia dell'arte* as a theatrical style of the Russian avant-garde is discussed with circumspection in the Soviet Union, and then generally in the context of the "crisis" of modernist theatre in Russia.[25] Yet the Russian *commedia dell'arte*, which blended the energy and colour of Italy and the irony and grotesque of Germany, added a unique theatricality to the annals of *commedia dell'arte* in the history of world theatre. In the way it subverted theatrical conventions and stimulated the fantasy of actor and audience alike, it was the most revolutionary art of all.

University of Ottawa

NOTES

1 Ettore lo Gatto, "La Commedia dell'Arte in Russia," *Rivista di studi teatrali*, 9/10 (1954), 176–86; Virginia Bennett, "Russian *pagliacci*: Symbols of Profaned Love in the Puppet Show," in James Redmond (ed.), *Drama and Symbolism* (Cambridge: Cambridge University Press, 1982), 141–78; Olle Hildebrand, *Harlekin Frälsaren: Teater och verklighet i Nikolaj Evreinovs dramatik* (Uppsala Slavic Papers, 1; Uppsala, 1978).

2 Not 1896 as Bennett has it. See P. A. Markov (ed.), *Teatral'naia entsiklopediia*, IV (Sovetskaia entsiklopediia: Moskva, 1965), 298.

3 See Edward Braun, *The Theatre of Meyerhold* (London: Eyre Methuen, 1979), 30–31 for details of this production and a photograph of Meyerhold in this role.

4 A detailed description of this production is to be found in P.P. Gromov, "Raniaia rezhissura Vs. E. Meierkhol'da," in *U istokov rezhissury: ocherk, iz istorii russkoi rezhissury kontsa XIX–nachala XX veka* (Leningrad: Leningradskii gosudarstvennyi institut teatra, myzyki i kinematografii, 1976), 172–73.

5 *Der gestiefelte Kater* was later translated by V. Gippius as *Kot v sapogakh* and published in Meyerhold's journal *Love for Three Oranges* (*Liubov'k trem apel'sinam*, 1916, No. 1, 7–62)—a testimony to the importance of this play for Russian work on *commedia dell'arte*. Sergei Eisenstein later worked on designs for a production of the play which never materialized. See Marjorie Hoover, *Meyerhold: The Art of Conscious Theater* (Amherst: University of Massachusetts Press, 1974), 94–95.

6 J.L. Styan, *Max Reinhardt* (Cambridge: Cambridge University Press, 1982), 18. For information on Reinhardt's work with the *commedia dell'arte*, see Leisler, Edda, and Gisela Prossnitz (editors), *Max Reinhardt und die Welt der Commedia dell'arte* (Salzburg: Otto Müller Verlag, 1970).

7 Georg Fuchs, *Revolution in the Theatre: Conclusions Concerning the Munich Artists' Theatre*, translated by Constance Connor Kuhn (Ithaca: Cornell University Press, 1959). Another important German source for the theoretical basis of Russian *commedia dell'arte* was the translation of an article by Oscar Heller

[Oskar Geller], "Pantomima," *Teatr i iskusstvo*, 1909, No. 21, 375–77.

8 Vsevolod Meyerhold, *Meyerhold on Theatre*, translated with a commentary by Edward Braun (London: Methuen, 1969), 125.

9 The playbill of the original Viennese production is reproduced in Heinrich Schnitzler et al., *Arthur Schnitzler: Sein Leben. Sein Werk, Seine Zeit* (Frankfurt am Main: S. Fischer, 1981), 95.

10 M.M. Bonch-Tomashevskiii, "Pantomima A. Shnitslera v 'Svobodn. Teatre,'" *Maski*, 1913–14, No. 2, 52.

11 D.N. Filosofov, "Printsessa Brambilla," reprinted in *Liubov' k trem apel' sinam*, 1915, No. 4–7, 191–92. Filosofov, who apparently was not by any means sympathetic to Meyerhold, confirms the importance of Gozzi for Hoffmann, and in turn the importance of them both for the Russian director: "Somewhat later, in the following generation or so, Hoffmann turned into a teacher, a theoretician, from whom one must learn. The genius dilettant was transformed into a man of learning, the eternal improviser into a professor. I have in mind the 'studio' of V.E. Meyerhold and Dr. Dapertutto's journal. *Commedia dell' arte* is the ideal of this school and Count Carlo Gozzi its idol"(ibid., 192).

12 For a detailed discussion of this production, see Thomas J. Torda, *Alexander Tairov and the Scenic Artists of the Moscow Kamerny Theater, 1914–1935*, diss., Univ. of Denver, 1977, 39 and 162–67. Other early *commedia dell' arte* productions by Tairov were Jacinto Benavente's *Los Intereses creados* (translated as *Iznanka zhizni*) at the Reineke's Russian Dramatic Theatre in December 1912, and Goldoni's *Il Ventaglio (Veer)*, the fourth production by Tairov at his own theatre, the Kamernyi, in January 1915.

13 P.A. Markov, "O Tairove," in A.la. Tairov, *O teatre: Zapiski rezhissera, stat' i, besedy, rechi, pis' ma* (Moscow: Vserossiiskoe teatral'noe obshchestvo), 12–13.

14 Ju. Baltrusajtis, *Liliia i serp* (Paris: YMCA Press, 1948), 62.

15 The cult of Gozzi in Germany is discussed in Hedwig Hoffmann Rusack, *Gozzi in Germany* (New York: Columbia University Press, 1930); of especial interest are the chapters "Gozzi and Ludwig Tieck" (117–38) and "Gozzi and E.T.A. Hoffmann" (144–72), which document in considerable detail the references to Gozzi by these writers, and their use of motifs and devices from Gozzi's works.

16 V. Zhirmunskii, "Komediia chistoi radosti," *Liubov' k trem apel' sinam*, 1916, I, 85–91.

17 For details of this production, see Rusack, 110–14.

18 Vasilii Sakhnovskii, "*Assambleia* i *Printsessa Turandot*," *Maski*, 1912, No. 2, 55. The enthusiastic tone of this review, with its stress on the colourful spectacle of the production echoes that of Reinhardt's production by Siegfried Jacobsohn (reprinted in Rusack, 111–12).

19 A description of this production, including reviews and photographs, can be found in Torda, 260–71.

20 I have relied for the account of the production, including the quotations from

reviews and memoirs, on Torda (308–31). A discussion of the tale and its
relationship to Gozzi's *fiabe* is to be found in Rusack, 150–54. Rusack writes:
"It is very apparent that Hoffmann had Gozzi continually in memory when he
wrote his fantastic fairy story" (151).

21 Carlo Gozzi [Karlo Gotstsi], *Printsessa Turandot*; Teatral'no-tragicheskaia ki-
taiskaia skazka v piati aktakh Karlo Gotstsi (Moskva-Petrograd: Gosizdat,
1923). The same year saw the publicaton of the first collection of Gozzi's
plays in Russian: *Skazki dlia teatra* (Moskva: Vsemirnaia literatura, 1923).

22 A. Matskin, *Portrety i nabliudeniia* (Moskva: "Iskusstvo," 1973), 349.

23 Nikolai Evreinov, *The Theatre in Life* (New York: Brentano, 1927), 240. For a
discussion of the popularity of meta-theatre in Russian drama in the 1920s, see
J. Douglas Clayton, "The Play-within-the-play as Metaphor and Metatheatre
in Modern Russian Drama," in Lars Kleberg and Nils Åke Nilsson (eds.),
Theatre and Literature in Russia 1900–1930 (Stockholm: Almqvist & Wiksell
International, 1984), 71–82.

24 An English translation of the play, which was produced widely in the West
by such directors as Pirandello, is to be found in Nikolai Evreinov, *Life as
Theater: Five Modern Plays* (Ann Arbor: Ardis, 1973), 33–118.

25 See, for example, Iu. Gerasimov, "Krizis modernistskoi teatral'noi mysli v
Rossii," *Teatr i dramaturgiia* (*Trudy Leningradskogo gosudarstvennogo insti-
tuta teatra, myzyki i kinematografii*, 4; Leningrad, 1974), 202–44. In the name
of a realist, progressive aesthetic, Gerasimov thoroughly debunks all the tendencies towards experimentation and manipulation of theatrical convention in
Russian modernist theatre by such practitioners as Meyerhold and Evreinov.

Giulio Ferroni

L'Ossessione del raddoppiamento nella *commedia dell'arte*

Una riflessione sui meccanismi di raddoppiamento nella commedia dell'arte rischia subito di essere tautologica, di coincidere con una riflessione sulle caratteristiche più generali di quella grande tradizioone teatrale o sui fondamenti della comunicazione teatrale *tout court*. E' facile avvertire che l'ossessione del raddoppiamento nella commedia dell'arte non fa che portare alla più esplicita evidenza, al più lineare e schematico gioco comico, una dimensione costitutiva del movimento e della parola teatrale, e cioè la necessità dell'incastro di ogni personaggio-figura-oggetto scenico con almeno un altro personaggio-figura-oggetto scenico: la comunicazione teatrale si dà solo nello sdoppiarsi della catena verbale e gestuale, nel continuo aprirsi di un rapporto con l'"ombra"; la voce e il gesto di ogni identità scenica devono scindersi e specchiarsi nella voce e nel gesto di qualche "altro," devono ripercuotersi fuori di sé, trovando in altre voci e in altri gesti il proprio riflesso e la propria alienazione. E non è un caso se alle origini di molti dialoghi e di molti scambi teatrali si dà il ben noto rapporto padrone-servo, di cui si può seguire la varia fenomenologia soltanto partendo da una distinzione tra diverse forme di comunicazione teatrale e prima di tutto tenendo conto della distanza tra forme teatrali di tipo esplicitamente mitico o religioso e forme approssimativamente definibili come "laiche."

Nello svolgimento dal teatro comico "regolare" del Cinquecento alla commedia dell'arte l'evidenza esemplare del rapporto padrone-servo crea una ininterrotta serie di variazioni sull'ombra che il servo costituisce per il padrone e il padrone per il servo: le numerosissime coppie servo-padrone vi si intrecciano con ampia possibilità di scambi provvisori di posizione, di trasformazioni, cancellazioni, giochi simmetrici. Proprio su una coppia del genere è del resto basato uno dei documenti posti canonicamente alla fondazione della commedia dell'arte, a cioè il "duetto di Magnifico e Zanni": e tanto si è detto e scritto sull'azione dei servi-maschere nella commedia

dell'arte e sul suo intreccio con quella dei padroni; e infine alcune delle
più affascinanti riflessioni moderne sul "doppio" si sono concentrate proprio su quel frutto estremo ed assoluto della tradizione della commedia
dell'arte che può essere considerato il rapporto Don Giovanni-Leporello
nel capolavoro mozartiano.[1]

Questa struttura di doppio originaria e costitutiva data dal rapporto
tra padrone e servo, Magnifico e Zanni, si moltiplica e si espande, nella
commedia dell'arte, in altri raddoppiamenti, che in vario modo hanno la
loro origine nella commedia "regolare" del Cinquecento e assumono il
carattere di strutture costanti. Si tratta delle varie coppie formate dai due
padroni, dai due servi, dai quattro innamorati, tra cui si intrecciano tutta
una serie di legami di tipo orizzontale, verticale or trasversale, che permettono di vedere all'opera diversi tipi di rapporti binari: nel gioco degli
intrecci e nella successione delle scene gli scambi tra questi personaggi di
base permettono la formazione di tutti gli accoppiamenti possibili, creano
nuovi raddoppiamenti che interagiscono tra loro, anche grazie all'aggiunta
di personaggi e situazioni supplementari, di elementi irregolari capaci di
agire sul quadro generale con un forte effetto di amplificazione. E, anche
se ci si limita soltanto a seguire i movimenti delle quattro maschere fondamentali, quelle dei due vecchi e dei due servi, si può facilmente vedere
come i diversi orientamenti dei loro rapporti, verticali, orizzontali o tra-
sversali, conducano a complicare e a moltiplicare quel "kind of twin-sided
mirror" che il Nicoll ha visto manifestato da ciascuna delle due coppie.[2]

Seguendo proprio le complicazioni e le moltiplicazioni di questo gioco
di specchi, si può subito avvertire che la combinatoria a coppie della
commedia dell'arte mira a far balzare in superficie il gioco stesso dell'in-
trecciarsi e del corrispondersi delle parole, dei gesti, dei movimenti, delle
figure, degli oggetti. E' un processo che ci porta molto lontano dalla commedia "classica" cinquecentesca, dove pure esso ha la sua origine e in cui
era comunque essenziale la concentrazione sull'intreccio drammatico, sul
suo rigore e sulla sua razionalità. Nella commedia del Cinquecento il gioco
combinatorio, le duplicazioni e gli accoppiamenti scenici, gli incastri tra
personaggi, si collegavano sempre ad una assolutizzazione del modello
progettuale, della sua organicità; si imponeva con forza il carattere funzionale dell'intreccio, sempre tendente, anche se in mezzo a momenti di
scatenata e gratuita comicità, verso una chiusura, una sistemazione crea-
trice di equilibri (spesso con spostamenti simmetrici delle situaziooni e
dei rapporti dati all'inizio): e ciò anche nelle esperienze di tipo "manieri-
stico," che attraversavano quella razionalità strutturale assolutizzandola e
così corrodendola dall'interno.

Nello stesso legame della commedia "regolare" cinquecentesca con la novella boccaccesca e con la tradizione della beffa si poteva vedere all'opera questa combinatoria di tipo "razionalistico," questa tensione verso un risultato, verso una saldatura progettuale: scambi e raddoppiamenti della novella italiana e della commedia cinquecentesca ricavavano sempre i loro caratteri comici dalla loro stessa funzionalità, dal loro legarsi all'affermazione risolutiva di un personaggio o di un gruppo di personaggi su altri personaggi, e insieme dal loro tendere ad una "chiusura" razionale del discorso, tale da far riconoscere nell'oggetto drammatico qualcosa di ben definito e compatto, inseribile in un'organica prospettiva letteraria.

Nella commedia dell'arte gioco combinatorio e moltiplicazione dei raddoppiamenti sono invece dettati dan una automatica necessità di creare infinite variazioni, di dar luogo ad una libera e plurale serie di corrispondenze, di incastri, di accoppiamenti: e tutto ciò si articola per lo più indipendentemente da ogni dimensione progettuale, da ogni tensione verso una sistemazione, una saldatura finale. Il trionfo finale delle coppie di innamorati è un punto d'arrivo meccanico e scontato, un perno strutturale automatico a cui si può mirare in modi diversi, con combinazioni casuali ed eterogenee, e intorno al quale si possono innestare in più imprevedibili pretesti di movimento scenico: ma ogni situazione di ogni commedia, affidandosi a qualcuna delle svariate possibilità di raddoppiamento, sembra cercarne la giustificazione in se stessa, nel proprio momentaneo configurarsi, nel proprio propagarsi e ripetersi. Lo sguardo verso il punto d'arrivo finale è cosa troppo facile, risaputa, esteriore, per avere un rilievo funzionale: la *pièce* non deve essere mai un organismo, ma un parossistico inseguirsi di combinazioni, in un gioco teatrale dato dal puro affrontarsi di voci e di gesti, dallo sfiorarsi continuo di figure, ciascuna delle quali può essere ombra dell'altra, per ciascuna delle quali è possibile uno scambio, un gioco di raddoppiamento con ciascuna delle altre.

Proprio in un tipo di teatro in cui i ruoli sono fissati in modo nettissimo, definiti dalle maschere o dal ripetersi di posizioni strutturali fisse (come quelle degli innamorati), proprio nel continuo ripresentarsi di figure sempre uguali a se stesse, in mezzo ad una galleria-catalogo di immagini cristallizzate del comportamento umano e dei rapporti sociali, si dà così, paradossalmente, un aprirsi di ogni figura-personaggio verso una totale possibilità di scambio, di contatto, di confusione di posizioni con ogni altra figura-personaggio. La presenza teatrale della persona-maschera-ruolo non è qui mai chiusa in se stessa, nel regolato rilievo della propria indentità, ma si apre fisicamente (nella parola, nel gesto, nel contatto scenico) a mutevoli e variabili convergenze e interferenze con altre persone-maschere-ruoli.

Si può vedere, per esempio, quante libere (e scabrose) possibilità siano
date dagli scenari per ciò che riguarda il rapporto reciproco tra i due mem-
bri della coppia dei vecchi e tra essi e le altre coppie di personaggi (servi,
innamorati, innamorate). La situazione più semplice è quella in cui i due
si trovano a coprire in modo relativamente normale i loro ruoli di padri
e vengono messi in contatto soprattutto dai rapporti di vicinato e dagli
amori tra i rispettivi figli (la più schematica situazione-limite, piuttosto
rara allo stato puro, è quella in cui il primo ha una figlia e un figlio che
rispettivamente amano un figlio e una figlia dell'altro). Ma questi nitidi
ruoli di padri (in cui i due si fanno da specchio l'un l'altro e mantengo-
no rigidi rapporti verticali con la generazione dei giovani) si complicano
subito per i diversi rapporti che si creano col mondo dei servi e per le
collisioni a cui le azioni di questi e quelle dei giovani danno luogo. Inoltre
quasi sempre i due vecchi aspirano a rompere i limiti della loro condizione
paterna, facendosi trascinare da desideri e da tensioni verso le figure delle
serve o addirittura verso quelle delle fanciulle delle nuove generazioni.
Questi desideri modificano anche variamente la natura del loro rapporto
reciproco: si può avere una sfogatura nei loro atteggiamenti (uno dei due
può essere un padre serio e severo, che rimprovera l'altro delle sue incon-
grue scappatelle), o una loro convergenza in una allegra vita godereccia
(così, ne *La gelosa Isabella* dello Scala, Pantalone e Graziano si presentano subito come una coppia di allegri crapuloni); una loro collaborazione
in iniziative erotiche, o una loro concorrenza nell'amore verso la stessa
serva o la stessa fanciulla (così, ne *Lo specchio* dello Scala, sia Pantalone che Graziano aspirano alla mano di Flaminia, che alla fine toccherà a
Flavio, figlio di Pantalone). Per questa via si può giungere ad una serie di
interferenze nei rapporti che i due hanno con i rispettivi figli: frequentissimi i casi in cui l'uno aspira alla figlia dell'altro (col suo consenso, con
la sua indifferenza o con la sua opposizione). Si tratta naturalmente di
casi in cui la maschera del vecchio si espone totalmente all'aggressione
più spietata da parte della generazione dei giovani e dei servi che con essi
collaborano; e il tutto si complica ancora di più quando questi desideri
verso le giovani sfiorano una dimensione incestuosa (il padre desidera una
fanciulla che poi, alla fine, si rivela essere sua figlia), o quando i vecchi
si trovano ad essere mariti di giovani esuberanti, esponendosi ancora più
automaticamente all'aggressione da parte della giovane generazione e al
gioco del *cocuage*.

Anche per ciò che riguarda le coppie degli innamorati, si dà una variabi-
lissima possibilità di interferenze e di scambi: non soltanto per l'intervento
di concorrenti esterni (si tratti di vecchi, di capitani o di altri giovani fuori

dal gioco delle coppie) o per la frequente opacità della situazione iniziale (due giovani possono amare la stessa fanciulla, o qualcuno di essi può essere nascosto sotto un falso sembiante), ma anche e soprattutto per il darsi di una serie di contatti a più direzioni tra tutti i portatori del desiderio amoroso. In molti casi si dà una collaborazione tra il giovane di una coppia e la fanciulla dell'altra coppia, che vengono ad offrirsi sostegno e aiuto per la realizzazione dei rispettivi amori con l'altra fanciulla e con l'altro giovane (per esempio, ne *Li duo vecchi gemelli* dello Scala, Isabella, che ama Flavio, e Orazio, che ama Flaminia, si offrono reciproco appoggio per la felice riuscita dei loro amori): ed è evidente come queste collaborazioni prospettino momenti di comicità, che quasi sembrano aprirsi sulla possibilità di configurare coppie diverse e intrecciate, con uno scambio di posizioni nel gioco dei rapporti erotici. In modo più esplicito questo scambio di posizioni viene più volte sfiorato tramite gli equivoci scenici più casuali e banali, come quelli dati dalle scene notturne, che permettono momentanei congiungimenti, fino a trasgredire comicamente tutti i rapporti erotici assestati nello schema della *pièce*. Un esempio di particolare nitidezza è dato all'inizio del terzo atto dello scenario di Basilio Locatelli, *La commedia in commedia*, in cui un progetto di fuga amorosa da parte delle due coppie di amanti si realizza (per semplice effetto del buio notturno) con le posizioni scambiate; il Capitano, che crede di fuggir con Ardelia, si ritrova in realtà con Lidia (di cui, come si verrà poi a sapere, è addirittura fratello), mentre Lelio, credendo di fuggire con Lidia, si ritrova con Ardelia (anche questa sua sorella!):

Capitano, di strada (finge notte), dice non saper quale sia la casa d'Ardelia; dice esser ora di ritrovarsi, secondo si sono data la posta. In questo
Lidia, di casa (fingendo notte oscura la scena), credendo il Capitano sia Lelio, e il Capitano credendo che Lidia sia Ardelia, si abbracciano e partono per la strada.
Lelio, di strada (fingendo notte), dice voler vedere la sua Lidia, e tenerla in casa d'una sua amica. In questo
Ardelia, di casa, fa il cenno; si credono l'una il Capitano, l'altro Lidia: senza parlare s'abbracciano e partono per la strada.[3]

Lo scambio resta senza gravi conseguenze, perché gli amanti si accorgono subito dell'errore e, senza nessun pregiudizio dell'"onore," le coppie vengono presto rimesse a posto: ma intanto si è concesso un significativo spazio ad una fantasia comica di scambio e turbamento dei rapporti, di facile permutabilità delle coppie.[4]

Questi errori casuali, originati dal buio notturno o da semplicistiche inavvedutezze, ci introducono al più vasto repertorio dei travestimenti, delle trasformazioni, degli scambi di persona legati a propositi beffardi o a tentativi di dar luogo ad incontri erotici altrimenti irrelizzabili. Qui naturalmente la commedia dell'arte opera incessanti variazioni sui materiali della tradizione cinquecentesca, nella quale si possono distinguere sei schemi generali: 1) sostituzione senza mascheratura, 2) travestimento senza scambio di sesso, 3) sostituzione nel rapporto amoroso, 4) travestimento con scambio di sesso, 5) gemellarità, 6) gemellarità bisessuale.[5] Non ripercorrerò ora tutte le variazioni e le moltiplicazioni che questi schemi subiscono negli scenari della commedia dell'arte; devo limitarmi piuttosto a sottolineare come ad essi sia comunque attribuita una funzionalità assai ridotta, il loro legame con l'organismo generale dell'intreccio e col processo di soluzione della *fabula* sia in genere piuttosto labile e casuale. Travestimenti, trasformazioni, scambi di persona non si saldano mai ad una vera dimensione progettuale e programmatica, ad un lucido gioco di spostamento di rapporti e di creazione di nuove simmetrie: nella maggior parte dei casi essi tendono invece a creare nuove occasioni di confusione e di apertura scenica, a produrre replicate sovrapposizioni ed interferenze, a rendere più aleatori i rapporti e i limiti dei personaggi e della loro presenza scenica. Ogni gioco di scambio si concentra insomma sul proprio emergere, sulla propria comica gratuità, e non su di una funzionale ricerca di scopi e risultati: si può porre e si può cancellare istantaneamente, per il puro piacere di esserci e sparire. Certo non mancano quasi mai delle motivazioni occasionali, legate alla realizzazione di un desiderio o alla messa in opera di qualche beffa: ma quello che ne risulta è sempre il piacere di una fantastica ripetizione di contatti irregolari, abnormi, assurdi, impossibili.

Uno degli schemi più seguiti, ripetuti e ricombinati, è quello del personaggio che si inserisce sotto una falsa identità in una situazione che serve ad allontanare un pericolo o a creare nuovi rapporti con oggetti desiderati: uno schema che risale alla commedia nuova greca, che aveva avuto ne *I Suppositi* dell'Ariosto la prima esemplare sistemazione cinquecentesca (con la figura del falso servitore che si inserisce in casa dell'amata) e che aveva trovato la sua variante più fortunata, collegandosi allo schema della gemellarità bisessuale, negli *Ingannati* degli Accademici Intronati di Siena e nella *Twelfth Night* di Shakespeare.[6] Ne *Il marito* dello Scala lo schema è complicato e stravolto attraverso la figura del finto marito di Isabella, un tal Cornelio, con cui ella ha contratto un falso matrimonio in attesa del ritorno dell'amato Orazio. Questo Cornelio è in realtà la serva Franceschina, che si è finta morta e poi si è travestita in abiti maschili: la situazione dà luogo ad una serie di divertenti recitazioni del falso rapporto matrimoniale tra Isabella e il falso Cornelio, da cui sprigionano una serie di possibili allusioni sessuali, in un continuo gioco tra fantasia omosessuale e scherzo sull'impossibilità di un vero rapporto erotico tra i due sposi. Il secondo atto si chiude, ad esempio, su di una sfasatura, densa di possibilità comiche, tra quello che Isabella e il falso Cornelio si dicono, stanchi ormai dell'inganno, e il loro entrare "abbracciati" in casa:

> Cornelio arriva; Isabella gli accenna il seguito e che sarà tempo di scoprir l'inganno; e qui, dicendo ognuna che la natura patisce, abbraccciati entrano in casa, e qui finisce l'atto secondo.[7]

Questo stesso scenario (in cui, tra l'altro, Pantalone e Graziano desiderano tutti e due la giovane Flaminia, che è in casa di Pantalone, come sua pupilla, e che il tutore vorrebbe dare in moglie proprio al concorrente Graziano, ma per poterla poi "godere" a proprio comodo) presenta una esplosione ininterrotta di fantasie di spostamenti e trasgressioni, che culminano in una incredibile scena notturna, organizzata da Pedrolino, che gestisce tutta una serie di incontri erotici, con contatti diversi, alcuni abnormi ed irregolari, deludenti e beffardi, altri felici e desiderati; e lo stesso Pedrolino, che regola tutti gli incontri altrui, incappa in un incontro imprevisto, che prima gli appare spaventoso, ma poi felice e trionfante. Pantalone, che crede di andare ad incontrare Flaminia, viene accoppiato con Arlecchino, che a sua volta crede di incontrare Olivetta; Graziano, che anche lui crede di incontrare Flaminia, viene accoppiato con Olivetta; le giovani coppie sono dirette secondo i loro desideri, Flaminia col Capitano e Isabella con Orazio; per non lasciare vuoti, Pedrolino deve mettersi a letto con il marito di Isabella, il falso Cornelio, ma, vedendosi insieme a Franceschina, da lui amata e creduta morta, teme in un primo momento che si tratti di un fantasma. Tutto questo gioco notturno viene presentato in due movimenti opposti; i vari personaggi vengono prima fatti entrare da Pedrolino, uno dopo l'altro, nei luoghi dei loro attesi convegni; poi uno dopo l'altro escono fuori in camicia, rendendo conto della diverse situazioni in cui si sono trovati:

Notte

Pedrolino vede gli amanti, li fa ritirar, dicendo che allora saranno contenti; essi si ritirano. Pedrolino fa il cenno dato.

Arlecchino vestito da donna. Pedrolino lo pone in disparte e poi fa il cenno a Pantalone.

Pantalone fuora; Pedrolino li dà Arlecchino per Flaminia et egli la conduce in casa. Pedrolino fa il cenno al Dottore.

Graziano fuora. Pedrolino lo fa ritirare, poi fa cenno ad Olivetta.

Olivetta fuora. Pedrolino la dà al Dottore per Flaminia; egli la conduce in casa sua. Pedrolino fa cenno a Flaminia.

Flaminia fuora; Pedrolino le consegna il Capitano, quali vanno in casa a godersi. Pedrolino fa cenno a Isabella.

Isabella fuora; Pedrolino le consegna Orazio; essi entrano a godersi, e Pedrolino anch'egli entra per mettersi accanto a Cornelio.

Pantalone con lume, in camicia, e col pistolese, correndo dietro ad Arlecchino.

Arlecchino fuggendo, alla fine dice come Pedrolino l'ha tradito, avendoli promesso di metterlo con Olivetta. Pantalone: d'aver sentito romore in casa; entra. Arlecchino rimane; in quello

Pantalone di dentro grida: "arme, arme, vicinanza!"; in quello

Capitano in camicia con Flaminia, dicendo esser marito e moglie, sposati *[Flaminia]* da Pedrolino; in quello sentono romore

Olivetta fuggendo, Graziano dietro; si trovano burlati da *[Graziano]* Pedrolino. Sentono di nuovo romore; in quello

Orazio in camicia con Isabella; danno la colpa a Pedrolino, *Isabella* essendo ripresi da Graziano. Sentono di nuovo romore; in quello

Pedrolino in camicia, fuggendo

Cornelio dietro a Pedrolino, il quale, per vederlo con le treccie, lo crede lo spirito di Franceschina.[8]

Segue più da vicino la traccia degli *Ingannati* un altro scenario dello Scala, *La gelosa Isabella*, in cui mentre Isabella, presa da un attacco di gelosia, si traveste da maschio per cercare Orazio e per dirgli il fatto suo, appare Fabrizio, il gemello della stessa Isabella, creando tutta una serie di equivoci (specialmente in rapporto al padre Pantalone) e dando poi luogo ad un incontro erotico tra Fabrizio e Flaminia, che l'aveva fatto entrare in casa credendolo Isabella travestita. L'uso dello schema gemellare, sia con scambio tra i sessi (come in questo caso), che secondo la traccia del più lineare modello dei *Menaechmi* plautini, è diffusissimo in ogni genere di scenari: esso dà, del resto, la forma di raddoppiamento più esplicita e insieme più radicata in un sotterraneo fondo di suggestioni mitiche. Basta fare solo un provvisorio e quasi casuale elenco di titoli di scenari (a cui occorrerebbe aggiungere vari titoli di commedie secentesche comunque legate all'esperienze dei comici dell'arte), per rendersi conto dell'estensione di questo schema: oltre i due scenari dello Scala *Li duo vecchi gemelli* e *Li duo capitani simili*, ricordo *I due Arlecchini*, *Le due Flaminie simile*, *Li due fratelli simili con la pazzia d'amore*, *Li due Pantaloni*, *Li due Pulcinelli simili*, *Li due simili d'Andreini*, *Due simili con le lettere mutate*, *I due simili*, *Li due Trappolini*, *Quattro Pollicinelli simili*, *Li quattro simili di Plauto*, *Li sei simili*, *Zanni incredibile con quatro simili*, ecc.[9]

Questa così vasta diffusione dello schema gemellare si svolge in complicazioni di vario tipo, con giochi di raddoppiamento interno che germogliano dal nucleo di base: così, ad esempio, nel secondo atto de *Li duo vecchi gemelli*, la vecchia Pasquella arruola lo schiavo Ramadan, che ella ignora sia Pantalone, gemello di Tofano, perché reciti la parte di se stesso, apparendo come il redivivo Pantalone de' Bisognosi, padre di Flavio (e cioè ciò che lui è realmente) all'interno di una falsa scena magica. Come suggeriscono alcuni dei titoli sopra elencati, si possono poi dare casi di raddoppiamento e di triplicazione delle coppie gemellari, su di una linea di invenzione che ha alla sua radice l'*Amphitruo* plautino e un allucinato punto di arrivo in *The Comedy of Errors* di Shakespeare.

Ma, anche da questo punto di vista, complicazioni e moltiplicazioni della commedia dell'arte non si concentrano mai sulla struttura globale delle singole *pièces*, non arrivano mai a fare delle figure dei gemelli dei veicoli per una compartizione funzionale dello spazio scenico, per la creazione di un meccanismo drammatico fatto di bilanciamenti, di scissioni e di equilibri. I gemelli della commedia dell'arte tendono soprattutto a far ripetere, amplificare, prolungare le occasioni di indistinzione e di confusione che si danno sulla scena: e gli scenari tendono a concentrarsi, più che su ogni altro effetto del comico gemellare, sulle singole scene di equivoco date dall'apparizione successiva e separata, sulla scena, dei due diversi gemelli, di fronte ad uno stesso personaggio o gruppo di personaggi, con cui, ovviamente, si crea una catena di malintesi, continuamente smetiti o confermati, secondo la vera identità del gemello che volta per volta appare. Come accade ne *Li duo vecchi gemelli* un personaggio può dare ad uno dei gemelli una lettera, per recapitarla da qualche parte; poi può trovarsi di fronte l'altro gemello, interrogandolo sull'avvenuta consegna della lettera, e sentendosi rispondere che quello non ne ha sentito nemmeno parlare; poi, andando via quel secondo gemello, può tornare il primo, dicendo che tutto è stato fatto come comandato e suscitando un ulteriore turbamento dell'interlocutore; e il gioco può continuare così anche molto a lungo. Nell'atto finale de *Li duo capitani simili*, questo semplice schema di equivoco viene messo alla prova con una indiavolata successione di entrate e di uscite sceniche, in cui i due capitani si danno il cambio, sorprendendo gli altri personaggi con la continua modifica del loro comportamento, fino al momento in cui tutto esplode con uno scontro armato tra i due, che si contendono Isabella, moglie di uno di loro.[10]

Un ulteriore ed affascinante meccanismo di raddoppiamento, abbastanza raro nella commedia "regolare" del Cinquecento, è costituito, negli scenari, dal gioco di specchi dato dalla riflessione-ripetizione, entro l'azione, dell'azione stessa da un diverso punto di vista, o dall'esibizione del "teatro nel teatro": ed è stato opportunamente notato come negli scenari dello Scala siano frequenti i ripiegamenti del disegno drammatico su se stesso o le presentazioni, dentro la vicenda scenica, del mondo dei comici e dello spettacolo.[11] Uno degli esempi più affascinanti e quello de *Lo specchio*, nel cui atto finale tutte le vicende, i desideri e le situazioni della *pièce* vengono raccontate, riassunte, ripetute e svelate nella loro verità, attraverso lo sguardo di uno specchio magico, in cui successivamente si speccchiano Pedrolino, Arlecchino e Fabrizio, che in realtà è Isabella, che, nelle consuete sembianze di finto paggio, si era collocata al servizio del proprio padre Pantalone.[12]

Per ciò che riguarda il gioco del teatro nel teatro, tralasciando i numerosi scenari in cui si presentano azioni sceniche frammentarie, momenti di spettacolo mimico o musicale, personaggi che fanno i "comici" di mestiere, ecc., mi limito a ricordare lo scenario già citato, *La commedia in commedia*, in cui ha luogo la recitazione di una commedia per le nozze che Pantalone vuol imporre alla figlia Lidia col vecchio Coviello: Graziano e il Capitano si presentano in veste di comici, ma la loro rappresentazione viene interrotta quando, mentre il Capitano sta manifestando in scena il suo amore per una Isabella, Lelio tra gli spettatori raccoglie un guanto lasciato cadere da Lidia, suscitando l'ira di Coviello e un parapiglia generale, che per fortuna fa rinviare anche le nozze. Tra le varie agnizioni che si avranno alla fine, ci sarà anche quella degli attori: Graziano ritroverà il proprio ruolo di dottore, e il Capitano si scoprirà essere Orazio, figlio di Pantalone. La commedia recitata ed interrotta apre un forte squarcio nell'azione della commedia, nei rapporti tra i personaggi: ma l'attenzione viene concentrata non tanto sull'effetto che quella commedia che chiameremo "di secondo grado" può fare sulla commedia "di primo grado," quanto sul loro interagire, sovrapporsi, scontrarsi, e sui possibili giochi creati da queste interferenze. Commedia di secondo grado e commedia di primo grado non sono due specchi separati che si corrispondono (come in certi celebri giochi shakespeariani di *play within a play*, e prima di tutti quello di Amleto), ma due universi che interferiscono, due scene aperte che si sovrappongono e si combinano, che esaltano la comicità del loro scontrarsi ed esplodere in un parapiglia generale.[13]

Tutti i meccanismi di raddoppiamento a cui ho accennato meriterebbero un approfondimento legato ad una schedatura totale degli schemi presenti in tutto il repertorio disponibile (schedatura che, a che io sappia, non è mai stata adeguatamente fatta). Una tipologia più precisa e delle vere conclusioni potranno ricavarsi solo da un lavoro del genere, a cui occorrerebbe aggiungere un'altra direzione di ricerca, a cui non ho nemmeno accennato, e cioè quella relativa ai raddoppiamenti dati dai lazzi, dalle tecniche fisiche e verbali del comico, dagli schemi dialogici, dall'invenzione dei motti di spirito, dai giochi concettuali e metaforici (e anche qui il materiale a disposizione non è mai stato sottoposto ad una adeguata schedatura globale).

Si potrà intanto convenire su di uno stretto collegamento tra questa ossessiva presenza del doppio e la bivalenza di fondo su cui si regge la stessa tecnica drammatica e lo stesso darsi della comunicazione teatrale nella commedia dell'arte. E' la bivalenza tra il sistema dei modelli (il repertorio tematico, retorico, linguistico) su cui essa si fonda e il suo tradursi nel sempre rinnovato ed inafferrabile emergere della parola e dell'azione "improvvisa"; una bivalenza che così suggestivamente viene indicata dall'Apollonio:

Questo obbligo di tener sempre presente la regola, di giudicare limpidamente la lunghezza del passo che si tenta fuor dalla via battuta, questa possibilità di abbandonarsi apparentemente nel vuoto, ma tenendosi stretti ad un invisibile sostegno—la tradizione vicenda dell'azione—sono, mi sembra, elementi dell'arte classica.[14]

Certo non si potrà accettare questa riconduzione ad una dimensione di tipo "classico"; occorrerà invece insistere sul rapporto tra un abbandono sul vuoto e un invisibile sostegno, avvertendo però tutta la distanza che separa la commedia dell'arte sia dalle forme teatrali classicistiche o manieristiche del Cinquecento sia dai più marcati atteggiamenti "barocchi" del teatro secentesco. L'inquietante individualità della commedia dell'arte la sottrae, del resto, al vincolo di ogni definizione storiografica troppo stretta, di ogni tranquillizzante uso di concetti di periodizzazione: essa è proprio in quel difficile incontro tra una combinatoria articolatissima e la casualità del puro evento teatrale, in quell'incessante confronto tra la schematizzazione assoluta (che ci viene offerta da maschere, scenari, repertori delle "parti," ecc.) e la sempre gratuita apertura del gesto e della parola "improvvisa," del loro ingiustificato essere scenico.

La commedia dell'arte è insomma come una vasta enciclopedia del teatrabile, che la scena trasforma ogni volta in qualcosa di assolutamente gratuito, come casuale. In ogni emergere del presente scenico si dà sempre un'automatica allusione agli schemi, al catalogo che sorregge tutta la struttura: ma il piacere comico della scena si regge sul tradursi di quel catalogo in emergenza avventurosa, sul suo svolgersi come infinita trasgressione e infinita, provvisoria casualità.

Da questo punto di vista si appropria all'esperienza della commedia dell'arte il termine di *vertigine*: dalle più assoluta superficialità dell'emergere scenico essa guarda verso la sotterranea profondità del sistema e del catalogo, dell'enciclopedia di strutture in cui sono congelate le maschere, le situazioni, i movimenti; e ogni volta, nel tradursi in occasionale presenza, in gratuito affiorare del comico, quell'enciclopedia viene ricordata e dimenticata (e l'ossessivo affacciarsi del doppio ne è proprio un segno essenziale). Si tratta della *vertigine* del teatro, del pericoloso ed inestricabile rapporto tra il suo darsi nell'immediatezza del presente e il suo inserirsi in un sistema di comunicazione, in una predeterminata griglia strutturale: nella commedia dell'arte questa *vertigine* si dà con una gioia, con una leggerezza, con una incantata superficialità, che ovviamente resteranno ignote a tutte le esperienze novecentesche che tenteranno di affacciarsi su quell'inafferrabile vuoto.

University of Rome

NOTES

1 Mi riferisco ai lavori di O. Rank, *Die Don Juan-Gestalt* (Leipzig, Wien, ZVerlag, 1924) e di W. H. Auden, *Berlam and the Ass.*

2 A. Nicoll, *The World of Harlequin. A Critical Study of the Commedia dell'Arte* (Cambridge University Press, 1963) p. 42; il Nicoll ha indicato anche l'approfondirsi di queste complicazioni attraverso la varietà dei rapporti numerici dati dal *patterning* della commedia dell'arte. Per la definizione del modello dei rapporti possibili tra tutte le parti del canovaccio-tipo, è essenziale il contributo di L. Zorzi, "Struttura-fortuna della fiaba gozziana," *Chigiana*, XXXI, 1974.

3 Cfr. *La commedia dell'arte. Storia-tecnica-scenari*, a cura di E. Petraccone (Napoli: Ricciardi, 1927) p. 354.

4 Una delle più antiche radici novellistiche per lo schema dello scambio erotico per errore o inavvedutezza dovute al buio notturno è offerta dal *Novellino*, XCIX.

5 Per questa distinzione rinvio al mio saggio "Tecniche del raddoppiamento nella commedia del Cinquecento," in *Il testo e la scena. Saggi sul teatro del Cinquecento* (Roma: Bulzoni, 1980) pp. 43-64.

6 Negli scenari dello Scala è frequente la situazione della fanciulla in abito da paggio-servitore, più direttamente legata agli *Ingannati* (oltre a *Lo specchio* e a *La gelosa Isabella*, di cui si parlerà più avanti, ricordo almeno *Li tappeti alessandrini*): il legame degli scenari dello Scala con gli *Ingannati* è del resto fortissimo, come mostra gran parte del repertorio dei nomi dei personaggi dei giovani, che ricombina con qualche variazione proprio quello degli *Ingannati*.

7 F. Scala, *Il teatro delle favole rappresentative*, a cura di F. Marotti (Milano: Il Polifilo, 1976) p. 106. Molto interessante il confronto tra lo scenario de *Il marito* e la commedia *Il finto marito*, tendente ad una deludente "letterarizzaione" (cfr. le indicazioni di F. Marotti nell'*Introduzione* pp. LIX-LXII).

8 F. Scala, *Il teatro delle favole rappresentative*, pp. 108-09.

9 Questi (e altri numerosi) titoli di scenari possono ricavarsi dall'utilissima "Handlist of scenari," in appendice a K. M. Lea, *Italian Popular Comedy. A Study in the Commedia dell'arte, 1560-1620, with special reference to the English Stage* (Oxford: Clarendon Press, 1934) vol. II, pp. 506-554 (è un repertorio che meriterebbe di essere aggiornato e perfezionato).

10 Dal punto di vista della storia e del significato dello schema gemellare nella commedia dell'arte, l'uccisione in scena dello sciocco Zanetto ne *I due gemelli veneziani* di Goldoni verrà ad acquistare un sorprendente peso simbolico, proprio come celebrazione scenica dell'aspirazione di Goldoni ad eliminare la confusione e il pericoloso gioco di interferenza della commedia dell'arte.

11 R. Tessari, *La commedia dell'arte nel Seicento. "Industria" e "arte giocosa" della civiltà barocca* (Firenze: Olschki, 1969) pp. 109-135.

12 Un primo esempio di questi ripiegamenti interni del disegno drammatico si poteva trovare in una scena degli *Ingannati* (V, 2), in cui Clemenzia convince Flamminio ad amare Lelia col raccontargli la sua stessa storia, come se fosse accaduta ad altri; tra gli scenari dello Scala *Il vecchio geloso* presenta un *récit speculaire* dello stesso tipo, ma con funzione opposta, con cui Burattino rivela a Pantalone il suo *cocuage*.

13 Di tipo diverso, in un più tortuoso gioco di sovrapposizione e di rispecchiamento, è la doppia presenza del teatro nel teatro nella commedia di Giovan Battista Andreini, pubblicata nel 1623, *Le due commedie in commedia*, in cui vengono fatti rappresentare, entro la vicenda scenica, uno spettacolo di accademici e uno spettacolo di "comici," che in modi diversi vengono a richiamare in luce eventi passati, a scoprire rapporti perduti tra personaggi, in un'inquietante azione reciproca tra scena di primo grado e scene di secondo grado (data anche dal fatto che alcuni personaggi della prima recitano nelle seconde delle parti che "ripetono" eventi a loro accaduti nella stessa scena di primo grado): siamo sulla strada che porta al Pirandello dei *Sei personaggi*, di *Ciascuno a suo modo*, di *Questa sera si recita a soggetto*.

14 M. Apollonio, *Storia della commedia dell'arte* (Roma-Milano: Augustea, 1930) p. 182.

Steen Jansen

Sur la segmentation du texte dramatique et sur quelques scenarios de Flaminio Scala

0. Mon propos ici sera de discuter du problème de la segmentation du texte dramatique en général, à partir de quelques affirmations sur le rôle de celle-ci; ensuite j'essaierai brièvement de montrer comment on pourra envisager l'analyse d'un scénario de Flaminio Scala.

Avant de commencer, je voudrais préciser pourtant que je parlerai du *texte dramatique écrit*, et des problèmes que la *lecture* de celui-ci fait naître; je ne discuterai donc ni du spectacle théâtral ni du rapport entre texte et scène. On peut évidemment discuter ce choix préliminaire; ici je me limiterai à citer Marotti, qui à propos des scénarios de Scala dit:

Questo valore dei 'soggetti' . . . li pone anche come centro di un crocevia per l'esame del critico che può indagarli come 'commedie' autosufficienti nello spazio della pagina, e come notazioni su spettacoli perduti (1976:LV);

il envisage donc de voir le scénario soit comme texte écrit à lire soit comme texte à utiliser pour un spectacle, ou une mise en scène (pour une discussion plus détaillée voir Short 1981 et aussi Jansen 1983:92-95).[1]

1. Dans toutes les études structuralistes classiques (Propp, Lévi-Strauss, Greimas et d'autres, cf. Hamon), la segmentation du texte constitue une phase fondamentale et décisive de l'analyse, en ce sens que l'opération de segmentation détermine d'abord des unités d'expression et de contenu dont traite ensuite une classification, opération complémentaire de la segmentation, pour rendre compte du système de signification (regardant et l'expression et le contenu) qui caractérise ce texte.

Aujourd'hui, ce rôle de la segmentation est de plus en plus souvent mis en question.

Ainsi De Marinis exprime fortement son scepticisme en ce qui concerne la tentative même de vouloir segmenter le texte théâtral: il dénonce la "recherche mythique de l'unité théâtrale minimale" et pertinente (1979:4; cet article traite de la segmentation de façon bien plus détaillée que De Marinis 1982:95ss).

La critique de De Marinis porte en premier lieu sur le fait que formuler ainsi le problème signifie ne pas tenir compte de la complexité qui, à son avis, est le propre du spectacle, à savoir que celui-ci met en oeuvre, simultanément, plusieurs codes différents, plusieurs matières expressives différentes et plusieurs dimensions ou canaux sensoriels différents.

Il traite donc du texte spectaculaire, c'est-à-dire du spectacle (la performance, la mise en scène) et non pas du texte dramatique au sens étroit, tel que je l'entends: texte écrit et lu, et il ne dissimule pas qu'il doute assez fortement de l'intérêt même d'une analyse de ce texte (1979:4). Mais dans ses affirmations théoriques, il y a des éléments qui ne peuvent qu'intéresser aussi une telle analyse.

De Marinis ne nie pas qu'une segmentation du texte théâtral puisse être utile, mais il soutient que les segments qui en résultent ne peuvent être que des "parties du texte" seulement commodes, où l'analyse pourra plus facilement étudier l'organisation des significations, et alors qu'ils ne constituent en rien des unités minimales pertinentes. En effet, De Marinis va jusqu'à affirmer, semble-t-il, avec un renvoi à Barthes, que la segmentation de l'expression matérielle ne peut être qu'arbitraire (ibid:8).

D'autre part pourtant, et malgré le doute qu'il exprime envers l'intérêt même d'une analyse du texte dramatique en tant que tel, De Marinis propose aussi une caractéristique de la spécificité de celui-ci, qu'il oppose aux hypothèses formulées par Serpieri (1978), reprises et développées ensuite par Elam, auquel je reviendrai. Pour De Marinis donc

La specificità del testo drammatico scritto (. . .) va (. . .) cercato (. . .) (i) nella sua struttura dialogica che prescrive sempre, istituzionalmente, l'indicazione dei pseudo-soggetti dell'enunciazione; (ii) e inoltre (. . .) nella sua natura di "insieme di istruzioni *facoltative*" (. . .) (ibid:4 note)

Je ne pense pas que la seconde partie de cette définition soit correcte: ce n'est pas ainsi que le lecteur (que De Marinis ne mentionne pas d'ailleurs) lit et comprend le texte (cf Jansen 1983:86); la première partie par contre peut parfaitement bien constituer, à mon avis, la base d'un principe pertinent de segmentation en ce qu'on pourra appeler macro-séquences, et qui n'exclut pas du tout, à mon avis, la segmentation proposée par Serpieri; j'y reviendrai.

Si De Marinis peut affirmer qu'il n'y a pas de principes pertinents de segmentation, d'ordre général, pour le texte théâtral ou dramatique, c'est au fond parce qu'il considère les unités du code et les segments du texte comme des entités de type tout à fait différent et sans rapport entre eux autrement que par coincidence (ibid:4). Il dissocie ainsi (comme fait Barthes dans *S/Z*) à priori et de façon presqu'absolue signifiant et signifié; mais cela revient, je crois, à esquiver ce qui, à mon avis, est le problème fondamental de la sémiotique, à savoir d'écluder comment "certaines choses" ou entités concrètes, matérielles (mais pas toutes), deviennent pour nous (ou pour un groupe social donné) des "signes" (ou signifiants de signifiés) (cf Rossi-Landi 1980).

En réalité, le vrai problème ici, à mon avis, n'est pas de savoir si la segmentation a nécessairement ou non un caractère arbitraire; à elle seule, la théorie ne pourra jamais formuler qu'une hypothèse sur ce qui est censé être le meilleur principe de segmentation; ce sont les analyses de textes particuliers, fondées sur cette hypothèse, qui devront montrer si, du principe adopté, il résulte ou non des segments adéquats ou pertinents.

Dire qu'un principe de segmentation ne pourra jamais être qu'une hypothèse, ne signifie pas qu'il est nécessairement arbitraire, tel que j'entends ce terme, et, surtout, ne dispense pas de le motiver et de le formuler de façon aussi précise et non-ambiguë que possible. Bien au contraire.

La position de Keir Elam est légèrement différente: il semble admettre que l'analyse, pour être une analyse, doive nécessiarement segmenter le texte théâtral, et de façon non arbitraire:

the chief problem is theoretical and methodological, namely the establishing of agreed analytic *criteria* by which to undertake the semiotic division or *découpage* of the performance. In the words of Marcello Pagnini "one immediately comes up against the *punctum dolens* of every research of a semiological nature, namely that of the segmentation of the continuum into discrete units" (Elam 1980:47)

Pourtant la complexité du spectacle est telle que, jusqu'à présent, aucun critère, ou principe de segmentation satisfaisant n'a été formulé; pour Elam, il s'ensuit qu'il faudra aujourd'hui se contenter de chercher des critères qui regardent, séparément, chaque texte partiel dont le spectacle est composé (ibid:49).

Lorsqu'Elam choisit ensuite un texte partiel pour une analyse plus détaillée, c'est celui du discours théâtral (les répliques, ou les dialogues et monologues). Reprenant et développant les hypothèses formulées par Serpieri (1978), il propose pour le discours théâtral une segmentation en *micro-séquences*:

Within a given dramatic macro-sequence—say, an exchange between two characters—a number of micro-sequences will be distinguishable according to the deictic strategies manifested by the participants (ibid:145);

les répliques se présentent alors comme formées d'une suite d'*actes de parole* qui sont des unités d'orientation déictique-performative et des segments du texte de la réplique.

Dans la perspective que j'ai adoptée, celle de la lecture du texte dramatique, cette analyse et ces principes sont très importants; mais il faudra préciser d'une part que le discours théâtral qu'analyse Elam est formé des répliques seules, et il n'est donc pas identique au texte dramatique écrit, qui comprend aussi les didascalies, indispensables dans la lecture de ce type de texte; d'autre part, la suite de micro-séquence qui résulte de la segmentation que propose cette analyse, "atomise" à l'extrême le texte (comme on le voit dans l'exemple concret que donne Elam, sur les premières 79 lignes d'*Hamlet* (ibid:184-207)), et peut difficilement en constituer, à elle seule, la base d'une compréhension d'ensemble, je veux dire sans l'intermédiaire de quelques macro-séquences placées à un niveau entre celui des micro-séquences et celui du texte entier.

En simplifiant, sans doute, les idées de De Marinis et d'Elam, je les opposerai ici, pour les besoins de la cause, comme suit: d'une part, l'affirmation de l'impossibilité, ou de la non pertinence de la segmentation, d'autre part, l'affirmation qu'on doit essayer de résoudre le problème de la segmentation, pour complexe que soit le spectacle, et, par conséquent, la proposition, l'exemplification d'une hypothèse qui regarde un texte partiel du spectacle, le discours théâtral.

Dans *Le strutture e il tempo* (1974:24ss), Segre propose de distinguer deux types de segmentation qu'il oppose d'une façon qui n'est pas sans rappeler cette opposition entre les positions de De Marinis e d'Elam. Les deux segmentations, l'une linéaire et l'autre linguistique-formelle, sont présentées ainsi:

la prima operazione da attuare per l'analisi del discorso è la segmentazione. La segmentazione può proporsi almeno due obiettivi principali: 1) preparare le sequenze che, riordinate secondo la cronologia del contenuto, costituiranno la *fabula*; 2) individuare le zone di convergenza tra i vari tipi di funzioni discorsive e di linguaggio. Abbiamo insomma una segmentazione lineare e una segmentazione per classi linguistico-funzionali. (Segre 1974:24)

Ceci doit signifier que Segre, en distinguant entre deux sortes de segmentation, distingue aussi entre deux points de vue selon lesquels peuvent être conçus les éléments du texte narratif: d'abord celui qui regarde les deux premiers niveaux du texte (le discours et l'intrigue, bases de la fabula), et ensuite un autre qui englobe l'ensemble des quatre niveaux de la narration (discours, intrigue, fabula, modèle narratif).

Pourtant la clarté apparente, et l'utilité, de cette distinction, en tant que distinction, semble disparaître lorsque Segre affirme tout de suite après, en soulignant lui-même, que *"L'interesse della segmentazione lineare sta nella sua impossibilità"* (ibid:25), affirmation quelque peu énigmatique, ou pour le moins paradoxale: comment une chose qui est impossible, peut-elle présenter un intérêt?

Mais en essayant d'expliquer la différence, l'opposition qu'il y aurait ainsi entre les deux types de segmentation selon Segre, peut-être pourrait-on résoudre l'opposition qu'il y aurait entre De Marinis et Elam (ou Serpieri): la segmentation à laquelle pense le premier, et dont il nie la pertinence, serait-elle ce que Segre appelle une segmentation linéaire, tandis que le second cherche à montrer ce que pourrait être une segmentation linguistique-fonctionnelle?

Selon Segre (ibid:27-28), la segmentation linguistique-fonctionnelle concerne les modes de communiquer le contenu et est en ce sens reliées à l'*énonciation*, tandis que la segmentation linéaire regarde le rapport entre la narration et le référent, c'est-à-dire l'*énoncé*.

Or dans le texte narratif, il y a une énonciation de base, celle du narrateur (qu'il ne faut pas, à mon avis, confondre avec l'auteur; cf Soelberg 1985:69-70), qui organise la suite d'énoncés qu'est le texte narratif, et c'est bien cela qui fait dire à Segre que la segmentation linguistique-fonctionnelle exclut, ou de toute façon rend secondaire la segmentation linéaire. Mais est-ce que le même raisonnement est valable lorsqu'il s'agit du texte dramatique?

Pas nécessairement, à mon avis, et cela parce que le texte dramatique n'est pas formé d'énoncés pris en charge par une énonciation d'ensemble, mais d'une suite d'énonciations, "distribuées" sur différents personnages, mis face à face dans une succession de situations, que le texte présente comme une suite d'unités.

Je dirais alors que, si l'énoncé, dans le texte narratif, "s'insère" dans l'énonciation, pour le texte dramatique, c'est l'inverse: là, il y a une suite d'énonciations, correspondant à des micro-séquences, qui sont des éléments d'un "énoncé," une macro-séquence, manifestation ou réalisation d'une "situation"; le texte est alors une suite de tels "énoncés," organisée bien sûr, mais non par une énonciation semblable à celle du texte narratif et qui serait décisive pour la compréhension du texte.

Cette conception de la structure du texte dramatique est aussi une conséquence, ou un aspect, de ce que De Marinis appelle "la structure dialogique" du texte dramatique écrit (et lu); mais j'ajouterais que je ne pense pas qu'il y ait lieu de considérer les personnages du texte dramatique comme des "pseudo-sujets" de leur énonciation; de toute façon, ils ne le sont ni plus ni moins que ne l'est le narrateur du texte narratif de la sienne.

Si l'on entend maintenant par présence la manifestation, ou la possibilité de manifester une énonciation, on pourra dire que la présence, en ce sens, d'un ou de plusieurs personnages dans le lieu scénique que le texte présente au lecteur, sert à fonder une unité dans le texte dramatique, un "énoncé" dans lequel certaines énonciations sont possibles et d'autres non. (Cette unité, et le segment qui la manifeste, peuvent correspondre, mais ne correspondent pas nécessairement à la "scène" du texte dramatique traditionnel (voir *Acte sans paroles* de Beckett (cf Segre 1974:253ss), et *Le mensonge* de Nathalie Sarraute (cf Jansen 1976, dont l'analyse pourrait sans doute être réinterprétée selon cette conception: les silences prolongés y dénotent l'absence (ou non-présence) des personnages))).

La segmentation d'un texte dramatique comportera donc deux phase pour ainsi dire: d'abord on trouvera les macro-séquences qui correspondent à des situations et qui déterminent certaines "figures de présences," ensuite on découpera chacune de ces macro-séquences en micro-séquences correspondant aux actes—de parole ou de fait—qui, à l'intérieur d'une certaine "figure de présences," déterminent les relations qui s'y établissent entre les personnages.

Récemment, dans un chapître de *Teatro e romanzo* (1984:85ss) qui examine les nombreuses études faites sur le point de vue du texte narratif, Segre a repris le modèle à quatre niveaux présenté dans *Le strutture e il tempo*, pour suggérer une idée qui permettrait d'y intégrer la notion de focalisation (et plus généralement celle de "cette *régulation de l'information narrative* qu'est le mode" (ibid:97) élaborée par Genette). Il en résulte la formalisation simple que voici:

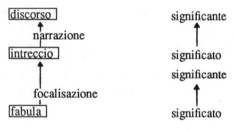

(Segre 1984:98)

Un modèle semblable, et aussi simple, pourrait être proposé comme une première structuration des problèmes que fait naître la lecture (et/ou l'analyse) du texte dramatique; j'y maintiendrai l'idée de trois niveaux distincts et de deux relations (ou fonctions) différentes qui relient ces niveaux, mais je remplacerai les termes de Segre par ceux employés dans ce qui précède (dont le modèle sera aussi un résumé alors):

discours dramatique
  ↑ |
  | ↓ dramatisation (mise en actes (de paroles))
"intrigue" (suite de situations/macro-séquences)
  ↑ |
  | ↓ "focalisation dramatique" (régulation de l'information dramatique)
"fabula" et univers dramatique

Si l'on adopte un tel modèle, on pourra faire correspondre les deux phases de la segmentation dont il a été question plus haut, à la "focalisation" et à la "dramatisation" respectivement. C'est-à-dire: un texte donné présente au lecteur un certain univers; lorsqu'on cherche à y relever les situations qui composent le texte, c'est (aussi) pour voir quelles sont les situations, parmi toutes les situations possibles que comprend cet univers (et la fabula), qui sont présentées directement au lecteur (ou qui sont "focalisées" par le texte); lorsqu'on essaie d'y relever les micro-séquences dont sont formées les macro-séquences, c'est (aussi) pour voir comment sont "dramatisées," en actes—de parole ou de fait—, les relations qui s'établissent entre les personnages.

Tout en étant encore très provisoire, le modèle conduira à poser des questions telles que: que peut signifier de façon plus précise la notion de "focalisation dramatique" (cf à ce propos Dodd et Pugliatti)? qu'est-ce qui la distingue de la focalisation narrative? ou plus généralement, est-ce qu'on pourra employer (et de quelle manière) la notion de "mode" lorsqu'on a affaire au texte dramatique? Peut-être pourrait-on montrer un jour si la différence texte narratif *versus* texte dramatique est ou n'est pas seulement une différence "de surface," comme on l'affirme parfois (par exemple Longacre et Levinsohn: "Drama, not mentioned above, is essentially a narrative whose surface structure form proceeds by means of dialogue." (Dressler 1978:104)), et si elle regarde aussi une organisation du contenu (et donc de la compréhension) du texte qui intervient avant que la "dramatisation" organise en discours les unités du niveau des situations.

D'autre part, ce modèle formalisera la conception de la compréhension du texte dramatique adoptée ici, de sorte qu'il y aura trois niveaux: du discours, des situations et de l'univers, et deux relations distinctes qui les relient.

Par la première relation, du premier au second niveau, le lecteur reçoit, du discours, des informations sur l'univers (et la "fabula") à construire (ou à découvrir); et en même temps cette relation fait du discours une suite d'énonciations insérées dans et déterminées par la situation dont elles font partie.

Chacune des situations, comprenant ou déterminées par un certain lieu, un certain moment et certain(s) personnage(s), présente au lecteur une partie, un aspect (un "côté visible") de l'univers dramatique; au fur et à mesure que la lecture s'avance le long du texte, la relation entre le niveau des situations et celui de l'univers permet au lecteur de construire une "synthèse mémorisée" (Segre 1974:17) qui est la base de sa compréhension du texte.

Cette "synthèse mémorisée" comprend, ou est formée de structures de connaissance (y comprises celles qu'apporte le lecteur, indépendemment du texte) et de structures d'attente, qui conditionnent l'interprétation (ou l'évaluation) des informations "reçues" (des énonciations) du discours.

Ces structures de connaissance et d'attente sont dominées par certaines contraintes, par exemple des contraintes fondées sur la grammaire (lexique et syntaxe) de la langue du discours, mais aussi des contraintes dues à la "forme" des situations: ainsi la présence de certains personnages d'une situation donnée fait prévoir (ou attendre) certaines énonciations (ou actes (de paroles)) et non pas d'autres.

Enfin, on pourrait, avec ce modèle, concevoir la relation entre les deux premiers niveaux comme une relation d'énonciation et celle entre les deux derniers comme une relation d'énoncé: d'une part, en effet, c'est la situation avec ses possibilités d'établir des orientations déictique-performatives qui permet de voir le discours dramatique comme une suite d'énonciations (ou d'actes de parole), et d'autre part, la situation, en présentant au lecteur une partie de l'univers dramatique, se présente aussi, dans le jeu de la lecture, comme référence à un pseudo-référent ("un referente che, in un racconto inventato, non esiste," Segre 1974:27), et comme telle avec les caractéristiques d'un énoncé.

2. Pour une étude qui cherche surtout à formuler une théorie du texte dramatique écrit (et lu), les scénarios de la *commedia dell'arte* ne sembleraient pas à première vue devoir susciter un intérêt. Mais lorsqu'on se met à lire ces scénarios, et en particulier ceux du recueil de Flaminio Scala: *Teatro delle favole rappresentative*, on s'aperçoit vite qu'ils présentent, bien au contraire, plusieurs caractéristiques intéressantes.

Une de celles-ci est ce que j'appellerai la relative simplicité des scénarios par rapport à d'autres textes dramatiques, c'est-à-dire comme la proposition simple par rapport à la proposition complexe, ou comme le conte populaire par rapport au roman moderne.

Cette simplicité—toute relative donc—du scénario de la *commedia dell'arte*, se trouve à tous les niveaux; par exemple: le système des rôles-types ou fonctions (les vieux, les jeunes amoureux, les serviteurs) auquel peuvent être reliés les différents personnages du scénario particulier; le conflit typique commun à presque tous les scénarios, et que Tessari appelle "l'unico Canovaccio davvero rappresentato dalla Commedia dell'Arte" (1981:102; cf aussi Nicolls (1963:40) pour une conception autre du conflit typique); la forme traditionnelle, et simple des situations, où l'entrée/sortie des personnages est (sauf rares exceptions) clairement marquée (cf Perrucci, cit. in Tessari 1981:150); la forme particulière qui abolit la distinction texte primaire *vs* texte secondaire (pour décrire la différence entre répliques et didascalies), mais non pas le caractère dramatique du texte puisque celui-ci présente toujours des personnages dans des actions qui doivent, ou peuvent, "dirsi e farsi dal recitante all'improvviso" (Perrucci ibid:149; cf aussi Jansen 1973:247 et ce que dit Constant Mic à propos de l'improvisation et du texte dramatique en général (1927:156-159)); enfin la langue des scénarios qui utilise un vocabulaire et une syntaxe "schématisés" et en ce sens assez simple.

On pourrait encore sans doute mentionner d'autres caractéristiques, mais je m'arrête ici; en somme, les scénarios de la *commedia dell'arte* présentent un intérêt certain pour une théorisation du texte dramatique à la fois parce que ce sont des textes concrets, ou "naturels," c'est-à-dire non pas construits pour et par la théorie (même s'ils sont déjà en eux-mêmes plus "formalisés" que d'autres textes dramatiques), et parce qu'y sont reliés un discours dramatique et un univers dramatique ayant tous les deux une structure, ou forme également simple. A mon avis, les scénarios pourraient sans doute jouer le même rôle pour l'élaboration d'une théorie du texte dramatique que le conte populaire a joué pour celle de la théorie du texte narratif.

Ceci vaut aussi parfaitement bien pour les scénarios de Scala; mais à cela s'ajoute (outre le fait qu'ils forment un corpus bien délimité) qu'ils réalisent la forme commune, caractéristique de la *commedia dell'arte* de manières tellement variées (variété qui justifie pleinement le terme de "sperimentalismo" avec lequel Tessari ailleurs caractérise Scala (1969:109)), que chaque texte apparaît comme une "oeuvre" individuelle, et pas seulement comme une copie.

Il y a donc de fortes chances pour qu'une analyse des scénarios de Scala puisse d'une part contribuer à l'élaboration d'un modèle du scénario de la *commedia dell'arte*, et d'autre part permettre d'appliquer ce modèle à un assez grand nombre de textes suffisamment variés pour que la validité du modèle puisse être discutée.

Selon l'hypothèse que j'adopte ici, chaque situation d'un scénario pourra être vue comme composée d'une ou de plusieurs *actions typiques* ayant pour fonction d'établir des relations entre les personagges présents dans la situation. Un scénario donné sera alors formé d'une suite de situations composées de réalisations particulières d'actions typiques, et le lecteur organiserait sa compréhension du texte du scénario en établissant entre les personnages des relations selon les actions typiques qu'il trouve manifestées dans le discours et, probablement, en résumant ou réorganisant sa compréhension lorsque les personnages changent, c'est-à-dire chaque fois qu'il passe d'une situation à la suivante.

Cela présuppose qu'il existe, et que le lecteur connaisse un système (ou code ou "grammaire") qui permette de construire, à partir du discours dramatique d'un scénario donné, un univers dramatique particulier. Il peut certainement y avoir plusieurs systèmes différents (dont résulteraient différentes compréhensions ou interprétations d'un même scénario), mais probablement ils doivent comprendre, au moins, une "grammaire" du discours dramatique qui indique comment on passe des termes manifestés de celui-ci aux actions typiques dont sont formées les situations, une "grammaire" des situations qui dise comment celles-ci peuvent se grouper, se répéter, s'enchaîner etc., et une "grammaire" de l'univers dramatique qui donne l'ensemble des éléments dont celui-ci peut être composé, avec leurs caractéristiques (ou fonctions ou les relations entre eux). Une telle distinction entre trois "grammaires" différentes sera peut-être seulement provisoire parce que les trois dépendront certainement les unes des autres; mais elle pourra être utile dans une première phase de l'élaboration d'un modèle (ou théorie) du scénario de Scala, qui sera en quelque sorte une description formalisée de ces "grammaires."

Dans la "grammaire" du discours dramatique, on trouvera alors une description formalisée du texte de celui-ci en fonction des actions typiques qu'il manifeste.

On peut envisager plusieurs types différents de formalisation (et de notation) des actions typiques; le plus simple sera probablement de les noter comme des "propositions logiques" (cf Genot 1984) dont le prédicat est une action typique et qui comprend quatre arguments: un sujet et un patient (deux personnages présents, celui qui "produit" et celui qui est "visé" par l'action),[2] un thème (explicitement mentionné dans le texte; le thème pourra être, et est souvent, une action typique) et une attente (de la part du lecteur; ce sera una liste des conséquences que l'action typique actuelle fait prévoir ou attendre). Pour le début d'un scénario, cela pourra donner une notation comme celle-ci:

s(Orazio,Capitano,d(Orazio,Isabella,amour,_),

   (c(Orazio,un Vieux,T,_),

   r+ (Orazio,Isabella,amour,_)));

elle signifie qu'Orazio (qui "produit" l'action) *fait savoir* (=s: action typique[3]) au Capitaine ("visé" par elle) que lui, Orazio, a un désir amoureux envers Isabella (thème) et que le lecteur (qui connaît la description du conflit typique de la *commedia dell'arte* faite par Tessari (1981:102)) s'attend maintenant à en voir surgir un contraste où s'opposent Orazio (le jeune) et un des vieux à propos du thème déjà mentionné (ici noté comme T) et à voir un résultat obtenu, qui sera la satisfaction du désir d'Orazio; dans les actions typiques "secondaires," l'attente du lecteur est indéterminée (ou "neutralisée").

Il doit y avoir une liste finie de telles actions typiques (et peut-être appartiendra-t-elle plutôt à la "grammaire" de l'univers dramatique); alors on pourra avoir dans un dictionnaire-encyclopédie de mots-clés du texte, appartenant à la "grammaire" du discours dramatique, une liste des verbes (ou expressions verbales) qui manifestent l'une ou l'autre de ces actions typiques (comme celle que donne Perruccci des mots du scénario qui indiquent l'entrée/sortie des personnages: "in questo," "in quello," "via" etc. (cit. in Tessari 1981:150)); ainsi "dire," "discorrere," "narrare," "raccontare," "scoprire" indiqueront l'action typique FAIRE SAVOIR, expressions qui contiennent les mots "amore," "amare," "godersi" celle d'un DÉSIR, "offrirsi" un APPUI, "attaccare," "minacciare," "riprendere," "scacciare" un CONTRASTE, etc. Ce ne sont là que des indications qui doivent être précisées et développées: le dictionnaire doit montrer par exemple que "dare a" (une personne) signifie un CONTRASTE, mais "dare / qualcosa / a" peut signifier cela et puis aussi un APPUI ou un RÉSULTAT obtenu. D'autre part, il y aura dans le dictionnaire, des mots-clés qui n'indiquent pas des actions-typiques, mais des relations (autres que celles qu'établissent les actions typiques, mots tels que "padre," "figlio," etc.) ou des thèmes (mots tels que "amore," "maritare," "dinari," etc.); il y aura également des noms propres avec indication de leurs rapport aux rôles-types, etc.

A côté du dictionnaire, il y aura une syntaxe, ou ensemble de règles disant comment peut être utilisé ce dictionnaire-encyclopédie devant le texte, ou discours dramatique, d'un scénario donné.

Une première règle (ou hypothèse à vérifier sur l'*ensemble* des scénarios de Scala) dit que chaque action typique est manifestée par une période
du texte, c'est-à-dire une phrase ou suite de phrases qui se termine avec
un point, et que l'action typique sera spécifiée à partir du verbe principale de cette période. D'autres règles trouvent ensuite les éléments qui
doivent remplir les postes de sujet, de patient—à savoir deux personnages
présents—et de thème. Il faudra certainement ici pouvoir avoir recours à
une analyse grammaticale (au sens traditionnel) de la période, mais sans
que celle-ci ait besoin d'être le fondement de l'ensemble de l'analyse du
discours dramatique.

Enfin certains règles doivent opérer non plus sur le texte, mais sur la
formalisation faite jusqu'ici, pour spécifier ce qu'on peut s'attendre à la
suite de l'action typique actualisée ici, et aussi, probablement, pour pro-
poser une (ou plusieurs) action-typique(s) dominante(s) de la situation; ici
plus qu'avant sans doute, pourra intervenir la compréhension "mémorisée"
des situations qui précèdent.

Voici comment on pourra, dans cette perspective, imaginer la formalisation des premières situations de *Il cavadente* et de *Il marito* (pour
monter aussi la différence qu'il y aura, malgré la réduction que comporte
la formalisation:

IL MARITO

Texte:

ORAZIO racconta al Capitano la cagione dello
(CAPITANO) starsene sconosciuto nella città, l'amor d'Isabella e voler veder di
parlarle innanzi che si scopre al padre. Capitano cerca di distorlo da cotal
amore, essend'ella maritata. Egli: di non poter ciò fare. Capitano gli offerisce
la casa, e parte.

Formalisation:

[s(Ora,Cap,(d(Ora,Isa,amour,_),s-(Ora,padre,prés.,_)),
    (c(X,Ora,T,_),r+(Ora,Isa,amour,_)))
c(Cap,Ora,(T,r+(X,Isa,mariage,_)),
    (c(mari,Ora,T,_),r?(Ora,Isa,amour,_)))
c(Ora,Cap,T,(c(mari,Ora,T,_),r?(Ora,Isa,amour,_)))
a+(Cap,Ora,(T,s-(Ora,padre,prés.,_)),
    (c(mari,Ora,T,_),r+(Ora,Isa,amour,_)))]

IL CAVADENTE

Texte:

PANTALONE dice a Pedrolino l'amor che porta ad

(PEDROLINO) Isabella vedova, e dubitar che Orazio, suo figlio, non sia rivale, e che, di ciò dubitando, aver risoluto di mandarlo allo studio. Pedrolino lo riprende, tenendo da quella d'Orazio. S'attaccano di parole e di fatti: Pantalone dà a Pedrolino e egli le morde un braccio, mostrando d'averlo morduto forte. Pantalone, minacciando, parte, dicendo che per suo conto parli con Franceschina, via.

Formalisation:

[s(Pant,Pedr,(d(Pant,Isa,amour,_),d(Ora,Isa,amour,_),
    d(Pant,Ora,-prés.,_)),
  (c(Ora,Pant,d(Isa,X,amour,_),r+(Ora,Isa,amour,_)))
c(Pedr,Pant,a+(Pedr,Ora,d(Ora,Isa,amour,_),_),
  (c(Ora,Pant,d(Isa,X,amour,_),r+(Ora,Isa,amour,_)))
c(Pant,Pedr,-respect(?),c(Pedr,Pant,blessure,_))
d(Pant,Pedr,s+(Pedr,Fran,d(Pant,Isa,amour,_)),
  (s-(Pedr,Fran,d(Pant,Isa,amour,_),_),
  c(Pedr,Pant,X,_),c(Ora,Pant,d(Isa,X,amour,_),_)))]

Note:

Les prédicats/actions typiques ici sont: s:faire savoir (ou communiquer), d:désirer (ou demander), c:contraste (ou conflit) et r:résultat (ou réalisation); ils peuvent être affirmés (+), niés(-) ou incertains (?). Parmi les arguments, il y a un X=quelqu'un ou quelque-chose, et un _ qui veut dire que l'argument reste indéterminé, imprécis (probablement non-formulé par le lecteur). "amour," "près." (=présence), "mariage," etc. sont des mots-clés indiquant des thèmes,; "T" (dans *Il marito*) est mis pour "d(Ora,Isa,amour,_)" pour abréger; le "(?)" (dans *Il cavadente*) après "-respect" (=manque de respect) signifie que je ne suis pas sûr de cette interprétation. (Cf. aussi plus haut, p 18).[4]

Il n'est pas du tout exclu que cette description formalisée puisse, et doive être modifiée à la suite de discussions dont elle sera peut-être l'objet, mais je crois qu'elle correspond *assez* bien à une compréhension intuitive des deux situations: dans la première, un personnage, qui est jeune, raconte à un autre ses déboires d'amoureux; l'autre essaie de le dissuader de son projet, mais le premier insiste et finit par obtenir l'aide du second; dans la seconde situation, un personnage, qui est vieux, raconte à un autre, son serviteur, ses problèmes d'amoureux; il en résulte un conflit très fort entre eux; le vieux pourtant demande au serviteur de fair connaître à un troisième personnage les problèmes en question.

Il est évident que ces "schémas" des deux situations "cachent" un très grand nombre de problèmes qui restent encore à résoudre avant qu'on puisse parler d'une formalisation réelle; mais j'ai au moins esquissé les directions qu'il faudra suivre, à mon avis, afin d'arriver à une telle formalisation.

A certains égards, cette formalisation de la situation isolée peut rappeller un peu l'analyse en micro-séquences proposée par Elam, mais quand-même, comme on voit, grandement et volontairement simplifiée (du moins pour ce qui regarde la formalisation, même si la notation de celle-ci peut sembler compliquée): l'une et l'autre se proposent de rendre compte de la "dramatisation" à l'oeuvre dans un texte dramatique. Dans un autre contexte, il faudra examiner quel pourra être le rapport entre les deux, par exemple en confrontant cette formalisation d'un scénario, *Il marito*, avec une analyse d'un texte "régulier" correspondant, *Il finto marito*.

L'analyse se poursuivra à un second niveau pour formuler les règles d'une "grammaire" des situations qui aideront à relever ensuite les relations qui s'établissent entre les situations précédemment formalisées. A la base de ces relations il y aura probablement des caractéristiques, ou notions, comme statique/dynamique, -/+changement ou continuité/discontinuité et les règles en question pourront alors être fondées sur la recherche, et le relevé d'éléments communs à la situation actuellement lue et à celles qui précèdent (ou plutôt à leurs actions typiques, et peut-être surtout à celles qui ont été marquées comme dominantes), d'éléments nouveaux et de relations entre eux. A partir d'un tel relevé seront établies les relations entre les situations.

Reste ouverte la question de savoir si cette "grammaire" des situations doit comprendre aussi une sorte de dictionnaire: une classification des situations, ou répertoire des situations-types possibles (analogue par certains côtés, à ceux qui se trouvent dans les "zibaldoni" des comédiants). Si les situations sont "construites," dans la lecture du scénario, à partir du groupe de personnages présents et d'une liste (ou répertoire) des actions typiques possibles, il n'est pas sûr que la compréhension du texte se fonde sur un dictionnaire des situations. (Mais voir aussi ci-dessous, à propos de la focalisation et de la distinction entre situations présentées directement et situations possibles.)

Dans la "grammaire" de l'univers dramatique, par contre, dominera sans doute une sorte de dictionnaire; là seront fixés le système des rôles-types, celui des différentes "maisons," les rapports familiaux et sociaux possibles qui en résultent, etc.

Les règles (de la syntaxe) de cette "grammaire" de l'univers dramatique, et de la fabula, seront des règles reliées à un conflit typique dont il sera présupposé qu'il est unique et commun à tous les scénarios (cf ce qu'en dit Tessari, cité plus haut), donc des règles d'ordre très général, peu spécifiques et différenciant peu; c'est là un aspect de la "simplicité" du scénario de la *commedia dell'arte*. Pourtant il y a certainement de telles règles, simples mais fondamentales, à l'oeuvre dans l'"emploi" des règles des deux autres "grammaires," ainsi par exemple lorsque le lecteur "construit" l'attente de telle ou telle action typique.

Enfin c'est une "grammaire" de l'univers dramatique qui permettra de se faire une idée assez simple de ce que peut signifier la "focalisation" dans un texte dramatique: connaissant une telle "grammaire" (ou le conflit typique qu'elle formalise) on pourra opposer la ou les situation(s) présentée(s) directement par le texte, à celle(s) qui aurai(en)t été possible(s), ou on pourra confronter deux textes différents à l'aide d'une "mesure" commune, pour voir comment la "focalisation" se réalise concrètement.

Ainsi, lorsqu'on compare le premier acte d'*Il marito* avec celui d'*Il cavadente*, on y verra comment l'opposition de base du conflit typique (entre jeunes et vieux) est présentée différemment: de la part du Jeune et de la part du Vieux, et de sorte qu'une différence apparaît aussi dans la composition du premier acte: dans *Il marito*, il y a une sorte de composition en "contre-point" où l'amour qu'Orazio porte à Isabella obtient l'aide du Capitaine (qui se transforme de personnage secondaire en jeune amoureux, et heureux), puis celle de Flaminia et aussi de Pedrolino, et pourtant—malgré les efforts et les inventions de ce dernier, tout dévoué à son jeune maître—conduit à un conflit entre les deux jeunes amoureux; dans *Il cavadente* par contre, le premier acte fait presqu'oublier l'opposition de base et les amours des jeunes, pour montrer comment se construit (se prépare, se met en oeuvre et se conclut) une intrigue basée sur l'opposition entre les vieux et les serviteurs.

3. Pour terminer je résumerai brièvement ce que je pense avoir fait dans cette intervention:
a) j'ai assumé qu'on puisse, et qu'il soit légitime de *lire* le scénario de la *commedia dell'arte*, et que l'analyse du scénario dans cette perspective puisse être utile pour l'élaboration d'une théorie du texte dramatique;
b) j'ai assumé que le texte dramatique—et donc aussi le scénario—soit formé d'une suite de situations, et que la compréhension du texte se fait à partir d'une compréhension de chacune de ces situations dans l'ordre où le texte les présente au lecteur;
c) j'ai proposé l'hypothèse d'une description formalisée de la situation ainsi conçue;
d) enfin j'ai esquissé une hypothèse concernant les relations entre les situations de l'ensemble qui constitue un texte dramatique, et j'ai distingué

entre une dramatisation et une focalisation, notions qui regardent respectivement la structure (structuration/composition) de la situation et la structure du texte entier.

University of Copenhagen

NOTES

1 Cf également la position de Pirandello, que A. Alessio a citée dans son intervention.
2 La scène à deux personnages est en effet, comme l'a montré T. Fitzpatrick dans son intervention, la configuration la plus habituelle dans les scénarios de Scala.
3 Cf encore l'intervention de T. Fitzpatrick, qui a relevé cette action typique, ou acte de parole, comme la plus fréquente.
4 J'ai noté, dans la formalisation d'*Il marito*, que le lecteur s'attend à voir un contraste (ou conflit) se développer entre un mari (d'Isabella) et Orazio; un autre lecteur, qui, comme celui que G. Ferroni a présenté dans son intervention, sait qu'il s'agit d'un *faux mari*, fera probablement d'autres prévisions; mais il ne me semble pas que le texte dramatique qu'est ce scénario présuppose en soi ce savoir chez le lecteur.

TEXTES CITÉS

De Marinis, M 1979: "Lo spettacolo come testo (II)" in *Versus* 22;
_____1982: *Semiotica del teatro*, Milano.
Dodd, W 1983: "Incipit ed esposizione" in AAVV: *Interazione, dialogo, convenzioni*, Bologna
Dressler (ed.) 1978: *Current Trends in Textlinguistics*, Berlin/NY
Elam, K 1980: *The Semiotics of Theatre and Drama*, London
Genot, G 1984: *Grammaire et récit*, Nanterre
Hanon, Ph 1974: "Analyse du récit: éléments pour un lexique," Urbino
Jansen, S 1973: "Qu'est-ce qu'une situation dramatique?" in *Orbis Litterarum* XXVII
_____ 1976: *Analyse de la forme dramatique du "Mensonge" de Nathalie Sarraute*, Copenhague
_____ 1983: "Fondamenti per una teoria del testo drammatico" in AAVV: *Interazione, dialogo, convenzioni*, Bologna
Marotti, F 1976: Introduzione in Scala 1976
Mic, C 1927: *La commedia dell'arte*, Paris
Nicolls, A 1963: *The World of Harlequin*, Cambridge
Pugliatti, P 1983: "*Given* and *new* nelle *histories*" in AAVV: *Interazione, dialogo, convenzioni*, Bologna
Rossi-Landi, F 1980: "I residui dei segni" in AAVV: *Scienza, Linguaggio e Metafilosofia*, Napoli

Scala, F 1976: *Il teatro delle favole rappresentative* (a cura di F. Marotti), Milano

Segre, C 1974: *Le strutture e il tempo*, Torino

———— 1984: *Teatro e romanzo*, Torino

Serpieri, A 1978: "Ipotesi di segmentazione del testo teatrale" in AAVV: *Come comunica il teatro*, Milano

Short, M H 1981: "Discourse Analysis and the Analysis of Drama" in *Applied Linguistics*, vol. II

Soelberg, N 1985: "Le paradoxe du JE-narrateur. Approche narratologique de *l'Etranger* de Camus" in *Revue Romane* 20,1

Tessari, R 1969: *La commedia dell'arte nel '600*, Firenze

———— 1981: *La commedia dell'arte: la maschera e l'ombra*, Milano

Domenico Pietropaolo

Improvisation as a Stochastic Composition Process

Improvisation has long been regarded as the chief defining feature of the *commedia dell'arte* but only in the past few years has there been a concerted effort to elucidate the conceptual content of the term and to establish the exact parameters of the historical phenomenon that it designates. Modern scholarship, in its *pars destruens*, has done much to correct various misconceptions, which had been generated by amateurish approaches to the subject and by the easy approximations of popularising accounts, but in its *pars construens* it has not yet determined the precise form of improvisation and has not yet seriously broached the question of whether this notion in the theory of the *commedia dell'arte* is a special case of a more general idea of improvisation, equally applicable to diverse art forms, such as other types of comedy and buffoonery, lyric poetry, mime and music. The latter and more ambitious task, however, cannot be fruitfully undertaken until the question of the form of improvisation has been adequately answered, since it is clearly on the level of form alone that the theoretical implications of analogy among heterogeneous art objects can be pursued with any degree of rigour.

This paper is an attempt to formalise the notion of improvisation in the *commedia dell'arte* tradition and to describe its distinctive features without making substantive references to the factual content of specific realisations in practice. Formalisation is here understood as the replacement of the common-sense description of this phenomenon, which is inevitably open to subjective input, with a set of clearly definable variables and with a law of association which relates them to one another and organises them into a coherent whole. This in effect means circumscribing the notion's formal aspects and ridding them of all accidental references to actual content, since such references would anchor our understanding of improvisation to specific cases and ultimately invalidate any claim to generality.

The starting point for such a formalisation is the now well-known fact that improvisation is a text-building process which is as far from the recitation of a fixed written work as it is from the spontaneous sort of creation *ex nihilo* that amateurs and romantics have at times imagined it to be. In recent years several scholars have pointed out—on the strength of contemporary theoretical accounts, such as those of Cecchini and Perrucci, and of detailed surveys of the texts and contemporary critical literature available on them—that in the *commedia dell'arte* improvisation is principally a question of collaboration among the cast for the purpose of conjoining signs drawn from the repertoires of the individual actors and harmonised into a plot-creating strategy.[1] It is, in other words, a process of composition—aiming, that is, at the formation of composite units by the addition of discrete parts. And this means that improvisation is not an elementary and self-contained notion but a relational concept. In the simplest case possible in a dialogue situation, it involves at least two variables, which it grafts onto one another in the formation of stimulus-and-response elementary units of communication: given the stimulus produced by one character, the process of improvisation must determine the textually appropriate response of his interlocutor, which is then regarded as another stimulus, itself awaiting a response in the evolving script.

In this context it is significant that contemporary theoreticians—as if to stress the stimulus-response nature of all textual segments and the discreteness of their components—forbid an actor to speak at the same time as another and to leave the performance space before his interlocutor has finished his response, since in the first case overlapping would render both utterances unintelligible, and in the second case the absence of the stimulus-emitting actor would cause a loss of continuity and consequently of textual coherence. It seems, in other words, that improvisation is a compositional function which, upon application to an actor's communicational stimulus, assigns to it a sequel from the repertoire of the other actor, in such a manner that the formation of stimulus-response composite units of communication has the intrinsic goal of contributing to the logical configuration of the text and the extrinsic one of immediately gratifying the audience.

In the case of two characters, which must have been by far the most common in the entire tradition, the form of this composition process may be charted in the following manner:

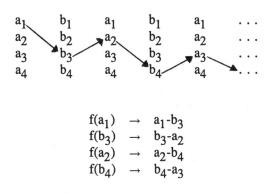

$$f(a_1) \rightarrow a_1\text{-}b_3$$
$$f(b_3) \rightarrow b_3\text{-}a_2$$
$$f(a_2) \rightarrow a_2\text{-}b_4$$
$$f(b_4) \rightarrow b_4\text{-}a_3$$

$$a_1 b_3 a_2 b_4 a_3 \ldots$$

The columns, arranged horizontally in temporal sequence, designate paradigmatically the sets of physical and verbal signs available respectively to actors a and b. The segments $a_1 - b_3, b_3 - a_2, a_2 - b_4, b_4 - a_3$ are examples of composite units of communications produced in a stimulus-response exchange when the compositional function f is applied to the first of the two variables. And finally the syntagmatic chain $a_1 b_3 a_2 b_4 a_3 \ldots$ represents the subsequent performance text in the process of formation. In more complex cases, the paradigmatic principle remains exactly the same—another column needs to be added for the third character—but the syntagmatic principle must take into account a much greater number of possibilities resulting from the different forms of collusion available to the characters.

From this schematism, which represents the minimum formal apparatus of improvisation, it is very easy to see that, as a composition process, improvisation has several interesting properties, all of which can now be formally established. The most basic of them, of course, is the length of the columns, which is a graphic indication of the *potential* range of competence of each actor in the company and hence of the company as a whole, since the number and complexity of plot situations that the company can collectively sustain is directly proportional to the combinatorial possibilities of each actor's inventory in the formation of composite units of communication. Of course the *actual* range of competence of an actor in the composition process depends on personal factors as well, and especially his power of quick recollection, which he needs in order to scan with his mind the entire collection of verbal and physical expressions before formulating his response to a given stimulus. The strength of memory required also varies directly with the fullness of the repertoire. It is significant in this context that several accounts of the *commedia dell'arte* from the seventeenth and eighteenth centuries describe memory as one of the most important assets of a performer. Even the historian of literature Francesco Saverio Quadrio—who, however, cannot be credited with having understood the historical development of the *commedia dell'arte*—saw very clearly on this point, and labelled "luoghi topici" all such repertory terms.[2] And it is scarcely necessary to recall that topics, to which Quadrio alludes, was that branch of rhetoric on which rested the very concept of artificial memory, and hence of memory as a skill that could be acquired by technical training.[3]

Furthermore, since all the elements in an actor's collection are conceived as possible responses to some stimulus, which is itself found in the inventory of another actor, it follows that none of them has a gratuitous purpose. Ideally every single verbal and gestural structure available to a member of the cast can be generated on stage as the second element of a composite unit of communication. The ideal company, therefore, is a perfectly co-ordinated system engaged in the collective assemblage of a performance, since, as a composition process, improvisation is necessarily and at once a function of individual competence and a function of concerted teamwork.

A corollary that immediately follows from this consideration is that a *commedia dell'arte* company cannot be very large, since each of its members must be thoroughly familiar with the verbal and gestural repertoires of the other actors with whom he might be on stage. Historically this was in fact the case. We know from Luigi Riccoboni that whereas in the rest of Europe the average company had at least thirty members, in Italy that number was never greater than eleven.[4] A second corollary is that the average *commedia dell'arte* actor can enjoy little potential mobility from company to company—since this is logically neither in the interest of the groups concerned nor in his own—and that a company that suffers the loss of a member is in serious trouble. And this too is corroborated historically. In 1700 Evaristo Gherardi observed that the replacement of an actor in a *commedia dell'arte* company was an extremely difficult task, since—we may add—the new actor would very quickly have to become acquainted with the improvisational possibilities of his new colleagues and they, in turn, with his.[5]

In formal and abstract terms, a perfectly co-ordinated company, whose members have distinct and necessary roles to play in the collective improvisation of the text, may be described as a system of interrelated parts which, from an initial state of rest at the beginning of a scene, goes through a series of transformations that take it from a state, in which it is dominated by an actor performing a segment of his repertoire, to another, in which a second actor claims the spotlight, and so on, until one of them engenders a verbal or gestural expression which cannot be further elaborated without causing a discontinuity in stage configuration, thereby marking the text's transition to another scene. A performing company engaged in stage improvisation is a system of interrelated components moving in concert through a succession of states, which constitute the improvised text as perceived by the audience.

The question now arises whether there is a general principle which conditions the occurrence of a given segment at a particular point in the textual sequence. Because at any given time the possible states that the system can enter are all items in actual repertoires, they must have all occurred in various combinations in the theatrical tradition prior to the performance in question, and this means that their formal history as second elements in composite units of communication can be expressed as relative frequencies of occurrence in the verbal and gestural language of the *commedia dell'arte*. Relative frequency, however, is just another name for probability. If in the theatrical tradition the composite units $a_i - b_i, a_i - b_{i+1}, a_i - b_{i+2}$, where i is any number, have all occurred, though with different frequencies, they may now recur with the corresponding probabilities in a performance that purports to be part of that tradition. This may be represented graphically as

$$a_i \rightleftharpoons \begin{matrix} b_i \\ b_{i+1} \\ b_{i+2} \end{matrix}$$

The resulting sequence $a_i - b_i, a_i - b_{i+1}, a_i - b_{i+2}$ is ordered according to decreasing probability of occurrence.

The system's progression through a succession of states until it enters one that is not susceptible of change—or, in other words, the production of linked textual segments until the end of the scene—in some way involves the relative probability of occurrence of each state in the series. Stated in technical language, all of this is equivalent to saying that *commedia dell'arte* improvisation is a stochastic composition process with an absorbing barrier.[6] It is a process for the production of colligated theatrical signs conditioned by the relative probabilities with which they occur in the sign universe of the entire *commedia dell'arte* tradition. Once activated at the beginning of a situation, whose general character and orientation as defined in the scenario delimit the subset of that universe in which appropriate elements are to be found, the system composes paired units of communication and, by assigning to each of its components the double function of stimulus and response, harmonises them into a structurally coherent series. The series finally comes to an end when it reaches a sign which cannot function as a stimulus unless the system's field of operation is shifted to a different subset, corresponding to a new stage situation. The stochastic nature of the process warrants that the statistical distribution of individual signs and composite segments prior to the performance in question may be regarded as a basis for predicting the chance of their recurrence or for estimating the degree to which their presence in the evolving text may be expected by the audience.

Of course, this description of improvisation as a stochastic process does not imply that each member of the cast must become an accurate calculator of probabilities every time that he has to respond to an interlocutor and that he automatically or mechanically gives the response with the highest probability value. Nor does it suggest that other personal and creative factors—such as an intuitive knowledge of what is appropriate at a given time—do not play significant roles in the company's collaborative production of text. Since we are dealing with the formal possibilities of an exact model and not with the specific realisations of individual companies in the context of local traditions, we are not compelled to take into account precise numerical data—which are not available in any case—but only relative proportions, such as may be familiar to the cast through training and experience. But the label "stochastic process" does however imply that the reception that is accorded to a performance by the audience is definitely governed by the frequency distribution of each stage expression in the theatrical tradition familiar to the audience, and this in turn affects an author's choice of response.

A performer must, in fact, decide whether to surprise the audience by producing the least expected response or to give them exactly what they expect along with the pleasure that comes with the sense of having made an accurate prediction. Clearly the problem cannot be resolved once and for all and then mechanically applied to every textual situation. Between the two extremes of, on the one hand, predictability—which is perceivable only as structural regularity in accordance with the standards of tradition—and, on the other hand, unpredictability—which instead consists in the recognition of a disruptive random element in the predicted configuration of composite units—there may already be a number of repertory options available to the actor, who can, in any case, give rise to a quasi-continuum of solutions by making small modifications to his standard responses in order to make them suitable for the occasion. The difficulty lies in striking the correct balance each time. Excessive order is as annoying as excessive randomness. Slight deviations from convention are a sign of originality and have the merit of enriching the vocabulary of tradition; major deviations from standard responses may easily appear to be gratuitous novelty and are in any case artistically unintelligible in the context of tradition. There can be no doubt that some controlled randomness is artistically desirable in the evolving text, since the audience's sense of surprise, intrigue and comic suspense depends entirely on the disruptive force that animates an otherwise fully predictable assemblage of signs. But neither can there be any doubt that unless the performance makes an abundant enough use of the code familiar and artistically acceptable to the audience, it will be considered either an unsuccessful and wasted effort or else a scheme to subvert tradition. And since the comic effect of a performance depends very little on the story and very much on the individual details of each plot situation, such considerations will have to be made by the cast in the formation of every composite unit, whose second component will ultimately depend on the actor's perception of what the audience anticipates as the most likely sequel in each case.

Now all of this demonstrates that, within the restraints of the plot line, improvisation, as a stochastic process, has another important formal feature, which is that the chance of occurrence of a given state depends on the occurrence of the previous one alone—intrinsically because it has the character of a response to the stimulus represented by the previous state, and extrinsically because the audience's anticipation of the occurrence of a given sign is based on its frequency in the stage vocabulary in combination with the one that immediately precedes and provokes it. Processes that satisfy this condition are known as Markovian chains and constitute a special class of stochastic systems whose usefulness as a conceptual apparatus in the development of composition and performance models is potentially great. There are in fact several art forms (music and farce, for instance) in which compositions and performances involve random variables that satisfy the Markovian condition and that can hence be analysed by means of the elaborate formalisms that have been developed in the theoretical exploration of simple stochastic processes as well as by means of the theories that have been developed through their application.[7]

In particular, information theory is a powerful tool for the analysis of all composition processes, including *commedia dell'arte* improvisation viewed as a plot-building strategy.[8] In the taxonomy of this theory the correlative of structural predictability is internal redundancy while that of randomness is entropy and, consequently, information itself, which is a function of entropy. This being given, the plot-building aspect of improvisation may be described and analysed as a process moving toward cumulative redundancy, since from a high entropic situation at the beginning of the action, when the plot-building aspect of composite units is charged with consequential information, we come to the final resolution of the action in a scene that has very few surprises to offer. The most immediate corollary of this is that—on the theoretical level at least—improvisation requires greater skill in the initial scenes, when, in addition to pleasing the audience, the actors must create a situation laden with the comic tension necessary to trigger off the action, than it does in the final ones, when the number of ways in which the action can come to an end, as a consequence of what precedes it, is so limited that the actual choice will be a structural redundancy. In the ideal situation entropy and redundancy are inverse proportions, not only in the first and final scenes, but all throughout the text, although their serial and cumulative values must clearly change from one composite unit to the other.

The need to strike the right balance, on the one hand, between predictability and surprise in order to gratify the audience, and, on the other hand, between structural redundancy and entropy, in order to give the sense of consequential resolution to the plot, and the further need to do so at all transition points between composite units of stage communication always in concert with the rest of the company—these things make improvisation an extremely difficult technique to acquire. After inventing the death of one of his masters, Goldoni's Truffaldino comments with comic *sprezzatura* on his own technique of improvisation: "I say the first thing that comes to my mouth."[9] But Truffaldino, as Brighella knows, is scarcely the fool he appears to be. The great actor Antonio Sacchi, who improvised the part of Truffaldino before Goldoni turned the scenario into a full text, may well have said those very words with the purpose of making a metatextual reference to his own celebrated skill as an improviser and an allusion to a well-known improvisational canon of tradition. In the late seventeenth century Andrea Perrucci had written in his manual on improvisation that only the best actors can say "quidquid in buccam venit" without faultering at some point.[10] Like Truffaldino and Antonio Sacchi, the improvising performer strives to give his improvisation the appearance of a spontaneous and effortless act, but both he and the audience know that beneath his mask his mind is moving much faster than his tongue and working even more strenuously than his muscles.

University of Toronto

NOTES

1 See especially Roberto Tessari, *Commedia dell'Arte: La maschera e l'ombra* (Milano: Mursia, 1984), pp. 75–95; Cesare Molinari, *La Commedia dell'Arte* (Milano: Mondadori, 1985), pp. 37–42.

2 *Storia e ragione d'ogni poesia* (Milano: 1744), quoted by Ferdinando Taviani and Mirella Schino in *Il segreto della Commedia dell'Arte* (Firenze: Usher, 1982), p. 318.

3 On the art of memory in the Renaissance see Frances Yates *The Art of Memory* (Harmondsworth: Penguin, 1966).

4 Luigi Riccoboni, *Histoire du "Théâtre Italien"* (Paris: Guerin, 1738), p. 36.

5 Evaristo Gherardi, *Le théâtre italien* (1700) in Taviani and Schino, p. 310.

6 On stochastic processes see Fred Attneave, "Processi compositivi stocastici," in *Estetica e teoria dell'informazione*, ed. Umberto Eco (Milano: Bompiani, 1972), pp. 119–130; E. S. Wentzel, *Operations Research*, tr. M. G. Edelev (Moscow: Mir, 1983), especially chapter V.

7 See for example Domenico Pietropaolo, "La farsa de Zöhan Zavatino di Gian Giorgio Alione," *Studi piemontesi* III (1974), pp. 264–275.

8 On information theory, see C. E. Shannon and W. Weaver, *The Mathematical Theory of Communication* (Urbana: The University of Illinois Press, 1949); J. R. Pierce, *An Introduction to Information Theory* (New York: Dover, 1980).

9 III,ii. "Digo quel che me vien alla bocca"—"Il servitore di due padroni" III.ii, *Tutte le opere di Carlo Goldoni*, 4th ed., 14 vols. (Verona: Mondadori, 1959) 4, p. 63.

10 Andrea Perrucci, *Dell'arte rappresentativa premeditata e all'improvviso*, ed. G. Bragaglia (Firenze: Sansoni, 1961), p. 159.

Tim Fitzpatrick

Flaminio Scala's Prototypal Scenarios: Segmenting the Text/Performance

Many factors have inhibited detailed critical discussion of the scenarios of the *commedia dell'arte*. First, scholars of dramatic literature with an unshakeable belief (however ill-founded) in the completeness of the fully-scripted playtext as a basis for discussion of character, plot and action are repelled by the synthetic brevity of the scenario format. Next, with the exception of Flaminio Scala's *Teatro delle favole rappresentative* (published in Venice in 1611), the large collections remain substantially unpublished.[1] Then, the myth of the *commedia dell'arte* as a predominantly gestural theatre has ensured that the scenarios have been plundered for their *lazzi*, rather than analysed as elements in a performance-structure. And finally, despite the fact that Scala's published collection clearly reflects the work of some of the major professional companies active in the late sixteenth century[2] and is therefore of capital importance, critics have been reticent to examine it thoroughly in relation to performance precisely because it *was* published, and hence can be suspected of no longer reflecting accurately the actors' originals.[3]

This article is in response to such reticence, since I believe—and the reasons for my belief will become clear from the discussion which follows—that this reticence is unfounded, and that the scenarios as published do reflect substantially the original manuscripts used by the actors, thus constituting invaluable evidence of a particular performance practice. The scenarios derive from a form of theatrical production in which suitably trained actors performed plays with limited preparation,[4] the dialogue being provided not by a single playwright, but by the actors themselves in concert.[5] For this reason to speak of "Scala's scenarios" is a necessary oversimplification, the collective nature of the enterprise precluding any attribution to Scala of the sole responsibility for the dramaturgical solutions implicit in the scenarios which he published.

Scala's scenarios manifest what might be termed schematic pragmatism, a constant strategy which, I suggest, was directly related to performance: to simplify and schematise the dramatic action in such a way as to render less laborious the work of the actors. This pragmatism manifests itself primarily through techniques of segmentation of the scenario, or, more precisely, of the performance to which the scenario relates. In other words, the segmentation I am referring to is not necessarily and directly a segmentation of the published text (though at some levels this is so); I am suggesting rather that there are textual indications from which we can infer segmentation of the performance on both of its axes, namely the *diachronic* (an analysis of which concerns the manner in which the various elements of performance succeed each other in time from one moment to the next), and the *synchronic* (an analysis of which concerns the manner in which the various elements of performance are combined at any one moment).

It is this continuing dialectical relationship of interdependence between scenario and performance to which I am alluding in my title: analysis of the scenarios reveals performance-elements (especially in regard to the segmentation of performance) deeply embedded in their textual structure— so embedded that when performed the scenarios will inevitably re-embed such elements in the performance, thus strengthening not only the force of the performance elements, but also the force of the scenarios' own function as notation of, and hence determining element in, the performance-process.

The discussion which follows constitutes the first step in a long-term project which aims at the eventual collation and comparison of all the Italian scenarios on the basis of the presence and density of the sorts of performance characteristics which I have isolated in Scala's prototypal collection.

1)   The scene-unit—*primary diachronic segmentation*

The primary technique of diachronic segmentation of the dramatic action involves breaking up such action into a large number of small, manageable units each involving only a small number of characters. The fifty scenarios of Scala's collection are each divided into three acts, which are further subdivided into a large number of scenes (some fifteen or so).[6] This subdivision into scenes is signified typographically by a new line of text, and the basis of such subdivision is purely functional: the entrance of a new character. The functional nature of this subdivision (rather than a division based on thematic or plot units) is a first indication of the pragmatic nature of the scenarios. It is thus a simple matter to calculate the number

of characters involved in a scene, merely by adding the number of characters left on stage after the previous scene to the number of characters
indicated in the left-hand margin as entering for the new scene. But this
is not to say that all these characters are actually on stage for the whole
scene, since the *exit* of a character does not constitute a division into a
new scene (perhaps a further indication of the pragmatic organisation of
these texts);[7] in fact, in over one quarter of all the scenes in Scala's fifty
scenarios, at least one character will exit in mid-scene.

In order therefore to calculate the number of characters actually on stage
at any one point, it is necessary to go beyond the typographical distinctions
of the scenario, and work from the basis of a shorter scene-unit which takes
account of these mid-scene exits. If we take both entrances and exits as
markers of a basic scene-unit (i.e. by a stringent application of the "French
Scene") we find that on average, instead of fifteen scenes per act, we have
around twenty-two scene-units per act. More importantly, this enables us
to calculate more precisely how many characters are on stage at any one
time: this averages out at only three.

An average of only three characters on stage is significantly low, especially if it is borne in mind that these three are from what nowadays would
be considered a large cast comprising on average eleven named or prominent characters.[8] Thus on average barely a quarter of the available cast are
on stage at any one moment, and eight out of eleven are backstage; and if
we discount the final half-dozen scenes of Act III, in which there is usually an aggregation of characters culminating in the final marriage scenes,
the average drops to around 2.5—clearly much of the onstage action is
constituted by scene-units involving only one or two characters.

Thus the first characteristic of these scenarios and of the performance
which they imply is that of a large number of scene-units, many of them
(well over half, for example, in Day 27) involving only one or two characters; these units are punctuated by a large number of entrances and
exits. This pattern is so general to the collection that it is difficult to
escape the conclusion that we are dealing with a deliberate minimisation
of the number of characters involved in the action at any one time. This
indeed seems to be Scala's first technical discovery: to work on the basis of a scene-unit which often involves only one or two characters, thus
achieving a simplification of the action and (more importantly) of the interaction between the characters. Between two characters the interactional
possibilities are not complex; the relationship between Pantalone and Arlecchino may well have a multitude of aspects and be subject to subtle
shifts and changes, but it remains a single relationship. However, with the

addition of a third characters such as Franceschina, there is an immediate exponential explosion of possible relationships; as well as the single relationships (Arlecchino-Pantalone, Pantalone-Franceschina, Franceschina-Arlecchino) there are the triadic relationships in which alliances might be formed on the basis of sex (Arlecchino-Pantalone vs. Franceschina), social status (Arlecchino-Franceschina vs. Pantalone), or common sense (Pantalone-Franceschina vs. Arlecchino). Clearly the negotiation of such complexities on the part of actors using the techniques of rapid preparation of the *commedia dell'arte* is no laughing matter (a consideration which has led some Italian scholars, as we shall see below, to the conclusion that the actors cannot have afforded to indulge in much real flexibility in performance), since it requires a talent for ensemble playing, quick-wittedness and training of a very high order.

For this reason the utilisation of the small scene-unit with a maximum of two characters seems designed to minimise this sort of interactional complexity and its concomitant problems of "blocking."[9] Scala achieves this small scene-unit principally by the strategic engineering of exits; the use of an exit once the character has made his or her contribution to the dramatic action is obviously of greater strategic value than its alternative, that of minimising entrances.[10] In this regard Scala's scenarios are quite different to modern dramatic convention; whereas we are accustomed to exits which are motivated either from onstage (e.g. a character ordered off) or from offstage (e.g. a character called off), Scala makes extensive use of the unmotivated exit. Occasionally exits are motivated in the manners suggested above, but for the vast majority the scenarios offer no explicit motivating force, and indeed at times the exits seem to run against all normal logic.

In some cases motivated and unmotivated exits occur side by side, as in Day 16, Act I, Scene 13:[11]

FLAMINIA

[. . .] Laughing at him, she enters the house.

PANTALONE

He likewise, to do what Pedrolino has ordered.

While Pantalone's exit is motivated by the plot, Flaminia's is not, but is facilitated by the flourish of the exit-line, or in this case exit-gesture.

An almost cynical use of unmotivated exit occurs in Day 2, Act II, scene 3; Morat, a slave (actually Flavio in disguise) overhears Orazio talking to the Captain about his (Morat's) long-lost beloved. At the news that she is still alive, Morat faints, and is revived by Orazio, the Captain and Franceschina:

FRANCESCHINA

with vinegar; all crowd around and revive Morat (who was watching as Orazio was speaking to the Captain, hence the reason for his fainting). Orazio excuses himself to go and find Cintio to have Arlecchino released. The Captain asks Morat what is the matter, but he begs him not to inquire. the Capain asks Franceschina to kiss her mistress's hand for him, and exits. Franceschina flirts with Morat, and goes into the house. Morat rages against Love and Fortune.

This final soliloquy from Morat is the functional reason for the three preceding mid-scene exits, since it provides background information for the audience as well as developing the plot (as it is overheard by Pedrolino). The motivation for Orazio's exit is only marginally related to the plot (since Cintio has just, in Orazio's presence, promised to have Arlecchino released), the Captain is provided with a rhetorical flourish to cover an unmotivated exit, and Franceschina simply goes back into the house. It may well be that such an exit might have been motivated by the actress in her character's dialogue, so that what seems unmotivated in the scenario might well have seemed motivated in performance;[12] nevertheless the three characters seem to share a common assumption that Morat, once recovered, needs no further attention and some soliloquial privacy.

An excellent example of the manner in which the characters come and go with ease is provided in Day 16, Act I, scene 9:

CAPTAIN

struts around the two women, and exits. Laura sends Flaminia into the house, and stays to have some fun with the Captain. They play a love-scene.

The Captain's wandering across the stage to attract Laura's attention, and then exiting to enable her to get rid of Flaminia, is emblematic of a much wider pattern of movement in these scenarios. The stage represents a public space—a street or square—onto which face various houses, usually with doors and windows giving onto the stage.[13] The area represented by the stage is thus a very limited index, a small segment of a wider dramatic world in which the characters spend most of their time (since on average eight out of eleven are offstage). The characters periodically appear from this offstage "world," play out their scene, and return to it; the pull of this densely-populated offstage segment of the dramatic world will also affect the audience, enabling it to accept readily a convention of unmotivated exits which are more or less natural returns to "home base."

Thus, the ramifications of this pattern of absence are far-reaching. While it necessarily entails a large number of entrances and exits, at the same time it relieves problems of motivating such exits, so facilitating the minimisation of onstage characters and the segmentation of the dramatic action into a chain of miniscule units, many with only one or two characters. Each link remains small and manageable, the interpersonal transactions simple and straightforward.

In this light, that part of the dramatic action constituted by the loves of the four or more young lovers is particularly interesting. Mic has noted that this aspect of the *commedia dell' arte* has the characteristics of a chain: A loves B, but B loves C, who in turn is in love with D, who loves A. This pattern is by no means general in Scala's scenarios,[14] but it is reasonably common, occurring usually as a three-link chain in something over half the scenarios. However, it is very much the exception to find the three characters involved in the chain on stage at the same time. Marotti's indication of the "scena interzata" (Day 12, Act I, scene 8) as emblematic of the scenarios[15] is true in one regard: in general the complications of such chains sustain and constitute the principal dramatic action. But it is not at all emblematic of the way in which such chains are usually represented on the stage. In the scene in question, Isabella, the Captain and Flaminia are on stage together, but the indication that they do a "scena interzata" (*interzata* signifying a third element inserted between two others) signals an exception rather than a rule. This is a specific piece of set business being alluded to; we can only hypothesise as to how it might have been played, but the jargon itself indicates something very specific, a set piece to enable them to play this difficult and unusual scene involving three links in the amorous chain. Such examples are rare (another one will be discussed below), and are usually fight-and-exit scenes;[16] in general the love-chains are ostended two links at a time (A and B, B and C, etc.).

2) Within the scene-unit: further diachronic segmentation

When we move from an examination of the primary segmentation into scene-units to examine what happens *within* such units, we see a range of techniques developed to respond to the situation in which there are more than two characters on stage: once unnecessary characters have been eliminated by the techniques outlined in the previous section, what can be done to simplify the scenes which involve more than two characters?

The first of such techniques involves further diachronic segmentation of the dramatic action. I have posited a scene-unit marked by entrances and exits as the basic organisational unit of plot and dramatic action; but these scene-units are composed of even smaller segments or sub-units, each of which answers the question *"Who does/says what, to whom, next?"*, and so can be distinguished as constituted by a single act or speech-act combined with a change in deictic orientation.[17] An examination of a number of examples is the best way to see this sub-unit at work; a seemingly complex scene between three characters, such as Day 3, Act I, scene 1, is indicative:

PANTALONE, ORAZIO, FLAVIO

Pantalone learns from the two brothers that their father Graziano, though old, is in love with Franceschina, and that he is not finding suitable wives for them as he should be. Pantalone tries to calm them, saying that love is more appropriate in the aged than in the young. Flavio, knowing that Orazio is his rival in love, makes clear to him that their father has had him study in order to graduate, not to find a wife. In the end they beg Pantalone, as friend of their father, to dissuade him from his foolish ways, and they leave. Pantalone remains, admitting that he too is in love with Franceschina.

Scenes like this, with their markedly discursive style, have persuaded some scholars that Scala initiated a general revision of his source materials when preparing the scenarios for publication, to make them more accessible to a reading pubic.[18] But even a scene such as this is nothing more than a syntagmatic compilation of speech-acts punctuated by deictic changes, a pragmatic blueprint for the organisation of the scene by the actors involved. The single acts are easily identified:

1) The characters enter;
2) The young men beg Pantalone's help;
3) Pantalone tires to pacify them;
4) Flavio reminds Orazio of his personal priorities;
5) They both repeat their appeal to Pantalone;
6) The young men exit;

---

7) Pantalone confesses that he too loves Franceschina.

Note that in the first scene-unit (sub-units 1–6) there is a further principle of schematisation at work, whereby two of the three characters are treated as a single unit: the young men act, or are acted upon, together in units 2, 3, 5 and 6. But with only seven sub-units for around one hundred words, this is not one of Scala's more economical scenarios. Most of the scenarios have a far greater density, being composed of very brief sub-units of around six words each, rather than fourteen words per sub-unit, as is the case here. Despite the occasional discursive scenario, statistically

Scala's collection is very much in line with the other collections, putting paid to the myth that Scala generally revised and expanded the whole corpus to make the scenarios more accessible to a reading public.[19] The stylistic differences to the other collections are of another order, which will be discussed below.

Closer to Scala's statistical norm is Day 21, Act III, scene 3, where there are five characaters on stage. Orazio, Flavio and Pedrolino are joined by the Captain and his servant Arlecchino:

CAPTAIN, ARLECCHINO

Captain tells Arlecchino that he will get even with him; he greets the lovers, and tells them the Doctor has given him some excellent wine; he exits. Pedrolino sends Arlecchino into the house to tell the ladies they will soon be happy; then whispering in the young men's ears, he sends them to dress up as ghosts, using costumes from their friend's shop. They exit, Pedrolino remains.

The schematic and schematising force of the scenario is clearly based on a succession of speech-acts punctuated by changes in deictic orientation; first the scene is segmented into three scene-units by the mid-scene exits of the Captain and then Arlecchino; and each scene-unit is composed of a number of sub-units, distinguished by changes in illocutionary force (e.g. 6 and 7) or changes in deictic orientation (e.g. 2 and 3):

1) Captain and Arlecchino enter;
2) Captain threatens Arlecchino;
3) Captain greets the Orazio-Flavio unit;
4) Captain mentions the wine he has been given;
5) Captain exits;

---

6) Pedrolino instructs Arlecchino;
7) He sends him off;
8) Arlecchino exits;

---

9) Pedrolino instructs the Orazio-Flavio unit;
10) He sends them off;
11) They exit, leaving Pedrolino alone on stage.

A comparison of these two examples reveals simply that the former provides more explicit information for some of the sub-units; the heterogeneity within Scala's collection is the result of different dramaturgical practices at work in different scenarios, some of which provide the actors with more explicit detail.[20]

The key role of the *commedia dell'arte*, and of Scala's collection in particular, in the development of European dramaturgy (especially through Molière's and Goldoni's practice of writing out or "stretching" scenarios— *scrivere per disteso* is the Italian term) suggests that this might be an important line of investigation, with ramifications which go far beyond the scope of this article. It seems possible, for instance, to posit the scenario as the most direct and simple notation of what are essentially *performance-units* (the sub-units constituted by a single act or speech-act). While such performance-units seem easily deducible from this particular form of notation, the same cannot be said in regard to the full playtext. In it, the performance-units are atomised into even more microscopic units of dialogue-utterance and individual gesture, rendering much more difficult the reconstruction of the hypothetical performance-unit.[21]

3) Within the scene-unit: synchronic segmentation

Cutting across this diachronic segmentation of the scene-unit into sub-units is another group of techniques which can be isolated by analysis of the synchronic axis of performance implicit in the scenarios. These are techniques of synchronic segmentation, the aim of which is to minimise, formalise and schematise triadic interpersonal relationships, to reduce triadic to diadic where possible. Such schematisation is achieved either by dividing up the characters in particular ways, or by dividing up the stage itself into contiguous, but not necessarily interacting, sub-spaces.

3a) *Grouping of characters*

i) *Characters in unison*: this technique has already been noted in the first example in the previous section. It involves a number of characters being treated as a unit rather than as individuals. Their role can be passive, as addressees, or active, as they participate in concert to corroborate each other's stories for, or attempt to persuade, a third party—as occurs in Day 9, Act II, scene 7:

ISABELLA
Isabella comes out of the house, and is encouraged by Pedrolino and Arlecchino to make Orazio happy. She shows reluctance, but is at last won over by their many requests, and agrees to speak to him.

Here the interpersonal transactions are strongly directed towards diadic rather than triadic patterns: the scene can be characterized either as a diadic relationship between the Pedrolino-Arlecchino unit and Isabella, or as an alternation between two diadic relationships, as first Pedrolino, then

Arlecchino attempts to persuade Isabella, the fixed focus of attention.

ii)   *Subordinate roles*: in many scenes a third character is relegated
to a role which is little more than that of an onstage audience, whose
presence is necessary either for plot or character reasons, but whose role is
marginal to the action. The most common example of this is the presence
of a servant in the company of his master (Arlecchino as servant and
companion to the Captain: Day 3, Act II, scenes 17, 19). There are
numerous cases in which a servant is on stage during a love-scene between
his master and the master's beloved (Day 9, Act II, scene 16; Day 11,
Act I, scene 7) where it might be suggested that the servant's role is
anything but subordinate; the onstage audience might very well have a
role as more or less ironic commentator on the love-scene. The third
character does not impinge on the interaction between the other two, but
provides a strand of parallel action; for the audience, this can lead to
complex counterpoint effects, but at the point of emission it involves a
simple schematic technique of two simultaneous but autonomous actions.
This technique will be discussed more fully below.

iii)   *Formal scenes*: one obvious method of grouping the characters to
simplify the interpersonal transactions and the complexity of blocking this
scene is to utilise formal patterns (set-pieces which might well be stock
elements prepared beforehand) to provide the actors with formalised set
moves to organise the action. These might take the form of processions
(Day 6, Act I, scenes 3, 10), most commonly the final marriage procession
at the end of Act III (Day 11, Act III, scenes 8–13, where the exact order
of the procession is specified). But such formal social rituals pervade
even less solemn moments, such as entering the house: "With appropriate
ceremonies, they all enter Pantalone's house" (Day 10, Act I, scene 4). The
formalisation of the action, as well as enabling the actors to have recourse
to prepared material, provides them with a set and limited repertoire of
formal gestures and movements from which to draw, effectively limiting
and simplifying the choices to be made in the preparation and performance.

iv)   *Set business*: this involves the use of a set routine as an element
of the dramatic action (not, as some scholars have seen it, as a temporary
deviation *from* the action, enabling the actor to demonstrate his bravura).[22]
This is a simple means of structuring the action in such a way that each
character has a specific, prepared and rehearsed role in the action or dialogue.

This constitutes the *lazzo*, a term much-used in later collections of
scenarios to indicate either a verbal or physical gag. The term is generally
thought to derive from *l'azione*, and, while Scala does not use the term,

such a derivation is supported by his practice. On a number of occasions he uses *atti* in this sense: "Isabella fa atti d'allegrezza" (Day 20, Act III, scene 8); "Graziano cade in terra imbriaco, dopo molti atti imbriacheschi" (Day 21, Act II, scene 19).

In this one regard Scala's collection is often fuller than later collections; instead of simply indicating that at a certain point a certain character "fa il lazzo di Cuccagna," Scala will indicate in detail how the gag is to be played, as occurs in Day 4, Act I, scene 12:

TWO CROOKS
Two crooks greet Burattino, and stand on either side of him. One of them starts telling Burattino that he is from the country of Cuccagna, and, as he describes the wonderful food to be had there, his companion eats Burattino's food.

More often than not, however, Scala's scenarios are just as synthetic as the later collections, indicating merely the type of action required: "Arlecchino plays a ridiculous scene" (Day 12, Act I, scene 6); "They play a scene of anger" (Day 15, Act III, scene 18); "They do a swagger" (Day 18, Act I, scene 6). Such indications were sufficient to enable the actors to decide which set elements from their repertoire to draw on, but remain just as indecipherable as the formulaic jargon of the later collections. The real difference between the earlier and later scenarios is merely one of style; the later may seem more compressed and less accessible than Scala's and the other early scenarios, but statistically they are not. The false impression is created by their greater use of jargon, a jargon which simply had not yet evolved when Scala published his collection.[23]

v) *Fights*: this is a particular case of the previous category, and as well an extremely effective exit-technique, since it is usual for the characters to exit fighting, as in Day 1, Act III, scene 3:

ARLECCHINO
Arlecchino to revenge Pedrolino's slap; he sees him and beats him up; everyone draws a weapon, and they go off up the street fighting.

Alternatively, the fight has begun offstage, and the combattants are separated by a third party who, in an explicit stage-direction, comes between them, as in Day 2, Act III, scenes 14–15:

ORAZIO, CAPTAIN
Orazio, Captain both enter, fighting; at that Cintio comes between them, so does Flavio.

Fight scenes draw on a very limited lexicon (enter fighting, draw, beat, fight, come between, flee, chase, exit fighting), which creates a false impression of perfunctory combat; it must be borne in mind that the summary notation of the scenario reflects what were in all likelihood elaborate set-pieces. Nevertheless the schematising force of such a limited lexicon, channelling the action along certain present syntactical paths, is itself a significant technique.

vi) *Limited lexicon*: the formulaic character of the scenarios governs not just fights. So schematic and homogeneous is the lexicon that it provides a very strong restraint on the characters in terms of the range of possible options available to them at any one moment. This is an aspect of the scenarios that requires a great deal more study than can be dedicated to it here, but it needs to be indicated as a particularly effective method of limiting and simplifying the choices available to the actors in performance. Thus its inclusion under the heading *Grouping of Characters*, since it pre-programmes the possible channels of interaction between given characters, providing a restricted range of possible topics and types of action.

The key words in this regard are the verbs, which denote the acts and speech-acts which carry forward the dramatic action. They can be categorised into verbs designating sharing of information,[24] argument and discussion, movements about the stage, emotional reactions, social rituals, fights, orders, requests, plotting, perceiving, sexual activities and festivities.[25]

The manner in which these general categories interact, and verbs from different categories set themselves in standard syntactical chains (as exemplified in the previous section) is a vast and unexplored field of enquiry.

3b) *Dividing the stage*

i) *The use of windows*: the simplest method of actually cutting up the stage-space into separate and not necessarily interacting areas is by the use of the different stage-levels required by the scenarios. The paucity of the iconographic evidence regarding performance of the *commedia dell' arte* reflects the temporary nature of the theatre buildings (most often rented halls)[26] used by the travelling companies, but Scala's collection, like most of the others, requires an upper level—the windows of the houses in the comedies, battlements or the like in tragedies.[27]

Usually the character at the window participates in the action taking place below, as in Day 22, Act II, scene 11:

FLAMINIA

Flaminia at the window, tells Orazio that his mother is angry with him. [. . .] Pedrolino confirms what she says.

The window provides an obvious advantage in terms of the blocking of the scene: one of the characters is fixed, providing a ready-made focus for the moves of the other characters; the effective choices available to the actors in their organisation of the scene are thus limited, simplifying and reducing the decisions to be made in rehearsal and performance. This particular characteristic of the window is well-illustrated in Day 3, Act I, scenes 12–13, where the fixity of Flaminia at the window gives rise to a piece of set business which depends on the careful positioning of her two suitors on the stage below. Flaminia at her window, Orazio on the stage, are joined by Flavio:

FLAVIO, PEDROLINO

Flavio stands behind Orazio, so that Orazio is in the middle. Orazio greets Flaminia who, pretending to return his greeting, greets Flavio, with whom she is in love. [. . .] At this point Pedrolino enters, and realises that Flaminia is only pretending to speak to Orazio, while really speaking to Flavio; he goes up to Orazio, and quietly asks him whom Flaminia is talking to. Orazio: she is talking to him. Pedrolino shows him Flavio standing behind him. Orazio, on seeing him, gets angry and draws his sword; Flavio does likewise, and they exit fighting.

It is the fixity of the character at the window, and the positioning of the other two characters in relation to the window, which creates this piece of set business and effectively schematises the action so as to avoid a triadic structure betweeen the three links in the love-chain: interaction between the two men is precluded until Pedrolino alerts Orazio, and the two rivals exit fighting—the third side of the interactional triangle is completed offstage.

It is also common for the character at the window to act as passive observer of the stage action, without participating, as occurs in Day 15, Act I, scenes 13–14:

PEDROLINO, FLAVIO

Pedrolino comes from Flavia's house, eating. [. . .] The Doctor asks what he is doing in that house. Pedrolino: that shortly he will be master of it, and relates everything he has heard Orazio and Flavia saying. The Doctor beats him in anger, and takes him off up the street. Flavia who has heard everything from the window, despairs.

Flavia, the tacit onstage observer, merely watches and listens until the other characters exit, and only then bursts into her lament. She will nevertheless be reacting during Pedrolino's speech, creating a counterpoint which automatically adds complexity to the action without the three characters becoming involved in a complex triadic relationship. Instead there are two simultaneous strands of action, two sets of information processed by the audience which draws complex inferences as to the interrelationships between the two distinct strands. But in terms of their theatrical production, the two strands have been simply and schematically juxtaposed. More developed examples of parallel action will be considered below.

ii) *Withdrawing*: another technique of juxtaposing distinct strands of action (to be wound into a single signifying whole by the audience) is that of withdrawing—presumably to one side—to watch unobserved the central action. Sometimes this division is achieved by means of an unobtrusive entry (Day 22, Act II, scene 19), but more commonly characters will withdraw to listen (Day 16, Act I, scene 7: "Hearing someone coming, they withdraw."). In Day 8, Act II, scene 11, Orazio and Pedrolino, who have just been told by Bigolo that he has poisoned Isabella, Orazio's beloved, overhear a scene between Pantalone and the Doctor, respectively Isabella's father and promised husband:

PANTALONE, DOCTOR

> Pantalone, Doctor come out of the house, lamenting the death of the bride-to-be; they go off to find doctors to establish the cause of death. Exit crying. Orazio, having heard all this, goes mad, and runs off up the street.

In this scene, then, Orazio overhears confirmation of his beloved's death from her own father and from his rival for her hand. But the two strands (Pantalone-Doctor, Orazio-Pedrolino) are kept separate; a major triadic scene between the three men most involved in the tragedy is avoided, and the onset of Orazio's insanity is delayed until the other two have left the stage. Clearly all Orazio and Pedrolino are to do while Pantalone and the Doctor commiserate with each other is to limit themselves to minor reactions to be read in counterpoint to the principal action.

iii) *Slowsightedness*: an equally conventional segmentation of the stage is implicit in this common technique. It involves one or more characters on stage, and the entrance of a further character or characters. The entering characters fail to notice those already present (hence the title), and communicate information either in direct address to the audience, or in dialogue with their entering companion. This having been done, only then do they notice the presence of the others.

This is not necessarily a case of characters overhearing information vital to the plot (e.g. Day 1, Act III, scene 16), and even when it is vital, they do not necessarily overhear, as in Day 8, Act II, scene 10 (the scene immediately preceding the example in the previous section). Orazio and Pedrolino are on stage when Bigolo (Flaminia in disguise) enters:

BIGOLO
Bigolo happy to have poisoned Isabella when she requested a drink; hints that there is still some poison left. She sees Orazio and Pedrolino, reveals herself, rebukes Orazio for his love, and says she has poisoned his beloved; berating him, she exits. They remain, astonished.

Clearly Orazio and Pedrolino do not hear the first announcement, since they show amazement only on the second recounting; it is equally clear that their state of suspended animation (until they are brought into play by being "seen" by Bigolo) is by no means brief, since Bigolo has to communicate the fact, her joy, the means by which she has accomplished the fact, and the information that there is still some poison left. This is a highly conventional device: "seeing" is equivalent to "drawing into the action."[28]

iv) *Asides*: an equally conventional means of communication, this technique often implies the same sort of division of the stage as does the previous one; one character draws another to one side to speak privately to him: "Burattino enters, and draws Orazio to one side, saying. . . " (Day 6, Act III, scene 4). Such a synchronic spatial segmentation is not absolutely necessary, however; we have seen in Day 8, Act II, scene 11 (where Pedrolino tells Orazio that Flavio is standing behind him) that an aside might merely require a sub-grouping of characters, since here the aside between Pedrolino and Orazio takes place while they are standing *between* Flavio and Isabella.[29]

v) *Parallel actions*: the previous four techniques have in common the tendency to employ two simultaneous strands of action. In its extreme form, this technique implies the audience receiving two autonomous emissions which do not depend on each other for their decoding (as is usually the case in the preceding sections), but which are simply perceived in counterpoint. In Day 21, Act I, scenes 12–13, for example, two sets of lovers hold two separate conversations at two separate windows:

ISABELLA, FLAMINIA
Isabella at her window, plays a love-scene with Flavio; Flaminia at her window, speaks with Orazio, complaining of the pains her pregnancy is

causing her; Isabella says likewise. Orazio tells the ladies of Pedrolino's plan.

Interaction between the four characters is limited until Orazio's speech draws the two strands together. An even more extreme example of parallel dialogue occurs in Day 13, Act III, scenes 14–15; Orazio and Isabella do simultaneous laments for love, without *hearing each other*:

> ORAZIO, ISABELLA
> Orazio in desperation, laments; at that point Isabella at her window; here, without hearing each other they do a dialogue together, railing against Love. At the end Orazio falls into a dead faint. Isabella says that it sounded like Orazio's voice; she withdraws.

It is only in retrospect that Isabella recognises the other voice that has been in counterpoint to her own; this highly conventionalised set-piece (two simultaneous monologues rather than true dialogue) works by simple juxtaposition. Complexity is achieved by the audience, who weave an intricate web of meanings on the basis of the two schematically juxtaposed strands.

4) Conclusions

The single factor which has most inhibited critical attention to Scala's scenarios is probably Luigi Riccoboni's comment that the collection

n'est pas dialogué, mais seulement exposé en simple canevas, qui ne sont pas si concis que ceux dont nous nous servons et que nous exposons accrochés aux murs du théâtre par derrière les coulisses.[30]

This has been oft-quoted by Italian scholars who, in an admirable attempt to attribute a literary status to the collection (and thus render it an appropriate object of critical discourse), have inevitably impugned its usefulness as documentation of performance-practice.[31] If these scenarios are considerably fuller than the performance originals used by Riccoboni's company, what real insights can they provide into the practice of the actors in the companies with which Scala was associated?

It must be remembered that the performance-practice reflected in Scala's scenarios anticipates Riccoboni's work by more than a century. By the time the latter brought the Italian actors back to Paris in 1716, the Italian comedy had evolved into a highly codified traditional theatre-form, in which it is quite probable that the actors, performing what were by then traditional scenarios with set roles and routines, needed only the barest plot-indications affixed backstage.[32] Whether the same can be said for Scala and his fellow-actors is another matter.

There is some evidence of development towards brevity in the later collections of scenarios, but this is restricted, as noted above,[33] to one aspect; the increasing use of specific jargon, which creates a false impression that the scenarios as a whole are less discursive than Scala's. In fact the overall statistical similarity of the vast majority of other scenarios to Scala's is further confirmation of Scala's trustworthiness regarding performance, since the later collections, though many of them have been copied for a variety of reasons,[34] have not been subjected to possible contamination in a process of publication.

It will be clear from the foregoing discussion that I do not believe that Scala's scenarios diverge greatly from the originals; he may have eliminated some shorthand, but this is a minor and limited intervention. Apart from the glaring presence of explicit stage-directions,[35] which would surely have been the first elements to disappear in any thorough-going revision for publication with readers rather than performers in mind, these scenarios exhibit numerous characteristics whose main justification would seem to be a close connection to a performance-practice involving brief rehearsal. The different techniques discussed above, whether used singly or in concert on either or both of the axes of performance to schematise the dramatic action and simplify the work of the actors, are inescapably obvious to a reader attuned to theatrical rather than literary devices.

The scenarios do reflect performance-practice, and, as they reflect it, so they throw light on it, revealing a rudimentary but effective model of dramatic action which relies heavily on diadic relationships and counterpoint rather than on the subtle interplay of personal politics which so quickly comes to the surface with triadic relationships.

What emerges from the preceding discussion is above all the importance of the scenario as a powerful and practical commanding form for the dramatic action, a stable basis on which the actors can organise their performance, and prepare quickly the *commedia all'improvviso*. In this light, the vision of the *commedia dell'arte* as an opposite of normal practice, a predominantly gestural, improvised actors' theatre, can be put into perspective. Italian scholars have justifiably reacted to exaggerations as to the nature and extent of improvisation in this form of theatre, but have perhaps tended to err in the opposite direction, minimising the importance of the actors' freedom to treat offhandedly the creation of dialogue, the surface-level of a performance which is structured on the scenario and on the preparation, both short and long-term, to which the actors subjected themselves.[36] Ludovico Zorzi addressed the problem of improvisation in these terms:

> The solo performer improvising, stringing together monologues, is in reality merely following an outline prepared beforehand; anyone with even the slightest practical experience knows that improvisation can work with a duo (comic and straight-man: Franco Franchi and Ciccio Ingrassia). Once you have a trio, it becomes absolutely impossible, even with the greatest actors, trained to work in close harmony.[37]

The preceding discussion, which has focused on those characteristics of the scenario which enable it to control and direct the dramatic action so as to limit the dangers of complexity which might arise should the actors be given freer rein to explore the exponential possibilities of interaction, might seem to substantiate Zorzi's view of limited presence of improvisation in the *commedia dell'arte*. However, it is important not to see the scenario as having a predominantly limiting function; the characteristics discussed above, rather than inhibiting improvisation, seem designed to facilitate it, by bringing about those very situations correctly indicated by Zorzi as potentially improvisational: the presence of just one or two characters, or (should there be more) the division of characters into sub-groups of one or two.

Franco Franchi and Ciccio Ingrassia, Eric Morecombe and Ernie Wise are using a combination of punctilious preparation and improvisational techniques which were first codified by Flaminio Scala. His collection of scenarios encode certain principles of segmentation and organisation of performance which favour a flexible, improvisational approach to the generation of dialogue and action.

University of Sydney

NOTES

1 All the other collections are in manuscript, many from later periods, and some reflect amateur rather than professional practice. Cf. Vito Pandolfi, *La Commedia dell'Arte. Storia e testi*, 6 vols. (Florence: Sansoni, 1957–61), vol. 5, pp. 291ff.; Ludovico Zorzi was preparing a critical edition of the collections at the time of his death in 1983. This article is part of a long-term project of collation and comparison of the Italian collections, the first results of which were published in 1985 under the title "Segmentation of *Commedia dell'Arte* Performance: the Scenarios of Flaminio Scala," as a supplement to the *Renaissance Drama Newsletter* of the Graduate School of Renaissance Studies of the University of Warwick.

2 Ferruccio Marotti, in his introduction to Scala's *Il teatro delle favole rappre-sentative* (Milan: Il polifilo, 1976), pp. xlv-xlvi, links Scala with the Uniti, the Accesi and Desiosi, and later the Confidenti.

3 Cf. Marotti, pp. lii ff.

4 Ferdinando Taviani and Mirella Schino, *Il segreto della Commedia dell'Arte* (Florence: Usher, 1982), make this the distinguishing note: "Un perfezion-amento dal punto di vista della velocità e della maneggiabilità della pro-duzione." (p. 425). Andrea Perrucci, *Dell'Arte rappresentativa premeditata ed all'improvviso* (Naples: Mutio, 1699; ed. A. G. Bragaglia, Florence: San-soni, 1961) says it was customary to perform with about an hour's preparation (p. 159).

5 Constant Mic (Konstantìn Miklasevski), *La Commedia dell'Arte, ou le théâtre des comédiens italiens des XVIe, XVIIe et XVIIIe siècles* (Paris: Schiffrin, 1927), p. 26, refers to "création collective." Flexible group-developed performance is more accurate than improvisation as a description of the phenomenon.

6 This holds not only for the comedies, but also for the ten mixed works (pas-torals, tragedies, etc.) which conclude the collection.

7 The actors, consulting the scenario backstage before entering, needed a clear textual indication of their point of entrance; but once on stage were beyond the help of the scenario, so any further textual distinctions indicating points of exit would have been superfluous.

8 Statistically Scala's scenarios conform both to Luigi Riccoboni's observation (quoted in Taviani and Schino, p. 305) that the Italian companies used only a total of eleven actors and actresses, and to Zorzi's structural model, with eight fixed roles (two old men, two servants, four lovers) and three changeable roles (e.g. Captain, maidservant, courtesan). Cf. Ludovico Zorzi, "Intorno alla Commedia dell'Arte," in Donato Sartori and Bruno Lanata, *Arte della Maschera nella Commedia dell'Arte* (Florence: Usher, 1983), p. 70.

9 Normally a most time-consuming rehearsal activity, this working out of the moves and positioning of the characters is a physicalisation of the interpersonal relationships.

10 With an average cast of eleven, it will be difficult to avoid a large number of entrances to enable each character to take part in the action.

11 Quotations from Scala are my translation, based on the original and on Marotti's critical edition (cf. note 2). An error-riddled English translation of the collection has been published: Henry F. Salerno, ed., *Scenarios of the Commedia dell'Arte* (New York: New York University Press, 1967); it is not to be trusted under any circumstances.

12 However the number and frequency of such exits would preclude such a pos-sibility in all cases; attempts to motivate exits by reference to non plot-related elements ("I need to go and see a man about a dog") could bring a large number of confusing red herrings into the audience's attempts to construct *fabula* from plot.

13 The best-known evidence is from the Corsiniana manuscript in the library of the Accademia dei Lincei in Rome (Cod. 976).

14 Mic's model (p. 73) is based on a later collection published by Adolfo Bartoli; the original is ms. 2800 in the Riccardiana library in Florence.

15 Cf. Marotti, p. lvi.

16 Cf. Day 10, Act III, scene 6; Day 17, Act I, scene 3.

17 Cf. Keir Elam, *The Semiotics of Theatre and Drama* (London: Methuen, 1980), pp. 145–8, 156–70 on the role of deixis and the speech-act in dramatic discourse. Roberto Tessari, *La Commedia dell'Arte nel seicento* (Florence: Olschki, 1969), p. 116 alludes to this characteristic of the scenario as a type of theatrical notation "tutta intesa a restituire sequenze di atti fonici e atti mimici."

18 Cf. Tessari, pp. 113–5; Marotti, p. lxii. Scala states in his preface (Scala, p. 4) that his publication of the scenarios relates directly to performance: he wishes to assert his authorship of material being used by other companies. Likewise the preface which the famous Captain Spavento, Francesco Andreini, added to his friend and colleague's work (cf. Scala, pp. 12–13) refers directly to the performance, rather than the literary orientation of the collection. Nevertheless Tessari sees an overriding commitment to a reading public in a single sentence of this latter; Andreini suggests that Scala's scenarios "serviranno nell'ore oziose del giorno e della notte per passar via la noia, e per dar onesto e piacevol trattenimento a Dame e Cavalieri, che di simili spettacoli sono tanto bramosi." Tessari, omitting the last clause, with its specific reference to *performances* as entertainment for "Dame e Cavalieri," interprets Andreini as referring to *reading* as entertainment (Tessari, p. 114).

19 Tessari (p. 115) supports his claim that the distinctive style of Scala's scenarios is determined by his literary aims with a quotation from Day 2, one of the most discursive of Scala's scenarios; a quotation from Day 10, which (despite the fact that is consists of roughly the same number of scenes) is less than half the length of Day 2, would give a very different picture. My statistical comparison of Scala's scenarios to each other and to the other collections is based on the assumption that simple overall length is not an adequate basis of comparison; detailed comparison must take into account three different factors:

1) the average length of scenes,
2) the number of sub-units per scene,
3) the number of words per sub-unit.

On this basis, Scala's scenarios can be tabulated thus:

Type of scenario	Words per average scene	Sub-units per average scene	Word per sub-unit
more discursive	55	7	8
average	40	6	7
more summary	25	5	5

Overall, in comparison to the other collections, Scala's is in the middle of a narrow range, the extremes of which are represented by one of the Naples collections and by the Perugia collection:

Ms XI.AA.41			
(Nat. Lib., Naples)	30	6	5
Scala	38	6	6
Ms. A. 20			
(Com.Lib., Perugia)	60	8	7

20 Days 1, 2, 36–40, 42 are considerably longer than the bulk of the scenarios; Days 7, 8, 10, 11, 18 considerably shorter. More work needs to be done on possible groupings within Scala's collection, perhaps from different original sources (the different companies with which Scala was associated?).

21 Clearly the *commedia dell'arte* actors atomised the sub-units of the scenario in an analogous manner; cf. Marotti's comparison of Scala's scenario *Il marito* (Day 9) with Scala's own fully scripted *Il finto marito*, based on the scenario (Marotti, pp. lx ff.).

22 Cf. Taviani and Schino, pp. 224, 268, 270.

23 Emilio Re, "Scenari modenesi," *Giornale Storico della Letteratura Italiana*, vol. LV, 1910, p. 329 endorses a similar explanation for an analogous lack of jargon in *La schiava*, a scenario which pre-dates Scala's collection (republished in Marotti, pp. xciii ff.).

24 The absolute predominance of *dire*, by far the most commonly occurring verb, provides proof, if any were needed, that we are not dealing with a predominantly gestural theatre.

25 These tentative categories are listed in descending order of lexical richness and verb-frequency.

26 Cf. Mic, pp. 201–1; Taviani and Schino, pp. 358–9; Tessari, p. 36.

27 Cf. Day 41, Act I, scene 3: "The King of Fessa, on the walls."

28 Even more conventional is Day 3, Act III, scene 8, where it is the onstage character Pedrolino who sees the Captain enter, talks to the audience about him and only then "sees" him and addresses him.

29 These two last-discussed techniques also imply a diachronic segmentation of the action, being specific cases of segmentation on the basis of changes in deictic orientation.

30 Luigi Riccoboni, *Histoire du Théâtre Italien* (Paris, 1730) pp. 39–40.

31 Cf. note 18; nevertheless Marotti maintains that the scenarios are "immediatamente riferibili, e riferiti, allo spettacolo." (Marotti, p. xxxiv).

32 Cf. Taviani and Schino, pp. 296ff. for a discussion of this phase of the *commedia dell'arte*.

33 Cf. section 3a, technique iv.

34 Some of the single scenarios may be actors' originals, but the collections, at least in Zorzi's opinion (cf. Zorzi, p. 69), are transcriptions. Nevertheless none

of these various copying processes seem to introduce deviations significant enough to disqualify the texts as evidence of performance-practice.

35 The most eloquent of these occurs in Day 42, Act III, scene 28: Pantalone, Graziano, Pedrolino and Burattino beg forgiveness of Oronte, King of Athens. He "reassures them one by one, to stretch out the scene." It is clear that the scene needs to be stretched out for technical reasons. Immediately prior to this, Altea has been condemned to death, and the following scene features her headless body carried across the stage on a cart; obviously some time was required to set up the technical effect.

36 Taviani's discussion of improvisation in these terms is enlightening: Taviani and Schino, pp. 410–19.

37 Zorzi, p. 72.v.

Pamela D. Stewart

Disguise and the Masks: from the *commedia erudita* to the *commedia dell' arte*

My contribution will deal only marginally—I was about to say, hypo-
thetically—with the *commedia dell' arte*. On the basis of a study I have
already carried out on disguise and on the lusory character of so-called
erudite comedy,[1] I will simply suggest a possible vantage point from which
to look at the *commedia dell' arte*.

The theme of disguise is certainly not a characteristic exclusive to dramatic literature. But due to its particular affinity with the theatrical world
of pretense and counterfeiting, disguise does seem to have the right to oc-
cupy a place of particular privilege on the stage. This is particularly true
of Italian comedies of the sixteenth century, mostly *commedie d'intreccio*
and not *commedie di carattere* (or to use the classical terminology echoed
by Leone de' Sommi, *commediae motoriae* rather than *comediae statariae*[2]
), in which the emphasis is on a fixed repertory of recognizable human
types and of intricate but recurring situations. "Pray do not be angry,"
pleads the apologetic Prologue in one of these plays, "if, having already
seen appear on stage a young lover, an old miser, a scheming servant and
similar such things (from which there is no escape for those who wish to
write for the stage), you should see them appear once again."[3] Whatever
their moral and educational value or their function as an exposure of contemporary mores, these comedies were conceived of as an elaborate game,
whose rules and conventions (as with all games) were known in advance,
and in which the audience was expected to participate with knowing and
amused attention. This provides a precise explanation for the many references to theatrical pretense and counterfeiting, and for the frequent direct
addressing of the spectators by the characters on stage to be found not
only in prologues and envoys—where this is to be expected—but also in
the course of the plays. These are, of course, devices already present in

the classical tradition, but now put to more frequent use, as if to draw
attention to the theatrical fiction as fiction.

In Ariosto's *Suppositi*, the Senese's servant cannot manage to remember
or even to repeat correctly the newly assumed mane of his master, who
is pretending to be Filogono of Catania. To overcome the difficulty, the
dim-witted servant offers to play the mute, citing as precedent this role in
an earlier play:

Servo: Di questo nome strano mi ricordarò male; ma quella Castanea non mi
dimenticarò già.
Sanese: Che Castanea? io dico Catania, in tuo mal punto.
Servo: Non saprò dir mai.
Sanese: Taci dunque; non nominare Siena, né altro.
Servo: Voi tu ch'io mi finga mutolo, come io feci un'altra volta?

(*Suppositi* II.2, 18–25)[4]

This is an obvious reference to a similar character in another of Ariosto's
plays, the servant Trappola in *Cassaria*, and perhaps also to the actor who
might have played that part.[5] But what is more relevant to our discussion
is the reference in the text to the situation of the actor who, while playing his part, doubles himself, like a shadow, and considers with amused
detachment the part he is playing. The prologue to the second version of
Il Negromante, developing a device in Plautus,[6] refers to the use of the
same scenery—the fixed stage set of the Ducal Theatre in Ferrara—and
the same costumes already used for the performance of *La Lena*:

So che alcuni diranno ch'ella è simile,
E forse ancora ch'ella è la medesima
Che fu detta Ferrara, recitandosi
La Lena; ma avvertite e ricordatevi
Che gli è da carnoval, che si travestono
Le persone; e le fogge, ch'oggi portano
Questi, fur ier di quegli altri, e darannole
Domane ad altri; et essi alcun altro abito,
Ch'oggi ha alcun altro, doman vestirannosi.
Questa è Cremona, come ho detto, nobile
Città di Lombardia, che comparitavi
E' inanzi con le vesti e con la maschera
Che già portò Ferrara, recitandosi
La Lena. Parmi che vorreste intendere
La causa che l'ha qui condotta: dicovi
Chiar ch'io nol so, . . .

(*Il Negromante*, II red., Prologo 14–29)[7]

The prologue is the prescribed place for questions of theatrical poetics. The particular interest that this prologue presents (and this is why I am mentioning it here) is its insistence on the fictitious, conventional, but also festive, nature of the theatrical operation, resulting from the use of the same scenery and costumes, and from the analogy between theatrical and carnival disguises, and including in the general amusement, players, spectators and the playwright himself, on whose behalf the Prologue speaks.

Very often a character will refer to other characters in other comedies, classical or modern: the servant Corbolo in *La Lena* recalls servants of the classical theatre and remarks that they had a much easier time of it than he, because of the gullibility of their aged masters;[8] in Aretino's *Talanta*, Orfinio is at pains to distinguish himself from Fedria, a character in Terence's *Eunuchus*;[9] in Della Porta's *Fantesca*, Panurgo, who plays the part of a servant, tells his young master Essandro to trust in him and his cunning, and quotes in his own support the resourcefulness of the Davi, Sosi and Pseudoli of the ancient comedies;[10] in Giannotti's *Vecchio amoroso*, the Prior of Saint Nicholas complains that nowadays priests and friars are put into plays and made to conduct the most unseemly affairs.[11]

Frequently a situation is pointed out as being typical of the theatre. Of the many examples I will quote only one, which I find particularly significant, taken from Firenzuola's *Trinuzia*:

Dormi [one of the servants]: Questa mi pare là tra 'l quarto e 'l quinto atto d'una comedia, ch'ogni cosa è confuso, intricato, avviluppato, e scompigliato.
Uguccione: Sì, ma c'è questa differenza, che le comedie si rassettano, e questa matassa non la ravvierebbe tutto 'l mondo.

(*Trinuzia* IV.5)[12]

Now, this exchange takes place a little after the second half of Act IV, and the difference pointed out between theatre and real life is mentioned in jest: in fact, it forecasts the play's happy ending where everything is ostentatiously made to fall into place:

Messer Florio ha ritrovato la Lucrezia sua nipote e 'l marito della nipote, che è Giovanni, e un nipote, che è Uguccione, che viene a essere fratello della Lucrezia; e la Lucrezia ha ritrovato il marito, il fratello e 'l zio; Giovanni ha ritrovato la moglie, un cognato, e un zio della moglie; Uguccione ha ritrovato la sorella, il cognato, e 'l zio; Alessandro s'ha trovato una moglie, e Uguccione un'altra; mona Violante e la Marietta un bel marito per uno. E messer Rovina, che non importa poco, ha ritrovato se medesimo. Oh potevasegli accozzar meglio?

(*Trinuzia* V.8)[13]

As for the explicit addressing of the audience from the stage, many examples could be quoted from *La Calandra, La Mandragola, Gl'Ingannati*,[14] and other plays of the period. But perhaps the play where this devise is used most often is Piccolomini's *Amor costante*, where the two maid servants, Lucia and Agnolella, carry on a one-sided conversation, at times with the female spectators, at times with the male spectators, and sometimes with the whole audience.[15] The men in the audience, for instance, are warned against the ladies of the town:

Vi vo' contare a voi uomini: acciò che voi sappiate la maccatelle di queste cittadine che ci voglian tôr le nostre ragioni a noi fantesche; perché i garzoni dovrebbon di ragione esser nostri, non loro, l'engorde che sono!

(III.7)

And similarly further on:

Voi non rispondete? Non volete che queste cittadine vi vegghin parlare con le fantesche, eh?

(V.6)

In the envoys, as I have said, it is normal to address the spectators directly. But the envoy of Bruno's *Candelaio* is unusual in that when the time comes to announce the end of the play, the play instead continues with the inclusion of the audience within the players' space. Manfurio, the pedant, robbed, beaten and deprived of his cap and gown—symbols of his academic dignity—deprived even of the short cape which had been given to him in exchange for his own clothes, hears somebody calling him:

Ascanio [the young page]: Olà, mastro Manfurio, mastro Manfurio.
Manfurio: Chi è, chi mi conosce? chi in questo abito e fortuna mi distingue? chi per nome mio proprio m'appella?

He is humiliated and bewildered. To see where he is, he puts on his spectacles, or as he calls them his "oculari," and realizes he is in a theatre. The play is at an end, and there he is in that attire, an object of ridicule for all:

Manfurio: . . . voglio applicarmi gli oculari al naso. Oh, veggio di molti spectatori la corona.
Ascanio: Non vi par esser entro una comedia?
Manfurio: *Ita sane*.
Ascanio: Non credete d'esser in scena?
Manfurio: *Omni procul dubio*.

Ascanio: A che termine vorreste che fusse la comedia?
Manfurio: *In calce*, in fine: *neque enim et ego risu ilia tendo.*
Ascanio: Or dunque, fate e donate il *Plaudite*.

Which Manfurio finally consents to do, even if only to avoid having the play start up all over again:

> *Ascanio*: Donate, dico, il *Plaudite*; e forzatevi di farlo ancora voi, e fate il tutto bene, da mastro ed uomo di lettere che voi siete: altrimente tornarrà gente in scena, mal per voi.
>
> (*Il Candelaio* V.26)[16]

The comic effect arises here precisely from the theatrical fiction, from the very condition of the theatre, and from the presence of the spectators who are, at one and the same time, the cause of and the reason for the fun. The finished play continues on and even threatens to start all over again to the detriment of the one character who remains serious amid the general hilarity. This is perhaps the best scene of the whole play. It realizes and throws into relief one of the extreme conditons of this theatre, in which players and spectators—and even the authors in some cases—all tend to be, to a lesser or greater degree, both producers and consumers of comic amusement.

We could, therefore, apply to the Italian comedy of the Renaissance the label "non-illusory theatre" used, in reference above all to Elizabethan drama, by J. L. Styan.[17] This is, however—and here is its drawback—a negative formula. It excludes the realistic illusion but does not indicate in any way the reasons, the actual characteristics, the acutal meaning of these plays. Formula for formula, I would perfer "lusory theatre," and would rely for its meaning on the notion of theatre as "play," as organized amusement, as a sophisticated game, in the sense I have tried to explain and illustrate. I will recall here the main points:

1) denunciation and acceptance of the theatrical fiction as fiction, with all its rules and conventions;
2) a high degree of predictability as to the characters' behaviour and the unfolding of the plot;
3) a bond of complicity between author, actors and spectators in view of the common goal of fun and amusement, over the heads of the characters and at the expense of their adventures or misadventures.

Disguise is a kind of theatre within the theatre, a play within the play. But while the play within the play usually serves to reinforce by contrast the realistic credibility of the framing play, disguise in the Italian comedies of the sixteenth century strengthens and reinforces their lusory character, their tendency towards the condition of a sophisticated game. This is why disguise cannot simply be dismissed as a tiresome and threadbare device. Even if we do not take into account the cases of hidden or mistaken identity or substitution of persons, there are not many comedies of this period where disguise is not used. In many cases disguise is central to the plot as, for instance, in *Suppositi, Calandra, Mandragola, Clizia, Anconitana, Moscheta, Ingannati, Marescalco, Geloso, Talanta, Filosofo, Assiuolo, Candelaio, Fantesca*, etc. Very frequently it is the main source of comic effects as in *Cassaria, Cortigiana, Trinuzia*, etc. It may even be used more than once in the same play: in *La Cortigiana*, Maco, Zoppino, Grillo, Togan, Erculano, Rosso and Romanello Giudeo all appear in disguise; in *La Talanta*, we have Antino, Lucilla, Oretta, Fora, Costa; in *L'Assiuolo*, Oretta, Violante, Ambrogio, Giannella, Giulio; etc.

The affinity, the homology, of disguise with theatrical performance and especially with role-playing, is all the more evident if we take into account that very rarely does disguise aim simply at hiding a character's true identity: in *La Mandragola* Ligurio and Siro, who take part in the nocturnal expedition, are among the few examples of "neutral" disguise. The same, however, cannot be said for the others in the group, Nicia, Callimaco or even Fra Timoteo.[18] Usually disguise requires a change of identity, a change of role. Very often the new role, the new identity, is in direct opposition to the previous one: servants dress as masters and masters as servants, men dress as women, and women as men, old men as youngsters and sometimes young men as old, ladies as courtesans, and courtesans as ladies, cheats and swindlers as honest merchants, as pedagogues, or even as law-keepers, and so on. This change or complete reversal of role is above all an occasion for innumerable comic slips, but it is also what epideictic was frequently for the orator: a pretext for a show of virtuosity—in the case of the actor, an opportunity to centre attention on his acting skills.

Now it is precisely the lusory character of this theatre with its frequent resorting to disguise—almost to the point of obsession—that provides, in my opinion, the most profound and significant link between the *commedia erudita* and the *commedia dell'arte*. This is not to say that I wish to dismiss the studies on the sources and precedents, in the erudite comedy, of *commedia dell'arte* masks and scenarios, a subject to which, though with some cautious reservations, the late Ludovico Zorzi returned recently.[19] Nor would I want to downplay the very considerable differences between these two types of theatre, their audiences and the social milieu in which they flourished. It remains true that the mask seems to come at the end of the line in the development of disguise, and that the theatre of the masks, the *commedia dell'arte*, would appear to be the point of arrival of the sophisticated game that is at the heart of the *commedia erudita*. The *commedia dell'arte*, to use an expression of Mario Baratto's, is theatre in the second degree, "teatro di secondo grado,"[20] theatre that does not attempt to conceal its bond with the stage. It has been said that *commedia dell'arte* is essentially not an aesthetic or artistic notion, but a professional, industrial, almost trade union concept.[21] This statement—in a certain sense too obvious—overlooks the fact that the rise of the professional actor goes together with an increasing awareness of the significance of the theatre as theatre, with a vindication of the autonomy of theatre.

But I would not like to conclude without mentioning at least one scenario. The one I have in mind I hope will illustrate what I have said about the *commedia dell'arte* as theatre in the second degree. It is about the multiple disguises of a mask. The *Metamorfosi di Pulcinella* is one of the 22 scenarios included in his *Zibaldone* by the Benedictine friar Don Placido Adriani. It was staged at Saint Peter's in Perugia in 1730 and Don Placido played the leading role. It was published in 1914 by Del Cerro[22] and then, in 1927, by Petraccone.[23] To further the love affairs of Orazio and Luzio, Pulcinella assumes seven different and quite improbable disguises in the attempt to deliver a message to the jealously guarded young ladies who are the object of the amorous attentions of the two young men. He first pretends to be a piece of furniture, in the form of a blackamoor supporting a table top ("Pulcinella da moretto statua a uso di tavolino"); then dresses up as the learned astrologer Chiaravalle di Milano, then as a statue on a pedestal, and next as Cicco Bimbo, the washerwoman's baby:

Pulcinella: suoi lazzi di cacca, di pappa; Dottore voler prendere una ricotta o altro. Pulcinella fa lazzi; donne gridano; Dottore entra con la ricotta, le sgrida, poi imbocca Pulcinella. Rosetta va a prendere biscottini e torna; donne imboccano Pulcinella, e finiscono l'atto.

As the action proceeds it becomes increasingly difficult to persuade Pulcinella to persist in his efforts, since he keeps getting discovered and beaten. The fifth disguise has him all wrapped up as an Egyptian mummy. The sixth has him appear as a body-guard, and he finally manages to deliver the message. The crowning disguise, which will permit the joining of the couples, is that of Pulcinella as King Tiratappiatacù accompanied by his friend Coviello as Prince Sangoriccio and the two young men as princes Guagnao and Barabao, the sons of King Tiratappiatacù.

In the erudite comedy disguise provides a source of comic amusement because of its programmed incongruity: either because dress is out of joint with the face, form, voice or gestures of a character, or more rarely, because its conformity reveals indiscretely an aspect of a character's nature, or even because of its unexpected and undesired consequences. In place of programmed incongruity, the *commedia dell'arte* substitutes programmed absurdity. But this is not to be interpreted as just the result of gross *exaggeration*. It is a further development, a *transformation* that has its inner logic and a definite meaning.

McGill University

NOTES

1 This study has now appeared in my volume *Retorica e mimica nel "Decameron" e nella commedia del Cinquecento* (Florence: Olschki, 1986), pp. 161–247.

2 *Quattro dialoghi in materia di rappresentazioni sceniche*, ed. F. Marotti (Milan: Il Polifilo, 1968), p. 25.

3 "Però non abbiate a sdegno se, altre volte avendo visto venir in scena un giovan innamorato, un vecchio avaro, un servo che inganni el padrone e simil cose (delle quali non può uscir chi vuol far commedie), di nuovo gli vedrete." The quotation is from the prologue to *Aridosia* by Lorenzino de' Medici, in *Commedie del Cinquecento*, ed. I. Sanesi, Reprint ed. by M. L. Doglio (Bari: Laterza, 1975), II, p. 127.

4 *Tutte le opere di Ludovico Ariosto*, ed. C. Segre, Vol. IV, *Commedie*, ed. A. Casella, G. Ronchi and E. Varasi (Milan: Mondadori, 1974), p. 215.

5 *Tutte le opere di L. A.*., p. 1046, note 69.

6 See the prologue to *Menaechmi*:
    Haec urbs Epidamnus est, dum haec agitur fabula;
    Quando alia agetur, aliud fiet oppidum.
    Sicut familiae quoque solent mutari<er>;
    Modo hic agitat leno, modo adulescens, modo senex,
    Pauper, mendicus, rex, parasitus, hariolus.

7 *Tutte le opere di L. A.*, Vol. IV, pp. 449–450.

8 *Lena* III.1. 578–591, *Tutte le opere di L. A.*, pp. 570–571.

9 *Talanta* I.14.1, P. Aretino, *Teatro*, ed. G. Petrocchi (Milan: Mondadori, 1971), p. 372.

10 *Fantesca* I.5, *Commedie del Cinquecento*, ed. N. Borsellino, Vol. II (Milan: Feltrinelli, 1967), p. 480.

11 D. Giannotti, *Vecchio amoroso* III.7, *Commedie del Cinquecento*, ed. N. Borsellino, Vol. I (Milan: Feltrinelli, 1962), p. 55.

12 A. Firenzuola, *La Trinuzia*, ed. D. Maestri (Turin: Einaudi, 1970), p. 67.

13 Firenzuola, p. 83.

14 *Calandra* III.1, *La Calandra*, ed. G. Padoan (Padua: Antenore, 1985), p. 115; *Mandragola* IV.10, N. Machiavelli, *Tutte le opere*, ed. M. Martelli (Florence: Sansoni, 1971), p. 887; *Ingannati* IV.5, *La Commedia degli ingannati*, ed. F. Cerreta (Florence: Olschki, 1980), pp. 205–206.

15 See A. Piccolomini, *Amor costante* II.4, III.7, IV.13, V.6, V.9, *Commedie del Cinquecento*, ed. N. Borsellino, Vol. I (Milan: Feltrinelli, 1962), pp. 350, 376, 403–404, 420, 423.

16 G. Bruno, *Candelaio, Commedie del Cinquecento*, ed. N. Borsellino, Vol. II (Milan: Feltrinelli, 1967), pp. 450–451.

17 *Drama, Stage and Audience* (London: Cambridge University Press, 1975), pp. 180–223. Styan quotes many examples, taken from English drama of the sixteenth and seventeenth centuries, of direct references, within plays, to the theatrical fiction, to the actor's profession and to the audience. The difficulty with his expression "non-illusory theatre," becomes evident when he attempts to define its meaning. After declaring that "illusion is the province of the theatre" and that "a favourite activity of the theatre is to play with the idea of illusion itself, to mock the very thing it most tries to create—and the audience that accepts it," he continues: "The term 'illusion' is obviously an embarrassment for criticism, and has been for years. The theatre which pretends an illusion, whether of real life or of fantasy, is to be distinguished from that which simply makes the occasion for imaginative activity, some of which may be illusory. The basis of Ibsen's theatre is illusory, at its best making an audience believe in the images it creates on stage, while the basis for Sophocle's theatre is non-illusory, never expecting belief in what is seen. The former mode is circumscribed by what is plausible, the latter has infinite flexibility" (pp. 180–181).

18 Nicia chooses a disguise which he thinks will make him look younger than he is (IV.7, 8), Callimaco must dress up as the "garzonaccio" (IV.2, 9), Fra Timoteo has to pretend to be Callimaco in disguise (IV.2).

19 "Intorno alla Commedia dell'Arte," *Arte della maschera nella Commedia dell'Arte*, ed. D. Sartori and B. Lanata (Florence: La Casa Usher, 1983), p. 67.

20 *La Commedia del Cinquecento* (Vicenza: Neri Pozza, 1975), p. 141.

21 See B. Croce, "Intorno alla 'Commedia dell'Arte,'" *Poesia popolare e poesia d'arte*, 4th ed. (Bari: Laterza, 1957): *"commedia dell'arte* non è, primariamente, concetto artistico o estetico, ma professionale o industriale. Il nome stesso dice questo chiaramente: commedia dell'arte, ossia commedia trattata da gente di professione e di mestiere: ché tale è il senso della parola 'arte' nel vecchio italiano" (p. 507). A different but less convincing interpretation of the term 'arte' is to be found in Allardyce Nicoll, *The World of Harlequin* (Cambridge: Cambridge University Press, 1963), pp. 25–26.

22 E. Del Cerro (pseud. of Nicola Niceforo), *Nel regno delle maschere: Dalla commedia dell'arte a Carlo Goldoni*, con prefazione di Benedetto Croce (Napoli: Perrella, 1914).

23 E. Petraccone, *La Commedia dell'Arte: Storia, tecnica, scenari* (Napoli: R. Ricciardi, 1927).

Gianrenzo P. Clivio

The Languages of the *commedia dell'arte*

1. Introduction

The vast and constantly growing number of books and articles devoted to the Commedia dell'Arte are indisputable evidence of the importance which is attributed to it by theatre specialists and literary scholars in general not only within the sphere of Italian culture, but also in the wider realm of European intellectual life, so that—for instance—contributions in French or German are plentiful.[1]

Perhaps the salient characteristic of the Commedia dell'Arte—also known as *Commedia all'improvviso*, or simply *Improvvisa*—is the fact that the various characters of a play (the *maschere*, whose traits and roles were largely fixed or at least predictable according to established tradition) expressed themselves not in the same language, but each in a different dialect of Italy, so that linguistic codes as radically distinct as Venetian and Neapolitan could coexist in any given *commedia*, along with Tuscan Italian and a variety of other dialects, Latin, Spanish, and even, in some cases, French, German, Greek and Hebrew.[2] The multilingual character of the Improvvisa has so far been investigated very little and certainly not from the point of view of modern sociolinguistics. Two essential observations must be made at this point before proceeding.

Firstly, the plays of the Commedia dell'Arte, being improvised on the stage, have generally not come down to us in a completely written out form: rather, we possess only a number of the so called *scenari*, or plot outlines, which were penned in a rather colourless, hasty and often ungrammatical Italian: the actors, having each memorized the overall sequence of actions and events, were then to develop the *scenario* into an actual play relying on improvisation.[3]

Secondly, the non-Italian reader in particular must be reminded of the profound linguistic fragmentation of Italy, which was mirrored, until as late as 1860, by lack of political unity: mutual intelligibility between dialects of different regions is by no means assured, and in the case of the northern versus the southern dialects (say Venetian or Lombard versus Neapolitan or Calabrian) totally precluded by marked phonological, morphological, syntactical and especially lexical differences.

Several problems and questions arise from the above considerations. First of all, while we know from a variety of sources that different dialects were employed within the same comedy, lack of the complete text of any given play makes it impossible to analyse those dialects in order, for instance, to establish whether there was any deliberate attempt to attenuate their original traits in the direction of a more easily understandable koine, nor are we in a position—without additional information—to determine what vertical or horizontal variety of any given dialect was chosen. Upper class and lower class Neapolitan, for example, vary quite considerably. Secondly, one wonders at the absence or rarity of certain dialects, notably Milanese,[4] Piedmontese[5] and Genoese[6] vis-à-vis the predominance of others—but in this regard it is quite certain that political and other extralinguistic factors must have played a decisive role. Still, this question has not been satisfactorily addressed.

Even more than the presence or absence of some dialects—or the frequency or infrequency with which some of them were employed—as well as the problem of vertical varieties, one must ask a very fundamental question, namely *why* the dialects were used in such bewildering variety and *how* the audience could decode the message. Even though the dialects in today's Italy show a tendency to reduce their differences because of the influence of standard Italian (which has lead to the obsolescence of a number of traits, especially lexical, now felt as rustic, vulgar or archaic), it is a fact that a play in Milanese or Piedmontese would be totally unintelligible south of the La Spezia-Rimini line, just as Neapolitan or Calabrian would not be understood north of it. Furthermore, one must add that in today's Italy the dialects of regions other than one's own are generally disliked and speakers are unwilling to make any kind of effort to try to understand them. All of this leads one to believe that—on the one hand—the sociolinguistic situation of Italy in the 16th and 17th centuries (when the Improvvisa was in its heyday) must have differed quite considerably from the present one. Furthermore, since standard Italian was then spoken only by a very negligible minority of the population, it stands to reason that at least a passive knowledge of dialects other than one's own was much more common then than it is at present. However, it is unreasonable to postulate such widespread knowledge of other regions' dialects as to guarantee the full decodification of any message whatever linguistic medium it was couched in. Nonverbal factors must indeed have played a not insignificant part: the fixed and predicatable roles of the various characters, which must have been well known to audiences, as well as the famous *lazzi*,[7] or comic gags and explicit body language, surely contributed in a decisive manner to the correct decoding of multilingual dialogues on the part of regionally diverse audiences.

As already mentioned, sources for a detailed investigation of these and other related problems are extremely scarce: for instance, Luigi Riccoboni's promisingly titled *Discorso della commedia all'improvviso*, written approximately between 1720 and 1730, devotes only a few passing remarks to the use of different dialects in the Commedia dell'Arte.[8] Riccoboni regards the dialects—or at least some of them—as a very positive component of the Italian theatre:

Per le Comedie in prosa, quando ancora fossero scritte in buon Toscano, il Pantalone trasportando la sua parte nella Veneziana Lingua, il Dottore nella Bolognese, ed i servi nella Lombarda, non perderebbero niente delle bellezze loro, ma goderebbero del vantaggio di quei mascherati, che aggiungano Grazia e spirito a l'attore, e danno alla Comedia Italiana un caratto [*sic*] di merito superiore ad ogni altra straniera, come tutti confessano.

And a few lines below, he adds:

Né si potrebbe temere che la Veneziana o la Lombarda Lingua facessero torto ad una bella Comedia, se il Maggi nelle sue in versi introduce la Lingua Milanese, anzi la più vile e bassa, e Ruzante tutte le più barbare dell'Italia.

Riccoboni thus, though he spends only a few words on the matter, shows no hesitation concerning the advantage of employing the dialects, and it is significant that he quotes Maggi, who at times used lower class and rustic varieties of Milanese[9] just as Ruzante, whom Riccoboni also mentions, had recourse to equally plebeian varieties of Paduan and other northeastern dialects.[10] But neither Maggi nor Ruzante can be regarded as Commedia dell'Arte's authors, though the latter in particular must have been very influential.[11]

On the topic, however, Riccoboni has nothing else to say and it may be worth only to point out that he makes no reference to any southern Italian dialects. In fact, there certainly existed a *lombarda* or northern Commedia dell'Arte (in which Venetian, Bolognese and Bergamask predominated) as opposed to a *meridionale* or southern variety, which surely reduced the problem of intelligibility, but doubtless did not eliminate it, for the dialect of the Bergamo mountains, often spoken by the *zanni* or servants, and that of the city of Venice differ at least as much as Copenhagen Danish and northern Norwegian, and almost the same can be said of Neapolitan and the dialect of Bari.

2. Andrea Perrucci's *Dell'arte rappresentativa premeditata ed all'improvviso*

The only ample and reasonably reliable source that we possess to investigate the problem of language and languages within the Commedia dell'Arte is a treatise by Andrea Perrucci, entitled *Dell'arte rappresentativa premeditata ed all'improvviso*, published in Naples in 1699, which—in spite of its very great importance—had been practically forgotten until A.G. Bragaglia's 1961 new edition.[12] We shall now turn to Perrucci and his treatise in order to examine it in some detail. In addition, since several of the major actors of the Commedia dell'Arte—such as Giovan Battista Andreini (1576?-1654), Silvio Fiorillo (dates unknown, but active between 1589 and 1634), Pier Maria Cecchini (1563–1645), and others[13] —published a number of comedies which may be regarded as fully developed *scenari*,[14] reference will be made to them as additional sources of information, though the published texts of these actors-authors surely do not reflect the Commedia dell'Arte version of their respective plays with complete exactness.

Perrucci was born in Palermo in 1651 and died in Naples in 1704, leaving us a not inconsiderable number of works in Italian and in various dialects, chiefly in Neapolitan. Most of his writings are of a theatrical nature, but he also acquired a considerable reputation as a poet in Neapolitan.[15]

In order to understand the stature that Perrucci achieved during his life as a poet, scholar, playwright, actor and director, it is worth quoting from Antonino Mongitore's brief biography which appeared three years after Perrucci's death:

Andreas Perruccius Panormitanus, Iurisprudentiae Doctor, ac Poeta eximius. Natus Panormi I. Iunii 1651 . . . annum agens octavum una cum Patre Neapolim petit; ibique humanas litteras. . . , philosophicas vero disciplinas, ac theologiae partem . . . non sine eximii ingenii laude accepit. Inde iurisprudentiae studiis admotus, in publico Neapolitano Lyceo sub diisciplina celebrium Iurisconsultorum . . . didicit . . . Poeticu ingenium nactus, a pueritia cum Musis ludere coepit . . . Musa ne dum Etruscas et Latinas, verum etiam Hispanas, Siculas, Neapolitanas, et Calabras egregie coluit . . . Per annos plurimos Parthenopeo Theatro Sancti Bartholomaei presuit . . . multaque ad illius theatri splendorem edidit . . . His accessit uberem omnigenae eruditionis copiam: et his omnibus praeclarum sibi nomen comparavit. In celebrioribus Italiae Academiis ascriptus fuit . . . Neapoli decessit . . . non sine Literatorum dolore.[16]

Even allowing for a fair degree of laudatory exaggeration on the part of Mongitore, it cannot be doubted that Perrucci had achieved very considerable literary fame and success during his life.[17] Still, it was not to be of the lasting kind and his treatise *Dell'arte rappresentativa*, published when the Commedia dell'Arte was approaching its decadence, undeservedly fell into oblivion, so much so that no more than perhaps three or four copies of the original edition are extant.[18] Bragaglia's edition has made this treatise available again, and a long and valuable essay by Pietro Spezzani has contributed to make it known,[19] but so far only to a limited extent since, for example, two of the most recent books on the Improvvisa—respectively by F. Taviani and M. Schino, and by C. Molinari—mention Perrucci a few times, but merely in passing.[20] Even M. Apollonio, in his well known *Storia della Commedia dell'Arte*, had devoted a mere six pages to Perrucci and did not deal with linguistic questions at all,[21] nor did I. Sanesi in the two long chapters of his *Commedia* devoted to the *Improvvisa.*[22] Yet Perrucci's work, which constitutes the first Italian comprehensive treatise on the theatre of the 16th and 17th centuries, is conceived in a systematic manner and has explicit normative and didactic intents.

Perrucci's *Dell'arte rappresentativa* consists of a series of rules, illustrated by numerous examples, many of which are stock in trade speeches, witticisms, pleasantries, jests and songs which the actors could exploit time and again to flesh out the often repetitive plots outlined by the *scenari*, and to obtain the expected comical or dramatic effects. These samples apply to the various characters of the Improvvisa, and are thus written in the dialect[23] that each one of them was supposed to speak, in accordance with a well established tradition to which Perrucci explicitly refers.

On one fundamental point Perrucci does not favour us with an explanation: namely, why the Commedia dell'Arte was of necessity to be multilingual. It evidently was by then an accepted fact, requiring neither justification nor discussion. He does, however, comment quite extensively on aspects of the linguistic situation in Italy. In the first place, he starts by asserting "che nella nostra Italia non vi sia chi perfettamente parla è cosa più chiara del sole istesso" (p. 106) and immediately disposes of the Florentines' claim to linguistic superiority:

I Fiorentini, che si gloriano padri della perfetta lingua sono tanto difettosi, che nulla più; poichè oltre che proferiscono nella gola, dicendo invece Cavallo Xhavallo,

per Duca DuXha, e gli è tanto difficile a levarseli questo difetto, hanno ancora
tanti vocaboli ostrusi, e contorti, che fanno un sentire molto barbaro all'orecchio
. . . Ecco che peccano in lingua quegli stessi, che ne vogliono dar norma al Mondo
tutto; Mi si dirà esser questo un parlare del volgo, e plebe di Firenze, bene rispondo
io. Dunque in loro non è buona la lingua naturale, se coltivata dallo studio non
viene . . . (ibid.)

Perrucci clearly found the so called "gorgia toscana," namely the spirantiz-
ation of intervocalic voiceless stops,[24] as strongly distateful and unacceptable: he hastened to add that not only the Florentines but other Tuscans as
well are subject to it, "benchè i Senesi qualche poco meno de' Fiorentini."

He then went on to enumerate and deprecate those which he regarded as
pronunciation faults peculiar to speakers from the various regions of Italy:
he, for instance, criticizes the Lombards for failing to pronounce "double"
or long consonants as well as for replacing the palatal sibilant with a dental;
disapproves of Neapolitans and Sicilians because they confuse open and
closed vowels[25] and substitute *nd* with *nn*; concerning the Bolognese and
the Genoese, Perrucci regards them as so bad as not to be worthy of
discussion.

Perrucci's diatribe on the lamentable pronunciation habits of the Italians is essentially nothing new, since countless purists before and after
him were prone to indulge in similar observations.[26] It must however be
pointed out that Perrucci's comments are fundamentally ambiguous, since
he does not explicitly state whether he is deploring, say, the Lombards'
way of pronouncing Italian, i.e. a language not their own, or whether he
is criticizing their native dialect on obviously subjective esthetic grounds.
The latter would seem to be the case when he refers to the Bolognese and
the Genoese, about whom he says: "I Bolognesi, e Genovesi gli rilascio
alla discrezione del benigno Lettore, che fatica ci voglia, a far che siano
sane quelle lingue, che sono meze per natura?" (p. 108) Thus, there appears to be a confusion between regional dialects and what we would call
nowadays "regional Italian," namely the way in which Italian is spoken
in any given region.

Be that as it may, Perrucci is willing to admit that good language
is to be heard in Rome, however not from the common people, to be
sure, but only from the courtiers who "studiano una lingua pulita, culta,
e bella: ma per dirla, alle volte affettata, perchè non sanno scompagnarsi
dall'adulazione." (p. 109)

Perrucci, who in addition to his various other occupations, was also an
actor, could of course not avoid being profoundly concerned with language
from a normative point of view: but his conclusion is that good Italian is

nowhere native and can be acquired only through study and, in fact, by means of a peculiar linguistic grafting:

La lingua dunque più tersa, e buona per rappresentare in buon linguaggio Italiano, sarà la Senese per li vocaboli, affinata nella Corte di Roma per toglierli il difetto della gola. (p. 109)

Perhaps, part of the reason why the various dialects played such a significant role in the Commedia dell'Arte is the quite obvious impossibility, except perhaps on the part of a very few, of meeting such an incredibly artificial standard, especially in the absence of the modern mass media! The dialects, on the other hand, possessed—at least each in its own geographical sphere—the qualities of spontaneity, genuineness and authenticity so that, Perrucci's assertions notwithstanding, it would stand to reason that audiences perceived them as more pleasing to the ear, in spite of possible comprehension problems.

3.   The characters of the Commedia dell'Arte and their languages

3.1   The lovers

In fact, when Perrucci comes down to specifying how the characters of the Commedia dell'Arte should speak, he prescribes literary Italian, based on Tuscan, only for the *innamorati*, the lovers, while all others were to express themselves in dialect. But in the case of the lovers Perrucci is quite insistent on the need for what he regards as linguistic perfection:

studino di sapere la lingua perfetta Italiana, con i vocaboli Toscani; se non perfettamente, almeno i ricevuti, ed a questo conferirà la lettura, così de' buoni libri Toscani, come gli Onomastici, Crusca, Memoriale della lingua del Pergamino, Fabrica del Mondo, Ricchezze della lingua, ed altri Lessici Toscani . . . (p. 163)

The *innamorati* must thus adopt a bookish language that they were to learn artificially by studying, and Perrucci includes numerous passages as examples of conceits, dialogues, monologues, etc., for the use of the lovers, which demonstrate what type of language he had in mind, namely a very literary, rather archaic, stilted and often pompous Italian, which surely could not be regarded as the living idiom of the Tuscans, be they Florentines or Siennese. The following brief soliloquy, in which an unhappy lover laments his fate, can be regarded as typical:

Io dunque posi le speranze in una donna, volubile di mente, tronca di mani, cieca di lumi, sorda d'udito, ignuda di virtù, d'abito cangiante, calva di chioma, e barbara d'azioni? A guisa degli stolti Romani le alzai Tempj di fede, le porgei preghiere,

l'incensai con sospiri, le consecrai vittime; ma che pro? se come volubile mi
deluse, come priva di mani non può porgermi aita, come cieca non rimira le mie
rovine, come sorda non ascolta i miei lamenti, come ignuda m'impoverisce di
gioie, come cangiante solo è varia a' danni miei, come calva giamai mi porge il
suo crine, e come tiranna del mio tormento sol gode: chi brama di sapere chi sia
costei,
    Che contro di me tante miserie aduna?
    E' una donna, è una Furia, è la Fortuna. (p. 168)

Lexical items such as *lumi*, *ignuda*, *chioma*, *guisa*, *stolti*, *aita*, *crine*,
brama, *aduna*, etc., have a marked archaic flavour and it is doubtful that
they could be easily understood by the uneducated, which in the 16th
and 17th centuries constituited the vast majority of the population.[27] One
should also notice the rather complex syntax of the quoted passage: the
language of the *innamorati* is characterized by hyperboles, excessive use
of adjectives, emphatic exclamations and rhetorical questions, just as is
the case in the literary theatre of the Cinquecento.[28] In fact, the *innamorati*
are one of the traits d'union between the Commedia dell'Arte and the so
called "Commedia erudita" of the Cinquecento.

Concerning the other characters of the Improvvisa, Perrucci does not
only specify which dialect or dialects each *maschera* may or must use,
but he often comments on the various dialects and sometimes (as in the
case of Calabrian) he even specifies which variety must be adopted. On
the whole, however, he is rather vague and his observations can be quite
perplexing.

3.2 *Pantalone*

Among the *maschere*, one of the most important ones was Pantalone, an
avaricious old man, often mocked and deceived by his servants and by
his son, and ridiculously in love with a much younger woman. Pantalone
spoke invariably in Venetian and, in fact, Perrucci—indulging once again
in his penchant for linguistic perfection—specifies that "chi rappresenta
questa parte ha da avere *perfetta* la lingua Veneziana, con i suoi dialetti,
proverbj, e vocaboli" (p. 195, emphasis ours). It is somewhat puzzling
what Perrucci could mean by "dialetti" in this context,[29] though it seems
likely that he was referring to vertical varieties of Venetian, intending to
have Pantalone speak in a more vulgar or more elevated form according
to circumstances. The three fairly long passages which Perrucci provides
as examples of stock in trade speeches (not without asking his readers'
forgiveness "della favella non naturale") are written in equally passable
Venetian, but some stylistic differences are apparent, especially with re-

spect to lexical choice. The first passage, the "Conseglio," in which Pantalone is supposed to be dispensing his advice to a prince, is characterized by an elevated vocabulary and a solemn syntax:[30]

. . . chi vol raccoger el fruto da quel c'ha semenao l'è necessetae, che se vada dal semmenaor del consegger per cogniosser el tempo che sia ben a farlo. Chi vol alzar l'Edifizio della Politica, el se serva del fondamento de la rason perchè senza questa anderà per tera tuta la machina. El comandar a la orba xè un voler cascar drento un fuogo de disgrazie; per no star a scuro bisogna aver el moccolo del giudizio. El xè bisogno che el timon governi la Galìa del Regno per no dar into i scoggi, e inte le secche d'un Mar pericoloso, l'aque avelenae dale Bisse dele turbolenze le no se fà chiare, che col corno del Lioncorno. E el Caval del Governo no anderà mai dreto se nol vien governao dal cavezon del consulto. Fa ben donca V. Zelenza come Pluton a servirse del Zimier del conseggio . . . (p. 196)

In the second passage, the "Persuasiva al Figlio," in which Pantalone scolds his son for his dissolute life and exhorts him to mend his ways, the lexicon has more of an everyday quality and is thus more typically Venetian:

. . . e no ti cognosi che i Buli xè tante sansughe, che tanto le te sta tacae, in tanto che le te ha zupegao el sangue e dale vene, e dela scarsela. Le scarabaze xè come i cagaori, che dopo che gh'avè fato i vostri bisogni le spuzza. El ziogo el xè un Lovo, che quanto più el divora più vol magnar . . . (p. 197)

Here is a sample of the third passage, the "Maledizione al Figlio," linguistically the more plebeian of the three:

. . . se ti vorrà nuar te posi niegar coma le Simie, se ti vorà magnar le Arpie te caga into a le vivande; le Mosche te cortezi come una carogna, le Zeraste quando ti bevi te posa pisar in tel vin; e i vermi te fazza l'acqua putrida, e i sorzi te devora il formento . . . E zà, che ti contro el Pare te si mostrao una Bestia . . . posi eser orbo come fa le Topinare . . . posi cagare el to mal como el Tordo, posi portar il fuogo da drio como la Luciola, posi perder l'aculea come la Ave . . . ti posi strapar i genitai como el Castor, te posi brusiar como la Parpaia de note, e per fin posi correr la fortuna del Cavreto, o de morir picinin, o de ingrandir beco cornuo . . . (p. 198)

Though stylistic differences, especially in the matter of vocabulary, are quite striking, the three passages do have in common certain rhetorical devices, especially the use of metaphors and comparisons, which are of a grandiloquent and almost bombastic nature in the first passage, more down to earth in the second and frequently vulgar or obscene in the third. Thus, it is obvious that Perrucci intended that Pantalone be able to adjust his linguistic register in such a way as to obtain amusing results whether by means of an excessively pompous language or a markedly plebeian one, spiced by scurrilous double entendre. It is worth noting that Perrucci's Venetian shows little influence from Tuscan, especially in the last two passages, although he occasionally introduces a Tuscan word instead of the genuine Venetian equivalent. For instance, in the long list of animals which are mentioned in the third passage (Pantalone in cursing his son says "te sia contrarie tute le Bestie del Mondo"), Perrucci includes the *luciola* "firefly" (Tuscan *lucciola*) and the *donola* "weasel" (Tuscan *donnola*): in this case, he is trying to make two Tuscan words sound Venetian simply by eliminating the double consonants, since the true Venetian terms are respectively *lusariola* and *martorèlo*.[31] This, however, is certainly not to be seen as an indication of a desire to Tuscanize Venetian in order to make it more comprehensible, but rather to be attributed to Perrucci's avowed imperfect knowledge of this dialect.

A role similar to Pantalone's could also be played by other *maschere*, less well known, such as Pasquariello or Cola, both of whom however spoke in Neapolitan, and Cassandro d'Aretusi, who expressed himself in lower class Florentine. Perrucci does not supply any examples of speeches by these latter characters, and in fact they are far less important than Pantalone within the Commedia dell'Arte. The part of the old man could also on occasion be assigned to a Neapolitan *maschera* called Tartaglia, whose name suggests his characteristic stammering way of speaking.[32]

3.3   The Dottore

While Pantalone's northern Italian dialect had to be "perfetto," Perrucci's prescription was somewhat different in connection with another major fixed character of the Improvvisa, also an older man, namely the Dottore or Physician, a learned but rather pompous and garrulous individual, commonly called Graziano, whose "linguaggio ha da esser *perfetto* Bolognese" (p. 198, emphasis ours). Though Perrucci does not abstain even in this case from demanding linguistic perfection (let us recall his very negative remarks on the qualities of Bolognese quoted earlier), in this instance he hastens to add

ma in Napoli, Palermo, ed altre Città lontane da Bologna non deve esser tanto stringato, perchè non se ne sentirebbe parola, onde bisogna moderarlo qualche poco, che s'accosti al Toscano, appunto come parla la Nobiltà di quell'Inclita Città, e non la Plebe, di cui appena si sente la favella; onde allora ch'ebbi la fortuna di esservi, al mio Compagno sembrava d'esser fra tanti Barbari, non intendendo punto quella lingua. (pp. 198–199)

Though Perrucci does not specify the regional origin of his travelling companion, we may assume that he was a southerner like Perrucci himself, so that this quotation affords us further proof that, indeed, mutual understanding of geographically remote dialects could be very problematic.

As the rest of the Gallo-Italic dialects, Bolognese shows the well known tendency to drop unstressed vowels, but even more markedly so than, say, Milanese or Piedmontese, so that its phonemic economy differs drastically from Italian and the southern dialects, and even Venetian: abundant heterorganic consonant clusters, a complex metaphonic system affecting the surviving tonic vowels which may be phonemically long or short (a fact not indicated by the normal spelling), apart from lexical peculiarities, contribute to making genuine Bolognese a very difficult language to other Italians.[33] Hence, it is not surprising that Perrucci advised that the speech of the Dottore be Tuscanized somewhat as needed. In the opinion of the actor Pier Maria Cecchini, the Dottore was to adopt

una lingua Bolognese in quella forma, ch'ella viene essercitata da chi si crede, che non si possa dir meglio, & poi di quando, in quando lasciarsi (con qualche sobrietà) venir di bocca di quelle parole secondo loro più scielte; ma secondo il vero le più ridicole, che si ascoltino; come sarebbe a dire interpretare per impetrare, urore per errore, secolari (credendosi di parlar Toscano) per scolari, & altre simili . . .[34]

Thus, according to Cecchini, the Dottore was not only to use a Tuscanized version of Bolognese, but also to create comical effects by Tuscanizing incorrectly, and such an expedient must have worked very well when the part was played in Tuscany. The Dottore, however, also introduced another language in the Commedia dell'Arte, namely Latin: he was supposed to give tangible evidence of his erudition, bordering on pedantry, by frequent Latin quotations, more or less correct and appropriate, which surely could not be understood by the uneducated, although they were accustomed to hearing Latin spoken in church. Perrucci provides several passages as examples of the type of speeches the Dottore might hold in any comedy, but he apologizes if "la lingua non è perfetta Bolognese . . . per non havervi fatto particolare studio" (p. 209), and in fact it would appear that quite often Perrucci is content to use normal Italian words with the final vowel omitted. The following is an example of Graziano's speech as rendered by Perrucci:

Lè l'hom al Mond senz'al saver, *sicut Asinus sine capistro*, perche se non ha el cavezon, ch'el mena per la strada de la virtù el va a scavezacol al prezipiz. Le appunt *sicut Porcus in luto*, che se non s'ingrassa col beveron de la dutrina, al resterà sempr' secc, e magr com stornel, el no sarà bon per ingrassar la minestra de

220 GIANRENZO P. CLIVIO

la Conversazion; al è un Papagal int'al Bosc' ch'al non *articulat verba*, de muod che se dal Maestr non l'è post int la gabbia, e vien ammaistrà ad articolar i azzient, non l'è pericol che sippa ne gotta. A l'è al Boja mal prattic' che non savendo struzar la ignoranza al se espon al pericol de la sassà del Popol. (pp. 207–208)

Apart from the Latin phrases, it is readily seen that this is a sort of Sprachmischung which would identify a speaker as being from the north of Italy in general, rather than from Bologna in particular, though a few lexical items—such as *int*, *muod*, *sippa* and *ne gotta*—are more definitely Bolognese. In fact, if one examines the approximately nine pages (200–209) which Perrucci devotes to exemplifying the Dottore's language, one can come to the conclusion that it is a cross between Tuscan and Venetian, with some other northern Italian elements and a few typically Bolognese features: thus—while shortening of long consonants, voicing of intervocalic occlusives and assibilation of palatals are very common—word internal unstressed vowels are normally preserved[35] as is the case in both Venetian and Tuscan, whereas they are dropped in word final position in contexts in which Venetian preserves them[36] but Bolognese does not. The lexicon shows a mere sprinkling of truly Bolognese items, the rest being words common to Italian and a number of dialects. A comparison between Perrucci's Venetized and Tuscanized Bolognese and the language of more or less contemporary Bolognese dialect writers, such as Giulio Cesare Croce,[37] would immediately show that the Dottore's language, while still identifying him as a native of Bologna, was far removed from genuine Bolognese.[38] The same hybrid linguistic traits characterize the two "Tirate del Dottore" first published by E. Petraccone,[39] which are also heavily interlarded with Latin words and phrases.

3.4 The Capitano

Apart from the lovers, Pantalone and the Dottore, the other main characters of the Commedia dell'Arte were the Captain, the first and second male servants or *zanni*, and the female servants or *fantesche*.

These characters were not as closely identified with a specific dialect, but their name often varied according with the dialect they spoke, except that the *Capitano* always retained his military title. He could be called Capitan Spavento,[40] Capitan Matamoros,[41] Capitan Tremimarte,[42] Capitan Spezzaferro, Capitan Terremoto, Capitan Rinoceronte,[43] Capitan Sbranaleoni or by other similar fierce sounding names, which however Perrucci does not mention. Whatever name the Capitano might assume, his was, according to Perrucci,

. . . una parte ampollosa di parole, e di gesti, che si vanta di bellezza, di grazia, e di ricchezza; quando per altro è un mostro di natura, un balordo, un codardo, un pover'uomo, e matto da catena, che vuol vivere col credito d'esser tenuto quello che non è . . . (p. 210)

This descendant of Plautus' *Miles gloriosus* could speak in various languages or dialects but, according to Perrucci, above all in either Spanish—a language not so very foreign in Italy because of political events in the 16th and 17th centuries[44] and at any rate not too difficult to understand for an Italian—or Calabrian, or even in a mixture of the two. Apparently, it was also not uncommon for the Capitano to speak in Neapolitan or Sicilian.

Perrucci provides three passages to exemplify the type of speeches in which the Capitano was wont to indulge in within the Commedia dell'Arte: the first one is in reasonably correct Spanish, the other two in Calabrian, a dialect which Perrucci regards as being endowed with "ridicolosissimi vocaboli" (p. 211). Here is a sample of Perrucci's Calabrian:

Bin haia lu Suli leiuni, voi chi ti mpacchia tridici centu curramati a li catrei? chi t'anca ssa cicogna? ti sparpagna cu nu vietti ssi spalli? chi ti fazza cruscula, pispici, e zunzumia? (p. 211)[45]

Perrucci then gives a "Saluto Calabrese alla Donna con bravura" (pp. 211–212) accompanied by an Italian translation "perché non tutti sanno i vocaboli strani di quella lingua" and goes on to specify that in the dialect of the Capitano "si mischiano i vocaboli dell'una e dell'altra Calabria Citra, ed Ultra" in order to make it richer, but that "l'enfasi haurà da esser tolta da i Casali di Cosenza, ch'è la più stretta" (p. 212). It is worthwhile stressing that—while in the case of the Dottore Perrucci insisted on the need to Tuscanize his Bolognese so as to render it reasonably understandable—he does not at all show the same concern in the case of Calabrian, though he dwells on its strangeness. One is entitled to doubt, however, that the part of the Capitano was often played in Calabrian in the north of Italy. In Naples, on the other hand, Calabrian—though probably considered uncouth and ridiculous—was not so incomprehensible, especially the northern variety.[46]

Thus, in this particular case, Perrucci prescribes a specific horizontal variety of Calabrian, namely Cosentino, a northern Calabrian dialect spoken north of the isogloss which divides into two very distinct linguistic areas the region of Calabria.[47] The isogloss runs south of the Sila mountains, roughly from just north of Crotone on the Ionian coast to just below Gizzeria on the Thyrrenian coast, leaving to its south the city of Catanzaro. The dialects spoken south of this isogloss are closely related to Sicilian, while those of northern Calabria show features of the Neapolitan type. Cosentino, which belongs to this latter group, lacks the simple perfect tense ("passato remoto") instead of which only the present perfect ("passato prossimo") is used, while preserving the infinitive which, in southern Calabrian has been by and large lost and substituted by the construction *mu + present indicative* (a Greek syntactic calque) except after the verb *potere*. Lexical differences between the two groups are quite marked, partly due to a very strong Greek substratum in the provinces of Catanzaro and Reggio.[48]

A brief examination of the "Saluto Calabrese alla donna con bravura" written by Perrucci shows that he does in fact mix the two varieties of Calabrian[49] : in the first line we find the word *vitti*, the simple perfect of *vidiri* "to see," a typically southern Calabrian form totally foreign to Cosentino, while the next two lines contain examples of the present perfect (*hannu zirniatu, hannu tripatu*) which would not be possible in southern Calabrian. Other instances of the simple perfect to be found in the passage are *mpacchiasti*, *misi* and *fici*, together with various other examples of the present perfect. On the other hand, the infinitive is used throughout in contexts where southern Calabrian would show the *mu* construction, such as *voi chi ti fazza, fazzu sautari*, etc.

The lexicon too shows elements of both northern and southern Calabrian. The term *vefida* "wasp" (probably erroneous for *defida* or *vedisa*)[50] is restricted to the provinces of Catanzaro and Reggio, while *sanceri*[51] "blood sausage," which occurs a few lines below, is used only in northern Calabria. The word *melizofidu* "melissa" (a plant) is a variant of *melizzòfudu*,[52] strictly southern, just as *pirria* "robin" and *secula* "coditremola," whereas *fravetta* "beccafico" is both northern and southern.

From the point of view of phonology, one finds that the northern Calabrian features predominate: in particular, *ll*, which in the south generally goes to a retroflex *d* (either long or short depending on the dialect), is mostly preserved (e.g. *alluma, chilli, stilli, illi*, etc.); *nd* is replaced by *nn*, a typically Cosentino feature (e.g. *sparannu, cumannami*, etc.); and Latin *fl* is reflected by *i* (*iuri* "fiore") rather then by *hj* as in southern Calabrian.

It can thus be concluded that the language of the Capitano is indeed a highly artificial form of Calabrian, resulting from a mixture of features drawn from both the northern and the southern dialects of the region, and thus likely to strike as very strange even a native Calabrian. How it could have been readily understood by the audiences of the Improvvisa is difficult to say, but it is worthwhile stressing that, in contrast with other

characters who spoke a pure dialect, the Capitano was characterized also
by the foreignness of his language, be it Spanish or Calabrian.

3.5 The servants

Of fundamental importance within the Commedia dell'Arte were the roles
of the male servants or *zanni*, of whom there were as a rule two and, according to Perrucci, "il Primo ha da essere astuto, pronto, faceto, arguto,
che vaglia ad intricare, deludere, beffare, ed ingannare il Mondo" (p. 215),
whereas the second one "deve essere sciocco, balordo, insensato di maniera,
che non sappia qual sia la destra, o la sinistra" (ibid.).

As far as the dialect to be spoken by the first servant, the matter was
of no great concern: Perrucci states that the part could be done "in qual-
sivoglia lingua" but especially in Milanese (by which he probably means
Lombard in general), Bergamask, Neapolitan or Sicilian. However, Perrucci then furnishes examples only in Neapolitan for the *maschera* known
as Coviello, though he specifies that the same passages could be translated
in Bergamask or in another dialect. Coviello's language is pure Neapolitan
and requires no special comment, but the following quotation will show
that, while it was far more intelligible than the Capitano's Calabrian, it
would have taxed a northern audience (*sh*, as was the case in 17th cent.
Neapolitan orthography, stands for palatal *s*):

St'azzione a lo shiore dell'huommene, a lo schiecco de Napole, a lo sfuorgio de
li Giuvene, a lo spamfio de la bellezza, a lo capo troppa de li smargiasse, a lo
Prencepe de li guattare, a lo Cuonsolo de li mbrogliune, a lo Quarto dell'arte
de l'ammasciature amoruse? Dare sto smacco a mè na Ciantella, Cacatronola,
Vommeca vracciolle, cierne pedeta, scola vallane, piede de papara, tallune fatte
a provola, scumma vruoccole, semmena pezzolle, jetta cantare Nzelle che tenze.
(p. 219)

As for the second servant, Perrucci again states that "di varie lingue
sogliono farsi i Secondi Zanni," but he then adds that in Lombardy and
in most of Italy the preferred dialect is Bergamask, in particular the variety spoken in the mountains of Bergamo. Here again a precise horizontal variety of a given dialect is prescribed, which Perrucci declares to
be particularly ridiculous and amusing. However, unfortunately, in this
instance he includes no examples of Bergamask speech, other than a single sonnet (p. 225), possibly because, as he himself states, he did not
know it sufficiently well. We are informed from other sources, however,
that Bergamask servants (Arlecchino and Brighella, though not mentioned
by Perrucci, where the two most famous ones) often tended to mod-

ify their dialect in the direction of Venetian, in order to make it more comprehensible.[53] In Naples, on the other hand, the second zanni was customarily played by the *maschera* known as Pulcinella, who of course spoke in Neapolitan and for whom Perrucci provides three passages as examples of the kind of speeches Pulcinella could utter on the stage. Pulcinella was to be a decidedly hilarious character and, among other things, Perrucci recommends that he should create laughter by misinterpreting and mistranslating Latin phrases,[54] and this was another way in which Latin could enter into the Improvvisa.

Finally, the roles of the maidservants or *fantesche* could be played in various dialects, including Tuscan, and in Naples "nell'idioma della plebe, imitando le Donne che fondachiere si chiamano" (p. 226), that is in the lowest vertical variety of Neapolitan. Perrucci exemplifies with three passages in Tuscan and two in Neapolitan, a total of five, of which four are in verse. Within the Commedia dell'Arte, the *fantesca* or *serva* could be either young and pretty, in which instance she often had an affair going with a male servant, or old and ugly, and then she generally played the role of a procuress, ready to assist in trick and intrigue. In either case, the part of the *fantesca* was apt to create very comical effects. A dialogue between a male and a female servant could involve two different dialects, and of this Perrucci gives an example in a later chapter, entitled "Delle Scene in Metafora e continuate, Equivoche, ed altre" in which the man speaks Neapolitan and the woman Tuscan (pp. 246–248). In this dialogue, the maidservant shows no difficulty in understanding such Neapolitan words as *sceregaziune, messiato, padeare, vommecare, appe, nchiasto, veppeta, mmescà, golio*, etc., all of which correspond to radically different words in Tuscan and would be unintelligible nowadays in northern Italy. The bilingual dialogue obviously implies a passive knowledge of Neapolitan on the part of the woman and, conversely, of Tuscan on the part of the man; when staged, it required at least a passive knowledge of both dialects on the part of the audience as well. It would seem likely that decoding would have been close to total in southern Italy, but only partial in the North where, however, the part of the male servant might have been played in Bergamask or another northern dialect.

3.6 *Songs and a* xaccara *in Calabrian*

Finally, in Perrucci's treatise of linguistic interest is still the chapter entitled "Delle azzioni ridicole, gesti travestimenti, Scene di notte, e canzoni" (pp. 249–255). Concerning the songs, Perrucci states: "Saranno anche ridicole le canzoni delle parti buffe in Scena, se saranno de' Zanni Berga-

maschi, Napoletani" (p. 252), and he furnishes as examples a song in
Neapolitan, one in Calabrian and a *xaccara*, written in a mixture of Calabrian and Spanish. The first song is in pure Neapolitan and requires
no further linguistic comment. The second one, in Calabrian, is written
in a composite dialect similar in every regard to the Capitano's peculiar
Calabrian already examined above, but it is worth quoting in full,[55] since
it was meant to be sung by a servant and is therefore a text of a different
nature:

> Chi Viennira? Chi Lena? Sti frattagghi!
> Nun ci nnè biella comu sta quatrara,
> Chi mi vruscia lu cori e li *ntramagghi*,
> Quannu da*dd*'occhi li tizzuni[56] spara.
> Tu comu nzunza mi consumi e squagghi,
> O comu lu cravuni *adda* carcara.
> Ma *sucavi*[57] li susti e li travagghi,
> Si mi ncucchiu cu tia, biella *litrara*.

Underlined elements are typically southern Calabrian (whether from a
phonetic, morphological or lexical standpoint), the rest may be regarded
as Cosentino or as Pancalabrian. Perrucci does not add a translation of
this song, but it can be rendered into Italian as follows:

> Che Venere? Che Elena? Queste frattaglie!
> Non ce n'è bella come questa ragazza,
> Che mi brucia il cuore e le interiora,
> Quando dagli occhi i tizzoni spara.
> tu come sugna mi consumi e squagli,
> O come il carbone alla fornace.
> Ma succhiai le molestie e i travagli,
> Se con te mi accoppio, bella fannullona.

Stylistically, this song befits a person of very limited education, just as a
servant, and—apart from the initial commonplace mythological references
—one easily perceives in its vocabulary and images the concrete flavour of
everyday life (cf. such lexemes as *ntramagghi*, *nzunza*, *cravuni*, *carcara*,
etc.) A simple comparison between the Calabrian original and the translation will show that a knowledge of Italian alone would surely not suffice
to understand this song, yet Perrucci shows no concern in this regard.

The last example of Sprachmischung which Perrucci supplies is the
xaccara "ove è ridicolosamente misto lo Spagnuolo col Calabrese." The
substantive *xaccara* may be reasonably assumed to be connected with the
verb *xaccari* "spaccare," which is common to both southern and northern
Calabrian, and would thus appear to have the meaning of "spacconata,

rodomontata (boasting, bragging)," and—though I have not found it attested elsewhere—it would seem to have been a well known contemporary term, since Perrucci does not bother to explain it at all. The *xaccara*
seems to be meant as a hilarious parody of those who attempted to speak
Spanish and unwittingly mixed it with their own dialect, or conversely
of those Spaniards who made an effort to express themselves in Italian,
with obviously amusing results. This hybrid language, Spanish-Calabrian
or Spanish-Italian, must thus be regarded as another, primarily satyrical,
component of the linguistic repertoire of the Improvvisa.

Though Perrucci refers to it more than once, he provides no examples
of *pezzi di repertorio* in Sicilian, and the same can be said of Milanese.

4. Conclusions

Our examination of those portions of Perrucci's treatise which are of
linguistic interest, along with the few bits of information that could be
gleaned from other sources, allows us at this point to answer some questions and to draw several conclusions.

It must of course be born in mind that Perrucci lived in the second
half of the 17th century and that *Dell'arte rappresentativa* appeared in
1699: thus it reflects the Commedia dell'Arte, including its linguistic
characteristics, as it was during that period, rather than, say, as it may
have been in its earlier Cinquecento stage.

4.1 The dialects of the maschere

The first consideration is that the use of the dialects was absolutely necessary and very extensive: there is no indication whatsoever that they
tended to merge towards a koine that might have been more understandable throughout the Peninsula. In fact, the distinction between Italian and
any one of the dialects was quite sharp.

Of all the characters of the Commedia dell'Arte, only the lovers were
obligatorily to speak in Italian (or literary Tuscan, which at the time was
synonymous with it), though several other characters, in particular the
Capitano, could do so optionally. Certain characters, on the other hand,
could speak exclusively in a specific dialect, with which they were thoroughly identified. Thus, the old man Pantalone spoke only in Venetian
and the Dottore could be done only in Bolognese though (if necessary) in
a Tuscanized and Venetized form of it, obligatorily spangled with abundant Latin formulae and quotations: this made Latin one of the languages
of the Commedia dell'Arte, which however was used only for "special

effects," e.g. to confer gravity and dignity to the Dottore or to create comical misunderstandings on the part of the servants.[58] Certain masks, such as Coviello and Pulcinella, were possible only in Neapolitan.

The remaining *maschere* were not as invariably identified with one single dialect, though certain restrictions applied. The Capitano, for instance, spoke mostly in Spanish, Calabrian or Italian, occasionally in Neapolitan or Sicilian, and there is no indication whatsoever that he could have been done in Bergamask or Venetian. In fact, these dialects were probably considered unsuited to his role (the reason would have to be determined on the basis of an historical investigation on the origin of this character).[59]

Concerning the servants, they spoke primarily in Bergamask or in Neapolitan, probably depending on where the comedy was staged (though Perrucci does not so specify explicitly), but Tuscan was also possible, especially for the female servants.

4.2   The qualities of the dialects

Two of the dialects of the Commedia dell'Arte, beside Tuscan, were always to be spoken in a pure form, namely Neapolitan and Venetian.[60] According to Perrucci, this applied to Bergamask as well, but other sources suggest that, in fact, this dialect tended to be more or less mixed with Venetian.

In several cases, Perrucci specifies which vertical or horizontal variety of a given dialect was to be selected, primarily in order to obtain greater comical effects. Thus, the *zanni* or male servants, if done in Bergamask, were to use its rustic, mountain variety, not the urban dialect of the city of Bergamo; the female servants, if played in Neapolitan, were to adopt its lowest horizontal variety; Cassandro d'Aretusi, a not very common Tuscan equivalent of Pantalone, was to use lower class Florentine; and, finally, the Capitano, if played in Calabrian, was to use the Cosentino horizontal variety.

The case of Calabrian, however, is much more complex, as we have seen. Though it was supposed to be based principally on the Cosentino variety, it was in fact an artificial and composite dialect, at least as reflected by the exemplificatory passages provided by Perrucci, and it could also be employed in a Sprachmischung form mixed with Spanish. It is noteworthy that in his exemplifications Perrucci is quite generous with Calabrian, a dialect not generally included among the most relevant of the Improvvisa, while—as already noted—he offers no samples of Sicilian. The matter is somewhet puzzling, since Perrucci was a native of Palermo and, though he had moved to Naples at a young age, surely he would have encountered no difficulty with Sicilian given the fact that he easily managed to write passages in several northern dialects. One is thus led to believe that in Perrucci's estimation Sicilian was of no great consequence within the linguistic economy of the Commedia dell'Arte[61] while, on the other hand, Calabrian must have been often employed, at least in Naples, the capital city of southern Italy, to which many Calabrians had naturally immigrated. The matter requires further investigation.

4.3   The problems of multilingualism

Concerning the reasons for the multilingual character of the Commedia dell'Arte, Perrucci limits himself to stating that "La diversità delle lingue suole dare gran diletto nelle Comedie" (p. 194) and, as Tessari observes,

in questo, dunque, la Commedia dell'Arte non si discosta dall'atteggiamento consueto a tanto teatro rinascimentale, anzi sviluppa con altissimo zelo l'intenzionalità comica del suo aspetto linguistico, ognora concentrando in una sola trama scenica quanti più idiomi è possibile . . .[62]

The extent to which the Italian dialects differ among themselves at all levels—phonetic, morphological, syntactic and lexical—has been stressed above at various points and, in connection with the Commedia dell'Arte, Perrucci's own specimens are good evidence of it. Yet, in the Cinquecento and the Seicento their use for artistic purposes was extensive, not only within the Improvvisa, but also in the more erudite, literary theatre of the times. One of the questions we raised at the beginning of this paper was how the audience could decode messages cast in such a bewildering, if often amusing, assortment of tongues.

While no conclusive answer has emerged from our examination of Perrucci's treatise and of other evidence available to us, three assumptions may confidently be made.

Firstly, given the fact that only a very few could speak Italian in the 16th and 17th centuries, the inhabitants of the Peninsula must have been accustomed to hearing dialects other than their own to a much greater extent than is the case nowadays. Contrary to the present day state of affairs, all social classes, regardless of wealth and education, spoke dialect at all times, though of course not necessarily the same vertical variety. Consequently, passive knowledge of various dialects must have been widespread, especially in places where persons of different regional origin lived together, such as large cities and the various courts of Italy. The attitude towards the dialects of others must have been on the whole positive, though certain low vertical varieties or rustic horizontal varieties must have been the source of amusement for people who spoke, or thought they did, a more refined language, and of this the Commedia dell'Arte took full advantage. As in other ways, it was linguistically a *speculum vitae.*

Secondly, as Perrucci explicitly prescribes for Bolognese, so too for the other dialects certain adjustments must have been made more or less intuitively depending on the locality and the environment in which the actors found themselves staging their plays, and the lexicon, at least, must have been tempered with lexemes of wide geographical distribution and, therefore, general intelligibility.

Thirdly, imperfect decoding surely still occurred on the part of the audience as well as, for effect, on the part of the actors, and of this some evidence can be found in the published plays of the period.

In the first scene of the first act of Pier Maria Cecchini's *L'amico tradito* (1633), Pantalone and the Dottore are having a heated argument concerning their respective sons. Part of the dialogue goes as follows:

DOTTORE: Putana d' mi, an sidi in la gran colra, e sì ha parladi tant'alterad, ch'al s' comprend ch'avidi pers 'l giudizi, e sì an savidi quel ch'an dsì.[63]

PANTALONE: Come, se so quel che digo, se mio dir xe fondao su 'l far de mio fio?

DOTTORE: Vostr fiol ha del far? Mo a lu andrà ben, perché l'è car quest ann. E chi gh' l'ha dà a Virgini? Ah furb, al m' l'ha rubà a mi! Dadm un poch al mia far, via prest al mia far.[64]

PANTOLONE: No se intendemo, sior capochia.

DOTTORE: Com ch'an v'intend? al se declina hoc far farriis al furment triticum tritidici . . . An intend molt ben mi![65]

PANTALONE: Nol xe el far nome, el xe el far verbo, che significa far poltronarie come fa vostro fio, e che sia la veritae, eccolo ch'el vien in qua con una putana. (E si ritira)[66]

We have here an example of an equivocation that occurs between characters who are speaking two different dialects, both of which are *northern.* The Dottore takes the word *far* to mean "spelt (a type of wheat)," whereas in Venetian it is the infinitive of the verb "to do, to make" and, used as a substantive, it can mean "behaviour, way of acting." But, in Bolognese, the equivalent of Venetian *far* is *fer* (phonemically /fǽːr/),[67] hence the misunderstanding. In the same comedy, Act III, Sc. XII, the Capitano bluntly declares that he does not understand the Dottore (whose Bolognese, in this play, is on the whole quite genuine):

CAPITANO: Voi Dottore? esercitate l'avvocato? o siete giudice? o pur un uomo vestito così per far ridere?

DOTTORE: A son Dottor, a so far l'avocat, e sì a spier d' far al zuds per mandarv

GIANRENZO P. CLIVIO

in galea a farv pianzer.[68]

CAPITANO: Io non intendo la scabrosità di questa vostra lingua.[69]

In this instance, it is a Tuscan speaking character, the Capitano, who encounters difficulties with Bolognese, while an audience to whom this dialect was fully familiar would surely have found the Dottore's words and the Capitano's failure to understand them very hilarious. Of similar expedients the art of buffoonery, of which the actors of the Improvvisa were masters, took full advantage. But, as already mentioned,[70] the Commedia erudita of the Cinquecento, and in general the literary theatre of the 16th and 17th centuries was not at all averse to employing misunderstandings (though these usually involved Latin rather than the dialects) as a device to create amusement.

It is in fact quite clear that the Commedia dell'Arte has numerous aspects in common with the regular theatre of the Cinquecento and the Seicento, multilingualism being surely the most obvious trait.[71] Further research on the linguistic dimension of the Commedia dell'Arte will have to be carried out in conjunction, therefore, with similar research on the languages of the regular theatre, so far not analysed from a linguistic and sociolinguistic point of view, as well as with an effort to investigate the actual everyday linguistic behaviour in the Italy of the Renaissance and the Baroque periods, quite apart from the higher manifestations embodied in literature. As observed by Grayson, "le nostre conoscenze sono ancora troppo limitate ai livelli superiori dell'espressione letteraria e alle disquisizioni di un''élite,' per permetterci uno sguardo veramente complessivo delle lingue di quell'età in tutte le loro manifestazioni."[72]

University of Toronto

NOTES

1 See for instance C. Miclachevsky, *La Commedia dell'Arte ou le théâtre des comédiens Italiens des XVI, XVII et XVIII siècles* (Paris: Schiffrin, 1927); G. Attinger, *L'esprit de la Commedia dell'Arte dans le théâtre français* (Paris: Librairie Théâtrale, 1950); W. Krömer, *Die italienische Commedia dell'Arte* (Darmstadt: Wissenschaftliche Buchgesellschaft, 1976); R. Spörri, *Die Commedia dell'Arte und ihre Figuren* (Wadenswil: Stutz, 1977). Contributions in other languages as well, such as Spanish, though less common, are by no means lacking. Very useful, in English, are K.M. Lea, *Italian Popular Comedy: A Study in the Commedia dell'Arte, 1560–1620* (New York: Clarendon Press, 1934), and the two books by A. Nicoll, *The World of Harlequin: A Critical Study of the Commedia dell'Arte* (Cambridge: University Press, 1963) and *Masks, Mimes and Miracles: Studies in the Popular Theatre* (New York:

Cooper Square Publishers, 1963). See also T.F. Heck, *Commedia dell'Arte: A Guide to the Primary and Secondary Literature* (New York: Garland, 1988). In Dutch, see R.L. Erenstein, *De geschiedenis van Commedia dell'Arte* (Amsterdam: International Theatre Bookshop, 1985).

2 French and German appear to have been used only in a pidgin form (see for instance M. Cortelazzo, "La figura e la lingua del "todesco" nella letteratura veneziana rinascimentale," *Scritti in onore di Giuliano Bonfante*, Brescia: Paideia, 1976, 173–182), whereas (a form of) Hebrew is spoken in a few comedies by characters playing the role of Italian Jews, as is the case in Orazio Vecchi's *Amfiparnaso* (Venice, 1597)—on which see M. Scherillo, *L'opera buffa napoletana* (Milan: Sandron, 1917), 5–15—and in Giovan Battista Andreini's *Lo schiavetto* (Milan, 1612). On the case of Greek, see especially L. Lazzerini, "Il "greghesco" a Venezia tra realtà e "ludus": saggio sulla commedia poliglotta nel Cinquecento," *Studi di filologia italiana* 35 (1977), 29–95, as well as the works by M. Cortelazzo, *L'influsso linguistico greco a Venezia* (Bologna: Il Mulino, 1970), and "Nuovo contributo alla conoscenza del grechesco," *L'Italia dialettale* 35 (1972), 50–64.

3 According to L. Fassò, about 800 scenari have survived (see his *Teatro dialettale del Seicento*, Turin: Einaudi, 1979, 219). See also A. Bartoli, *Scenari inediti della Commedia dell'Arte* (Florence, 1880).

4 Although the use of Milanese is attested only very rarely in the Commedia dell'Arte, various Commedia dell'Arte companies performed in Milan during the 17th century (see A. Paglicci Brozzi, *Contributo alla storia del teatro: il teatro a Milano nel secolo XVII*, Milan, 1891, and S. Pagani, *Il teatro milanese*, Milan: Cescina, 1944). See also below, n. 9.

5 In Piedmont however, though the Commedia dell'Arte does not seem to have flourished particularly in the region, examples of multilingual theatre are by no means lacking. The most important author is by far Giovan Giorgio Alione, who wrote primarily in the Astesan variety of Piedmontese, but also introduced in some of his "farse" (published in 1521) characters who expressed themselves in Milanese, French and other rural varieties of Piedmontese (see the modern edition by E. Bottasso, *L'opera piacevole*, Bologna: Palmaverde, 1953). Later in the same century, a certain Bartolomeo Brayda wrote a *Comedia pastorale*, published in Turin in 1556, in which one of the characters, a "villano," speaks in rural Piedmontese. Of great interest, at least from a documentary point of view, would probably have been the *Margarita*, a pastoral tragicomedy by Marcantonio Gorena, whose unpublished manuscript has been lost. We know, however, that it was staged in 1608 and that it contained characters who spoke in various dialects, including Piedmontese, Venetian and Bolognese (see L. Collino, *Storia della poesia dialettale piemontese*, Turin: Paravia, 1924, 43–44). To the 17th century belongs also the *Cont Piolet*, a rather pleasant comedy by Carlo Giambattista Tana (1649–1713), bilingual in Piedmontese and Italian, which was not published until 1784. On this play, B. Croce commented very

favourably in *Quaderni della critica* 9 (Nov. 1947), 30–40, and subsequently there have been several modern editions (see for instance the one included in L. Fassò's *Teatro dialettale del Seicento*, op. cit. (above, n. 3), 117–214).

6 Paolo Veraldo's *Mascherate et capricci dilettevoli, recitativi in comedie & da cantarsi in ogni sorte d'istromenti* (Venice, 1672) contains a song in Genoese (see V. Pandolfi, *La Commedia dell'Arte*, Florence: Sansoni, 1957–1961, IV, 164). Aside from the Commedia dell'Arte, poetry in Genoese was indeed being written in the first half of the 17th century (the best known author is Gian Giacomo Cavallo, who published *Ra cittara Zeneize* in 1636).

7 See the *Spiegazioni delli lazzi* in E. Petraccone, *La Commedia dell'Arte: storia, tecnica, scenari* (Naples: Ricciardi, 1927), 263–272.

8 The *Discorso* was not published during the author's lifetime and the only edition we have is the one by Irene Mamczarz (Milan: Il Polifilo, 1973). See pp. 27–28 for the remarks on the dialects.

9 On C.M. Maggi, the major 17th century Milanese author, see D. Isella, "I volgari milanesi di C.M. Maggi," *Studi di filologia italiana* 20 (1962), 315–363, "Le rime milanesi di C.M. Maggi," *Studi secenteschi* 6 (1965), 67–264, as well as Isella's edition of Maggi's theatre, *Il teatro milanese* (Turin: Einaudi, 1964), of which part of the introduction has been reprinted with the title "Il dialetto come strumento di verità e di moralità: Carlo Maria Maggi" in G.L. Beccaria, ed., *Letteratura e dialetto* (Bologna: Zanichelli, 1983), 50–59.

10 On Ruzante see L. Zorzi's edition of the *Teatro* (Turin: Einaudi, 1969²). On his language, see R. Wendriner, *Die paduanische Mundart bei Ruzante* (Breslau, 1889), and M. Milano, "Note sulla lingua del Ruzante," *Atti dell'Istituto Veneto di Scienze, Lettere ed Arti* 123 (1963–64), 517–542.

11 Gianfranco Folena aptly observed that the Commedia dell'Arte, just as tragedy in Piedmont, "ha percorso in un altro stato di confine, quello veneziano, la sua più luminosa parabola, quella che ha ai suoi estremi Ruzzante e Goldoni" (p. xix of the *Introduzione* to L. Vanossi et al., *Lingua e strutture del teatro italiano del Rinascimento* (Padua: Liviana, 1970).

12 A. Perrucci, *Dell'arte rappresentativa premeditata ed all'improvviso*. Testo, introduzione e bibliografia a cura di Anton Giulio Bragaglia (Florence: Sansoni, 1961). Bragaglia's edition reproduces the original without any attempt at modernizing and normalizing punctuation and capitalization, nor are typographical abbreviations resolved or misprints corrected. In quotations, a few obvious errors will be rectified, but we shall otherwise reproduce the text as given by Bragaglia.

13 A list of plays published by the professional actors and actresses of the Commedia dell'Arte is provided by K.M. Lea, op. cit. (above, n. 1), 462–464.

14 See L. Falavolti, *Commedie dei comici dell'Arte* (Turin: Utet, 1982), in which five such comedies are edited with an introduction and ample bibliographical information.

15 His best known work in Neapolitan is a long poem in six cantos entitled

L'Agnano zeffonnato (Naples, 1678) which already Ferdinando Galiani, the first historian of Neapolitan literature, regarded as "un grazioso poema . . . da annoverarsi tra i più distinti e preggevoli del nostro dialetto" (F. Galiani, *Del dialetto napoletano*, ed. by E. Malato, Rome: Bulzoni, 1970, 180; the first edition was published in Naples in 1779). See now Andrea Perrucci, *Le opere napoletane* ed. by L. Facecchia (Rome: Il Tornese, 1986).

16 See *Bibliotheca Sicula sive De Scriptoribus siculis* (Palermo, 1707), I, 32–34.

17 An annotated list of Perrucci's works is provided by Bragaglia, op. cit. (above, n. 12), 35–48.

18 Ibid., 26.

19 See "L'Arte rappresentativa di Andrea Perrucci e la lingua della Commedia dell'Arte," in L. Vanossi et al., op. cit. (above, n. 11), 357–438.

20 See F. Taviani and M. Schino, *Il segreto della Commedia dell'Arte* (Florence: Usher, 1982), and C. Molinari, *La Commedia dell'Arte* (Milan: Mondadori, 1985).

21 See M. Apollonio, *Storia della Commedia dell'Arte* (Rome: Augustea, 1930), 260–267. Even in his later *Storia del teatro italiano* (Florence: Sansoni, 1981, 2 vols.), which devotes about 80 pages to the Commedia dell'Arte, Apollonio mentions Perrucci only in passing and appears not to be aware of Bragaglia's new edition.

22 See I. Sanesi, *La Commedia* (Milan: Vallardi, 1954²) I, 501–633.

23 It should be noted that Perrucci does not use the term *dialetto* "dialect" in the modern sense of the word: he refers to Venetian, Neapolitan, Calabrian, Bolognese, Bergamask, Sicilian, Lombard, etc. as *lingue* "languages," just as he does when talking about Italian or Spanish. Though Perrucci employs *dialetto* a couple of times, the meaning he attributes to it seems to be that of vertical variety of a language. In Perrucci's times the modern meanings of *lingua* and *dialetto* had not yet become established, so that those which are now called *dialetti*, Perrucci calls *lingue*, or—for the sake of variety—at times *linguaggi* or *idiomi*, etc. On the history of the word *dialetto*, see M. Alinei,"*Dialetto*: un concetto rinascimentale fiorentino" in his book *Lingua e dialetti: struttura, storia e geografia* (Bologna: Il Mulino, 1984), 169–200.

24 The first of his examples, *Xhavallo* for *Cavallo*, is actually inaccurate, a case of hypercharacterization, since the *c* would not be aspirated in word initial position (aspiration occurs only intervocalically). The best comprehensive study of the "gorgia toscana" is H.J. Izzo's monograph *Tuscan and Etruscan* (Toronto: University of Toronto Press, 1972).

25 This distinction actually applies in Italian only to front and back mid vowels, each of which may occur as high-mid or low-mid. This difference is phonemic in Tuscany, but has a very low functional yield, though great importance was attached to it by purists in the past, in spite of the fact that it is not reflected by the standard Italian orthography.

26 See, for instance, Th. Labande-Jeanroy, *La question de la langue en Italie*

(Strasbourg: Istra, 1925); M. Vitale, *La questione della lingua* (Palermo: Palumbo, 1978²); B.T. Sozzi, *Aspetti e momenti della questione della lingua* (Padua: Liviana Editr., 1955); F. Ageno, "Sulle controversie linguistiche in Italia," *Giornale storico della letteratura italiana* 138 (1961), 9–100; and, in English, R.A. Hall Jr., *The Italian Questione della lingua* (Chapel Hill, N.C.: University of North Carolina Press, 1942).

27 On the very high incidence of illiteracy and extremely rare knowledge of standard Italian among the general population outside of Tuscany and Rome as late as 1860, see T. De Mauro, *Storia linguistica dell'Italia unita* (Bari: Laterza, 1963), 41. He comes to the conclusion that "negli anni dell'unificazione nazionale, gli italofoni, lungi dal rappresentare la totalità dei cittadini italiani, erano poco più di seicentomila su una popolazione che aveva superato i 25 milioni di individui: a mala pena, dunque, il 2,5% della popolazione."

28 See for instance the language used by Lelia in the anonymous *Ingannati*, one of the most famous comedies of 16th century Italian theatre, or by Messer Giannino in *L'Amor costante* by Alessandro Piccolomini (1536). Modern editions of both plays can be read in I. Sanesi, *Commedie del Cinquecento* (Bari: Laterza, 1912, 2 vols.).

29 See n. 23 above. Perrucci uses "dialetti" again in connection with Bergamask: ". . . porteremo un Sonetto in lingua Bergamasca . . . mi scusi bensì chi legge se mal prattico in quella lingua non accerto i suoi propri dialetti" (225). Here again it would seem clear that Perrucci is referring to vertical and horizontal varieties of a specific dialect.

30 Perrucci's spelling of Venetian is rather inaccurate: for instance, all double consonants, except for *ss* which represents a voiceless *s*, should be written single (Venetian has no long consonants), and *z* stands for *s*. Word division is also occasionally faulty.

31 See G. Boerio, *Dizionario del dialetto veneziano* (Venice, 1856), s.v.

32 Perrucci notes that "la parte di Tartaglia si prattica per lo più in Napoli dove si figura un huomo, che stenta a proferire le parole . . ." (209). Tartaglia appeared for instance in the comedy entitled *Convitato di pietra*, whose *scenario* was published for the first time by L. Fassò, op. cit. (above, n. 3), 233–242.

33 For further details, see A. Gaudenzi, *I suoni, le forme e le parole dell'odierno dialetto della Città di Bologna* (Turin, 1889), and F. Coco, *Il dialetto di Bologna. Fonetica storica e analisi strutturale* (Bologna: Il Mulino, 1970).

34 Quoted from the partial reprint of Cecchini's *Frutti delle moderne comedie et avisi a chi le recita* (Padua, 1628) provided by V. Pandolfi in *La Commedia dell'Arte*, op. cit. (above, n. 6), IV, 99.

35 As, to point out only one case, in *beveron* "zuppa," which should be *bevron* (see C. Coronedi Berti, *Vocabolario bolognese-italiano*, Bologna, 1869–1877, s.v.).

36 On the sound structure of Venetian see G.C. Lepschy, "Fonematica veneziana," *L'Italia Dialettale* 25 (1962), 1–22. A good general treatment of the dialects

of the entire Veneto region is A. Zamboni, *Veneto* (*Profilo dei dialetti italiani*, 5), (Pisa: Pacini, 1974).

37 On whom see for instance O. Guerrini, *La vita e le opere di Giulio Cesare Croce* (Bologna, 1879).

38 See for instance the texts published by B. Biondelli, *Saggio sui dialetti gallo-italici* (Milan, 1853), 321 foll.

39 See E. Petraccone, op. cit. (above, n. 7), 257–261.

40 The actor Francesco Andreini, famous for his skill in the role of the Captain, published a book entitled *Le bravure del Capitano Spavento divise in molti ragionamenti in forma di dialogo* (Venice, 1607), on which see C. Molinari, op. cit. (above, n. 20), 116–117.

41 This is the name of one of the two Captains, for instance, in Silvio Fiorillo's *La Lucilla costante, con le ridicolose disfide e prodezze di Pulcinella* (Naples, 1632). The second one is called Capitan Squarcialeone. On Fiorillo see G. Checchi, *Silvio Fiorillo in arte Capitan Mattamoros* (Capua: Museo Provinciale Campano, 1986).

42 In F. Andreini's *La Campanaccia*, a comedy in which the Capitano speaks Italian, while the Dottore, who expresses himself in Bolognese as normal, bears the unusual name of Campanaccio.

43 As in Pier Maria Cecchini's *L'amico tradito* (Venice, 1633).

44 In Piccolomini's *L'amor costante* (already mentioned above, n. 28), for instance, several characters speak in Spanish, as does Capitan Matamoros in S. Fiorillo's *La lucilla costante* (see above, n. 41). On the linguistic and literary consequences of Spanish domination in Italy, see G.L. Beccaria, *Spagnolo e spagnoli in Italia* (Turin: Giappichelli, 1967).

45 Perrucci hastens to add the following translation: "Ben' habbia il Sollione, vuoi che ti dia mille e trecento bastonate a gli omeri? che t'apra la zucca, ti misuri con un pezzo di legno le spalle? che ti faccia in pezzi, in minuzzoli, ed in brani?"

46 But Spanish was apparently the preferred language for the Capitano in the opinion of many others, including Pier Maria Cecchini, in his days a famous actor and the author of the already mentioned *Frutti delle moderne comedie* (above, n. 34), who states, concerning the Capitano, "questa iperbolica parte par che suoni meglio nella spagnuola che nell'italiana lingua" (quoted from the partial reprint in E. Petraccone, *La Commedia dell'Arte*, op. cit. [above, n. 7], 13). See also, in the same volume by Petraccone, L. Riccoboni's comments: "La domination des espagnols en Italie attira quelques comédiens de leur nation dans le pays et cela donna au théâtre des Capitans, qui parlaient purement la langue espagnole ou une mélange des deux langues" (59); taken from Riccoboni's *Histoire du théâtre italien*, Paris, 1727).

47 On the linguistic division of Calabria see G. Rohlfs's introduction to his *Nuovo dizionario dialettale della Calabria* (Ravenna: Longo, 1977) as well as his various articles collected in *Calabria e Salento* (Ravenna: Longo, 1980).

48 On the Greek substratum in Calabria see in particular G. Rohlfs, *Scavi linguistici nella Magna Grecia* (Galatina: Congedo, 1974) and *Nuovi scavi linguistici nella antica Magna Grecia* (Palermo: Istituto siciliano di studi bizantini e neoellenici, 1972).

49 We are here interested in examining the Capitano's Calabrian from a linguistic point of view. For an interesting stylistic analysis of the Capitano's speech, see R. Tessari, *La Commedia dell'Arte nel Seicento* (Florence: Olschki, 1959), 273–277.

50 See G. Rohlfs, *Nuovo dizionario*, op. cit. (above, n. 47), s.v. (238 and 759).

51 See ibid. s.v. *sangieri* (601).

52 Ibid., s.v. (411). The common name of the "melissa" in Cosentino is *ranghellu*, though this form is not given by L. Accattatis, whose *Vocabolario del dialetto calabrese* (Cosenza, 1898)—in spite of its title—reflects primarily the language of the "Casali" (i.e. surrounding villages) of Cosenza, to which Purrucci makes reference. Accattatis' dictionary, however, is based mostly on literary sources and is not always reliable.

53 See P. Spezzani, op. cit. (above, n. 19), 403–406. For later developments in the type of language spoken by the Bergamask *zanni*, see the two important articles by G. Folena, "Il linguaggio del Goldoni dall'improvviso al concertato," *Paragone* 8 (1957), 4–28; and "L'esperienza linguistica di Carlo Goldoni," *Lettere italiane* 10 (1958), 23–24 and 46–47.

54 Perrucci suggests, for instance, that Pulcinella could translate Virgil's line "Ancora fundabat naves et littora curvae" by "L'ancora sfonnava la nave e mannava na lettera co lo cuorvo" (224).

55 Since the text as given by Perrucci contains several misprints that must be corrected in order for it to be understood, we do so and also normalize punctuation and capitalization.

56 Bragaglia has "vizzuni" which is nonexistent.

57 Bragaglia writes in two words "su cavi," which makes no sense.

58 The use of Latin for various effects is by no means unusual in the literary theatre of the 16th and 17th centuries. See for instance Francesco Belo's comedy *Il pedante*, published in Rome in 1529, or Lodovico Dolce's *Il ragazzo* (Venice, 1541).

59 A number of useful considerations on the matter are offered by P. Spezzani, op. cit. (above, n. 19), 395–396.

60 It should be remembered that, by the 17th century, Venetian had become a language of not inconsiderable prestige which, because of political and economic circumstances, had spread far beyond the limits of the city of Venice. See G. Folena, "Introduzione al veneziano *de là da mar*" in A. Pertusi, ed., *Venezia e il Levante fino al secolo XV* (Florence: Olschki, 1973), I, 297–346. Venetian was also used in formal situations within the Venetian state: see N. Vianello, "Il veneziano lingua del foro veneto nella seconda metà del secolo XVIII," *Lingua nostra* 18 (1957), 68–73. As for Neapolitan, it was the parler *directeur* for the

whole of southern Italy: see A. Varvaro, "Bilancio degli studi sulla storia linguistica meridionale" in P. Giannantonio, ed., *Cultura meridionale e letteratura italiana* (Atti dell'XI Congresso dell'Associazione Internazionale per gli Studi di Lingua e Letteratura Italiana), (Naples: Loffredo, 1982), 25–37, especially 34–35.

61 However, Virgilio Verrucci's famous *Li diversi linguaggi* (Venice, 1609), for instance, has a Pedant who speaks in Sicilian, and Sicilian is the most important dialect in Vincenzo Belando's *Gl'amorosi inganni* (Naples, 1609). Both of these plays are very much within the tradition of the Commedia dell'Arte. Of the latter, see the recent edition in S. Ferrone, ed., *Commedia dell'Arte* (Milan: Mursia, 1985–87, 2 vols.).

62 See R. Tessari, op. cit. (above, n. 49), 254.

63 "Puttana di me, siete in gran collera e così avete parlato tanto arrabbiato, che si comprende che avete perso il giudizio, e così non sapete quello che dite."

64 "Vostro figlio ha del farro? Ora a lui andrà bene, perché è caro quest'anno. E chi gliel'ha dato a Virginio? Ah furbo, l'ha rubato a me! Datemi un po' il mio farro, via presto, il mio farro."

65 "Come non v'intendo? Si declina questo far farris, frumento da macinare . . . Vi intendo molto bene io!"

66 The text is taken from Falavolti's edition, op. cit. (above, n. 14), 692.

67 See Gaudenzi, op. cit. (above, n. 33), xii. In normal spelling, however, *fer* is frequently written *far*, since the tonic vowel (which is long) is phonetically intermediate between a central *a* and a low open *e*.

68 "Sono dottore, so fare l'avvocato, e così spero di fare il giudice per mandarvi in galera a farvi piangere."

69 See Falavolti, op. cit. (above, n. 14), 736.

70 See above, n. 58.

71 On multilingualism in the 16th century, see for instance G. Folena, "Le lingue della commedia e la commedia delle lingue" in *Scritti linguistici in onore di Giovan Battista Pellegrini* (Pisa: Pacini, 1983), 1485–1513, and I. Paccagnella, *Il fasto delle lingue: plurilinguismo letterario nel Cinquecento* (Rome: Bulzoni, 1984).

72 C. Grayson, "Le lingue del Rinascimento" in V. Branca et al., eds., *Il Rinascimento: Aspetti e problemi attuali* (Atti del X Congresso dell'Associazione Internazionale per gli Studi di Lingua e Letteratura Italiana), (Florence: Olschki, 1982), 335–352, quotation from p. 336.

Marco De Marinis

Appunti per uno studio diacronico della recitazione nella *commedia dell'arte*

Un silenzio paradossale

Lo studioso che decida di occuparsi della recitazione degli attori appartenenti alle compagnie italiane che, fra il XVI e il XVIII secolo, inventarono ed esportarono in tutta Europa quel modo di fare teatro chiamato poi Commedia dell'Arte, si trova subito di fronte a quello che, almeno in apparenza, costituisce un paradosso, uno dei tanti con i quali, per la verità, la Commedia dell'Arte ci costringe a fare i conti in sede di indagine storico-critica. Questo paradosso possiamo enunciarlo nel modo seguente: anche nel caso della Commedia dell'Arte, che pure fu incontestabilmente ed essenzialmente un teatro d'attore, e in cui quindi la recitazione, il *jeu*, era la componente principale, siamo alle prese con una quasi totale mancanza di documenti sulle tecniche e sul lavoro degli attori, sul loro addestramento, sulla loro preparazione fisica e vocale. E conviene aggiungere subito che non si tratta di una accidentale carenza documentaria ma di un silenzio premeditato dei comici riguardo ad alcuni elementi essenziali della loro arte (Taviani 1982:419). Se andiamo a sfogliare lo straripante materiale letterario tramandato dai comici (rime, scenari e commedie, testi di polemica e di difesa, autobiografie, epistolari con migliaia di lettere), troveremo informazioni su tutto: sulla vita nomade delle compagnie, sui loro viaggi, sulle vicissitudini interne (rivalità, gelosie, odi e meschinità) e sui rapporti con l'esterno (corti, città, autorità civili e religiose), questi ultimi improntati soprattutto alla difesa e alla promozione degli spettacoli. Ma non troveremo (se non eccezionalmente: si pensi ai diari scenici di Dominique Biancolelli [Spada 1969]) informazioni precise su quello che invece, con ogni verosimiglianza, doveva rappresentare la parte più importante della loro attività.

Beninteso, non è che i comici tacciano completamente del loro lavoro di attori ma—come osserva ancora Taviani (1.c.)—ne parlano solo per quegli aspetti in cui esso è assimilabile al lavoro dell'*oratore* o del *letterato*, cioè a lavori basati su tecniche conosciute e palesi; mentre passano sotto silenzio proprio ciò che il loro mestiere doveva avere di teatralmente specifico e di diverso rispetto agli altri.

Le rare volte che nelle testimonianze letterarie si apre uno spiraglio sull'attività interna delle compagnie dell'Arte quelli che ci vengono mostrati, più che attori di una troupe teatrale, sembrano—come è stato argutamente notato—"studenti agli esami o monaci in biblioteca." E' l'immagine che emerge, ad esempio, dalle parole della fantesca nell'VIII prologo di Domenico Bruni sulle *Miserie de' comici* (1621):

La mattina la signora mi chiama: -Olà, Ricciolina, portami la innamorata Fiammetta che voglio studiare. Pantalone mi domanda le lettere del Calmo. Il capitano le Bravure del Capitano Spavento. Il zanni le astuzie di Bertoldo, il Fugilozio e le Ore di Ricreazione. Graziano le sentenze dell'Erborense e la novissima Poliantea. Franceschina vuole la Celestina per imparare a fare la ruffiana. L'innamorato vuol l'opera di Platone e quasi in un punto chi mi comanda una cosa, chi un'altra.

Da Francesco Andreini a Pier Maria Cecchini, da Niccolò Barbieri a Andrea Perrucci, i comici italiani ci presentano il lavoro sulle "parti" soprattutto, se non soltanto, come un lavoro di letterati su materiali letterari, tacendo del tutto sull'almeno altrettanto importante attività di *training* fisico (gestuale e vocale) che quelle "parti" non potevano non comportare (si ricordi, in proposito, che non solo i servi eseguivano azioni acrobatiche e di grande impegno ginnico-atletico, ma anche il Capitano e il Magnifico, e inoltre c'era la danza che costituiva una componente di rilievo per quasi tutti i ruoli, compreso quello degli Innamorati).

Ad averne il tempo sarebbe interessante soffermarsi un po' sulle possibili ragioni di questa vera e propria strategia del silenzio messa in atto dagli antichi comici italiani.[1] Ma converrà invece passare subito a vedere in che modo è stato possibile, è oggi possibile, infrangere almeno parzialmente questo silenzio.

Indizi iconografici

Se, nonostante tutto, questa relazione sulle tecniche di recitazione nella Commedia dell'Arte non si arresta qua, in sostanza ancor prima di cominciare veramente, se insomma è possibile aprire almeno degli squarci nello spesso velo che avvolge, per loro stessa scelta, il lavoro interno dei comici—com'è noto—lo dobbiamo in massima parte al materiale iconografico piuttosto abbondante che ci è stato trasmesso sulle compagnie italiane fra XVI e XVIII secolo.

Si tratta, però, diciamolo subito, di un materiale eterogeneo e disegua-
le, un cui limite comune è inoltre quello di presentare quasi sempre delle
"scene tipiche," con gli attori in posa. Molto meno spesso esso mostra gli
attori in azione durante la recita e quasi mai il prima o il slopo dello spettacolo. Anche le pochissime eccezioni al riguardo, se si esclude la famosa
immagine satirica del 1670 con Élomire (Molière) allievo di Scaramouche (Fiorilli),[2] non mostrano mai attori al lavoro, preferendo in genere il
momento dell'arrivo dei comici sul luogo dello spettacolo, sia esso una
corte o una piazza cittadina.[3]

Nonostante che l'importanza fondamentale delle fonti iconografiche per
lo studio della Commedia dell'Arte sia riconosciuta da tempo,[4] c'è da
constatare come lo stato delle ricerche al riguardo sia ancora parecchio
arretrato. Manca tuttora un lavoro di raccolta e di sistemazione organica
di questi materiali[5] e ancora incerti e molto parziali risultano i rari tentativi di seria analisi critica (cfr., comunque, Beijer 1928, 1957; McDowell
1942; Sterling 1943; Adhémar 1945; Mastropasqua 1970; Rauhut 1972;
Povoledo 1975). Fino ad oggi ci si è quasi sempre limitati ad attingere in
maniera abbastanza casuale a questo caotico repertorio visivo, magari per
impreziosire un volume sull'argomento, trascurando così di porsi in modo
serio i problemi metodologici relativi alla utilizzazione documentaria di
tali materiali.

E' così successo spesso che si assumessero come fedeli fonti di informazioni storiche sulla Commedia dell'Arte dei dipinti, delle incisioni o
dei disegni che poi, ad un esame più attento, si sono rivelati il risultato
di una libera reinvenzione dell'artista, a partire da situazioni o maschere di questo teatro, o addirittura, talvolta, senza nessun rapporto preciso
con esso. Il caso più clamoroso in tal senso è rappresentato senz'altro
dai *Balli di Sfessania* di Jacques Callot, la celebre serie di ventiquattro
incisioni pubblicata a Nancy nel 1622. Si sa che queste incisioni, insieme
ad altre del Callot (i *Gobbi*, *Les Gueux*), sono state usate spessissimo per
illustrare il teatro dei comici italiani e a volte esaminate anche come se
possedessero un preciso valore documentario, mentr'invece—com'è ormai
assodato—con la Commedia dell'Arte esse non hanno molto a che vedere,
essendo state ispirate all'artista francese dalle figure di certi balli tradizionali napoletani (come appunto la Sfessania e la Locìa) sul disegno delle
quali egli appose dei nomi di maschere dei carnevali italiani, senza neppure curarsi bene della corrispondenza fra il nome e la figura (cfr. Apollonio
1940:604; Nicoll 1963:72–3; ma soprattutto Prota-Giurleo 1962:60–65 e
Taviani 1982:488).[6]

Un discorso simile può essere fatto per le notissime immagini di Claude

Gillot e di Antoine Watteau, di quasi un secolo posteriori, anch'esse comunemente utilizzate per visualizzare momenti e aspetti della Commedia dell'Arte e il cui valore documentario è invece ugualmente molto esiguo, trattandosi di solito[7] di "scene di fantasia" che rievocano il mondo del teatro delle maschere attingendo a fonti disparate e lontane fra loro: dai disegni appena ricordati di Callot, alle immagini del Carnevale, dai teatri della Foire, al *Recueil* del Gherardi (cfr. Taviani 1982:297; Molinari 1985:239–240). Fra l'altro, come ricorda Xavier de Courville (1945:197), la Commedia italiana dei pittori nasce proprio nel periodo di assenza della reale Comédie italienne, e cioè negli anni che vanno dalla cacciata dei comici da Parigi nel 1697 a loro ritorno nel 1716.[8]

Sia ben chiaro che l'inattendibilità documentaria di Callot, Watteau e Gillot non elimina affatto l'interesse teatrale delle loro immagini e non ne impedisce ovviamente l'utilizzazione in sede di indagine storico-critica sulla Commedia dell'Arte, a patto però di tenere sempre ben presente il tipo di rapporto che esse intrattengono realmente con questo teatro.

Per nostra fortuna ci sono stati tramandati anche dei repertori iconografici di ben maggiore credibilità filologica, soprattutto per quanto riguarda la prima Commedia dell'Arte (a parte l'ancora nebulosa fase delle origini). Si tratta di veri e propri cicli visivi (perlopiù serie di incisioni a stampa), i quali, per una somma di ragioni interne ed esterne (prima fra tutte una notevole concordanza intertestuale circa alcuni tratti stilistici fondamentali), sono ormai unanimemente considerati dalla storiografia come fonti di informazioni storiche piuttosto sicure sul teatro delle compagnie italiane verso la fine del '500 e agli inizi del '600, informazioni particolarmente preziose per quanto riguarda, appunto, la messa in scena e le tecniche della recitazione. Mi riferisco soprattutto ai seguenti tre complessi iconografici:
– le scene affrescate da Alessandro Scalzi, detto il Paduano, sulle pareti della *Narrentreppe* (la "scala dei matti") nel castello di Trausnitz in Baviera (questi affreschi, databili con sicurezza al 1578, secondo Rauhut [1972:254], si riferiscono molto probabilmente alle rappresentazioni di commedie all'improvviso che dei comici italiani, di dubbia identificazione, dettero alla corte di Baviera fra il 1569 e il 1575 per impulso del principe Guglielmo V);[9]

– le varie serie di incisioni incluse nel *Recueil Fossard* (dal nome del loro primo collezionista) e comprendenti, fra l'altro, le immagini di una farsa francese (recitata dalla troupe del celebre *farceur* Agnan Sarat) e ben diciotto stampe relative a uno spettacolo di comici italiani, già con tutti i personaggi principali della Commedia dell'Arte (questa raccolta, ritrovata da Agne Beijer in un grande volume in-folio presso il Gabinetto

delle Stampe del Museo Nazionale di Stoccolma, è di datazione incerta ma sicuramente compresa fra il terzultimo e il penultimo decennio del XVI secolo [cfr. Beijer 1928, 1957; Mastropasqua 1970; Gambelli 1972]);[10]
– le incisioni curate personalmente da Tristano Martinelli, il primo grande Arlecchino, per il suo volumetto burlesco (fatto di una settantina di pagine quasi del tutto bianche) dal titolo *Compositions de Rhétorique*, pubblicato a Lione nel 1601 e dedicato al re di Francia Enrico IV di Borbone.[11]

Gli indizi largamente concordi che emergono da queste testimonianze visive, al di là di varie e ovvie differenze,[12] insieme alle peraltro scarsissime informazioni di provenienza letteraria, consentono di delineare un quadro sincronico abbastanza attendibile per quanto riguarda lo stile recitativo dei comici italiani delle prime generazioni (in altri termini, per il periodo compreso fra la seconda metà del '500 e gli inizi del '600) e permettono di avanzare ipotesi piuttosto fondate circa le tecniche e le convenzioni che stavano alla base di quel tipo di recitazione.

Meno fortunati siamo invece per le fasi successive della Commedia dell'Arte, sulle quali il materiale iconografico non scarseggia, certo, ma—come ho già detto—pone quasi sempre grossi problemi di pertinenza e di attendibilità. Comunque, anche per il periodo che va dalla seconda metà del '600 alla fine del '700 esiste la possibilità di individuare dei supporti iconografici, delle stampe, in genere, che consentono di formarsi almeno un'idea delle trasformazioni profonde subite dalla recitazione dei comici dell'Arte nel lungo arco di tempo che va dall'epoca del massimo fulgore artistico e della più vasta affermazione internazionale a quella della cosiddetta "francesizzazione" e del successivo e definitivo tramonto. Per brevità non sto ad elencare adesso questi riferimenti visivi ma li citerò più avanti man mano che ce ne sarà bisogno.

Una nuova concettualizzazione: il corpo artificiale

A questo punto, però, sarà meglio dire che i materiali iconografici (anche con l'aggiunta delle poche informazioni scritte disponibili al riguardo) non avrebbero permesso, da soli, di arrivare a formulare le ipotesi, per altro parziali e provvisorie, che sto per presentarvi, riguardo ad alcune tecniche di base degli attori dell'Arte e sulla loro trasformazione-involuzione dalla seconda metà del XVI secolo in poi. A tal fine, infatti, si sono rivelate indispensabili alcune importanti ricerche recenti sull'attore, ricerche di biologia e di antropologia teatrale che da qualche anno stanno cambiando, o quantomeno arricchendo in maniera decisiva, il nostro modo di guardare scientificamente alle questioni della recitazione e della scena; e ciò soprattutto grazie all'individuazione, da parte loro, di una *base pre-espressiva* del teatro e della performance attorica: secondo Eugenio Barba, uno dei capifila di tali ricerche, questa base pre-espressiva consisterebbe nella messa in opera di un certo numero di *tecniche extraquotidiane* del corpo grazie alle quali l'attore acquisirebbe la capacità di affascinare lo spettatore e di trattenerne l'attenzione con la sua sola presenza, prima ancora che quest'ultima assuma particolari significati scenici, prima ancora, insomma, che l'attore cominci ad esprimere o a rappresentare qualcosa o qualcuno (cfr. Barba 1981; Savarese 1983).

Potremmo quindi parlare, in proposito, di tecniche della *presenza drammatica* o, ancor meglio, di tecniche del *corpo artificiale* (fino ad oggi misconosciute nel teatro di prosa occidentale e semmai più familiari, non a caso, presso generi non-verbali e non-rappresentativi quali la danza e il mimo); in effetti la loro individuazione (una vera e propria "scoperta") consente di mettere a fuoco tutta una zona intermedia compresa fra la vita quotidiana e la rappresentazione, cioè fra l'attore in quanto *persona sociale* e l'attore in quanto *maschera scenica, personaggio*: è appunto in questa specie di *no man's land* che l'attore, mediante l'impiego (più o meno consapevole, ma questo è un altro problema) di determinate tecniche fisiche, e anche mentali, procede—come dice Barba—a "mettere-in-forma" il proprio corpo quotidiano, caricandolo della energia e della precisione necessarie per attirare e trattenere lo sguardo dello spettatore anche quando non finge, non interpreta un ruolo, non racconta una storia.

Evidentemente non si tratta qui di elaborare una nuova metafisica teatrale, questa volta biologistica, da sostituire alle altre metafisiche (spiritualistiche, psicologistiche o, magari, semiotiche) più o meno correnti. In ogni caso non sarebbe questo il mio intento. Del resto, lo stesso Barba ci tiene a precisare che quello biologico costituisce solo *uno* dei tre poli fondamentali del comportamento attorico, gli altri due essendo il polo *storico-sociale*, relativo—sempre secondo le sue parole—alle "particolarità delle tradizioni e del contesto culturale" e il polo che egli chiama della *chimica personale* dell'attore, riguardante cioè la sua personalità, il suo talento, etc. (Barba 1985).[13]

Tuttavia, l'individuazione di un *fondamento biologico dei teatri* permette di cominiciare a fare luce—come dicevo prima—su tutta una zona del lavoro dell'attore che era rimasta in ombra fino ad oggi, e per esempio consente (tornando al nostro tema) di leggere in modo nuovo e stimolante le testimonianze letterarie e, soprattutto, figurative riguardanti la recitazione dell'attore occidentale fra XVI e XVIII secolo e, in particolare, quella dei comici dell'Arte.[14]

Tanto per anticipare sinteticamente su quel che mi accingo ad esporre, dirò che gli indizi inediti che tali documenti stanno cominciando a fornire, grazie appunto alla sollecitazione di nuove domande, consentono di delineare, per quanto riguarda la fase compresa fra la seconda metà del '500 e la prima metà del '600, i tratti di un tipo di recitazione che risulta quanto di più lontano si possa immaginare da quello stile pantomimico a cui è sempre stata impropriamente riferita la recitazione dei comici dell'arte: uno stile cioè gestualmente esuberante, e anche acrobatico, ma fatto soprattutto di movenze equilibrate e aggraziate, quasi da balletto, e in cui ha grande importanza anche la mimica facciale, con le sue *grimaces*. Ora, il riferimento alla pantomima può essere pertinente, al massimo, per quanto riguarda la tarda Commedia dell'Arte, oppure nel caso di attori fuori della norma, in ogni senso, come Tiberio Fiorilli, che fu grandissimo mimo nel ruolo di Scaramouche e che non a caso recitava senza maschera (Molinari 1985:219); ma esso risulta invece del tutto inesatto e fuorviante—e lo vedremo subito—per la recitazione delle compagnie italiane e dei grandi attori che inventarono l'Improvvisa e ne propiziarono il primo successo internazionale.

Allo stesso modo ritengo riduttivo e improprio identificare le tecniche extraquotidiane dei comici dell'Arte delle prime generazioni con quegli elementi acrobatici e coreutici sui quali invariabilmente insistono tutti gli studiosi (da Miklaševskij a Apollonio, da Nicoll a Tessari). Riduttivo e improprio—ripeto—innanzitutto perchè le tecniche extraquotidiane degli attori italiani non comprendevano soltanto tecniche del corpo (in ogni caso molto più sofisticate e teatralmente consapevoli di quelle dei saltimbanchi e dei buffoni) ma anche, e non meno, tecniche letterarie e declamatorie: quindi, come ho parlato, e parlerò ancora—per la recitazione all'improvviso—di tecniche extraquotidiane del corpo, allo stesso modo è necessario parlare anche di tecniche di artificializzazione e di deformazione extraquotidiana dell'eloquio, della sintassi e del lessico (soprattutto mediante l'uso vertiginoso della metafora e della paronomasia), della pronunzia, degli accenti e degli stessi modi di emissione della voce (per esempio, mediante i dialetti).[15] Inoltre, mentre l'acrobazia e la danza permangono, per testimonianza unanime, anche nell'ultima, manieratissima Commedia dell'Arte, ben diversa è la sorte di quelle che chiamo le tecniche extraquotidiane, le quali—come si vedrà fra poco—scompaiono progressivamente nel corso del '600, sottraendo energia e vitalità alla performance attorica.

Dalla "lingua energica" alla recitazione manierata

Rifacendomi a un' importante ipotesi del Taviani (1982:186–7), distinguerò tre fasi principali all'interno delle trasformazioni diacroniche subite dalle tecniche recitative dei comici dell'Arte nel corso di più di due secoli: 1) una fase della "lingua energica" (o extraquotidiana); 2) una fase del realismo elegante; e 3) una fase del manierismo lezioso.[16]

La "lingua energica". Questo tipo di recitazione caratterizza—come già anticipato—la prima fase della Commedia dell'Arte e trova le sue principali pezze d'appoggio figurative nelle tre serie citate precedentemente, in particolare, nel Recueil Fossard e nelle incisioni curate da Tristano Martinelli per le *Compositions de Rhétorique*. Per dirla sinteticamente con le parole di Taviani (cui spetta anche l'espressione "lingua energica"), questo tipo di recitazione era basato

su una sapiente composizione delle tensioni fisiche, su una deformazione consapevole e intelligente del corpo e del comportamento (p. 420).

In questa definizione, prima ancora che sui pur importanti sostantivi (composizione, tensione, deformazione), è sugli aggettivi (*sapiente, consapevole, intelligente*) che dobbiamo porre l'accento, perchè sono loro a fornirci la chiave per cogliere la netta differenza qualitativa che separa la recitazione energica degli attori dell'Arte dal più istintivo e irriflesso saper-fare gestuale del saltimbanco e dello zanni cerretano.

Purtroppo, in mancanza di ipotesi interpretative più sottili e pertinenti (come quelle che ci mettono oggi a disposizione le ricerche sulla pre-espressività) la intensa gestualità esibita dalle antiche incisioni è stata quasi sempre letta, riduttivamente e superficialmente, come un'eredità della coreutica e dell'acrobatismo buffoneschi degli zanni "saltatori;" cosicchè ci si è soffermati soltanto sulle manifestazioni più evidenti e, in fondo, più ovvie di questa esuberanza corporea (le *culbutes*, i trampoli, le cadute e le arrampicate, le risse, le baraonde, etc.) e non ci si è accorti che, in realtà, le tecniche extraquotidiane della recitazione energica sono all'opera molto più diffusamente, e molto più sottilmente, anche nelle posture e nelle movenze più semplici e tranquille, almeno in apparenza, sotto forma di un'ininterrotta, organica deformazione, da parte dell'attore, del suo modo di camminare, di tenersi in piedi, di star seduto, di gesticolare, addirittura di guardare, e questo sempre nell'intento di infondere energia alla propria presenza scenica, di rendersi interessante e seducente prima ancora di cominciare a recitare in senso proprio, cioè a rappresentare, fingere, raccontare (Taviani 1982:486).

Si vedano, ad esempio, le posture di Martinelli, quando lavora nel ruolo di Arlecchino, il suo modo di insaccare la testa fra le spalle rigide e di appoggiare le braccia alla bassa cintura, il gioco delle opposizioni fra le due gambe, l'una tesa e l'altra piegata; oppure si guardi la spropositata, squilibrante amplificazione delle camminate di Pantalone, non solo nel Recueil Fossard ma anche in altre due incisioni della stessa epoca (conservate alla Bibliothèque Nationale di Parigi, l'una e al Fitzwilliam Museum di Cambridge, l'altra[17]); oppure si osservi—sempre nelle stampe del Fossard—la torsione deformante che possiede i corpi di quasi tutti i personaggi, dallo stesso Pantalone ad Arlecchino, da Zany Corneto al Capitano, tenendoli nelle condizioni di un permanente disequilibrio: gambe esageratamente divaricate, corpi incredibilmente arcuati che vanno all'indietro mentre le gambe sembrerebbero sospingerli in avanti, o viceversa (è questo il caso, ad esempio, della incredibile scena di Arlecchino guerriero che, dinanzi a donna Lucrezia e con Zany Corneto alle spalle, indossando una corazza alla rovescia, esegue il lazzo di girare i gomiti in avanti [cfr. Mastropasqua 1970:108; Molinari 1985:96]).

Va però chiarito subito, a scanso di possibili equivoci, che recitazione energica non vuol dire affatto recitazione rozza, senza controllo (com'è ad esempio quella dei *farceurs* di Sarat raffigurati in un'altra serie di immagini del Recueil Fossard); al contrario, essa presuppone, almeno ai suoi livelli più alti, una grande sapienza tecnica e un elevato, consapevole controllo formale, il quale, lungi dall'allentarsi, si accresce proprio nelle movenze più innaturali e apparentemente più scomposte.[18]

Il realismo elegante. E' un dato di fatto incontrovertibile che questa recitazione energica, basata sull'uso cosciente delle tecniche extraquotidiane del disequilibrio, dello spreco di energia e della dilatazione delle tensioni corporee, scompare gradualmente negli spettacoli delle compagnie italiane, per lasciare il posto, alla fine, durante il XVIII secolo, a una recitazione affatto diversa, morbida e leziosa. Più difficile risulta invece proporre delle date e dei nomi precisi per scandire con una certa esattezza i momenti intermedi di questo passaggio. Sembra, però, possibile ipotizzare almeno una grossa fase intermedia, che chiamerei appunto del "realismo elegante," da collocarsi genericamente nel lungo periodo, più di un secolo, che intercorre fra le ultime testimonianze figurative della lingua energica e la massiccia diffusione dell'attore manierato. Questa fase del realismo elegante risulta in genere sacrificata nelle trattazioni, peraltro quasi sempre affrettate, che la storiografia ha dedicato alla recitazione dei comici dell'Arte; viceversa si tratta di un momento cruciale (e non soltanto per l'attore dell'Arte ma per l'attore moderno *tout court*), come ha messo in rilievo Taviani, che qui conviene citare estesamente:

Ciò che caratterizza questa fase intermedia—scrive dunque Taviani (1982: 486–
7)—è ciò che determina il destino dell'attore occidentale moderno: il passaggio
dalla tecnica extra-quotidiana del corpo ad una tecnica "superiore," cioè la scelta di
lavorare non sulla cosciente deformazione del corpo e dei suoi comportamenti, ma
sull'etichetta, cioè su quell'insieme di pratiche che la società codifica in vista di
un agire pienamente accettabile. Da un certo momento in poi—forse a partire dal
XVIII secolo—all' attore europeo viene insegnata, sostanzialmente, l'etichetta: il
suo sapere si edifica attorno all'esigenza di rappresentare *bene* ed *elegantemente*:
senza indipendenza (corsivi dell'autore).

Quindi, con l'avvento del realismo elegante ci troveremmo di fronte
non a un semplice cambiamento di tecnica espressiva o di stile esecuti-
vo ma ad una vera e propria *coupure* epocale, quella che separa appunto
l'attore moderno, e poi nostro contemporaneo, dai suoi antecendenti (ivi
compresi i primi comici dell'Arte), e che consiste in un radicale mutamento del metodo di lavoro dell' attore e della direzione e degli scopi di
questo lavoro. A partire dal XVII secolo, l'attore comincia a rinunciare
alla sua *diversità* socio-antropologica, e alla sua indipendenza creativa,
e accetta di integrarsi—come attore oltre che come uomo—nel sistema
culturale dominante, adottandone i modelli e i canoni rappresentativi.

Mi pare, comunque, che ci sia poco da aggiungere, almeno per ora,
all'analisi fatta da Taviani, se non per cercare di precisare qualche circostanza, soprattutto cronologica. In proposito, la già riportata indicazione
del Taviani ("forse a partire dal XVIII secolo") risulta troppo generica
e probabilmente anche troppo sbilanciata in avanti. Credo che le fonti
letterarie e iconografiche a nostra disposizione consentano (sia pure con
tutte le doverose cautele) di circoscrivere con un po' più di esattezza
l'epoca di inizio di questa vera e propria inversione di rotta rappresentata
dall'abbandono della lingua energica.

Innanzitutto le fonti letterarie, le quali evidenziano, già verso il terzo
decennio del XVII secolo, una chiara tendenza dei comici dell'Arte verso
l'adesione a quello che Pier Maria Cecchini (1628) chiama un "propor-
zionato verisimile:" si veda, ad esempio, dello stesso Cecchini, la critica
mossa a quegli attori

i quali con una pazza maniera girano gli occhi, allargano le braccia, e compongono
il corpo tutto in guisa tale, che uno molestato dalle colica, porgerebbe molestia
minore à chi lo mirasse (Cecchini, 1628);

o il Barbieri (1634) che, nel, corso della sua puntigliosa distinzione tra il
comico e il buffone, critica quanti, per "far ridere," si limitano a

una brutta smorfia, una strabocchevole caduta, un gesto d'una scimia, un giuoco d'un cagnolino, gatto e d'altro simile;

o infine, il Perrucci (1699), il quale inveisce contro coloro che, a suo parere, rovinano l'Improvvisa: e cioè:

la più vile feccia della plebe [. . .] i vilissimi ciurmatori e salt'in banco [i quali] vogliono rappresentare nelle pubbliche piazze comedie all'improviso, storpiando i sogeti, parlando allo sproposito, gestendo da matti, e quel che è peggio, facendo mille oscenità e sporchezze.

Anche se queste polemiche non sono dirette contro i grandi interpreti della recitazione energica ma hanno per (facile) bersaglio i suoi infimi epigoni nelle piazze e nelle fiere, tale circostanza non diminuisce certo la loro importanza di testimonianze relative e una decisiva variazione ideologico-culturale delle compagnie italiane, e al loro prevalente modo di intendere la recitazione, da un certo momento in avanti: non più come consapevole e controllata deformazione extraquotidiana della persona, in funzione soprattutto pre-rappresentativa, ma, ben diversamente, come abbellimento-impreziosimento di un modello quotidiano ai fini di una rappresentazione elegante e verosimile.[19]

Quanto alla documentazione iconografica della "svolta" realistica non c'è che l'imbarazzo della scelta: dai piccoli disegni acquerellati della cosiddetta raccolta corsiniana, *Scenari più scelti di istrioni* (databile, secondo Zorzi [1980:111], verso la metà del XVII secolo) alle illustrazioni contenute nei volumi del *Théâtre Italien* di Evaristo Gherardi (1700)[20] a molti dipinti e incisioni di Watteau e soprattutto del suo maestro Claude Gillot. Di quest'ultimo, particolarmente significative, ai fini del discorso che stiamo facendo, mi sembrano le quattro incisioni (risalenti al primo o al secondo decennio del '700) con "Arlecchino ghiottone," "Arlecchino sospirante," "Saluto di Arlecchino," e "Arlecchino piangente." A proposito di questa celebre serie di stampe, Molinari (1985:96) parla, correttamente, di un controllo formale che è ormai divenuto formalismo, una specie di realismo di secondo grado:

L'Arlecchino di Gillot non piange, non mangia, non saluta, ma letteralmente *esibisce il modo di* mangiare, piangere, salutare [corsivo mio].

E più avanti, nella stessa recente monografia, Molinari sottolinea il passaggio da quello che veniva chiamato il *jeu naturel* di Biancolelli alla composta stilizzazione geometrizzante di Evaristo Gherardi, propotipo del manierato Arlecchino settecentesco (p. 222).

Il manierismo lezioso. Questo terzo tipo di recitazione si afferma nel corso del '700 e coincide grosso modo con la fase del progressivo declino della Commedia dell'Arte. Ovviamente trascende i limiti del presente intervento il tentativo di precisare maggiormente, anche in termini cronologici, le fasi del trapasso dal realismo elegante a quelle che Apollonio (1940:566) chiamò una volta le "grazie raggentilite" della tarda Commedia dell'Arte.

Una cosa comunque è certa: le testimonianze figurative al riguardo sono tutt'altro che scarse, e persino troppo abbondanti, se è vero che—come ricordavo prima—proprio quella dell'attore lezioso e sdolcinato, con le sue movenze rococò, ha costituito fino ad oggi l'immagine più diffusa dell'Improvvisa e del suo stile recitativo. In ogni caso, per farsi un'idea più che sufficiente di ciò che bisogna intendere per "manierismo lezioso" della tarda recitazione dell'Arte, basterà richiamare alla mente qualcuno dei tanti Arlecchini di cui pullulano, nel '700, libri, stampe e dipinti, con le loro riverenze, i piedi in terza posizione e la mano graziosamente appoggiata al batocchio; oppure si pensi, per più consistenti visioni d'insieme, agli affreschi del castello boemo di Krumlov (metà del XVIII secolo), ai Pulcinella di Giandomenico Tiepolo in Ca' Rezzonico a Venezia (1791–93), o anche alle piccole sculture di porcellana, liberamente raffiguranti maschere e situazioni della Commedia dell'Arte, che varie manifatture tedesche produssero nel corso di quel secolo e una cui scelta è ora raccolta nel George R. Gardiner Museum of Ceramic Art di Toronto.

Tuttavia, mi sembra che, a livello storiografico, mentre esiste—e non potrebbe essere altrimenti—un sostanziale accordo circa i tratti caratterizzanti lo stile scenico dell'ultima Commedia dell'Arte, sia spesso frainteso, invece, il senso delle trasformazioni complessive che intervengono nella recitazione dei comici italiani dalla fine del '500 al '700 e che sfuggano—come ho già accennato—le implicazioni del doppio passaggio dalla recitazione energica al realismo elegante e da questo al manierismo lezioso. Di solito, infatti, si descrive questo doppio passaggio nei termini piani di una evoluzione (o involuzione) progressiva da una recitazione naturale e spontanea verso uno stile convenzionale e artificioso. Questa è ad esempio l'interpretazione del Miklaševskij (1927:124). Ora mi sembre superfluo far notare quanto una lettura del genere sia debitrice nei confronti di un'idea della prima Commedia dell'Arte come fenomeno aureo di libera e spontanea creatività: un'idea che—com'è noto—ha rivelato ormai da tempo la sua natura puramente mitica. In realtà, l'*élégance un peu lièvre* di cui parla il Mic per la Commedia Italienne settecentesca va spiegata—a mio parere—come l'estrema e forse inevitabile conseguenza della scelta che era stata alla base della svolta decisiva del realismo elegante: cioè—come si è già detto—la scelta, da parte dell'attore, di non lavorare più direttamente, e autonomamente, sulla propria pre-espressività corporea, sulla consapevole artificializzazione extraquotidiana della propria persona scenica, in funzione anche non-rappresentativa, per dedicarsi invece all "abbellimento," ai fini di una rappresentazione riconoscibile, di modelli di comportamento quotidiano già precostituiti e socialmente istituzionalizzati.

Questa svolta comportò per il comico dell'Arte (ma non solo per lui, evidentemente[21]) una graduale perdita di contatto con quello che Grotowski ha chiamato il "processo organico" dell'attore; produsse, in altri termini, la progressiva dissipazione di quel patrimonio di sapienza biologica (corporea e mentale insieme) che fondava la recitazione energica e che quella realistica seicentesca conservò ancora in parte, per un certo periodo. Ecco perchè il gesto (inteso qui nel senso più ampio del termine) dell'attore dell'Arte settecentesco sembra perdere di forza, si svuota, e diventa pura esteriorità, stilizzandosi infine secondo i dettami di una maniera estenuata e leziosa; ecco perchè tutta la recitazione dell'Arte (e non soltanto quella) passa dall'invenzione (che non era, comunque, conviene ribadirlo, libera e disordinata creazione *ex nihilo* ma—come già chiariva Apollonio [1940:579,590]—riappropriazione originale di "un linguaggio scenico ben determinato e tradizionale," ovvero attualizzazione concretizzante, mediante l'improvvisazione, di schemi astratti rigidamente codificati), alla ripetizione sempre più pedissequa di moduli ipercodificati, al *cliché*, allo stereotipo artificioso.

Ovviamente non è mia intenzione negare che nella crisi della Commedia dell'Arte durante il '700, e dunque anche nello scadimento della sua recitazione, intervengano molte altre circostanze e numerosi fattori concomitanti: dalla cosiddetta e più volte qua ricordata "francesizzazione," che cristallizza la Comédie italienne nelle forme immobili di uno pseudo-genere ideale (nel quale, fra l'altro, la scenotecnica la fa sempre di più da padrona rispetto al *jeu* dell'attore: si pensi al successo delle *pièces-à-machines* e delle *Comédies-ballet*, cui anche la Commedia dell'Arte deve convertirsi nel '700), ai vari ed esiziali tentativi di "salvataggio" (da Marivaux e Luigi Riccoboni a Carlo Gozzi), alla scomparsa di grandi talenti attorici, al mutamento dei gusti del pubblico. Ritengo tuttavia che il distacco dalle sue basi biologiche, con il conseguente abbandono delle tecniche extraquotidiane, abbia rappresentato, per un teatro eminentemente d'attore come la Commedia dell'Arte, un evento dalle enormi conseguenze, e dunque più che sufficiente a spiegare come mai le compagnie italiane—in

252 MARCO DE MARINIS

mancanza di punti d'appoggio altrettanto profondi e vitali, come ad esempio una grande drammaturgia—siano potute scivolare nel corso del XVIII secolo lungo la china di una decadenza rapida e definitiva.

University of Bologna

NOTE

1 In proposito mi accontenterò di rinviare a Taviani (1982:419), per il quale "il virtuosismo dei comici era un'arte dalla tecnica segreta."

2 Per la riproduzione di questa immagine, pubblicata allo inizio di una Commedia contro Molière, *Élomire Hypocondre* di Le Boulanger de Chalussay, cfr. ad esempio Molinari (1985:119).

3 Ved. ad esempio il dipinto attribuito a Marco Gheraerts il vecchio (1575), di proprietà di J. F. Montagu, Cold Overton Hall, Oakham (raffigura l'arrivo di una troupe teatrale, probabilmente italiana, ad un palazzo che, secondo qualcuno [Sewter 1940], potrebbe essere la corte elisabettiana); oppure il disegno a penna del XVII secolo, conservato alla Bibliothèque de l'Arsenal di Parigi, il quale mostra l'arrivo di una compagnia comica in una piazza cittadina, quasi sicuramente romana (Taviani 1982:423).

4 Nelle sue ultime pagine dedicate alla *Commedia dell'Arte*, le *Prelezioni* del 1968, il grande storico italiano Mario Apollonio scriveva che, per gli attori dell'Improvvisa, "unica sorgente d'informazione semiologica è il documento iconografico," dal cui studio soltanto può dipendere "un incremento singolare di conoscenze linguistiche (tenuto conto che il linguaggio dell'Arte è spettacolo, e che a spettacolo riduce anche le componenti più illustri, la retorica petrarchesca e le leggende devozionali dei secoli cristiani") (Apollonio 1968:189–190).

5 Un primo tentativo in questa direzione è rappresentato dalla recente monografia del Molinari (1985), cui ci riferiremo più volte in tal senso, e nella quale sono riprodotte, sia pure in maniera incompleta, molte fra le più importanti "monografie" iconografiche legate alla *Commedia dell'Arte*.

6 Come ho appena detto, immagini dai *Balli di Sfessania* compaiono in tutti i principali volumi sulla *Commedia dell'Arte*. Si vedano invece in Molinari (1985:125–32) le splendide riproduzioni a colori della serie di dipinti (conservati presso il Museo Teatrale alla Scala di Milano) che un Anonimo di scuola bolognese ha tratto molto fedelmente, verso la fine del '600, dalle stampe di Callot.

7 A parte le eccezioni di cui farò menzione più avanti.

8 Per le riproduzioni delle immagini di Watteau legate alle maschere e alle situazioni della *Commedia dell'Arte*, cfr. Macchia-Montagni (1968). Per quanto riguarda Gillot, cfr., ad esempio, Duchartre 1925 e 1955; Nicolini 1958, Pandolfi 1957–61, Molinari 1985.

9 Scorrendo (per esempio in Molinari) le riproduzioni di queste scene affrescate, è facile accorgersi che il pittore ha messo molta cura, spesso, nell'evidenziare

la maschere sui volti dei personaggi: si veda, ad esempio, lo zanni riconoscibile nella fig. 104 di Rauhut (1972), per il quale questo fatto "prova che si trattava di rappresentare non personaggi drammatici ma Commedianti che rappresentano personaggi" (Rauhut 1972:260).

10 Queste stampe sono state riprodotte in fac-simile da Beijer (1928). Quanto alla loro attendibilità documentaria piuttosto alta, una importante prova interna sembra essere fornita proprio dalle evidenti differenze stilistiche con cui il disegnatore e l'incisore hanno rappresentato la rozza recitazione dei *farceurs* francesi e quella, molto più raffinata e controllata, degli italiani (Mastropasqua 1970:100; Molinari 1985:96).

11 Le cinque incisioni sono state riprodotte dal Duchartre in appendice a Beijer (1928) e, successivamente, fra gli altri, da Pandolfi (1957–61: I, 265 sgg.).

12 Piuttosto evidenti appaiono, ad esempio, le differenze fra lo stile scenico dell'Arlecchino del Fossard e quello dell'Arlecchino di Martinelli, anche se non sappiano fino a che punto la minore raffinatezza di quest'ultimo dipenda dall'incisore piuttosto che dall'attore (Gambelli 1972:53). Certo è che vi sono differenze anche nel costume e, come ha notato Molinari (1985:108), nello stesso atteggiamento di base, cosa quest'ultima spiegabile, almeno in parte, con la circostanza che le xilografie delle *Compositions* ritraggono Arlecchino più in posa che in azione. In ogni caso, si tratta di differenze pressochè irrilevanti ai fini del presente discorso.

13 Per una discussione critica, anteriore alle loro ultime formulazioni, delle ipotesi di Barba sulla pre-espressività dell'attore, cfr. De Marinis (1984).

14 Le proposte che seguono sono largamente debitrici al Taviani, il quale, nel libro già più volte citato, è stato il primo ad abbozzare una analisi diacronica della recitazione dei comici dell'Arte sulla base delle recenti elaborazioni dell'antropologia teatrale (cfr, in particolare, Taviani 1982:486–7).

15 E' forse tempo ormai di chiarire definitivamente che la *Commedia dell'Arte* non fu, come si è spesso detto, frettolosamente, e come si ripete talvolta enfaticamente ancora oggi (Tessari 1981), un Teatro del Corpo e del Gesto, e che essa si basava, come sostiene ad esempio il Nicoll (1963:27), "su una combinazione di dialogo e di azione, non sulla sola pantomima." Ma in proposito si legga ora quel che scrive Taviani (1982:325–6) anche sulla base di una acuta quanto tendenziosa lettura del primo Prologo di Flaminio Scala alla sua Commedia *Il finto marito* (1618).

16 Per semplicità farò riferimento solo al *côté* corporeo-gestuale della performance attorica, e ciò evidentemente anche a causa delle caratteristiche e dei limiti dei documenti, visivi appunto, sui quali si fonda il mio discorso.

17 Per le riproduzioni, cfr. Nicoll (1963:69, 67).

18 Detto questo non mi pare di poter condividere né l'insistenza di Mastropasqua (1970:113–114) sull'"estrema misura della composizione di gruppo e dei movimenti" nello spettacolo italiano del Fossard, né, tantomeno, quella di Molinari (1985:96) sui "gesti di ricercata eleganza" esibiti da alcuni personaggi

della stessa serie. Precisione e controllo non implicano, necessariamente, misura ed eleganza; e le stampe del Fossard, a mio parere, lo provano. Quanto alla deformazione (gestuale, lessicale, vestiaria, etc.) come "costante stilistica" dello spettacolo dell'Arte, si rimanda naturalmente all'Apollonio (1968:177), per il quale essa aveva una basilare funzione di "stacco" tra la vita reale e lo spettacolo (tra quotidiano ed extraquotidiano, nei termini da me adottati) e di incorniciamento di quest' ultimo (Apollonio 1940:532, 577). Dal canto suo il Miklaševskij (1927:120) era andato molto vicino all'individuazione di un livello pre-espressivo della performance attorica quando aveva scritto: "Mais le corps, dans la comédie italienne, ne possedait pas seulement une valeur expressive; on accordait une très grande importance à la force, à l'habileté, à la souplesse corporelle dont l'acteur, *en dehors de toutes intentions expressives*, faisait montre dans des numéros de pure acrobatie" [corsivo mio].

19 Ma a questo proposito, a proposito cioè di quello che Taviani chiama, come abbiamo visto, l'apprendimento dell'"etichetta" da parte dell' attore europeo verso la fine del '600, siamo sicuri che si tratti veramente di un'acquisizione nuova e non sia invece, in gran parte, un ritorno al passato, un recupero di qualcosa che era già esistito ed era già stato teorizzato? Il "rappresentare bene ed elegantemente," prima di diventare l'esigenza dell'attore moderno non era già stato, in sostanza, l'ideale del teatro pre-ed extra-professionistico del '500, quello, intendo, sviluppatosi nelle corti e nelle accademie italiane, e i cui moduli rappresentativi e recitativi si codificano sulla base di un'implicita, e talvolta anche esplicita equazione attore-uomo di lettere-oratore, perseguendo ideali (retorico-comportamentali) di naturalezza, grazia e dignità a fini di onesto godimento estetico e di edificazione morale? Non esiste forse, sotto questo aspetto, un filo rosso che collega, quasi senza soluzione di continuità, la riflessione teorica del Rinascimento sullo spettacolo e sull'attore (da Giraldi Cinthio a De' Sommi, a Ingegneri) con gli scritti di Scala, Cecchini, Barbieri, etc., fino al Perrucci e oltre?

20 Per le riproduzioni degli acquerelli corsiniani, cfr., ad esempio, Pandolfi (1957–61:257 sgg.). Illustrazioni dal *Recueil* del Gherardi si trovano riprodotte un po' in tutti i principali volumi illustrati sul nostro argomento, da quelli del Duchartre, a quelli del Nicolini, del Nicoll e dello stesso Pandolfi.

21 E' chiaro infatti che da questa stessa scelta nasce anche l'attore del teatro di prosa moderno, con prevalente funzione illustrativa-rappresentativa nei confronti del testo drammatico e del personaggio; così come è evidente che il Grande Attore, da Talma alla Duse, più che una incarnazione "sublime" di tale modello, ne costituì una rara quanto prodigiosa eccezione.

BIBLIOGRAFIA

Adhémar, J. 1945: "French sixteenth century genre paintings," *Journal of the Warburg and Courtauld Institute*, VIII.

Apollonio, Mario. 1930: *Storia della Commedia dell'Arte*, Roma-Milano, Augustea (rist. anastatica: Firenze, Sansoni, 1982).

_____1940: *Storia del teatro italiano*, vol. II: *Il Teatro del Rinascimento*: *Commedia, Tragedia, Melodramma*, Firenze, Sansoni (ivi, 1981, vol.I).

_____1968: *Prelezioni sulla Commedia dell'Arte*, in AA.VV., *Contributi dell'Istituto di Filologia Moderna—Serie Storia del Teatro*, vol.I, Milano, Vita e Pensiero.

Barba, Eugenio. 1981: *La corsa dei contrari. Antropologia teatrale*, Milano, Feltrinelli.

_____1985: *El cuerpo dilatado*, relazione al Congresso Internazionale de l'Instituto del Teatro di Barcellona, 19–25 maggio 1985.

Barbieri, Nicolò. 1634: *La Supplica, discorso famigliare. . .* , Venezia, Ginammi, (ed. critica a cura di Ferdinando Taviani, Milano, Il Polifilo, 1971).

Beijer, Agne. 1928: *Recueil de plusieurs fragments des premiéres Comédies Italiennes qui ont été représentées en France sous le règne de Henry IV*, Paris.

_____1957. "Quelques documents sur les farceurs français et italiens," in *Revue d'Histoire du théâtre*, IX, 1–2.

Cecchini, Pier Maria. 1628: *Frutti delle moderne comedie et avvisi a chi le recita*, Padova, Guareschi.

Courville, Xavier de. 1945: *Un apôtre de l'art du théâtre au XVIII siècle: Luigi Riccoboni dit Lélio*, Paris, Droz.

De Marinis, Marco. 1984: "Il corpo artificiale: l' arte dell' attore fra biologia e cultura," *Prometeo*, IV, 14, giugno.

Duchartre, Pierre-Louis. 1925: *La Comédie italienne*, Paris, Librairie de France.

_____1955: *La commedia dell'arte et ses enfants*, Paris, Ed. d'Art et Industrie.

Gambelli, Delia. 1972: "Arlecchino dalla preistoria a Biancolelli," *Biblioteca teatrale*, 5.

Gherardi, Evaristo. 1700: *Le Théâtre Italien. . .* , Paris, Cusson et Witte, 6 vol. (una antologia di questa raccolta è stata pubblicata da Marcello Spaziani, Ed. dell'Ateneo, Roma, 1966).

Macchia, G. e Montagni, E.C. 1968: *L'opera completa di Watteau*, Milano, Rizzoli.

Mastropasqua, Fernando. 1970: "Lo spettacolo della collezione Fossard," in F. Mastropasqua-C. Molinari, *Ruzante e Arlecchino*, Parma, Studium Parmense.

McDowell, J.H. 1942: "Some pictorial aspects of early *Commedia dell'Arte* acting," *Studies in Philology*, XXXIX.

Mic, Constant (pseud. di Konstantin Miklaševskij). 1927: *La Commedia dell'Arte, ou le théâtre des comédiens italiens des XVIe, XVIIe et XVIIIe siècles*, Paris, Schiffrin, aux Editions de la Pléiade.

Molinari, Cesare. 1985: *La Commedia dell'Arte*, Milano, Mondadori.

Nicolini, Fausto. 1958: *Vita di Arlecchino*, Milano-Napoli, Ricciardi.

Nicoll, Allardyce. 1963: *The world of Arlequin. A critical study of the Commedia dell'Arte*, Cambridge, University Press (trad.it. *Il mondo di Arlecchino*, Milano,

Bompiani, 1965, 1980).

Pandolfi, Vito. 1957–61: *La Commedia dell'Arte. Storia e testi*, 6 vol., Firenze, Sansoni.

Perrucci, Andrea. 1699: *Dell'Arte rappresentativa premeditata e all'improvviso*, Napoli, Mutio.

Povoledo, Elena. 1975: "Bouffons et Commedia dell'Arte dans la fête venitienne au XVIe siècle," in AA.VV., *Les fêtes à la Renaissance*, vol.III, Paris, CNRS.

Rauhut, Franz. 1971: "La Commedia dell'Arte italiana in Baviera: teatro, pittura, musica, scultura" in AA.VV., *Studi sul teatro veneto fra Rinascimento e età barocca*, a cura di Maria Teresa Muraro, Firenze, Olschki.

Savarese, Nicola, ed. 1983: *Anatomia del teatro*, Firenze, La Casa Usher.

Sewter, A. C. 1940: "Queen Elizabeth at Kenilworth," *The Burlington Magazine*, LXXXVI, 444.

Spada, Stefania. 1969: *Domenico Biancolelli ou l'art d'improviser*, Napoli, Istituto Universitario Orientale.

Sterling, Charles. 1943: "Early paintings of the Commedia dell'Arte in French," *Bulletin of Metropolitan Museum*.

Taviani, Ferdinando. 1982: "Il segreto delle compagnie italiane note poi come Commedia dell'Arte," in F. Taviani–M. Schino, *Il segreto della Commedia dell'Arte*, Firenze, La Casa Usher.

Tessari, Roberto. 1981: *Commedia dell'Arte: la maschera e l'ombra*, Milano, Mursia.

Zorzi, Ludovico. 1980: "La raccolta degli scenari italiani della Commedia dell'Arte," in AA.VV., *La Commedia dell'Arte*, a cura di Luciano Mariti, Atti del convegno di studi di Pontedera (28–30 maggio 1976), Roma, Bulzoni.

Donato Sartori

Sviluppi e derivazioni della *commedia dell'arte*

Se volessimo o se si potesse scomporre la Commedia dell'Arte nelle singole componenti e nelle tecniche che costituiscono quello che è stato un fenomeno culturale che si impose in oltre due secoli in tutta Europa, si rimarrebbe certamente sconcertati dall'immensa versatilità della sua intrinseca costituzione. Analizzandone singolarmente gli aspetti compositivi ne risulterebbe un complesso organigramma, un composito reticolo di elementi legati tra di loro in un delicato equilibrio, tanto da formare un'unica essenza.

In esso convergevano le esigenze vitali e le pulsioni creative di gruppi eterogenei o di "famiglie" che sin dalla prima metà del Cinquecento svilupparono un modulo di comunicazione già da tempo esistente in forma larvata.

Piccoli nuclei girovaghi si spostavano di paese in paese proponendo la propria versatile estroversione. Si veniva così formando attraverso il carico delle esperienze una nuova professionalità. Era questo il prodotto di una simbiosi tra necessità legata alla sopravvivenza e la creatività quotidiana maturata nei simboli e nei feticci propri ad una popolarità difficile e complessa. L'energia dei comici andava così affinandosi nei sunti recitativi sull'essenza del gesto, sulle modalità dialogiche, sulle invenzioni di tematiche semplici, eppure universali, toccando le necessità sociali e le abitudini, ed entrando nella storia e nei credo politici. Comici appunto che riuscivano attraverso il veicolo comicità a produrre quello stupore e quell'emozione che, stimolando tematiche proprie all'ambiente in cui essi agivano, permetteva loro di aprire una breccia capace di accomunare l'eterogeneo pubblico delle strade e delle piazze che si riconosceva e si identificava con l'azione rappresentata nei palchi: analisi consapevoli (o inconscie?) che portavano all'elaborazione di azioni capaci di fendere le naturali diffidenze di un pubblico semplice, sottoposto ai rigori della Chiesa, vessato dal potere politico e da differenti interessi, soprattutto stranieri, ma per questo ben dotato di capacità immaginifiche.

Non resta quindi che interrogarsi su quali siano gli insegnamenti tramandati, pervenuti fino a noi, quali siano gli ipotetici sviluppi e derivazioni di un genere teatrale che seppe radicarsi così profondamente nel tessuto sociale e nelle abitudini della civiltà rinascimentale e barocca tanto da divenire modello per altri settori artistici, dalla letteratura alle arti visive, dalla musica alla moda. Questi espedienti così detti teatrali sono in realtà ben più complessi costrutti che fanno parte dell'articolarsi del sistema creativo: diremmo oggi la costituzione o la delineazione intuitiva di un'arte multi o pluridisciplinare per la stimolazione dell'elemento folla o pubblico suscitandone l'interesse attraverso la sollecitazione delle necessità, dei desideri e delle abitudini. Attraverso sintomi di varia natura il commediante avverte che il pubblico può liberare quell'energia da sempre latente o repressa. Certamente per poterci basare su di un'arte lasciata decadere, che serviva un tempo e che oggi non serve più, non basta desumerne gli aspetti formali, ma bisogna identificarne la componente essenziale, per trarne quella linfa vitale capace di infondere nuovo vigore agli elementi costitutivi di una nuova creatività.

Per questo attribuiremo grande merito ai pionieri del recupero storico della Commedia che sin dagli inizi del Novecento seppero dare, attraverso le loro ricerche ed analisi, impulso a nuove sperimentazioni artistiche. Copeau e Dullin, al Vieux Colombier, presero spunto da queste indagini per elaborare una nuova teoria sul mestiere teatrale.

A causa degli sconvolgimenti politici e bellici, questa nascente energia rimase però latente per un lungo periodo, e solo dopo la seconda guerra mondiale si risvegliò in un rinnovato interesse nei confronti delle proprie matrici storiche.

In Italia, per una strana fatalità, è proprio a Padova, patria del Ruzante e della "fraternal compagnia" di comici, che viene dato l'avvio a quella serie di esperienze che costituiranno il punto di partenza per una nuova teatralità. Riscoperta quindi di un modo che, faticosamente rigenerato da un remoto passato ricalcandone i primi incerti segni, dava finalmente la libertà di riscavare nella memoria delle proprie radici per trarne nuovo alimento. Non restava allora che riaddentrarsi nel problema maschera, nello studio di quell'elemento di cui si erano perdute le consuetudini dell'uso e della tecnica di costruzione, strumento simbolico che racchiude in sé il carisma di un arcano insito da sempre nella natura umana e nei significati della comunicazione.

Successivamente, nel mondo occidentale, una fioritura di coincidenze fece capire ai "creatori di teatro" che era necessario porre una singolare attenzione a quegli elementi plastici, ottici e sonori utilizzati nel teatro e nel rito primitivo. Arte rituale e magia, ed in molti casi la fascinazione mistica orientale, si combinarono con i mezzi e la moderna tecnologia per la realizzazione di un teatro totale o radicale.

Senza voler risalire all'origine storica di questo fenomeno, che situa le sue radici sin dal 1919 con le prime esperienze del Bauhaus, posiamo notare come nel teatro dell'ultimo ventennio si avverta una tensione difficilmente definibile connessa al ribaltamento dei principi politici, sociali ed umani. Lo spettacolo cambia fisionomia perché il pubblico la sta cambiando. Si cercano nel gioco e nella festa, nelle azioni spontanee ed irripetibili, la suggestione e non più la rappresentazione; non più convincere ma destare impressioni, comunicare al di fuori delle schematizzazioni strutturali. Si vuole sovvertire l'ordine dell'arte stabilitosi in secoli di cultura occidentale per rivolgersi verso una nuova improvvisazione. Atti provocatori, libertà di partecipazione, tendenza alla utilizzazione di elementi altri che la creazione artistica: dalla pittura alla scultura, dalla luce al suono, dalle variazioni del colore alle percezioni visive. Gli uomini di teatro cercano, allora, attraverso un uso polivalente dei media comunicativi, forme espressive capaci di catalizzare l'attenzione di spettatori in cerca di un ruolo diverso da quello in cui erano stati relegati da secoli di teatro borghese. Il pubblico vuole ora partecipare, prendere parte ad un'azione creativa, essere parte di un evento artistico. La maschera della Commedia dell'Arte simboleggiava un'epoca e ne esprimeva i desideri, le debolezze ed i peccati e la rabbia. La nuova Commedia crea altre maschere e realizza dei fantasmi che parlano di politica, di verità e di giustizia, e trattano alla pari con un pubblico che sta maturando una nuova coscienza.

Happening e provocazione, estetica ed ideologia, significavano una volta in più la penetrazione dell'arte nella vita, diminuendo la distanza tra realtà teatrale e realtà sociale. Questa "controcultura" nata nel sessantotto incarnava il sogno di tutti quelli che credevano fosse sufficiente riappropriarsi della propria forza creativa, attraverso la cooperazione, per risolvere ogni problema e realizzare un'utopica comunità.

Tutte queste attitudini vanno a cristallizzarsi in eventi che prendono il nome dagli aspetti propri a questo tipo di "teatro di strada," il quale risponde al desiderio di un pubblico che non sente più la necessità di un edificio culturale, rifiutando la convocazione premeditata e privilegiando azioni immediate nelle piazze, nelle strade, nei parchi e nei quartieri: "underground," sottoterra, prodotto di nascosto, ai margini del permesso o contro lo stabilito, o "teatro di guerriglia" per la somiglianza apparente a questo modo di aggredire il pubblico.

Una proliferazione di gruppi con caratteristiche similari costella il mondo
degli anni sessanta. In America il Performance Group, l'Open Theatre, la
San Francisco Mime Troupe, il Teatro Campesino, il Bread and Puppet, ed
il più antico di tutti, che data la sua fondazione dal 1946, il Living Theatre,
crearono un nuovo tipo di teatralità che toccava tutte quelle tematiche, dal
testo all'improvvisazione, dalla rappresentazione alla partecipazione, dal
teatro di strada al pacifismo ed alla lotta, alle quali attinsero i nuovi gruppi teatrali. In Europa, fra quanti trassero alimento da questa nuova onda,
solo alcuni impressero veramente una svolta personale alle tematiche, ai
contenuti ed agli insegnamenti.

Mentre in America l'esigenza di partire da nuove tecnologie e da realtà
concernenti un incombente potere economico fece sí che i gruppi doves-
sero comporre le loro proposte su aspetti contingenti, in Europa si tendeva
ad evolvere e a modificare i contenuti tematici desunti dal proprio passato.

In questi anni di profonda crisi politica e sociale si riflette e ci si in-
terroga sulla reale funzione della cultura: può ancora la sublimazione
dell'estetico o l'Arte in senso lato svolgere la sua opera di culturizzazione
in seno ad un clima di profondissima mutazione sociale?

Il dubbio presente nella cultura teatrale percorre anche le così dette
arti visive, intese come vere e proprie discipline; avviene così un rapidis-
simo mutamento che nello spazio di meno di un ventennio le disgiunge
da quel concetto di arte che in più secoli aveva fissato delle ineluttabili
consuetudini culturali.

Senza risalire alle avanguardie ormai storiche, ci riferiremo a quei movimenti che, sviluppatisi dall'astrattismo, non si rapportavano più a un
contenuto rappresentativo ma ad una tensione angosciosa che nasce dalla
consapevolezza della precarietà esistenziale dell'uomo stesso.

Se il pubblico più colto, ad un certo momento, rifuggiva le gallerie
di proposta contemporanea, ormai conscio di essere stato raggirato da un
gioco che vedeva il prodotto artistico solo come mezzo di tesaurizzazio-
ne, cioè come investimento di capitale, non rimaneva agli operatori che
rivolgersi al pubblico-massa, ricercando con nuove tecniche di pensiero di
accaparrarsi la sua fiducia. Molti sono per un lavoro associato, accentrato
su attività didattiche più responsabilmente socializzate.

Anche se le varie discipline creative tendono ad interessarsi di tematiche
comuni, interessi di diversa natura hanno impedito che un reale rapporto
di interscambio si instaurasse fra il mondo teatrale e quello delle arti visive. Ciascuno, racchiuso nella propria specialistica ideologia di settore
evolveva una ricerca sperimentale volta in senso comune, ma ignorando se
non addirittura criticando apertamente tutto ciò che non concerneva il pro-

prio ambito di azione, senza considerare i progressi che hanno coinvolto reciprocamente le diverse discipline artistiche, teatrali e musicali.

L'attività del Centro Maschere e Strutture Gestuali trae origine dalla constatazione che arti visive ed esperienze teatrali tendono ormai ad unificarsi in un'univocità di intenti. In questa situazione l'elemento maschera, che storicamente costituisce il punto di unione fra "produzione artistica" e "forma spettacolare," diventa il centro propulsore dal quale si irradiano i polivalenti interessi del Centro. A questi si aggiunge la consapevolezza che la volontà di partecipazione ricopre un ruolo la cui importanza è determinata dalla volontà di liberare la propria attività creativa. Nuova perché non risponde più alle esigenze di un singolo individuo ma al bisogno esistenziale ed etico che si manifesta nella domanda di massa di una espressività comune alla ricerca di rapporti umani meno inquinati. Si instaura così tra operatore e fruitore un rapporto non più di dipendenza culturale ma di corrispondenza creativa. L'artista si trasforma dunque in coordinatore e cooperatore, ovvero in provocatore di sollecitazioni operative.

Centro Maschere e Strutture Gestuali

Franco Fido

La scuola degli istrioni: Goldoni e le maschere *dell'arte*

1. Questa mi sembra una buona occasione per esplorare almeno una parte del territorio che si estende dietro il muro di due grossi luoghi comuni: luoghi comuni per altro giustificabili, come vedremo, ma troppo spesso accettati senza discussione. Il primo consiste nell'idea che la "Riforma" goldoniana—cioè le commedie scritte e fatte recitare fra il 1748 e il 1753 al Teatro di Sant'Angelo, e più ancora quelle prodotte al Teatro di San Luca fra il 1753 e il 1762—comportò la liquidazione della vecchia Commedia italiana, e segnò quindi la fine delle maschere, della recitazione all'improvviso, di un teatro fortemente stilizzato, ad altissimo coefficiente ludico e di scarso "contenuto" realistico.

Il secondo luogo comune riguarda l'immenso debito di Goldoni verso i comici dell'arte: tutto un patrimonio di situazioni, morfemi scenici, trucchi, personaggi, lazzi che il veneziano assimila dalla tradizione e ricicla nelle sue commedie "premeditate." E dietro quest'altro luogo comune c'è poi un dilemma, tra l'indubitabile presenza in Goldoni della suddetta eredità dell'Arte, e la mancanza di documenti sulla commedia dell'arte che abbiano la stessa consistenza testuale delle sue commedie, sì da rendere un paragone veramente possibile.

Si tratta, ripeto, di luoghi comuni in sostanza fondati, più ancora il secondo del primo: e da questo vorrei cominciare, scomponendo il problema nei suoi tre aspetti principali. La prima lezione che i vecchi comici trasmisero ai commediografi colti del Settecento, primo fra tutti il Goldoni, sta naturalmente nella consapevolezza di un pubblico che è lì, che ha pagato l'ingresso, e che vuol divertirsi a teatro: essa riguarda cioè un primo rapporto necessario, fra autore e spettatori.[1] Un secondo, ovvio legame tra la Commedia italiana e il teatro goldoniana sta nella struttura stessa delle compagnie, composte secondo i ruoli dell'Arte: due coppie di Innamorati, due Vecchi, due Zanni, una cameriera, e nell'attaccamento degli attori a questi loro ruoli—che era spesso incapacità di uscirne. Così la specializzazione dei comici predetermina in un certo senso il *cast*, e questo costituisce un dato che a sua volta influenza, o almeno limita, le possibilità dell'intrigo e della caratterizzazione dei personaggi. Questo secondo punto riguarda dunque il rapporto fra *autore* e *attori*. Più complesso è il terzo aspetto della questione, e cioè il rapporto fra l'*autore* Goldoni e i *personaggi* della Commedia italiana: di questo appunto cercherò fra poco di occuparmi in particolare.

2. Prima però vorrei proporre un'altra tassonomia, fondata questa su elementi spiccioli, concreti, testuali, dell'eredità della *commedia dell'arte* in Goldoni, in quattro punti.

I) Dalla tradizione italiana Goldoni prese talvolta intere trame per le sue commedie, quasi sempre su proposta dei comici stessi. Così, a richiesta del Truffaldino Sacchi, dallo scenario *Arlequin valet de deux maîtres* compreso nel *Nouveau Théâtre Italien* del Riccoboni Goldoni ricavò nel 1745 *Il Servitore di due padroni*,[2] e dallo scenario corsiniano *Pantaloncino* derivò per il D'Arbes *Il Frappatore*.[3] Pur senza rifarsi a un modello specifico, altre sue commedie—come ha dimostrato Ludovico Zorzi a proposito degl'*Innamorati*[4]—presentano lo schema binario tipico dei canovacci dell'arte.

II) Dopo l'intrigo, un secondo tipo di materiali tradizionali riciclati dal Goldoni si potrebbe riconoscere nelle *tirate*, in quei discorsi o sproloqui pieni di concetti, di sorprendenti o grottesche metafore, che ogni tanto i suoi personaggi pronunciano. Per esempio nella *Madre amorosa* (II, 4) Brighella offre una sua filosofia dei sessi, sostenendo che in amore gli uomini invecchiando si comportano come animali diversi:

Dai diese sina ai disdotto ho fatto l'amor co fa i colombini, zirando intorno alla colombina, ruzando pian pianin sotto ose, e dandoghe qualche volta una beccadina innocente. Dai disdotto sina ai vintiquattro ho fatto l'amor co fa i gatti, a forza de sgraffoni e de morsegotti. De vintiquattro me son maridà, e ho fatto come i cavai da posta. Una corsa de un'ora, e una repossada de un giorno. Adesso me tocca a far co fa i cani: una nasadina, e tirar de longo:

dove evidentemente l'autore conta sul riconoscimento da parte degli spettatori di un *topos* dell'arte per farsi perdonare la relativa volgarità delle immagini.

III) Un altro, ovvio espediente della vecchia commedia sfruttato dal Goldoni sono i lazzi, cioè quelle azioni, pantomime, serie di gesti che i comici compiono a rincalzo del dialogo. Gli esempi più numerosi e divertenti si trovano nel *Servitore di due padroni*, ma qui probabilmente i lazzi risalgono al primo interprete Sacchi,[5] per cui preferisco riferirmi ad altre commedie. Così il lazzo—fra i tanti descritti da Giorgio Maria Raparini nel suo poema *Arlichino* (1718)[6]—di Brighella finto sensale che vende a Pantalone una mummia egiziana dopo lunghe contrattazioni in supposta lingua armena col supposto proprietario è ripreso da Goldoni in una bella commedia dei primi anni della Riforma al Sant'Angelo, *La Famiglia dell'antiquario* (I, 17, e II, 12). Mentre un lazzo dello scenario del Gherardi *La Précaution inutile* sarà usato pari pari da Goldoni negli *Amanti timidi*: Colombina (nello scenario gherardiano) o Camilla (nella commedia) riceve da Arlecchino il ritratto dell'innamorato, fa vista di restituirglielo indignata e intanto lo scambia col suo (II, 6).[7]

Non appena ci mettiamo in traccia dei lazzi dell'Arte sfruttati da Goldoni ci imbattiamo nel quarto elemento della mia tassonomia spicciola, che è poi la traduzione concreta del terzo aspetto (rapporto fra autore e personaggi) del problema generale discusso in precedenza.

IV) Il lazzo, sia in Goldoni che nella tradizione dell'Arte, è indissolubilmente legato a certi personaggi, cioè alle maschere, e in particolare alle due più vivaci e comiche, gli Zanni. Si prenda uno dei più graziosi lazzi del teatro goldoniano, quello della *Gastalda* del 1751, in cui Arlecchino è incaricato dal padrone di riscattargli la *velada* o marsina data in pegno all'oste suo creditore, ma on ha naturalmente un centesimo, e pensa di "prendere a prestito" un candeliere d'argento in casa di Pantalone:

Corpo del diavolo! Cossa dirà el me pover padron, se non ghe porto la velada? El m'ha dit inzegnete, bisogna che m'inzegna. Gh'ho dito, se sgrafignasse? El m'ha dito inzegnete. Diavolo, se savesse come far. Zitto. Coss'è sta roba? (*guarda qua e là, e vede i candelieri d'argento*) Questo l'è arzento. Se portas un de sti candelieri all'osto? Credemo che el me das la velada? Oh, sior sì! Donca bisogna torlo. Se m'ho da inzegnar, quasta l'è l'ocasion. Ma l'oi da robar? Sior no, l'ho da tor in prestido. E lo torrò in prestido senza pegno? Sior no, vôi lassarghe el pegno. Sior taolin, me imprestela sto candelier? Sì? grazie. La vol el pegno? La gh'ha rason. Ghe lasso el me cappellin. Cussì fa i omeni d'onor. No i roba, no i tol in prestido senza pegno. Son un galantomo. Porto via el candelier, ma ghe lasso el me cappellin (II, 7).[8]

In questo caso, il lazzo non viene da uno scenario determinato, bensì direttamente da Arlecchino, la maschera carnevalesca che, fuor di commedia, passeggiava per Venezia, e andando al Ridotto, dove si giocava, prelevava cerimoniosamente un ducato, tra mille inchini e ringraziamenti, da ogni tavolo da gioco.[9]

3. Le cinque maschere italiane presenti in Goldoni sono come è noto i due Vecchi (Pantalone e il Dottore), i due Zanni (Brighella primo Zanni, e Ar-

lecchino, o Truffaldino, o Traccagnino secondo Zanni) e infine la servetta, con quattro o cinque nomi diversi.

Le coordinate sociolinguistiche e l'abito di queste maschere restano sostanzialmente in Goldoni quelli tradizionali: Pantalone vecchio mercante veneziano, il Dottore giurista, o più raramente medico bolognese, gli Zanni servitori bergamaschi, ecc. Ma la loro utilizzazione da parte del commediografo, o meglio il lavoro di rinnovamento dall'interno di questi personaggi, sotto il guscio del vestito a scacchi colorati e delle maschere di cuoio o di cartapesta, varia da caso a caso.

Meno importanti e interessanti, sia come numero di presenze sia come caratterizzazione psicologica, appaiono il secondo Vecchio, cioè il Dottore, e il primo Zanni, Brighella, spesso imborghesito nel ruolo di locandiere. Le tre maschere di gran lunga più notevoli nel teatro goldoniano sono Pantalone, il secondo Zanni e la servetta.

Delle 48 commedie scritte fino alla rottura coi Medebach e al passaggio dal Sant'Angelo al San Luca nel 1753, 44 contengono le maschere, e in 37 di queste le maschere hanno una parte centrale o importante. Se a queste 44 aggiungiamo le 8 commedie con maschere fra quelle scritte per il San Luca dal 1753 al 1762, e le 3 con maschere scritte in Francia, arriviamo a 55 commedie. Già questi primi rilievi statistici ci portano ad alcune conclusioni che possono sembrare sorprendenti se pensiamo al cliché di Goldoni "nemico" e "vincitore" delle maschere:

I) Metà circa delle commedie goldoniane contengono le maschere.

II) L'eliminazione di queste non avviene affatto durante gli anni della Riforma vera e propria al Teatro di Sant'Angelo fra il 1748 e il 1753. Delle 39 commedie scritte per i Medebach in quei cinque anni, 36 contengono le maschere. Fanno eccezione la *Pamela*, prima commedia senza maschere in assoluto, del 1750: qui il modello di Richardson e l'ambientazione inglese escludono ovviamente la presenza di Pantalone e di Arlecchino; *Il Molière*, per le stesse ragioni; e *La Locandiera*, dove però Mirandolina è una variante al tempo stesso imborghesita e intellettualizzata di Corallina, il ruolo di servetta in cui era specializzata la brava Maddalena Marliani.

III) Le maschere vengono abbandonate da Goldoni solo intorno al 1755, cioè dopo due anni di attività al Teatro di San Luca, e in coincidenza con nuove tendenze che si affermavano allora nel suo teatro, verso la commedia o tragicommedia esotica in versi martelliani, o meglio verso vari tipi di "esotismo": l'esotico per così dire storico del *Terenzio* e del *Torquato Tasso*, l'esotico politico-sociale del *Filosofo inglese* e del *Medico olandese*, e l'esotico geografico nella variante "orientale" delle tre commedie persiane del ciclo di Ircana, e nella variante "americana" della *Peruviana* e della *Bella selvaggia.*

Si potrebbe dire cioè che—prima dell'avvento di nuovi filoni nell'ultima grande stagione creativa di Goldoni a Venezia: vita popolare veneziana, aristocrazia in campagna, borghesia in crisi—le maschere cedano il campo ad altre forme di convenzione e di stilizzazione: le fiabe chiaresche, o filosofiche, o pseudoeroiche in versi martelliani.

4. La maschera che Goldoni trasforma più radicalmente dall'interno, fino a farne, come è noto, il personaggio portatore per eccellenza dei valori borghesi, e dunque il portavoce della Riforma, è Pantalone. Curiosamente, nelle prime commedie, quelle scritte per il Teatro di San Samuele prima del soggiorno pisano, e precisamente intorno al 1740, Pantalone appare meno frequentemente del Dottore: questo perché proprio in quelle commedie Goldoni utilizza il giovane "Pantalone" della compagnia, Francesco Golinetti, per il nuovo personaggio senza maschera del *Cortesan*, o giovane borghese veneziano.[10] Mi riferisco alle tre *pièces* dialogate solo in parte fornite alla compagnia Imer fra il 1738 e il 1741: *Momolo cortesan*, *Momolo sulla Brenta* e *Il Mercante fallito*, che saranno stese per intero più tardi, intorno al 1755, coi titoli rispettivi de *L'Uomo di mondo*, *Il Prodigo*, e *La Bancarotta.*[11]

Il Cortesan ha in potenza tutte le virtù che saranno poi quelle del vecchio mercante veneziano nelle commedie per il Teatro di Sant'Angelo, talché invecchiando il *cortesan* potrà riprendere la maschera, il naso a becco e la barba all'insù del primo Vecchio, e diventare il nuovo Pantalone goldoniano. Lo schema genetico del personaggio "riformato" potrebbe dunque essere questo:

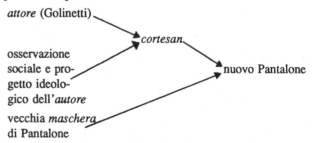

A partire dal *Padre di famiglia* (1751), il peso del *Mondo*, nel nuovo personaggio, è chiaramente superiore al peso del *Teatro*, cioè gli elementi che lo caratterizzano appartengono più all'ideologia goldoniana che alle connotazioni tradizionali (avarizia, libidine, ecc.) della maschera dell'Arte. Se dunque le commedie fra il 1750 e il 1753 rappresentano il momento di maggior frequenza di Pantalone, è anche da dire che in

esse Pantalone è sempre meno "maschera," e sempre più rappresentante
tipico ed esemplare della borghesia mercantile veneziana, eroe di quei valori di economia, prudenza, puntualitàa, buon senso, pace domestica, che
costituiscono l'assiologia della Riforma.

In questo caso quindi, l'*autore* prende nettamente il sopravvento sugli
altri elementi costitutivi del personaggio.

Una prova *e contrario* possiamo vedere in un testo assai poco noto del
1753, *Il Geloso avaro*, prima commedia rappresentata al Teatro di San
Luca, dove rispunta inopinatamente, dopo tanti Pantaloni saggi e buoni,
un Pantalone cattivo, non solo geloso e avaro come annuncia il titolo,
ma grossolano con la virtuosissima moglie, venale e spregevole: quasi
per riprendere da zero il rapporto coi Pantaloni viziosi della *commedia
dell'arte*, e insieme per un lontano presagio di quella crisi del personaggio borghese che all'altro estremo di questa fase al San Luca scoppierà
in personaggi come Sior Todero brontolon nella commedia omonima, che
questo Pantalone geloso avaro del 1753 anticipa per più di un verso, fin
dall'ingresso in scena dei due personaggi. Pantalone ordina a Traccagnino
di andare a vedere cosa fa sua moglie: "Va a véder se la laora, se la leze,
se la scrive, se la sta alla finestra" (*Geloso avaro*, I, 5), mentre Todero
tempesta di domande analoghe il vecchio servitore Gregorio: "Chi ghe xe
adesso in cusina? [. . .] Mio fio dove xelo? [. . .] Dove xe la putta?
[. . .] Cossa fala [. . .] Cossa laòrela?, ecc." (*Sior Todero*, I, 5). E si
veda ancora l'illusione comune ai due personaggi di poter vivere in eterno
e "sotterrare" tutti gli altri in famiglia (*Geloso*, I, 6; *Todero*, I 6 e 7); e
infine il loro ossessivo intercalare: "In casa mia son paron mi" (*Geloso*,
I, 12), "In sta casa no ghe xe altri patroni che mi" (*Todero*, I, 5).[12]

5. Se passiamo alla servetta, ci avvediamo subito che è più difficile stabili-
re la sua presenza in quanto maschera in questa o quella commedia, perché
si tratta di un personaggio che di solito parla toscano, e non porta come
i due zanni la mascherina nera sulla faccia, o un costume particolare: un
personaggio cioè le cui coordinate caratterizzanti sono soprattutto psicologiche (malizia, spirito pronto, ambizione di migliorare, intraprendenza,
ecc.). Come nel caso delle altre maschere, l'attrice specialista nel ruolo di
servetta conserva sempre il suo nome di scena da una commedia all'altra,
per cui quando in una compagnia di attori una nuova servetta viene a sosti-
tuirne un'altra, nelle commedie scritte per l'attrice nuova cambia il nome
del personaggio. Così abbiamo intanto Smeraldina nelle commedie scritte
per la compagnia Imer al Teatro di San Samuele, dove faceva la servetta
Anna Baccherini, di cui tanti anni dopo il vecchio Goldoni scriverà nei

Mémoires:

C'étoit une jeune Florentine, très-jolie, fort gaie, très-brillante, d'une taille arron-
die, potelée, la peau blanche, les yeux noirs, beaucoup de vivacité, et une pronon-
ciation charmante. Elle n'avoit pas le talent et l'expérience de celle qui l'avoit
précédée, mais on voyoit en elle des dispositions heureuses, et elle ne demandoit
que du travail et du tems, pour parvenir à la perfection. Madame Baccherini étoit
mariée, je l'étois aussi. Nous nous liâmes d'amitié; nous avions besoin l'un de
l'autre; je travaillois pour sa gloire, et elle dissipoit mon chagrin (I, 43).[13]

Per lei sarà scritta tra l'altro nel 1743 la *pièce de transformation* che Goldoni chiamerà spesso la "primogenita" delle sue commedie, *La Donna di
garbo*.

Dopo Smeraldina, nelle commedie scritte per i Medebach al Sant'Angelo a partire del 1748, viene Colombina, che non sappiamo chi fosse, e che
diventa un paio di volte Fiammetta, e una volta, come cameriera francese
di Rosaura *Vedova scaltra*, Marionette. Ma nel 1751 tornò coi Medebach,
cioè col marito Giuseppe Marliani che era il Brighella di quella compagnia,
la brava servetta Maddalena Raffi, in arte Corallina.[14] La transizione fra la
Colombina delle commedie precedenti e la Corallina di quelle successive è
documentata dalla *Donna volubile*, in cui Goldoni scrisse salomonicamen-
te una parte sia per Colombina che per Corallina, rispettivamente prima
e seconda cameriera in casa di Pantalone, e rivali sulla scena per l'amore
di Brighella come dovevano essere rivali nella compagnia per il ruolo
della servetta. Questo restò presto appannaggio esclusivo di Maddalena
Raffi Marliani, cioè di Corallina, per la quale Goldoni scrisse le più belle
parti di cameriera-protagonista, come quelle della *Gastalda* e della *Serva
amorosa*, finché—abbandonando il suo stesso nome d'arte, e trascenden-
do le solite coordinate del personaggio—la Marliani diventa l'intelligente,
inquieta, ambigua Mirandolina della *Locandiera*.

Al San Luca, fra il 1753 e il 1762, la servetta era Giustina Campioni,
detta sulle scene Argentina, e anche per lei Goldoni compose qualche bella
commedia, come *La Cameriera brillante* del 1753 o *La Donna di governo*
del 1758, dove per altro la serva-padrona si chiama Valentina.

Finalmente, Goldoni trovò in Francia l'ultima, e una delle più famose
servette del Teatro italiano, quella Camilla Veronesi per la quale furono
scritti gli scenari diventati poi la Trilogia di Zelinda e Lindoro.

Se ripercorriamo rapidamente questa amabile dinastia ancillare, da Smeraldina a Colombina a Corallina ad Argentina a Camilla, vediamo che nel
caso della servetta l'elemento distintivo, la sfacciataggine di Smeraldina
come il brio e l'eleganza di Corallina o il patetismo di Camilla, è lega-

to soprattutto alla personalità dell'interprete. Degli elementi costitutivi della maschera goldoniana—autore, attore, personaggio—è questa volta il secondo, *l'attrice*, a mantenere il sopravvento.

6. Arriviamo così ad Arlecchino; o meglio al secondo Zanni come conviene dire, perché ancora una volta abbiamo vari nomi per la stessa maschera. Il secondo Zanni compare 8 volte nelle commedie scritte prima del 1748, col nome di Truffaldino o di Arlecchino, 28 volte in quelle per i Medebach al Sant'Angelo, col nome di Arlecchino, 8 volte al Teatro di San Luca, col nome prevalente di Traccagnino, e 3 volte nelle commedie scritte a Parigi, di nuovo come Arlecchino: 47 volte in tutto, contro le 40 di Pantalone, e ancora le 40 della servetta. Il Truffaldino della compagnia Imer al San Samuele era il grande Antonio Sacchi; il Traccagnino del San Luca era Francesco Cattoli, e l'Arlecchino del Théâtre italien a Parigi Carlin Bertinazzi.

Come nel caso di Colombina, non sappiamo invece quale attore recitasse da Arlecchino nella compagnia Medebach. Nel *Teatro comico*, la commedia-programma del 1750, Goldoni lo chiama semplicemente Gianni, e neppure le ricerche dell'Ortolani sono valse a scoprirne l'identità. Il fatto che non sia restata memoria di questi due comici è un forte indizio della loro scarsa bravura. A sua volta, l'assenza di un secondo Zanni, e fino al 1751 anche di una servetta celebri, o almeno provvisti di una forte personalità, può essere stata una condizione favorevole per la Riforma goldoniana, e aver facilitato quell'imborghesimento della commedia che il veneziano affida in questi anni alla rinnovata maschera di Pantalone, impersonata invece di un bravissimo attore, il Collalto.[15]

Questo limita la portata dell'apparente paradosso che vede la maschera più refrattaria alla Riforma, la meno riducibile ai criteri di verosimiglianza e di *bienséance* borghese predicati nel *Teatro comico*, apparire come abbiamo visto nelle sue commedie più frequentemente di Pantalone. Bisogna aggiungere tuttavia che la presenza del secondo Zanni con funzioni teatralmente forti si verifica lungo un tempo più esteso di quella delle altre maschere, e sopratutto in commedie di particolare importanza per la loro posizione nel canone goldoniano, come quelle che potremmo chiamare "terminali."

Come è noto, esattamente all'inizio della carriera goldoniana il *Momolo cortesan* del 1738 era stato una specie di incunabolo di teatro borghese, perduto ma ricostruibile a partire dalla commedia che Goldoni ne ricavò più tardi, *L'Uomo di mondo*. Nello scenario del 1738, solo la parte del protagonista Momolo era dialogata per iscritto, mentre le altre, compresa quella del Truffaldino Sacchi, erano lasciate all'improvvisazione dei comici. Sette anni dopo, a Pisa, cade il risveglio dell'interesse di Goldoni per il teatro, con un altro scenario steso su richiesta dello stesso Sacchi, che era appena tornato da Mosca: *Il Servitore di due padroni*. Questa volta Truffaldino è naturalmente il protagonista, e quando, di nuovo, Goldoni stese per intero la commedia, certamente incorporò nei dialoghi battute e lazzi che il Sacchi aveva usato nel recitarla all'improvviso.

All'estremo opposto della carriera italiana del Goldoni, molti anni dopo il trionfo della Riforma e la conseguente supposta liquidazione delle maschere, egli scrive due curiose e pochissimo note commedie, *Il buon compatriotto*, rappresentata al San Luca nel dicembre del 1761, fra dei capolavori quali la trilogia delle *Villeggiature*, e il *Sior Todero brontolon*, e Il *Genio buono e il Genio cattivo*, scritta a Parigi dopo la trilogia di Zelinda e Lindoro e dopo *Il Ventaglio*—e dunque ultima in assoluto fra le commedie italiane di Goldoni—, e rappresentata nel carnevale del 1768 al Teatro di San Giovanni Grisostomo.[16]

Come il lontano *Momolo* all'altro estremo della stessa storia, anche *Il buon compatriotto* è una commedia mista, parte dialogata parte lasciata all'improvvisazione; ma esattamente al contrario del *Momolo cortesan*, qui tutte le parti sono scritte per intero meno quella del protagonista Traccagnino, libero di inventare il dialogo sulla traccia delle schematiche indicazioni dell'autore.

E' come se Goldoni si voltasse indietro, e si divertisse a un ricupero quasi archeologico del proprio esordio, tanto più che Traccagnino, figlio di un ciabattino, sta viaggiando in burchiello dalla natia Bergamo verso Venezia dove intende stabilirsi in proprio, provvisto com'è di un piccolo capitale e perfino (come i figli di Renzo nei *Promessi Sposi*) di qualche conoscenza scolastica che gli permetterà di tenere i conti. Al secondo Zanni sembra affidato un discorso sottilmente metateatrale, un viaggio dalla preistoria alla storia, dalle origini popolari e bergamasche della maschera verso la rispettabilità del personaggio inurbato e borghese.

Altrettanto interessante è da questo punto di vista *Il Genio buono e il Genio cattivo*, fiaba ragionevole con la quale Goldoni intendeva probabilmente rispondere a quelle strabilianti del Gozzi, in cui Arlecchino passa per opera magica dalla condizione iniziale di contadino innamoratissimo della moglie Corallina a quella di ricco e goffo turista a Parigi e a Londra, sempre pronto alle vanterie e alle facili imprese galanti, per poi tornare pentito ai suoi campi a sua moglie. A parte lo studio dell'azione corruttrice del denaro e dei privilegi, che può far pensare a un'influenza su Goldoni della *Double inconstance* di Marivaux,[17] anche questa commedia, all'estremo limite dell'itinerario goldoniano, sembra voler offrire una storia in nuce, una specie di sommario antropologico della nostra maschera.

7. Entro la gamma tematica e cronologica di eccezionale ampiezza che si estende fra i testi "terminali" appena ricordati, il secondo Zanni di Goldoni presenta delle costanti e delle variabili psicologiche e drammaturgiche. Così, egli indossa l'abito tradizionale a scacchi e losanghe policrome, e porta ancora (ma non usa più) il *batocchio* o spada/spatola di legno.[18] Parla ormai veneziano, con qualche stilizzata inflessione bergamasca (per esempio: *pader* per *padre* o *pare*), è sempre affamato, non sa né leggere né scrivere, è credulo, dice spropositi. Fin qui, le sue caratteristiche coincidono con quelle del grande Truffaldino Sacchi, per il quale furono concepite le prime parti goldoniane di secondo Zanni.

Un po' più tardi, al Teatro di Sant'Angelo, l'Arlecchino impersonato dal non meglio identificato Gianni della compagnia Medebach assume talvolta una funzione involontariamente e comicamente demistificatrice, come nel *Bugiardo*, dove le bugie dette dallo Zanni a imitazione delle "spiritose invenzioni" del suo padrone Lelio sono giudicate troppo pesanti persino da quest'ultimo (I, 14). Ancora, l'Arlecchino goldoniano è quasi sempre un domestico, talvolta un facchino, una volta, nel *Feudatario* del 1752, "servo della communità" o come diremmo oggi usciere, un'altra, nell'*Amante militare* del 1751, soldato per forza.

A differenza del *servus currens* della commedia latina e di quella rinascimentale, lo Zanni di Goldoni non ha di solito un peso risolutivo nello scioglimento della trama. La sua funzione è piuttosto quella di "controcanto" demistificante o di "spalla," un po' come il Leporello di Da Ponte/Mozart, probabilmente memore del resto dei servi goldoniani, oltre che del Catalinòn di Tirso, del Passarino del Cicognini e dello Sganarelle di Molière.

Parallele a queste costanti corrono le differenze, a documentare le quali userò di preferenza titoli che ho già ricordato, ma di cui potrei moltiplicare gli esempi. Così il Truffaldino impersonato da Antonio Sacchi può essere fannullone, senza scrupoli, aggressivo coi deboli e vigliacco coi più forti come quello del *Momolo cortesan* e dell'*Uomo di mondo* di cui *Momolo* dovette essere la sinopia, oppure pasticcione ma simpatico, e pieno di risorse fino all'invenzione geniale come il *Servitore di due padroni*. Tra i frequentissimi Arlecchini degli anni della Riforma al Sant'Angelo e quelli che più raramente compaiono nelle commedie scritte per il San Luca, il tipo prevalente è "un bon fiolazzo un poco semplice," come dice di lui Corallina nella *Gastalda*, ma abbiamo ugualmente una gamma di sfumature caratteriali assai estesa.

Ad un estremo possiamo incontrare il balordo e credulo Arlecchino dell'*Amante militare*, che fa il suo primo ingresso in scena capitombolando e spaccando la brocca d'acqua che dovrebbe far rinvenire Rosaura svenuta (I, 6), viene poi condannato a morte come disertore per aver cercato di lasciare l'esercito travestito da donna, ed è graziato all'ultimo momento. All'estremo opposto si trova l'Arlecchino del *Raggiratore* del 1757, forse il peggiore di tutti, tanto eccezionalmente odioso fra i secondi Zanni quanto il già ricordato *Geloso avaro* fra i Pantaloni: furbo, cinico, mezzano, imbroglione, maligno, eppure—eccezionale anche in questo— deus ex machina della commedia cui appartiene.

Al termine di questa lunga sfilata troviamo gli Arlecchini più complessi, come quello già ricordato del *Buon compatriotto* (1761), che come tanti suoi confratelli "xe un poco alocchetto" (dice Rosina, che poi lo sposerà), ma è anche un buon uomo, economo fino all'avarizia, laborioso, capace anche un pochino di leggere e far di conto, e insomma aspirante borghese; o quello debole e influenzabile, superficiale e ghiottone, ma sinceramente innamorato della sua Corallina e fondamentalmente educabile, che il Genio buono e il Genio cattivo si contendono nella commedia omonima.

8. Quando scriveva Il *Genio buono*, Goldoni aveva alle spalle le poche, ma interessanti e spesso raffinate *pièces* scritte per il grande Arlecchino degli Italiens, Carlin Bertinazzi. Di queste, i tre scenari *Les Amours d'Arlequin et de Camille*, *Les Jalousies d'Arlequin* e *Les Inquiétudes de Camille* del 1763 furono subito trasformati da Goldoni nelle tre grandi commedie italiane di Zelinda e Lindoro, dove però i protagonisti non sono più delle maschere, e richiederebbero un discorso diverso, allargato alla poetica della commedia sentimentale o *larmoyante* nel secondo Settecento.[19] Preferisco dunque chiudere questa rassegna attenedomi alle due altre commedie concepite inizialmente come scenari per il versatile Carlin, e poi stese, più fedelmente, per intero: *L'Amore paterno o sia la serva riconoscente* e *Gli Amanti timidi*.

Nella prima Arlecchino è un maestro di casa che si è arricchito rubando al suo padrone Stefanello, avido, duro con gli altri servitori e con la promessa sposa Camilla, addirittura brutale col povero Pantalone appena sbarcato a Parigi con due figlie, e lasciato senza sostegno dalla morte del fratello Stefanello che l'aveva invitato a raggiungerlo. Negli *Amanti timidi*, concepiti come scenario nel 1764 e poi stesi interamente per il Teatro di San Luca—e dunque probabilmente ultima commedia italiana del Goldoni, se consideriamo a parte la fiaba del *Genio buono*—l'Arlecchino protagonista è un servitore impulsivo e ingenuo, ma anche buono e fedele, caratterizzato soprattutto dalla timidezza che lo paralizza quando si trova davanti alla servetta Camilla, non meno timida e non meno innamorata di lui. Oltre che con la propria timidezza, Arlecchino deve sostenere un'altra doppia lotta, contro una lettera che ha ricevuto a che non sa leggere, cioè contro *la scrittura*, che lo ricaccia nella sua condizione di analfabeta, nel suo status di maschera ignorante; e contro un ritratto, o meglio due ritratti: quello del padrone, eseguito come regalo per la fidanzata e segno del diritto del giovane all'amore, e il suo proprio, "rubatogli" cioè eseguito di nascosto dal garzone del pittore (I, 4), possibile dono per Camilla e segno della velleità di Arlecchino all'amore ("caro sior patron, son de carne anca mi": I, 6).

Come vedremo fra un momento, il motivo quasi rousseauiano *avant la lettre* del ritratto rubato rinvia a quello più generale dell'identità di Arlecchino. Ma intanto nella maggior sottigliezza psicologica e grazia scenica di questo suo ultimo o penultimo Zanni possiamo ravvisare l'influsso della tradizione arlecchinesca francese, o meglio degli Italiens a Parigi, che è poi quella decisiva nella storia del personaggio: una storia che passa per le interpretazioni di Domenico Biancolelli ed Evaristo Gherardi nel Seicento, di Tommaso Visentini e Carlin Bertinazzi nel Settecento, via via raffinate dal contributo di grandi scrittori teatrali come Regnard e Marivaux,[20] e di eccezionali interpreti figurativi delle nostre maschere, come Claude Gillot e soprattutto—quasi altrettanto misterioso dei Mezzetini e dei Pierrot a lui cari—il grande Antoine Watteau.[21]

L'Arlecchino di Biancolelli e di Visentini, già italianizzato dal Goldoni durante i venticinque anni della sua attività teatrale veneziana, si arricchisce di nuove sfumature tornando alla Comédie italienne di Parigi: tornando a casa, se si vuole. Si tratta insieme di un ritorno alle origini e di una rivincita degli Italiens sul loro poeta presto deluso, e acerbo critico Carlo Goldoni. Ma come sempre, o quasi sempre, Goldoni sa trarre partito dalle esperienze più difficili. L'Arlecchino dei testi concepiti per Carlin Bertinazzi da un lato dà ragione a quel che di lui aveva osservato uno dei suoi più intelligenti interpreti tardo-secenteschi, il già ricordato Gherardi: "Arlecchino non ha un carattere distinto: è tutto quello che si vuole che sia."[22] Dall'altro esso resta inconfondibilmente e sempre lui attraverso tutte le varianti, furbo/sciocco, ricco/povero, grossolano/gentile di cui il suo inventore Goldoni e il suo interprete Bertinazzi sono capaci.

Nell'ultima scena degli *Amanti timidi* Arlecchino dichiara finalmente di voler sposare una certa *amiga* di Camilla, che sa di sicuro essere a sua volta innamorata di lui; spinta da tutti, Camilla finisce col confessare che l'*amiga* è lei stessa, e che l'uomo amato è quello del ritratto che tiene in mano:

(fa vedere il ritratto d'Arlecchino e si copre il viso) ARLECCHINO (da sé, giubilando): Son mi, son mi. Camilla xe l'amiga, e mi son mi (e tutti applaudiscono).

E' certamente un caso, ma non è per noi senza significato che il teatro italiano di Goldoni si chiuda praticamente con questa battuta di Arlecchino, quell'Arlecchino che nella *Pamela* del 1750—prima sua commedia senza maschere—l'autore aveva fatto scioccamente lodare dal fatuo cavaliere Ernold:

Oh se vedeste che bella maschera è l'Arlecchino! . . . Costui rappresenta un servo goffo ed astuto nel medesimo tempo. Ha una maschera assai ridicola, veste un abito di più colori, e fa smascellar dalle risa. Credetemi, amici, che se lo vedeste, con tutta la vostra serietà sareste sforzati a ridere. Dice delle cose spiritosissime. Sentite alcuni de' suoi vezzi che ho ritenuti in memoria. Invece di dir *padrone*, dirà *poltrone*. In luogo di dir *dottore*, dirà *dolore*. Al *cappello* dirà *campanello*. A una *lettera*, una *lettiera*. Parla sempre di mangiare, fa l'impertinente con tutte le donne. Bastona terribilmente il padrone . . . (I, 16).

Sembrerebbe una liquidazione senza appello, un antifrastico e ironico elogio funebre. Ma dopo un quarto di secolo, e dopo altre cento commedie, Arlecchino è ancora lì, e può trionfalmente ripetere: "Son mi, son mi. Camilla xe l'amiga, e mi son mi."

Se nella metamorfosi di Pantalone possiamo, come si è visto, riconoscere una piena vittoria dell'*autore*, che porta una poetica e un'etica nuove *dentro* il vecchio personaggio della Commedia italiana; e se nelle trasformazioni della servetta si impone invece anche, e in un certo senso soprattutto, la personalità dell'*attrice*, che riuscirà a portare nuove e vive figure di donna *fuori* della maschera tradizionale (Mirandolina la locandiera da Corallina, Valentina la governante da Argentina, la patetica Zelinda da Camilla), nella lunga storia dell'Arlecchino goldoniano l'ultima parola resta in definitiva al *personaggio*: "mi son mi."

C'è appena bisogno di aggiungere che le mie sono delle semplici metafore, dei tropi metateatrali. Chi vince sempre, anche quando accoglie e approfondisce genialmente la lezione degli istrioni dell'Arte, è naturalmente il Goldoni.

Brown University

NOTES

1 Per la consapevolezza, da parte di un drammaturgo colto, della forza spettacolare della Commedia dell'arte, e quindi della sua superiorità scenica sul teatro
 letterario, si veda per esempio la dedica di Pier Jacopo Martello a G. B. Recanati della sua commedia *Che bei pazzi*: "quando cotesti artegianelli o barcaiuoli
 vanno al teatro per ridere, più tosto il Dottore, il Pantalone, ed Arlecchino, e
 Finocchio, che la *Lena*, il *Negromante*, i *Suppositi*, la *Cassaria*, e la *Scolastica*
 vorrebbero ritrovarvi: conciossiacosaché nessuna commedia ridevole, per savia,
 piccante, e costumata che siesi, può alla commedia istrionica italiana resistere
 (. . .) confesso ch'io lascerei l'*Edipo* di Sofocle, e l'*Anfitruone* di Plauto per
 una di queste favole da valenti istrioni rappresentata." P. J. Martello, *Teatro*, a
 cura di Hannibal S. Noce (Bari: Laterza, 1980–82), I, 235–36.
2 Cfr. *Mémoires*, I, 50: in C. Goldoni, *Tutte le opere*, a cura di G. Ortolani (Milano: Mondadori, 1935–56—d'ora in poi: *Opere*), I, 224–26, e per altre notizie
 la "Nota storica" di E. Maddalena al *Servitore*, in C. Goldoni, *Opere complete*
 (Edizione del Municipio di Venezia, 1907–71—d'ora in poi: *Ed. Mun.*), I, 623–
 24. Il riassunto dell'*Arlequin valet de deux maîtres* riprodotto dal Riccoboni
 nel I tomo della seconda edizione del *Nouveau Théâtre Italien* (Paris: Briasson,
 1729) era già stato pubblicato nel *Nouveau Mercure* dell'agosto 1718.
3 Cfr. *Mémoires*, I, 51: *Opere*, I, 231–32. Per le circostanze dell'incontro col
 D'Arbes a Pisa vedi Francesco Bartoli, *Notizie istoriche de' Comici Italiani*
 (Bologna: Forni, 1978—ristampa anastatica dell'edizione di Padova, 1781–
 82), alla voce *D'Arbes, Ceasre* (I, 45–49). Sullo scenario del *Pantaloncino*
 o *Paronzino veneziano* cfr. la "Nota storica" di E. Maddalena al *Frappatore*,
 Ed. Mun., II, 77–78.
4 L. Zorzi, "Due schede di lettura: *L'amante militare* e *Gl'innamorati*," *Studi
 Goldoniani*, a cura di N. Mangini, 3 (1973), pp. 75–105:91–94.
5 Vedi ciò che scrive del Sacchi l'Autore a chi legge nella prefazione al *Servitore*: "Truffaldino ha una prontezza tale di spirito, una tale abbondanza di sali
 e naturalezza di termini, che sorprende: e volendo io provvedermi per le parti
 buffe delle mie commedie, non saprei meglio farlo che studiando sopra di lui
 (. . .) Affaticato mi sono a distendere tutti i lazzi più necessari . . . " *Opere*,
 II, 8–9.
6 Sul bolognese Giorgio Maria Raparini e sul suo rarissimo poema "in tre atti"
 L'Arlichino, cfr. Fausto Nicolini, *Vita di Arlecchino* (Milano-Napoli: Ricciardi,
 1958), pp. 89–96. Sul lazzo del mercante armeno, ivi pp. 309–10.
7 Cfr. Evaristo Gherardi, *Le Théâtre Italien* . . . (Paris: Briasson, 1741), I, scenario 11: e Nicolini, pp. 132 e 380–88.
8 Cito da *La Gastalda*, cioè dal testo primitivo della commedia, come fu presu-
 mibilmente recitata alla "prima" del 1751 e stampata nel t. VII dell'edizione
 Bettinelli (Venezia, 1753). Nell'edizione definitiva Paperini di due anni dopo
 (Firenze, t. VIII) Goldoni ridusse parecchio la parte di Arlecchino, sopprimendo
 tra l'altro il lazzo del candeliere: vedilo in *Opere*, IV, 1106–7.

9 Cfr. Nicolini (che desume la notizia dal Raparini), p. 141.

10 Vedi *Mémoires*, I, 40: *Opere*, I, 184–86.

11 Le tre commedie furono stampate per la prima volta nel t. X e ultimo dell'edizione Paperini (Firenze, 1757).

12 Sulla complessa figura di Todero e sul suo significato nella storia del personaggio borghese in Goldoni, vedi l'acuta "Lettura del *Todero*" di Mario Baratto, *La letteratura teatrale del Settecento in Italia (studi e letture su Carlo Goldoni)* (Vicenza: Neri Pozza, 1985), pp. 177–212.

13 *Opere*, I, 197.

14 Sui coniugi Marliani cfr. F. Bartoli, *Notizie istoriche* . . . , (II, 27–29).

15 Sia per il "Traccagnino" Cattoli ricordato più in alto che per il Collalto cfr. ancora le *Notizie* del Bartoli, I, 163–64 e 173–75 rispettivamente.

16 Per la genesi e le fortunate rappresentazioni veneziane del *Genio buono* vedi la "Nota storica" di G. Ortolani alla commedia, *Ed. Mun.*, XXII, 147–52, e sul significato della fiaba Jacques Joly, *Le désir et l'utopie. Études sur le théâtre d'Alfieri et de Goldoni* (Faculté des Lettres et Sciences humaines de Clermont-Ferrad, 1978), pp. 231–57.

17 *La double inconstance* fu rappresentata nel 1723, e stampata anonima l'anno seguente (Paris, F. Flahaut). Benché Goldoni, a quanto mi risulta, non nomini *mai* Marivaux nelle sue opere, è impensabile che non ne conoscesse il teatro. Fonte comune a Marivaux e a Goldoni potrebbe essere stato l'*Arlequin Sauvage* di Delisle de la Drévetière—rappresentato nel 1721 e stampato prima in estratto nel *Mercure* del giugno dello stesso anno, poi integralmente nel t. II del *Nouveau Théâtre Italien* (Paris: Briasson, 1733)—dove le rimostranze del protagonista a chi ha voluto "civilizzarlo" potrebbero benissimo essere rivolte dall'Arlecchino goldoniano al Genio cattivo: "pourquoi donc, scélérat, m'as-tu tiré de mon pays pour m'apprendre que je suis pauvre? Je l'aurait ignoré toute ma vie sans toi; je ne connaissais dans les forêts ni les richesses, ni la pauvreté; j'étais à moi-même mon roi, mon maître et mon valet (. . .) Je veux être homme, libre, et rien plus. Ramène-moi donc où tu m'as pris, afin que j'aille oublier dans mes forêts qu'il y a des pauvres et des riches dans le monde": citato da Mario Matucci, "Marivaux e l'*Arlecchino Selvaggio* del *Nouveau Théâtre Italien*," in AA. VV., *Studi in onore di Carlo Pellegrini* (Torino: SEI, 1963), pp. 289–99:293.

18 Per il costume dell'Arlecchino o secondo Zanni goldoniano si vedano le incisioni che illustrano le due grandi edizioni veneziane del Pasquali (1761–77) e dello Zatta (1788–95), ora comodamente raccolte in C. Goldoni, *Il Teatro illustrato*, a cura di F. Pedrocco e O. Pugliese (Padova: Marsilio, 1981), cfr. per es. pp. 35, 48, 97, 198, 201, 202, 209, 211, 222.

19 Sulla trilogia cfr. J. Joly, *Le désir et l'utopie* . . . , pp. 217–30, e il mio *Da Venezia all'Europa: prospettive sull'ultimo Goldoni* (Roma: Bulzoni, 1984), pp. 99–103.

20 Si veda in generale Gustave Attinger, *L'esprit de la "Commedia dell'arte"*

dans le théâtre français (Paris: Librairie Théâtrale e Neuchâtel: La Bacon-
nière, 1950), e in particolare di Alexandre Calame, *Regnard: sa vie et son
oeuvre* (Paris: PUF, 1960) i capitoli su "Le Théâtre italien" (pp.
141–259), e
Robert Niklaus, "La Comédie italienne et Marivaux," nei citati *Studi in onore
di Carlo Pellegrini*, pp. 279–87.

21 Cfr. il saggio di François Moureau, "Iconographie théâtrale" nel catalogo della
grande esposizione *Watteau 1684–1721* (Paris: Editions de la Réunion des
musées nationaux, 1984), pp. 509–28: e Herbert Dieckmann, "Claude Gillot
interprète de la Commedia dell'Arte," *Cahiers de l'Association Internationale
des Études Françaises*, 15 (1963), pp. 201–24; e in generale la bibliografia di
Allardyce Nicoll, *The World of Harlequin. A Critical Study of the Commedia
dell'Arte*, Cambridge University Press, 1963.

22 "'Arlequin,' said Gherardi, 'has no marked character; he is whatever one wishes him to be'": M. Wilson Disher, *Clowns and Pantomimes*, citato da Jackson
I. Cope, *Dramaturgy of the Daemonic. Studies in Antigeneric Theater from Ruzante to Grimaldi* (Baltimore & London: The Johns Hopkins University Press,
1984), p. 3. Il libro del Cope contiene la più recente e intelligente proposta di
"demonizzare" il secondo Zanni: si veda soprattutto il capitolo "Harlequin's
Reinvasion: Garrick, Goldoni, and the Germans," pp. 105–21, che si chiude
opponendo al precetto evangelico "Voi non potete servire a Dio e a Mammona"
la servitù di due padroni vittoriosamente praticata dal personaggio goldoniano: "'Ye cannot serve God and Mammon' (Matt. 6:24). But the old daemon
Harlequin can and did, breaking through the surface of social comedy in the
eighteenth century to flash signals of recognition across places and time to remind that comedy really pays the psyche double wages. It is order restored
by chaos rampant." Sul Gherardi si veda *Il Théâtre Italien' di Gherardi*, Otto
commedie di Fatouville, Regnard e Dufresny presentate de Marcello Spaziani,
(Roma: Edizioni dell'Ateneo, 1966), l'Introd. dello Spaziani alle pp. 9–51.

Brian Pocknell

The Théâtre du Vieux Colombier and the Renewal of the *commedia dell'arte* in France

The initial impetus towards the reform of the French theatre in the early years of this century came from Jacques Copeau's hostile reaction to the commercialism of the boulevard plays of the time. Others before him, Antoine, Fort, Lugné-Poe, had condemned the current fashionable theatre. The previous avant-garde movements, the Théâtre-Libre, the Théâtre d'Art, later the Théâtre de l'Oeuvre, had developed highly identifiable styles; Copeau aimed at a complete renewal of values, not so much a revolution as a renaissance.

His stated goal was to purify the theatre, free it from commercial interests, clear away much of the stage machinery that cluttered the acting areas, and improve the quality of acting. The choice of the Salle de l'Athénée Saint-Germain confirmed his rejection of boulevard theatre and its commercial style: the theatre was located on the left bank of the Seine, and contained only five hundred seats. His earliest appeals for help in establishing the Théâtre du Vieux Colombier, as the new company was called, make no direct reference to the *commedia dell'arte*. They promise to restore literary values to the theatre, a sign of Copeau's links with the *Nouvelle Revue Française* group, but they already indicate the trend of his thinking on staging plays:

Que les autres prestiges s'évanouissent, et pour l'oeuvre nouvelle, qu'on nous laisse un tréteau nu.[1]

The bare stage was an important statement of Copeau's policy; it became a characteristic of his productions. Clearly more than a protest against current trends which he had fiercely attacked as a drama critic, it marked above all a return to the sources of the art of drama from which his proposed renewal could develop. When later he discovered that Lope de Rueda had, according to Cervantes, used a bare platform stage constructed from four benches with planks across them, and a blanket drawn across at the back, Copeau rejoiced. He had found an ally from the past and through him he felt encouraged that the reforms he was proposing would bring him closer to the purer form of theatre he sought.

Copeau explained his decision to favour the bare stage in productions at his new theatre:

Mais est-il possible de revenir en arrière, de singer la naiveté, le dénuement primitifs? Je dis que cela est une nécessité . . . *Il faut*. Tout brûler. Que rien ne subsiste plus. Non pas modifier, améliorer, élaborer. Mais *supprimer*. Si je tends une toile grise sur la scène à la place du décor, ce n'est pas parce que je trouve cela plus beau, ni surtout que je pense avoir découvert une formule décorative nouvelle et définitive. C'est un remède radical, une purgation. C'est parce que je veux que la scène soit nue et neutre afin que toute délicatesse y paraisse, que toute faute s'y accuse, afin que l'ouvrage dramatique modèle dans cette ambiance neutre l'enveloppe personnelle dont il entend se vêtir.[2]

The Vieux Colombier company began its career with an Elizabethan play, Thomas Heywood's *A Woman Killed with Kindness*, played against a grey back curtain. On the same bill was a play that showed affinities with the *commedia dell'arte*, Molière's farce, *L'Amour médecin*, which involves no fewer than five physicians. A second Molière farce soon followed: *La Jalousie du Barbouillé*, concerning Gorgibus of Pantalone's "family," is a transcription of scenes that were improvised by Evariste Gherardi, one of the Italian actors in Paris and a famous Arlequin. These farces balanced the literary dramas, but they also helped Copeau to see more clearly the path his reforms should follow:

L'étude de Molière me conduisait à celle de la Comédie Italienne. J'entrevoyais le style de la farce et, pour en exalter les mouvements, la ramenais en esprit au tréteau de ses origines.[3]

With the *commedia dell'arte* now a discernible model, Copeau spent some time planning the formation of a new troupe of actors, "suffisamment intelligents, habiles et bien dressés pour improviser sur tel scénario proposé, et capables de raviver la *commedia dell'arte* à la manière italienne, mais avec des types nouveaux: le bourgeois, le noble, le marchand de vins, la suffragette remplaceraient Arlequin, Pierrot et Colombine. Chacun des types aurait son costume, son parler, son allure, sa psychologie. Et chacun des acteurs n'incarnerait qu'un type, s'y tiendrait et ne s'en départirait point, mais l'enrichirait et l'amplifierait sans cesse."[4]

Copeau explored the possibility of creating such a troupe further by visiting the Cirque Medrano where he admired the work of some of the clowns, especially the Fratellini, who were later to become instructors at the Vieux Colombier school, and Ceratto, a stammering clown, a direct borrowing from the Tartaglia of the *commedia dell'arte*.[5] Henceforward, Copeau kept a special notebook for recording his thoughts on improvised comedy:

C'est un art que je ne connais pas, que je vais étudier dans son histoire. Mais je vois, je sens, je comprends qu'il faut restaurer cet art, le faire renaître, l'aider à revivre, que lui seul nous rendra un théâtre vivant: une comédie et des comédiens.
Sortir de la littérature . . .
Créer une confrérie de comédiens . . . Des hommes vivant ensemble, travaillant ensemble, jouant ensemble. Mais j'avais oublié cet autre terme, auquel je devais fatalement aboutir: créant ensemble, inventant ensemble leurs jeux, tirant d'eux-mêmes et les uns des autres leurs jeux.[6]

The basis of his reform was to be broader, more attention was to be given to following the lines of the *commedia dell'arte*: building a troupe of actors, encouraging them in their improvisations, and building these improvisations into forms of entertainment, as Maurice Sand and his friends had done when they had attempted to revive the *commedia dell'arte*.

Copeau was aware of the traps. One was that he would appear to be a dilettante, a man of literature dabbling in an ancient art. Another was simply reconstituting the old *scenari* of the Italian comedy or the French farces.

Nous étudierons la *commedia dell'arte* et le Théâtre de la Foire. Nous connaîtrons l'histoire et le développement de l'improvisation, les moeurs, les procédés, et les particularités des comédiens qui l'ont pratiquée. Mais notre but c'est de créer une nouvelle comédie improvisée avec des types et des sujets de notre temps.[7]

The new characters would not, according to this plan, be related to abstract figures, characters in morality plays or symbols of the passions. They would be descendants of the characters of the *commedia dell'arte* and, while there would be some resemblance, the new characters would be dressed quite differently and capable of a wide range of human behaviour; they would also be able to act out a large number of situations, from broad farce to subtle comedy and drama.

Copeau saw his own role as that of a poet providing his actors with inspiration for their improvisations. The actors would not be allowed to research their characters for fear of being too erudite in their compositions.

Eventually they would become their characters and collectively create their plays; from this point on, Copeau's role would be reduced to that of critic. This improvised comedy now had a name, the *Comédie Nouvelle*, and the Vieux Colombier School was to be its nursery.

These notes on the improvised comedy were made while members of the company were in the army. The war did not prevent them from preparing for the *Comédie Nouvelle*. Louis Jouvet frequently sent long letters to Copeau with suggestions for training the new actors, and Roger Martin du Gard was planning the first of two *scenari*.

Despite these enthusiastic reactions, Copeau's concepts were not really understood. Jouvet's suggestions for example were often unacceptable. When he recommended that actors should study scenes from Henry Monnier's sketches of Joseph Prudhomme or base their improvisations on poems, in a way similar to that of Isadora Duncan who gave her interpretations of symphonies in improvised dance, Copeau refused. He was anxious that actors in the new comedy should not imitate others, and Jouvet's second suggestion was too "literary." The remedy that Copeau proffered for this over-zealous desire for documentation was simply to act out jokes: "Faire des blagues ensemble."[8]

While Jouvet was reading Gozzi, even as he was tending the wounded at the front, he was composing a series of outlines of sketches and devising exercises for improvisations based on proverbs and sayings: "Un personnage apprend à un autre à faire quelque chose. C'est comme dans la comédie italienne,—avant tout exploiter dans une scène un trait de caractère ou du type d'un personnage!"[9] Copeau agreed that this type of work would be appropriate.

Meanwhile, another member of the Company, Charles Dullin, was recruiting likely candidates for the *Comédie Nouvelle* at the front in the trenches. He wrote to tell Copeau that he had found three excellent prospects who had been able to improvise on sketches he had suggested so well that he imagined he was back at the Théâtre des Funambules. None of the three had had actor's training. Two had been in prison, which Dullin claimed had enriched their observation of life. Dullin made another important discovery in the trenches, a young man who, he said, would make a first-rate secretary for Copeau after the war, "un type tout à fait supérieur." This was Pierre-Louis Duchartre, who went on to become one of France's most eminent authorities on the *commedia dell'arte*.

Copeau received further encouragement for his project by reading of Meyerhold's work in the Russian theatre.[10] Meyerhold's essay *The Fairground Booth* had appeared in 1912, but Copeau had not learned of it until he read Alexander Bakshy's *The Path of the Modern Russian Stage*. Meyerhold's remedy for a theatre steeped in realism and "literature" was succinctly reported as "back to the booth and the *commedia dell'arte*"; Copeau made notes from his reading and wrote to his friends about this genuine move towards the renewal of theatre in Europe. Copeau was nevertheless on his guard. He would reject merely erudite forms of a ressuscitated *commedia dell'arte*, just as he disapproved of Schlegel's "transcendentale bouffonnerie." The temptation to recreate the achievements of the past was one pitfall; the temptation to create an impressive personal style was another.

For the opening of the Vieux Colombier company's first season at the Garrick Theatre in New York City in 1917,[11] Copeau chose a play that retains an important link with the *commedia dell'arte*. Just as he had chosen a farce by Molière to share the inaugural program of his first season, so he turned to Molière again on this occasion. *Les Fourberies de Scapin* is one of Copeau's most important contributions to play production. Not only did he underscore Molière's debt to the Italian comedy but he also used for the first time the portable platform stage designed by Jouvet and himself. This was installed on top of the permanent stage at the Garrick. It was on this "tréteau nu" that the action principally took place:

Nous avons tâché, dans la circonstance, de rapprocher cette comédie française de la tradition italienne et de lui rendre la violence et même la cruauté de son mouvement.[12]

The use of the platform stage aroused considerable interest among theatre critics, and the quality of the acting was praised. The *New York Herald* reported: "Copeau and his company delivered their lines with so vivid an expression and with such active and telling pantomime that the absence of scenery became a matter of no importance. Indeed, scenery would have cumbered the effect."[13] *The New York Times* in an article headed "Molière Reborn" dwelt on the use of the bare platform: "Purposeless, even eccentric, as this appears at first sight, it will probably be found to have a distinct and highly intelligent reason for being. Do the entrances of Molière seem to us moderns to be very poorly motivated? With this double playing space, this stage within and above a stage, the characters can wander on as aimlessly as you please until the time comes for them to break into the action, when they do so with far greater naturalness. Are there frequent asides and scenes in which two parties loudly converse unaware of each other's presence? Again, the double stage lends plausibility. It is effective, furthermore, to have action take place on different levels, for it renders possible many combinations in the grouping, all sorts of telling encounters."

Copeau himself saw the platform stage as an integral part of the dramatic action: "il matérialise la forme de l'action, et lorsque le tréteau est occupé par les comédiens, lorsqu'il est pénétré par l'action—même—il disparaît."[14]

A.G.H. Spiers in *The Nation* noticed how the platform stage drew the audience's attention to the actors' movements. Scapin controlled the proceedings on the platform. Whether lying down or crouching to play dice as in the *lazzo* with the other servant, Sylvestre, he remained entirely visible; he had mastery of the other actors when they were on the lower stage, and when they joined him on the platform, they became as prisoners, with the edges of the platform restricting their range of movement and cutting off their escape.[15] What Spiers had noticed was confirmed by Copeau: ". . . le tréteau est dans les *fourberies* un 'piège à vieillards,' il doit donner la sensation du péril . . ."[16]

Copeau himself played Scapin. He was dressed like Brighella, in a close fitting yellow costume with Brandenburgs, not like the Scapin of Callot's famous engraving who wears a loose fitting garment. Acrobatically, Copeau leapt on and off the platform, sometimes sitting on its edge, swinging his legs. He included several *lazzi*, such as Scapin's trying to catch a fly while the young lover Octave was talking, and failing to do so, a trick that had become known as the "'*lazzo* de la mouche,'"[17] or the valet Sylvestre, chewing sunflower seeds and blowing the remains from his mouth, or again, Géronte, the Pantalone figure, played by Jouvet, carrying a parasol which he used variously to protect himself from the sun, to twirl while pondering his words, and as a stick to keep his son Léandre at a distance.

Of the forty-four productions he staged in two years in the United States, this remained among the most satisfying for Copeau. It was conducted in the spirit of a tradition he admired and pointed to further possible developments.

Avec les *Fourberies* on a essayé une réalisation purement théâtrale et de pur mouvement. On a cherché ni excentricité ni même la nouveauté pour elle-même, mais, au contraire, par une certaine disposition des surfaces de jeu, par un certain renouvellement de la configuration et du relief scéniques, on a voulu rendre à une comédie immortelle sa configuration, son relief primitif, et se rapprocher ainsi d'une tradition perdue, dont l'esprit, s'il renaissait parmi nous, peut inspirer les talents éperdus d'aujourd'hui.[18]

The production was staged again in Paris when the Vieux Colombier Theatre, now refurbished with a new permanent stage and a movable platform stage as in New York City, reopened in 1920. The Vieux Colombier touring company took the production to some provincial towns, using the portable platform stage in the open air as itinerant actors had done centuries before. Subsequently Jouvet staged his version of Copeau's production when he became director of his own company, and Jean-Louis Barrault repeated it at the Marigny Theatre. As Jouvet said: "Tout ce qui a été tenté depuis Copeau emprunte à Copeau."[19]

Copeau's return to Paris meant that Roger Martin du Gard could now proceed to explain to him the work he had been preparing for the *Comédie Nouvelle* since Copeau had written to him to encourage such a project in 1916. Copeau had begun with the admonition: "Rompre avec tous les *genres* plus ou moins *littéraires* . . . Se mettre à faire des blagues gratuites et à chercher chacun son personnage."[20]

Martin du Gard named his project the *Comédie de Tréteaux*, the title being chosen to honour the platform stage designed by Copeau and Jouvet. It was to be "un spectacle naturel comme une improvisation mais achevé comme une fable, où un public passionné par les événements en cours viendrait se délasser et vivre sans arrière-pensée, aux irrésistibles drôleries de marionnettes vivants, qui lui seraient de longue date familières; d'un spectacle qui soulignerait d'une touche précise et rapide les travers les plus tyranniques de l'époque, la sottise des boniments à la mode, le péril de certains conflits quotidiens . . ."[21] Martin du Gard was already calling the *Comédie de Tréteaux* his modern replica of the *commedia dell'arte*.[22]

Martin du Gard created a series of social types. A group of bourgeois, including Hector Punais, apoplectic, pompous, engaging in corrupt business deals whilst proclaiming his honorable principles, and Carmen his enormous, overdressed, bejewelled, and highly predatory wife. The servants included Fric, an agile valet, quick-witted and enterprising, his girlfriend Miette, a "Colombine de faubourg"; a gangster, Malandrin, originally a speculator, later a chauffeur to the Punais, who prepared traps for his victims and waited for them to succumb. There was Falempin, a "matamore du trottoir," always embroiled in intrigues, whose language was the slang of the streets of Paris, and then Benênoist, the optimistic businessman, ever about to make a fortune but sinking into bankruptcies instead, and getting a beating at the same time. Martin du Gard made detailed notes for their costumes, for he wanted his characters to be recognizable as soon as they leapt on the platform stage, in the hope that they would soon become as familiar as the figures of the Italian comedy.[23]

Two plays were written for the *Comédie de Tréteaux*: *Malandrin secoue ses maîtres* and *Hollé-Ira*, the latter concerning the exploits of Fric.[24] Both failed to live up to Copeau's expectations. He found them lacking in spontaneous gaiety, their humour arising from the written witticisms of the author; Martin du Gard's work showed the influence of realist writers (Copeau named Octave Mirbeau), and was not suitable for the *Comédie Nouvelle*. Martin du Gard reluctantly agreed, but when Copeau explained to him his own plans for a farce, *Le Roi, le vizir et son médecin*, he found that no better than his own. It was, he wrote, too much influenced by Voltaire.[25] Martin du Gard did not pursue his project. Discouraged, he compared himself to Monsieur Jourdain attempting to learn to dance; he tried briefly to introduce some of the characters from the *Comédie de Tréteaux* into his second peasant farce, *La Gonfle*, as the manuscript of an early draft shows, but abandoned even that attempt.[26]

The inadequacy of the *Comédie de Tréteaux* as a part of Copeau's *Comédie Nouvelle* can be attributed to the fact that whereas Copeau had conceived his project whilst working with actors, in constant touch with the stage, Martin du Gard, notwithstanding his experience with the company (as an author of a peasant farce and even as an actor during the short tour of England) had composed the *Comédie de Tréteaux* in isolation; the result is that the plays are written works with too little room for the improvisation essential to Copeau's scheme.

Copeau too had invented a set of characters: Bonhomme, essentially French, Boche, essentially German, Monsier Paul, a salesman hawking everything from politics to manufactured goods, and an adolescent who had appeared in a text now lost, *La Comédie des Ressemblances*. He was carefully trying to eliminate "tout esprit de réalisme" from these; his chosen method was to include one character who would be the embodiment of realism, a character who would be an anti-comic factor, whose presence on the stage would be in such contrast to all the others that he would appear to belong to the audience. Copeau claimed that this was his own idea, and that it would be very useful.[27]

If Martin du Gard felt frustrated by the cool reception given his texts, Jules Romains persisted. Romains, the first director of the École du Vieux Colombier whose plays had been principally verse dramas up to this point, shared Copeau's enthusiasm for the *Comédie Nouvelle*. He invented Monsieur Le Trouhadec, a character inspired by the *Vecchi* of the *commedia dell'arte*. Le Trouhadec is a learned geographer, "un de ces hommes qui à une valeur personnelle nulle joignent une efficacité sociale."[28] He is assisted by Bénin, a young friend who is related to the *zanni*. Bénin orchestrates events, such as the meeting between the actress Mlle Rolande and the besotted old gentleman in *Monsieur Le Trouhadec saisi par la débauche*, who wins and loses a fortune at the Casino.

Romains was anxious to make the Monte-Carlo setting as abstract as possible: "aucun décor, ni accessoire. Le Tréteau. Pas de trace de 'comédie réaliste' ni 'théâtre libre.'" The play itself was, he maintained, pure comedy, "pas de vérisme ni di 'satire.'" It had been inspired by Copeau's production of Molière[29] and by the platform stage for which it was designed. The roles had been written to suit the talents of Louis Jouvet and Valentine Tessier.[30]

Despite these claims which appeared to make the play suitable for the *Comédie Nouvelle*, despite their long conversations and their correspondence about the play, Copeau was disagreeably surprised when he read it. "Je n'y vois pas du tout une farce de tréteau," he wrote.[31] He preferred to call it a "comédie de grand style." Althoug he had announced the play in his program, Copeau did not produce it. Romains gave it to Jouvet, who directed a production at the Comédie des Champs Elysées, playing the principal role, as intended by Romains and playing the same character in two further plays that Romains wrote for him, in accordance with a *commedia dell'arte* tradition.

Romains' most famous play, *Knock*, shows some interesting parallels with Copeau's *Comédie Nouvelle*, having links with both the Italian comedy and, more obviously, with Molière's farces, which were much in evidence at the École du Vieux Colombier.

The inspired practice of medicine is the driving force of the play. It absorbs time, space and all the action, giving Dr. Knock control of the whole community. There are two physicians here: Dr. Parpalaid, an older, bourgeois doctor who at the outset has sold a worthless practice to Knock at an inflated price, and Knock, a modern type, a physician nurtured in his charlatan ways by the methods of modern advertising, who convinces his clients—and everyone is a client—that being well is an imaginary condition of people who are in varying degrees of ill-health. He is surrounded by modern social types: the avaricious peasant, the pretentious bourgeoise, the ignorant country louts ready to mock modern science. The ages of the characters are not indicated, their names are not listed in the cast; they appear only as "la dame en noir," "la dame en violet," "les deux gars." If this offers an interesting link with Martin du Gard's types, there are further parallels with the *commedia dell'arte*. Romains' play bears a subtitle: *Le Triomphe de la médecine*. This is the title of a sketch performed by the Italian actors in France in 1674, according to C. and

F. Parfaict's *Histoire de l'ancien théâtre italien*; Dominique had played in it and had noted the *lazzi*.[32] Jacques Copeau had given Léon Chancerel the task of researching the material of the Italian comedy and he provided the outline for the Vieux Colombier. It was performed in the Spring of 1923 at one of the *Matinées classiques* with Copeau himself playing the part of the physician.

The sketch as performed at the Vieux Colombier concerns a doctor who convinces a healthy man who is trying to fish that he is ill:

MÉDECIN: Vous n'avez pas d'alcooliques dans votre famille?
HOMME SAIN: Moi? (*Pause*)
MÉDECIN: Vous avez encore votre grand-père? (*Silence*) Et votre grand'mère? (*Silence*) Votre père est mort? Aussi? (*Silence*). Vous êtes marié? Vous avez des enfants?
HOMME SAIN: Oui.
MÉDECIN: Pauvres petits! (*Un petit temps*). Tiens! tiens! tiens! Est-ce qu'il y a longtemps qu'il saute?
HOMME SAIN: Qui?
MÉDECIN: Votre oeil droit.
HOMME SAIN: J'ai l'oeil droit qui saute?

Le médecin le regarde en silence

HOMME SAIN: C'est pourtant vrai. Pourquoi saute-t-il?
MÉDECIN: Spasme du facial déterminé par un foyer hémorragique ou par des fibrolipomes . . .
HOMME SAIN: Sans blague.
MÉDECIN: . . . Vraisemblablement localisés sur le pied de la deuxième frontale. Posez votre ligne. Levez le bras. L'autre. Les deux. Bon. La jambe. L'autre. Les deux. Vous ne pouvez pas?

The sketch ends with the healthy man running after the doctor, pleading for help.

In *Knock* the physician tackles the first of two peasant lads who have come to make fun of him and convinces him that he is ill:

KNOCK: Etendez-vous là-dessus. Allons. Remenez les genoux. (*Il palpe le ventre, applique çà et là le stéthoscope*). Bien. Rhabillez-vous. (*Silence. L'homme se rhabille*). Vous avez encore votre père?
LE PREMIER: Non, il est mort.
KNOCK: De mort subite?
LE PREMIER: Oui.
KNOCK: C'est ça. Il ne devait pas être vieux?
LE PREMIER: Non, quarante-neuf ans.
KNOCK: Si vieux que ça!

Knock's use of technical jargon to convince the lady in black that she needs long, expensive treatment echoes the language of the Physician in *Le Triomphe de la Médecin*, which also overcomes the patients initial reluctance. He does not speak Latin as Molière's doctors do, but he achieves a similar effect.

The characters in *Knock* do not wear masks as their ancestors did, yet, in a manner somewhat similar to Molière's characters according to the famous study by W. G. Moore, it is as if they have absorbed a mask into their personality. Knock's charlatanism is a form of mask, one that he wears perfectly; he even confesses that he has so come to believe in his techniques of instant diagnosis that he avoids looking in mirrors. Jouvet's remarkable facial expression, complete with monocle and stethoscope conveyed something of a mask. Jouvet played the role over a thousand times, one of the clearest examples of an actor "owning" a character that the modern French theatre can offer.

Knock was not a "farce de tréteau"; it was not strictly suitable for the *Comédie Nouvelle*; there is no room for improvisation within its framework. It was moreover written about the period that Copeau decided to devote himself entirely to the Vieux Colombier School. He had decided that the way to create the *Comédie Nouvelle* lay through his own student actors, who were still young and unspoiled. As he had done with his fledgling troupe in 1913, Copeau took the students away from Paris, this time to Burgundy. According to Léon Chancerel: "C'est en grande partie pour créer cette forme de théâtre (la Comédie Nouvelle) . . . qu'il (Copeau) voulait partir avec quelques apprentis et des hommes comme Jean Villard, Suzanne Bing, Auguste Bovério et moi-même, qui auraient fourni les Personnages comme dans la *Commedia dell'arte* de cette comédie."[33]

The importance of the *commedia dell'arte* for the school is shown by the list of its activities: masks, mimes, improvisations and the compositions of different characters. The log-book of the school has an entry for March 18, 1925: "Le patron reprend toutes ses notes sur la *commedia dell'arte*." The new group of actors, known familiarly as Les Copiaus, performed a *parade* by Thomas-Simon Gueulette, *Les Sottises de Gilles*. It was, as Gontard has pointed out, entirely in keeping with the aims of the school: it contains the farce, the mime and the style of the *commedia dell'arte*. They performed Copeau's adaptation of Ruzzante's *L'Anconitaine ou Les Amoureux de Padoue*, they performed *Arlequin Magicien*, but the culmination of their research appeared in two works of their own devising: *La Danse des Villes et des champs*, concerning the attempts of a peasant to succeed in a town, and two comical townsmen unable to cope with country life, and *Les*

Jeunes Gens et l'araignée, a tragi-comedy in four acts, a dream performed with masks, mime and improvised characters. According to Mme Rose-Marie Moudouès, the Copiaus staged a *parade* in the local village of Meursault prior to their performance,[34] in keeping with the tradition of the itinerant Italian actors.

The legacy of the Vieux Colombier's attempt to renew the theatre of twentieth-century France through the *Comédie Nouvelle* continued after the closing down of the Copiaus, through the Compagnie des Quinze, led by Copeau's nephew Michel Saint-Denis and, in another sense, through Léon Chancerel's work with the scout group, Les Routiers, whose improvisations and mimes achieved recognition, and who produced some well known actors.

Copeau himself never realized his *Comédie Nouvelle* in the manner he had hoped. Yet much of his work towards that goal has given him the place that directors from Jouvet to Barrault have acknowledged as foremost among them. He was convinced throughout his life that the path to renewal lay along the route he had indicated. In 1941 he wrote: "Je ne dis pas qu'il faille refaire la *Commedia dell'arte*. Je ne le dis pas et ne crois pas que cela soit possible. Mais je dis que si nous devons retrouver un premier élan, rouvrir une veine exploitable et de quelque fécondité, ce sera dans les parages et sous l'inspiration d'un genre dont tant de poètes—et Goethe lui-même—ont eu et ont encore la nostalgie."[35] His own work for the *Comédie Nouvelle*, through Molière, the *commedia dell'arte* and the platform stage, has provided the principal impetus for a new movement spread over several years, but particularly since the publication of his *registres* began in 1974. A new generation of actors has listened eagerly to his words.

The Théâtre du Soleil, under the direction of Ariane Mnouchkine, has repeatedly acknowledged its debt to Copeau, and particularly in one of its major undertakings, *L'Age d'or*, in 1975. Staged in the vast bare space of the Cartoucherie de Vincennes, the work follows complex lines, through an action which takes place initially in eighteenth century Naples, with the Prince and Arlequin, the man designated to find the culprit responsible for introducing the plague, and then moves into contemporary France, with the arrival of an Algerian worker, Abdallah, at Marseilles in the year 2000. Between the arrival of "Arlequin-Abdallah," as he is now, when the naive immigrant is robbed of his exotic clothes and can only find space to sleep in the over-crowded hostel if he perches acrobatically on his hands, and his death which occurs when he is sent to work on the construction site in a high wind, the actors, mostly masked, act out through improvisation a number of situations: these convey the conditions of the poor immigrants, exploited by their employers and supervisors, and moments in the life of the rich and powerful classes, such as the dinner-party following a disaster on a building site or inspecting the beach so that it can be appropriated for a lucrative construction project. There are characters whose names provide links with the Italian comedy, such as the developer, Marcel Pantalon; there is M. Gueulette-Polichinelle, who reminds us of the French-Italian comedy; Pantalon's wife, Viviana, may belong to the family of Martin du Gard's Carmen Punais; some of the workers resemble his Malandrin in the *Comédie de Tréteaux*. The characters may retain some features in their costuming to indicate their ancestry, such as Polichinelle's overflowing shirt, but their dress is modified to suit the modern types they represent; Arlequin-Abdallah's headgear is a cotton cap, a sign of the immigrant worker.

Rather than a reconstitution of the *commedia dell'arte* Mnouchkine's work is closely allied to Copeau's in his search for the *Comédie Nouvelle*. If the "texte-programme" for *L'Age d'or* begins with a series of quotations from Copeau, it is because the production quotes Copeau—but not only Copeau—recurrently. In an interview with Denis Bablet, Mnouchkine suggests that Copeau would have modified his idea of completely replacing the characters of the *commedia dell'arte* by purely modern types if he had been able to try out his ideas more in practice.[36] From this it appears that Martin du Gard's approach to the *Comédie de Tréteaux* may have been an important point of contact between the Vieux Colombier and the Théâtre du Soleil if the project had been pursued through improvisations beyond the initial draft. A reading of the first volumes of Copeau's *Registres* and his correspondence with Roger Martin du Gard allows us to detect several parallels between the two companies, and some of these have already been explored.[37]

Currently the Théâtre du Soleil is performing a companion piece to *L'Age d'or*, a work which relates an aspect of contemporary history, in the idiom of its own new theatre form.[38] One reviewer introduced his analysis of this latest production with a lengthy quotation concerning the renewal of the theatre through a version of the *commedia dell'arte* taken from Copeau's *Registres*. There are signs that the process of renewal is continuing, then, and while we can only guess at Copeau's reaction to the emergence of the new comedy at the Théâtre du Soleil, it is possible to conclude that the sun is still shining on the spirit of the *commedia dell'arte* some seventy years after the doctors of *L'Amour Médecin* first trod the bare stage at the Vieux Colombier.

McMaster University

NOTES

1 *Registres I: Appels* (Paris: Gallimard, 1974), p. 32.
2 *Registres III: Les Registres du Vieux Colombier I* (Paris: Gallimard, 1979), p. 359.
3 *Souvenirs du Vieux Colombier* (Paris: Nouvelles Editions Latines, 1931), p. 76.
4 Gide's entry in his *Journal*, 21 janvier 1916. Quoted in *Registres III*, pp. 318–319.
5 A photograph taken in May 1925 of the students of Copeau, "Les Copiaus," shows Michel Saint-Denis dressed as Tartaglia carrying the school's banner through the streets of Demigny in order to publicize a performance. See Denis Gontard, *Le Journal de Bord des Copiaus* (Paris: Seghers, 1974), pp. 32–33.
6 *Registres III*, p. 323.
7 *Registres III*, p. 325.
8 *Registres III*, p. 338.
9 *Registres I*, p. 341.
10 *Registres IV: Les Registres du Vieux Colombier, II. America* (Paris: Gallimard, 1984), p. 523. Copeau's notes read: "Stupéfaction d'apprendre que Meyerhold (. . .) après un long travail de *vingt ans* en est arrivé aux conclusions que j'ai pressenties dès l'abord." See also *Registres I*, p. 361.
11 Copeau was sent to the United States by the French Government. He was allowed to have Jouvet and later Dullin with him.
12 *Registres IV*, p. 175.
13 *New York Herald*, 2 December 1917, III, p. 7. This and the following extract from the *New York Times* appear in M. Katz, *A Historical Study of Jacques Copeau and the Vieux Colombier Company at the Garrick Theatre in New York City, 1917–19* (Ann Arbor: University Microfilms, 1966), pp. 172–177.
14 Jacques Copeau, *Les Fourberies de Scapin de Molière* (Paris: Editions du Seuil, 1951), p. 17.
15 *Registres IV*, p. 179.
16 *Les Fourberies de Scapin de Molière*, pp. 20–21.
17 Léon Chancerel explains that the actor makes a buzzing sound and searches for the fly. In a similar way, Arlequin pursued butterflies. Dominique (Biancolelli) caught flies on the nose of Scaramouche whose nose was slapped in the process. Lafontaine used it in the *Fable de l'ours et l'amateur des jardins. Jeux Tréteaux Personnages*, No. 8 (15 April 1931), p. 216.
18 *Les Fourberies de Scapin de Molière*, p. 152.
19 *Les Fourberies de Scapin de Molière*, p. 17.
20 *Correspondance Jacques Copeau—Roger Martin du Gard* (Paris: Gallimard, 1972), I, p. 211.

21 *Correspondance*, p. 211, n. 2. Martin du Gard's 25 pages of notes on the project appear in the Appendix to letter 72, II, pp. 819–825.
22 *Correspondance*, p. 263. The extract is taken from Martin du Gard's *Journal*.
23 Roger Martin du Gard, "Souvenirs autobiographiques et littéraires" in *Oeuvres Complètes* (Paris: Gallimard, 1955), I, pp. lxxviii–lxxix.
24 See Appendix.
25 Fragments of this farce are extant (Fonds Copeau, Bibliothèque de l'Arsenal). It concerns a king who is suffering from eczema and who is cured not by the important people around him but by a poor peasant.
26 *Correspondance*, I, p. 364. Claude Sicard's notes confirm this.
27 Claude Sicard, p. 319 suggests the idea is comparable to Diderot's *anti-roman*. Curiously, it seems to foreshadow techniques used by Tom Stoppard.
28 "Deux êtres en marche" (Correspondance Jules Romains—Jacques Copeau), *Cahiers Jules Romains* (Paris: Flammarion, 1978), No. 2, p. 58.
29 *Cahiers Jules Romains*, pp. 132–133. In a note Romains states that Monte-Carlo should function as a distant background in a way similar to that of Naples or Venice in 18th century Italian comedies.
30 *Cahiers Jules Romains*, p. 126.
31 *Cahiers Jules Romains*, p. 137.
32 *Le Triomphe de la médecine* is mentioned in two articles by Léon Chancerel. The first appears in *Jeux Tréteaux Personnages*, No. 4 (15 décembre 1930), pp. 87–88; the second in No. 8 (15 avril 1931), pp. 217–218. The extract we offer is taken from the latter.
33 See Denis Gontard, *Le Journal de bord des Copiaus (1924–1929)*, pp. 29–30.
34 In a personal interview, June 1985 at the *Revue d'Histoire du Théâtre* offices. I should like to express my gratitude to Madame Moudouès, Madame Marie-Hélène Dasté, Madame Suzanne Maistre-Saint-Denis and Madame Roger Froment for their generous assistance with this project.
35 "Le théâtre populaire," *Registres I*, p. 310.
36 Denis Bablet, "Rencontres," *Travail Théâtral*, Numéro Spécial, février 1976, p. 100.
37 Apart from the special articles by Denis Bablet and Catherine Mounier in *Travail Théâtral*, février 1976, there is an interesting study by Elisabeth Hervic, "*L'Age d'or*, une rencontre Mnouchkine-Copeau," *Revue d'Histoire du Théâtre*, XXVIII, pp. 274–285.
38 *L'Histoire terrible mais inachevée de Norodom Sihanouk, roi du Cambodge.*

APPENDIX

A. *Comédie de Tréteaux*, by Roger Martin du Gard:
Malandrin secoue ses maîtres ou Les Croquants croqués
The characters in *Malandrin secoue ses maîtres* are sketched out as early
as 1917 (*Correspondance Jacques Copeau-Roger Martin du Gard*, II,
pp. 821–23).

The Bourgeois:

Hector Punais. A modern version of Joseph Prudhomme. Very wealthy as a
   result of his Stock Exchange transactions. Very portly. Grey vest, gold chain.
Carmen Punais. Fat, heavily powdered, former prostitute, now the overweight,
   worthy bourgeoise. Voluminous cherry-red dress. Peroxide blonde hair.
M. Commissaire. Judge, lawyer, policeman all at once. A leader of society.
Oui-dire. A parasite, a gossip, involved in all intrigues. Pointed nose, large
   cardboard ears.

The Rebels:

Malandrin. Called Falempin in the earliest notes, he is young, about sixteen, and
   speaks with a Parisian street accent. He wears a light overall, dark motoring
   goggles with a piece of green taffeta sewn beneath them to form a mask.
   Chauffeur, mechanic, a born revolutionary, an anarchist, a representative of the
   C.G.T. union. Good humoured.
Midinette. A little fairy-like Parisienne. In love with Malandrin. Once a maid
   to Carmen Punais perhaps.
Miteux. A sad bandit. Very thoughtful. An anarchist. Always at war with the
   police.
Chemineau. A light-hearted bandit. Quite sentimental about life and liberty.
   Gathers flowers and girls along the wayside whenever he can.

Synopsis
Malandrin secoue ses maîtres ou Les Croquants croqués

Act I

   Malandrin, uttering the password: "Tremble, société pourrie, crève,
société croupie!" summons his accomplices Miteux and Chemineau. His
employers, the Punais, overwork him. He knows all their secrets. That
night they are going out to dinner, and Malandrin will drive them home.
He will stage a break-down. The Punais will have to walk. Miteux and
Chemineau can rob them. Hector will be carrying a fortune in banknotes
which he will collect at the dinner for his part in a corrupt business deal.
Carmen will be wearing her diamond earrings, the size of bottle stoppers.
Malandrin does not want the money for himself, but acts out of political

convictions. No harm must come to the Punais. He also wants a long lock of hair that Punais has been cultivating for months.

As they walk home the Punais quarrel. They are afraid of attackers, but Punais has purchased, for an exorbitant sum, some protection: a union card for the Confédération Générale du Travail. This will give them immunity from attack. As planned, Miteux and Chemineau waylay them, knocking Puanis to the ground. Chemineau grabs Carmen, pulls her down and silences her cries with a kiss; she soon stops protesting. Oui-Dire sees Carmen going off with Chemineau. Miteux lets Punais rise, stands behind him and kicks him. Punais punctuates his groans with "C.G.T.!" (The passage is marked *lazzi*.) The union card does not impress his attacker. He hands over some money and falls to his knees to beg for mercy. Malandrin comes from behind to lower his employer's breeches, revealing wads of money, a cushion against the kicks he received from Miteux. Oui-Dire reappears with a passer-by. This man calls out "Justice!" He is promptly shot by Miteux. The lock of hair is removed. Chemineau has returned. The bandits leave, muttering, "Tremble, société pourrie, crève, société croupie!" Oui-Dire returns with Monsieur Commissaire and policemen. They take the Punais to be the criminals and tell the body to get up. They decide then that Punais is the murderer and proceed to beat him. (The passage is marked *lazzi*.) Malandrin reappears without his mask, accompanied by Midinette. Monsieur Commissaire recognizes her as the girl he has been trying to meet secretly. Malandrin identifies his employers as respectable bourgeois. Monsieur Commissaire is embarrassed. Punais prefers to lay no charges since his money was illicitly obtained; Carmen's diamonds were in fact false, and she was so well treated by her attacker that she too makes no complaint. They all agree to pretend that they discovered the body lying in the road.

Act II

The Courtroom. Three puppets, the jury, sit behind a counter. The bandits have been arrested after all. Malandrin plans to lure away the magistrate (Monsieur Commissaire) during the trial by using Midinette as bait. As the trial of Miteux and Chemineau begins, Midinette sends Monsieur Commissaire a message. He withdraws to meet her. Malandrin, disguised as the magistrate in Monsieur Commissaire's clothes, enters. He takes over the trial. The accused protest their innocence. Society is the real criminal, as anyone who has been to the Stock Exchange, Parliament or a newspaper office can see. Punais' criminal dealings are revealed.

Carmen's past career in a "house in the rue des Baisers" is related; for that she will not be condemned for she gave joy to others, but she has denied her past and has built a new virginity around herself in a rotten society. Malandrin now concludes: since no specific charges have been laid, and in the light of the evidence of the new crimes, there will be a new trial, with Punais and Carmen the accused. He activates the heads of the puppet jurors to obtain their consent. Miteux is a good citizen for retrieving the ill-acquired money from Punais, and Chemineau has exposed the fraud perpetrated by Carmen. Malandrin is interrupted by Monsieur Commissaire who has escaped from the closet in which Malandrin had confined him. Malandrin slips away and the trial resumes as soon as some clothes are brought for the magistrate. He orders the guilty parties to stand: everyone rises except the two bandits. Monsieur Commissaire nevertheless condemns Miteux and Chemineau and activates the jurors' heads to confirm the punishment: they will be cut off from society with the rapid, incisive means that are available. The Punais rejoice, the policemen beat the two bandits, who are led off muttering, "Tremble, société pourrie, crève, société croupie!"

B. *Comédie de Tréteaux*, by Roger Martin du Gard:

Synopsis
Hollé-Ira!

Characters:
Fric aged 17. Groom to Gomme-Persil.
Miette, aged 16. Maid to Dame Cloche.
Dame Cloche, aged 40. Palym's second wife, fat.
Palym, aged 50. Crude old man.
Gomme-Persil, aged 20. Palym's son. Affected. Wearing pyjamas.
Benenoit, aged 50. A hunchback, a schemer.
Martin du Gard suggests the roles should be played by dancers.

I. Fric enters shouting: "Hollé!" He flirts with Miette. She evades him. He catches her, lifts her up and carries her off crying: "Hollé-Ira!"
II. Benenoit tries in vain to interest Palym in some financial transaction.
III. Benenoit flatters Dame Cloche. She is trying to find Palym who has left her without money.
IV. Gomme-Persil is looking for Fric. He tells Benenoit he wants to change his idle ways and seeks his help in finding some work.
V. Fric describes his life as a servant to Benenoit. Benenoit explains he has to make some money. He asks Fric to help him make a loan to Gomme-Persil, to be repaid at high interest when Palym dies, which

he hopes will be soon. Fric only agrees to speak on Benenoit's behalf to Dame Cloche to get her to respond to his love.

VI. Fric informs Gomme-Persil that moneylenders like Benenoit end up taking half of an inheritance. He wants to help Gomme-Persil acquire some money so that they can both be free of Palym.

VII. Miette has read Dame Cloche's fortune in the cards. The lady is frustrated, for Palym ignores her charms, and he is miserly too. They talk of love. Miette tells her mistress to let love guide her actions. Left alone, she claps her hands, Fric appears, chases her, shouting "Hollé-Ira!"

VIII. Palym is worried. Everyone seems changed. his wife smiles, his son no longer asks him for money, and Benenoit has stopped stealing from him.

IX. Palym tries to flirt with Miette. She escapes, leaving him to fall over as he chases her. (The scene is marked *lazzi*.)

X. Palym refuses to tell Benenoit why he is sitting on the ground. They stay on stage for the next three scenes.

XI. Miette is angry with Fric. He has tried to arrange a rendez-vous for her with Benenoit.

XII. Gomme-Persil is angry with Fric. He shows him an account of his transaction with Benenoit. Half the interest is shown as going to Fric. He kicks Fric. Palym beats Benenoit over the head when he learns that he has lent his son money on the strength of his future inheritance. To escape further beating, Fric protests to his master that he was being paid only for advancing Benenoit's suit with a certain lady, whom he cannot name, but she now appears. Palym is horrified. Gomme-Persil shocked.

XIII. Dame Cloche rebukes Fric for being heartless. She has given herself to him, but he is chasing after her maid. Palym now emerges from his hiding place. Fric runs away, shouting "Hollé!" Palym beats Dame Cloche, then she beats Benenoit.

XIV. Miette would like to run away with Fric. Everyone is blaming him, she tells him. Off he runs.

XV. Fric is cornered by Gomme-Persil, Benenoit and Dame Cloche, armed with sticks and brooms. Fric, staying close to the edge of the platform, boxing and dodging blows, sees Palym enter, leaps on his shoulders shouting "Hollé-Ira!," then jumps off and away, as Palym staggers to the middle of the group and collapses. Miette sobs.

Antonio Alessio

Pirandello and the *commedia dell'arte*

On first glance one might feel inclined to identify Pirandello's position with that of the *commedia dell'arte*. The very title of the play *Tonight we improvise* would immediately recall the freedom and autonomy that the *comici dell'arte* claimed against the playwright: Life takes a stand against Literature.

Yet, at a careful reading of Pirandello's critical essays and plays, the convergences are limited to a common point of departure. Briefly, what they have in common is their reaction to tradition. After this Pirandello takes a totally opposite road to that of the *commedia dell'arte*.

The *commedia dell'arte*, as we know, rejected the written text, reacting against the *commedia dei letterati*, thereby putting a stop to the old fashion of imitating the classics which paralysed the Italian stage and prevented the growth and development of an Italian theatre.

Whether or not the *comici dell'arte* (beyond their undeniable professional qualities as actors and their autonomous ability of inventiveness) really revolutionised the theatrical scene is not the aim of this paper. It might nevertheless be useful to remember, as Silvio D'Amico pointed out,[1] that those who are against the *commedia dell'arte* still underline its dependence on classical comedy: one would find the same scene, the same square with houses facing one another, the same road. The characters themselves would be chipped from the old block: old men, young people in love, rascally servants, all involved in the same old intrigues. Even the so-called improvisation has been questioned, inasmuch as the actors did not really improvise but took their material from the *formulari* which they learnt by heart and used with extreme ability, giving them a character of originality and freshness. The only recognized novelty was the introduction of the masks.

Like the *comici dell'arte*, Pirandello claims immediacy and spontaneity in art. The phrase which occurs over and over again in his writing is *sincerity in art*, rejecting everything which constitutes a model. "One cannot imitate what cannot be imitated: style." For Pirandello every created work must be "neither old nor modern, but unique, the one which belongs solely to a particular work of art and cannot be another one, nor of any other work of art." Tradition must therefore be excluded right away, indeed "it should never have existed."[2] For Pirandello art must originate spontaneously within the spirit of the artist, rejecting every pre-established *formula*. "The old rhetoric has mummified—so to speak—the traditional forms, fixing laws and regulations with extreme rigour and preventing their natural evolution . . . Style has been turned into a sort of wardrobe where every manikin (call it comedy, tragedy, dialogue, short story, poem, etc.) chooses its costumes . . . Within every manikin there is a well-trained parrot which knows how to repeat with extreme ease and confidence passages from Homer, Horace, Plautus, Terence, Cicero, etc."[3]

Thus the vindication of the autonomy of the creative spirit would seem to be the common ground between the *comici dell'arte* and Pirandello.

The *commedia dell'arte*, however, tended to operate mainly within the limits of pure entertainment, absorbing as a consequence everything which was trivial, gross, even obscene. The *commedia dell'arte* did not aim at being a clear mirror of life, but was rather a free manifestation of the spirit; we might call it a mechanical operation of instincts.

For Pirandello a work of art "must never be a futile game or an insipid exercise in style."[4] In his essays Pirandello refers briefly on a couple of occasions to the *commedia dell'arte* and only as a comparison. These two comments seem even to be a slight contradiction. At one point he maintains that the *commedia dell'arte* is based on "a repertory of stereotyped phrases, of traditional typical jokes as if taken from a manual of etiquette"[5] whereas elsewhere he speaks of "embryonic scheme and free creation of the actor."[6]

I would say that one objection of Pirandello towards the *commedia dell'arte* concerns the presence of the mask. The mask automatically consecrates the fixity of characters; it establishes a precise indestructible role, specific functions. Although it allows free movement, it always presupposes certain conventions which the public wants and expects. The mask has freedom but within specific boundaries.

Pirandello, on the contrary, has broken with the mask, splitting the personality into one hundred thousand atoms *ad infinitum*.

In addition the actors of the *commedia dell'arte*, rejecting the written text (more instinctively than through an aesthetic elaboration), cut through the umbilical cord separating themselves from the author completely.

For Pirandello the problem was not so easy—if only because he himself was an author. This is where Pirandello—to my mind—departs from the *commedia dell'arte.* For Pirandello art must always be a clear reflection of life, strongly related to a specific content. "This content must respond to the particular spirit which animates our times in every field . . . The plays which do not accept in themselves this new spirit are nothing but bran . . . The writers, therefore, must always be directed towards particular problems outside of which there is no hope for building new and vital works."[7]

Pirandello, however, makes it clear that it is not the problems in life which should condition writers and induce them to write. In fact, he is against those writers who start from a certain specific situation and simply bring it on to the stage, "extracting a drama out of it, like a construction piece which is built according to a precise plan . . . through a process of drafting and arrangements. Nor could there be any art also where one starts from a general, abstract idea (whether suggested by an event or a more or less philosophical thought) and then through cold reasoning and study one proceeds to draw some images to be used as symbols . . . It is not the drama which makes the people, but the people who make the drama."[8] One must always start from the people, and from "free people." Open minds, creative spirits, find the problems "without looking for them; they deal with them even knowing them in their abstract terms, and they solve them without any study."[9]

The relation between author and actor was the problem which tormented Pirandello throughout his life. He realised that there is always an interference between the two, just as there is an interference between the director and actors. As the author (if he wants to create a work of art) has to identify himself with the character he wants to represent so that the two become one, the same thing should be done by the actor with the character he wants to portray. A faithful interpretation is however "very difficult, not to say impossible . . . It is always subjected to the personality of the actor. Apart from the fact that a perfect incarnation is often prevented by the physical aspect of the actor (something one could remedy in part by make-up) one would encounter more of an adaptation, a mask rather than an actual incarnation. However much the actor tries to penetrate into the intention of the writer, it will be difficult for him to see the character as the author has seen it, to feel the character as the author has felt it . . . to render it on the stage as the author intended. . . ."[10]

On one hand, we have the author who doesn't want to be betrayed by the actor; on the other, we have the actor who wants to defend his freedom, and any interference of the author would be considered an invasion. The actor would also tend to exploit in a play the elements which are more theatrical. "He does not want the written words to come out from his mouth like a mouthpiece, as from a phonograph." He would rather want to re-conceive the character for himself. The result is that the image produced by the actor is therefore altered. "The image is bound to be modified whenever it passes from one spirit to another. It could be called an approximate image, more or less similar, but never the same. That certain character on the stage will say the same words of the written text but it will never be the character conceived by the playwright. The actor has recreated it in himself, and what we experience would be his expression, his voice, his body, his gestures."[11]

This is what happens also with illustrators and translators. They too, like an actor, translate from one art into another. A translation is never faithful and is therefore inferior. "It might happen of course that the translation is better, but in this case it is the original which becomes a translation." So what does an actor do? "He chooses a *canovaccio* and infuses life into the stage . . . He does not want to be considered a mechanic or passive instrument of communication."[12]

One thing is a work of art (drama) already expressed and living on its own, and another thing is "its stage representation, translation and interpretation, a copy, which, although living in a material reality, is nonetheless fictitious and illusory . . ."[13]

Either the author or the actor is therefore bound to lose his independence. A compromise would seem to be impossible.

As in the *commedia dell' arte*, the actors of Pirandello want to establish absolute, complete freedom in the name of life. Indeed, Pirandello's *Trilogy of the Theatre in the Theatre* claims rebellion on all sides. In *Six Characters in Search of an Author*, the characters rebel against the actors and the director. In the play *Each in His Own Way*, it is the spectators who rebel against actors and author, whilst in *Tonight We Improvise*, the actors actually get rid of the director.

In the first mentioned play, the six characters want the actors to make them relive their lives on the stage not as masks but as living persons. Theatre as a show, a spectacle, must never overtake their desire to live as they really are. Theatre should not be a lie, a simple convention. They reject therefore the relation theatre-mask and all the ingredients of the traditional theatre. Also in *Tonight We Improvise* life ends up by defeating conventions and literature. Where the director considers writing superior to life, the actors claim that the time has come *not* to write but to live. *Tonight We Improvise* is in fact a parody on the pretences of the director who threatens the creativity of the actors. The latter eventually revolt against him. "Let's stop playing marionettes." The first actor shouts "We do not want the usual theatre anymore . . . I also want to cry aloud my passion."

In *Each in His Own Way*, the author tries to imitate a tragic event in life, but this will never be possible. When Morello slaps the first actress she simply affirms that abysmal difference which exists between theatre and life. The actors leave and the performance cannot go on.

Following this trend, Pirandello ends up by questioning even the validity of art itself. We see this in the play *Diana and Tuda*. For the old sculptor Giuncano, a work of art, however beautiful and perfect, remains ever fixed and dead. For this reason he decides to destroy all his works of art. Only life has value because life is in continual movement and eternally changeable.

Only a human being can be considered a true work of art, in this case the lady Tuda who poses as a model, not the statue which the young sculptor Dossi wants to make. Every work of art is destined to fossilize itself in forms of death, whereas for the young sculptor Dossi life must be completely subservient to form. Life for him is only a means through which the artist reaches perfection in his work. Everything must be sacrificed on the altar of art. Not only that, the sufferings and humiliations, which the girl Tuda encounters, are indispensable to obtaining the perfect result. Idealism is carried to extremes.

The exclusive, abstract, purely aesthetical ideal of art is the theme of *Each in His Own Way*. Here again the painter Giorgio Salvi, like Dossi, lives only by his art, ignoring every other human feeling. The girl Delia, like Tuda, realises the indifference of the artist who puts art above everything else. As a woman, as a human being, she rebels. For her, feelings are the only absolute values in life, not the work of art which, once made, remains eternally dead, a cold documentation. Between life and form compromise would not seem possible, just as there can be no compromise between freedom and slavery. This is understood by the Norwegian Nielsen in the play *Trovarsi* (*To find oneself*). Having fallen in love with the actress Donata, Nielsen suggests that she abandons everything and everybody. "We must get rid of everything . . . I won't permit you to go back to acting in the theatre . . . to give life to your puppets. . . . I shall give you the real life if you have never lived . . . and *you* will give it to me! I want to free you from these ties . . . We have to throw ourselves into life.[14] We must swim . . . a strong swish of the tail just like a fish . . . and we change direction . . . The sea is immense."[15]

The pirandellian *formula* which seems to bother so many critics "Either you live life or you write it" is very simple. It can in fact be extended and reformulated like this: "Life can be either lived or acted," or "either lived or painted" and so on.

Finally we come to the question: if life is irrepresentable, if one must choose between the motionless world of the forms and the perennial movement of life, is every artistic production useless?

Pirandello was aware that this would imply the negation of all his work, yet he felt a compulsion to write and work all his life. In the play *Trovarsi*, Pirandello seems to have found the solution to this major problem. He knows that an actor or an actress immobilises himself or herself in a form. When Donata, the actress, in the first two acts tries to reproduce in every little detail her relationship with Elj, the quality of her acting dies. But in the third act, when she succeeds in overcoming the level of exact transcription of reality, she reaches the height of true artistic creation. "I have freed myself . . . I have conquered the whole of my soul . . . I have found myself in life *as* in art."[16]

Trovarsi is for me a very important play with regard to the complex problem of art. The clash between life and art seems to find, through the character of Donata, its solution. When art expresses itself outside every pre-established rule, in absolute autonomy and freedom, in complete harmony with the inspiration which originally motivated it, not only does it acquire life but it identifies itself with life. "To copy nature is impossible. . . . Art is nature itself . . . From this derives the love of the artist for nature. He recognises himself in it. The work of art is created spontaneously within the spirit . . . The artist must therefore abandon himself to the free movement of life and, no matter how great his knowledge, can not graft on dead limbs to create a living body." The artist however, is not he who works through instinct only, through inspiration alone. "Every artist has a trade whose rules are not truly possessed until one applies them without thinking, until they become the instinctive form of thought and action. . . ."

The instinctive application of the rules must be accompanied by the free inspiration of the artist, inspiration which is necessary to guarantee originality which is, after all, the distinctive sign of art. In short, for Pirandello, technique is born with inspiration, spontaneously. "The acquired science cannot be used through reflection. Technique must have become almost an instinct . . . The first condition for a true artist is to appropriate technical language until he speaks it naturally."[17]

The actors of the *commedia dell' arte*, through severe discipline, had also succeeded in transforming their great technical ability into naturalness, but they had not gone beyond the boundaries of pure entertainment and enjoyment. To summarise, one might say that, like the actors of the *commedia dell'arte*, Pirandello reacted to the imitative character of the traditional theatre. As they rejected the text in the name of their artistic autonomy, Pirandello's characters and actors react to the conventions of the author and the director. Pirandello however dissociates himself from the *commedia dell'arte* inasmuch as the latter aims at confining itself to the ability of acting, to liveliness and movement, yet turning a deaf ear to the reality of everyday life.

Indeed, the strict relation between life and art which, for Pirandello is a *sine qua non* condition, would put him on the opposite side of the *commedia dell'arte*.

If any comparison were to be drawn, Pirandello's attitude and position would be much on the same lines as those adopted by Carlo Goldoni.

McMaster University

NOTES

1 Silvio D'Amico, *Storia del Teatro Drammatico*, (Milano: Garzanti, 1960).
2 Luigi Pirandello, *Saggi, Poesie, Scritti varii*, (Milano: Mondadori, 1977) 189. All translations are mine.
3 Pirandello 194.
4 Pirandello 183.
5 Pirandello 239.
6 Pirandello 224.
7 Pirandello 232.
8 Pirandello 1016.
9 Pirandello 233.
10 Pirandello 215.
11 Pirandello 216.
12 Pirandello 222.
13 Pirandello 224.
14 Luigi Pirandello, *Maschere Nude*, (Milano: Mondadori, Vol. 2 1981) 935.
15 Pirandello, *Maschere* 936.
16 Pirandello, *Maschere* 963.
17 Pirandello, *Saggi* 211.

Maristella de P. Lorch

Concluding Remarks

These observations represent my reaction to the meeting I have just attended. I did not read one single presentation. I am grateful to Domenico Pietropaolo for having invited me to listen. Listening was a pleasure from beginning to end.

A congress, from *cum-gredior*, implies simply a "moving together"; a conference, from *cum-fero*, more specifically an interaction through discussion. What I have attended during the past three days was more a *Congress* than a *conference*. I say this without regret since this way so much information could be brought to light on a topic which we are always trying to approach from different angles. This is precisely the reason, I discovered, for which our *impresario*, Domenico Pietropaolo, asked us to convene: is there something else that can be discovered about a mysterious kind of play called *commedia dell'arte*? Far back in 1968, in a beautiful essay (*Italian Quarterly*, XI:44) a "friend" of the *comici*, from Ruzzante to Goldoni, Franco Fido, wrote: "Today the *commedia dell'arte*, the old Italian *commedia a soggetto*, is perhaps closer than anything else to the ideal work of art dreamed of by some philosophical, creative critics: it is essence, rather than existence, a pretext, rather than a text, something out of which sophisticated writers and exuberant directors can make practically whatever they want. This is probably the reason why the *commedia dell'arte* is so popular in our time." (p. 3). Franco Fido is still right and our Congress proved it.

First, in line with what the *commedia dell'arte* is, we did not try to define the *commedia dell'arte*. Thus we tacitly admitted it escapes definition. What we aimed at instead is the possibility of approaching the phenomenon *commedia dell'arte* with the support of new methodologies. The historical section of the Congress preceded the theoretical. Two "general" results come immediately to mind: improvising is a most difficult technique which requires not only natural gifts but also a thorough preparation, and our present attraction for "improvisation" must be seen within

a totally different context from the "necessity" of improvising that motivated the Italian *comici dell'arte*.

More specifically, a new perception of the *commedia dell'arte* as a theatrical phenomenon emerged through lectures and performances. In the
lectures the basic constituents of the *commedia dell'arte* were analysed:
improvisation, language, disguise, structure of the scenario, play within
the play, the relation of the *commedia dell'arte* to its sources, the classical
plays and mostly the Italian *commedia erudita* or literary comedy. This
was done in the light of new methodologies with, at times at least, excellent results. Thus we have been made aware that the *commedia dell'arte*
has roots in the innate human desire for theatrical experimentation. The
commedia dell'arte never aims at becoming a unity (an *organismo*) but
is and will be—as it was in the past—an "inseguirsi di situazioni para-
dossali," a process of continuous tension dictated by a human instinctive
theatrical tendency (almost a necessity) "di creare intrecci all'infinito."
My first strong reaction to this perception was that it was not at all by
chance that the *commedia dell'arte* found its most genuine expression in
sixteenth century Italy. Therefore much of "what it was" could be understood by relating this theatrical phenomenon to the political and mainly
to the literary scene of the period: to the humanistic university fifteenth-
century farces in Latin and to the *poema cavalleresco*, not perhaps the
great productions, the *Orlando innamorato* and the *Orlando furioso*, as
the popular *cantari*, poems or novels in octaves. Most important would
be to study further the implications of what *laughter* signifies and what it
aims at.

Our Congress threw new light on the fact, usually taken for granted but
still worthy of further analysis, that this theatrical phenomenon acquired
a new aspect and a new creative élan when it crossed the Alps and was
"married" with the French theatre or French requests from the theatre.
What the *commedia dell'arte* became in Paris may explain some of the
"loves" it still inspires today and the role it played in our times in some
avant-garde experiments in Russia, Germany, in New York and in Italy
itself, with some most challenging solutions to the most puzzling problem
of "improvisation" and its motivation and aims.

New basic techniques aiming at the transformation of the body of the
actor *before* he acts, making it, so to speak, an *instrument* for the trans-
mission to the public of a special bodily energy, may help to envisage
the essence and the effects of some techniques of movements which were
so much a part of the *commedia dell'arte*. After all, the *lazzi* or bodily
tricks, that varied from plain kicks to the sophisticated *lazzo delle mosche*,

commonly practised by the hungry *zanni*, derive from *l'azzi* or *l'azzione*, action, movement, perennial movement on stage as the *condicio sine qua non* of theatre. While we should certainly welcome these new approaches, we should also make clear that they are not "influences" of the *commedia dell'arte* on modern theatre but rather inspirational motives from the little we know about the *commedia dell'arte*.

In further exploring this theatrical phenomenon we were rightly warned (Fido) not to consider the masks as one of the traits disappearing with the *commedia dell'arte's* decadence. The masks were actually absorbed into the written comedy. Goldoni, who is usually seen as the reformer who cut off the dead branches of a decayed *commedia dell'arte*, introduced the mask in more than 40 of his regularly written comedies, one third of his whole production! The same goes for improvisation. Also in this case Goldoni paid the greatest homage to the art of improvisation with his Truffaldino. Thus, *The Servant of Two Masters* remains the most viable document of the *improvisa*. Last night we heard a Torontonian Truffaldino exclaim in the middle of an improvised scene: "You see, I am learning my part!" Didn't the same Goldoni use Pantalone to create his most beloved character, his spokesman? Of the many avenues our conference opened for further studies, this last, in my opinion, should be kept in mind in our search for the "heredity" of a type of theatre, which—being tied to the performance, in action and words, of several generations of exceptional actors—cannot be exploited today in its extant documentation beyond what it can possibly give us.

But more about documents. The main motivation of the conference was most laudable: while we search for documents we should try to find in some of our theatrical techniques and even moods and inclinations a hint of the nature of the historical document we miss. I must admit that the word *science* in the title of the conference—"The Science of Buffoonery"—worried me at first sight. Attending the conference itself, however, I learned to give the word a flexible and more complex meaning than the one it suggests if it is taken literally. I began then to perceive the conference as a kind of play that unrolled in front of our eyes, a unity divisible into acts, each act into scenes. As a homage to the actors I shall now mention them (at least up to and including Act III) in order of appearance so as to better identify, within the whole, the message each tried to convey.

* * * * *

Act I—The Historical Scene 1.

The *commedia dell'arte* meets with the genres that have some affinity with it (a phenomenon of *agnition*?) Here Erasmi—a *Triestino* whom we found out at dinner can sing powerfully ballads and operas—stepped on stage with a series of questions: "Why not Aristophanes?" "*Why* were Machiavelli's *Maschere* lost?" "Why did the warning of Vespasiano da Bisticci, that there was a manuscript of Menander, go unnoticed?"—Fantham then danced through the *atellanae* and Plautus' comic devices to make us aware of how masks and other elements of the comic theatre of antiquity should be kept in mind in our search for the entity of the *commedia dell'arte*. An old time friend, Douglas Radcliff-Umstead, displayed examples of the relationship between the *commedia dell'arte* and the *commedia erudita*. Much of this was to be expected; still the novelty cannot be perceived if not through an individual example.

Act I, Scene 2

In a most charming way Detenbeck walked on the ground of *Antiparnaso* and of *Pazzia senile*, showing us how *strambozzare musicalmente* was an important constituent of the *commedia dell'arte*. Pugliese, an intelligent reader of the *Decameron*, reminded us that Boccaccio is present not only in the *commedia erudita* but in the *scenari* of the *improvisa* as well, where rhetorical act and verbal bravura play a decisive role. Finally, Meredith Chilton made us walk lightly among the elegant porcelain figures of her Museum: an epitome of eighteenth century elegance and charm.

Act II, Scene 1

We slowly move from the historical into the theoretical. Muratori, Maffei, Martello. Hannibal Noce led us with a sure hand to the discovery that even in the "enemy" ground of the *commedia dell'arte*, the "national theatre," there was at least one voice that highly praised improvisation. Christine Piechura remarked that at the birth of another national theatre, in Poland, *commedia dell'arte* played a relevant role. Most important, however, is what happened in France. Here David Trott, with complete control of voice and movement, portrayed the marriage Riccoboni-Fuzelier. The Italian princess, our *commedia dell'arte*, became then French by marriage; and a royal marriage it was with Marivaux. A problem however

arose sharply: what is the relation of an author's text to the actor's improvisation? At this point Douglas Clayton moved on stage with a *passo
doppio*. Holding on to *I Pagliacci* (which the romantic myth had made
the symbol of the life of a *comico dell'arte*), he led us into the acrobatics
of Russian cabaret theatre. The revolution brought along by the *commedia dell'arte* became integrated with the Russian avant-garde theatre, soon
to be set aside by the "real" revolution that introduced social theatrical
realism.

Act III

We are now definitely on the ground of what in the Programme is designated as "theory." Friend Ferroni performed for us a new version of a
motif we know is his favourite: "meccanismi di raddoppiamenti, rapporti
del personaggio con la sua ombra, gioco degli specchi." At the end of
his performance we felt in our bones that the *commedia dell'arte* with its
"nulla di programmato, ma solo il piacere dell'essere e dello sparire" uses
the comic mechanism without any specific aim or functionality. It just
aims at making you laugh. Thus it gives a unique theatrical possibility,
"la possibilità di abbandonarsi apparentemente nel vuoto attaccati ad un
invisibile sostegno." Besides, it offers us the widest "enciclopedia del
teatrabile che la scena trasforma." Applying the *commedia dell'arte* rule
of polilingualism, Jansen followed Ferroni with a new language, asking us
to envisage "une analyse du texte dramatique avec une segmentation de la
base linéaire." The message will become clearer in the written *scenario*.
Also in his personal performance the next actor, Pietropaolo, proved to
be the *impresario* that he was in directing the play. His message was a
clear, rational warning against using superficial amateurish approaches to
the subject in question, when today we have at our disposal all sorts of
new techniques and methods. Thus he made us aware that improvisation
implies the strongest kind of collaboration among the members of a given
cast. Far from being a self-contained notion, it implies two variables:
individual inventiveness and concerted effort. What a loss for a company
was the loss of an actor! Fitzpatrick, the Australian member of the cast,
recited his part through an intermediary, David Trott. He focused upon
the very significant problem of the dialectic inter-relation of *scenario* and
performance. He did so by a close *theatrical*, not literary, analysis of
a published *scenario* by Flaminio Scala. We were then convinced that,
when the Italian actors came back to Paris (after having been expelled)
in 1716, they needed only bare directions backstage; the *scenario* in Fitzpatrick's reading turns out to be a practical commanding form for dramatic

action. One postilla: the *scenario* never limits improvisation. Ludovico Zorzi, whom we all miss, was mentioned here for the second time. Finally Pamela Stewart came on stage. Her dance was classical, her performance impeccable. She claimed to offer only a vantage point from which to look at the *commedia dell' arte*, by conveying the feeling of what disguise, as play in the play, constituted for the written comedy as well as the *improvisa*. Another character was recalled among us whom we sorely miss, Mario Baratto.

At night *The Servant of Two Masters* translated into a tangible theatrical reality the work of Acts I–III: a whirlwind of acrobatics and *lazzi* with splendid costumes and an astounding *mis-en-scène*.

Acts IV and V have just taken place today, adding a linguistic dimension and bringing to light the influence of the *commedia dell' arte* in different fields and countries. We shall not forget Bouissac's "performance" and Sartori's masks.

With so much knowledge to enlighten us on . . . improvisation, I express the hope that another conference will soon follow in the same spirit and with the same cast.

Barnard College, Columbia University